The Cambridge Companion to Edgar

This collection of specially commissioned essays by experts in the field explores key dimensions of Edgar Allan Poe's work and life. Contributions provide a series of new perspectives on one of the most enigmatic and controversial American writers. The essays, specially tailored to the needs of undergraduates, examine all of Poe's major writings, his poetry, short stories, and criticism, and place his work in a variety of literary, cultural, and political contexts. They situate his imaginative writings in relation to different modes of writing: humor, Gothicism, anti-slavery tracts, science fiction, the detective story, and sentimental fiction. Three chapters examine specific works: *The Narrative of Arthur Gordon Pym*, "The Fall of the House of Usher," "The Raven," and "Ulalume." The volume features a detailed chronology and a comprehensive guide to further reading, and will be of interest to students and scholars alike.

CAMBRIDGE COMPANIONS TO LITERATURE

CAMBRIDGE COMPANIONS TO CULTURE

THE CAMBRIDGE
COMPANION TO
EDGAR ALLAN POE

EDITED BY

KEVIN J. HAYES

DECATUR PUBLIC LIBRARY

AUG 1 5 2004

DECATUR, ILLINOIS

CAMBRIDGE
UNIVERSITY PRESS

PUBLISHED BY THE PRESS SYNDICATE OF THE UNIVERSITY OF CAMBRIDGE
The Pitt Building, Trumpington Street, Cambridge, United Kingdom

CAMBRIDGE UNIVERSITY PRESS
The Edinburgh Building, Cambridge CB2 2RU, UK
40 West 20th Street, New York, NY 10011-4211, USA
477 Williamstown Road, Port Melbourne, VIC 3207, Australia
Ruiz de Alarcón 13, 28014 Madrid, Spain
Dock House, The Waterfront, Cape Town 8001, South Africa

http://www.cambridge.org

© Cambridge University Press 2002

This book is in copyright. Subject to statutory exception
and to the provisions of relevant collective licensing agreements,
no reproduction of any part may take place without
the written permission of Cambridge University Press.

First published 2002

Printed in the United Kingdom at the University Press, Cambridge

Typeface Sabon 10/13 pt.   *System* LATEX 2$_\varepsilon$ [TB]

A catalogue record for this book is available from the British Library

ISBN 0 521 79326 2 hardback
ISBN 0 521 79727 6 paperback

DECATUR PUBLIC LIBRARY

AUG 1 5 2004

DECATUR, ILLINOIS

For Myung-Sook

CONTENTS

CONTENTS

LIST OF ILLUSTRATIONS

CONTRIBUTORS

BENJAMIN FRANKLIN FISHER, Professor of English at the University of Mississippi, currently serves on the editorial board of *Poe Studies*, is an Honorary Member and past president of the Poe Studies Association, and a Life Member and Chairman of the Speaker Series in the Edgar Allan Poe Society of Baltimore. In 1993 he was awarded a Governor's Citation, State of Maryland, for his outstanding contributions to Poe studies. He has published widely on Victorian literature and on the Gothic tradition. A member of the Executive Committee in the International Gothic Association, he also serves on the editorial boards of multiple scholarly journals in the field.

TERESA A. GODDU, Associate Professor of English at Vanderbilt University, is the author of *Gothic America: Narrative, History, and Nation* (1997). Her essays and reviews have appeared in *American Literary History*, *South Atlantic Quarterly*, and *Studies in the Novel*. She is currently writing a book on anti-slavery literature.

KEVIN J. HAYES, Professor of English at the University of Central Oklahoma, has, among other books, written *A Colonial Woman's Bookshelf* (1996); *Folklore and Book Culture* (1997); *The Library of William Byrd of Westover* (1997), for which he won the first annual Virginia Library History Award; *Melville's Folk Roots* (1999); and *Poe and the Printed Word* (Cambridge University Press, 2000). In addition, he has edited previous collections of critical essays including *Henry James: The Contemporary Reviews* (Cambridge University Press, 1996).

RICHARD KOPLEY, Associate Professor of English at Penn State DuBois and Head of the Division of English for Penn State's Commonwealth College, is President of the Poe Studies Association. He is editor of *Poe's Pym: Critical Explorations* (1992), *Prospects for the Study of American Literature: A Guide for Scholars and Students* (1997), and *The Narrative of Arthur Gordon Pym* (1999); co-editor of the journal, *Resources for American*

Literary Study; and author of *Edgar Allan Poe and The Philadelphia Saturday News* (1991). He has recently completed a book-length study of the origins of *The Scarlet Letter*.

KENT LJUNGQUIST, Paris Fletcher Professor of Humanities at Worcester Polytechnic Institute, is the author of *The Grand and the Fair: Poe's Landscape Aesthetics and Pictorial Techniques* (1984), editor of *Nineteenth-Century American Fiction Writers* (1999) and *The Facts on File Bibliography of American Fiction to 1865* (1994), and co-editor of James Fenimore Cooper's *The Deerslayer* (1987). An Honorary Member of the Poe Studies Association and a Member of the American Antiquarian Society, he has also published essays on Poe, Cooper, Melville, and Thoreau.

MARK NEIMEYER, Maître de Conférences at the Université de Paris-Sorbonne (Paris IV), has published extensively on American literature and culture. His essays and reviews have appeared in *Journal of American Studies* and *Revue Française d'Etudes Americaines*. Currently, he is Associate Editor of the French Pléiade edition of the works of Herman Melville and is writing a book-length study of the Atlantic Cable.

SCOTT PEEPLES, Assistant Professor of English and Coordinator of American Studies at the College of Charleston, is the author of *Edgar Allan Poe Revisited* (1998). His essays and reviews have appeared in such journals as *American Literature*, *Biography*, and *Criticism*.

RACHEL POLONSKY, Research and Teaching Fellow at Emmanuel College, Cambridge (1994–2000), is the author of *English Literature and the Russian Aesthetic Renaissance* (Cambridge University Press, 1998). She has written a number of essays and reviews concerning early Russian and English literature and cultural history for the *Journal of European Studies*, *Slavonic and East European Review*, and *TLS*.

DANIEL ROYOT, Emeritus Professor of American Literature and Civilization at the Sorbonne, Paris and President of the American Humor Studies Association, has, among other books, authored or co-authored *L'Humour Américain: Des Puritains aux Yankees* (1980), *Images des U.S.A.: De l'Icône Populaire à l'Oeuvre d'Art* (1985), *Nouvelle-Angleterre* (1991), *Histoire de la Culture Américaine* (1993), and *L'Humour et la Culture Américaine* (1996).

GEOFFREY SANBORN, Assistant Professor of English, Williams College, Williamstown, Massachusetts is the author of *The Sign of the Cannibal: Melville and the Making of a Postcolonial Reader* (1998). His work on British and American literature has also appeared in the *Wordsworth Circle* and *Nineteenth-Century Literature*.

PETER THOMS teaches in the Department of English at the University of Western Ontario. He is the author of *Detection and Its Designs: Narrative and Power in Nineteenth-Century Detective Fiction* (1998) and *The Windings of the Labyrinth: Quest and Structure in the Major Novels of Wilkie Collins* (1992).

SANDRA TOMC is Associate Professor of English at the University of British Columbia. Her work on nineteenth-century American and contemporary culture has appeared in *American Quarterly*, *Canadian Literature*, *ESQ*, and *Essays in Theatre*, as well as in numerous collections of essays. She is currently completing a book on nineteenth-century American writers and the concept of leisured creativity.

JOHN TRESCH will receive his PhD in the History and Philosophy of Science from Cambridge University for a dissertation on Poe, Baudelaire, and French science. He is currently teaching at Columbia University in the Society of Fellows in the Humanities. His earlier work on Poe and science appeared in the *British Journal for the History of Science*.

KAREN WEEKES, Assistant Professor of English at Penn State Abington, has published essays treating nineteenth-century American literature in the *Georgia Review* and *Southern Literary Journal*.

1809	Edgar Poe is born 19 January in Boston, where his parents, Elizabeth Arnold Poe and David Poe, Jr., both actors, are performing.
1811	Elizabeth Poe dies 8 December in Richmond, Virginia. Since David Poe had abandoned the family prior to his wife's death, Edgar, his brother William Henry, and sister Rosalie enter different foster families. Frances and John Allan take Edgar into their family – without legally adopting him, however.
1815	John Allan moves his family to London, where he established a branch office of his mercantile firm, Allan and Ellis.
1816	Edgar enters a London boarding school run by the Misses Dubourg.
1818	Edgar becomes a boarding student at the Manor House School, Stoke Newington, run by the Reverend John Bransby, which would later serve as the model for the school in "William Wilson."
1820	His London business venture proving unsuccessful, John Allan takes his family back to Richmond, Virginia, where Poe begins studying with Joseph H. Clarke and also writes much poetry.
1823	Poe transfers to a Richmond school run by William Burke.
1825	John Allan inherits much of the immense fortune of his uncle, William Galt.
1826	In February, Poe enters the University of Virginia, where he studies ancient and modern languages. He incurs considerable gambling debts, which John Allan refuses to honor. Poe leaves school in December and returns to Richmond.
1827	Frequently bickering with Allan, Poe leaves Richmond for Boston, where Calvin F. S. Thomas publishes his first collection of verse, *Tamerlane and Other Poems*. Using the name Edgar

A. Perry, he enlists in the US Army and is ordered to Fort
Moultrie, South Carolina.

1828   Rising to the rank of sergeant major, Poe begins to seek
appointment to US Military Academy at West Point.
To that end, he becomes reconciled with John Allan,
who helps him obtain the appointment. Frances Allan
dies 28 February.

1829   Hatch and Dunning publish Poe's second collection of verse,
Al Aaraaf, Tamerlane, and Minor Poems at Baltimore.

1830   Poe enters West Point in May. John Allan remarries in
October 1830.

1831   Though endearing himself to fellow cadets, Poe generally
dislikes life at the Academy, deliberately disobeys orders,
and is court-martialed and expelled from West Point.
Before leaving, however, he solicits subscriptions for his
third collection of verse, *Poems*, which is published at
New York by Elam Bliss and dedicated to "The US Corps
of Cadets." He relocates to Baltimore, where he lives with
his aunt and cousin, Maria and Virginia Clemm. His brother
Henry, who also lives with the Clemms, dies on 1 August.

1832   Poe submits five tales to a contest sponsored by the
Philadelphia *Saturday Courier*: "The Bargain Lost,"
"A Decided Loss," "The Duke de L'Omelette,"
"Metzengerstein," and "A Tales of Jerusalem," which
publishes all of them.

1833   In October, "MS. Found in a Bottle" wins the first prize of
$50 in a literary contest sponsored by the *Baltimore Saturday
Visiter*, which also publishes "The Coliseum" this year.
The contest serves to introduce Poe to John Pendleton
Kennedy, who would prove to be an important literary
connection.

1834   "The Visionary" (later, "The Assignation") appears in January.
John Allan dies 27 March, yet leaves Poe nothing.

1835   Kennedy recommends that Poe begin contributing to the
Southern Literary Messenger and encourages its proprietor,
Thomas W. White, to hire Poe in an editorial capacity.
In August, Poe moves to Richmond, where he joins the
Messenger staff. His uncompromising reviews attract the
attention of literati throughout the nation. The stories he
contributes to the *Messenger* this year include "Berenice,"
"King Pest," "Lionizing," "Morella," and "Shadow: A

Parable." In October, Maria and Virginia Clemm join Poe in Richmond.

1836   Poe weds Virginia Clemm on 16 May. His contributions to the *Messenger* this year include the two-part "Autography" and numerous important critical essays including the "Drake-Halleck Review." Poe's editorial freedoms, combined with occasional drinking bouts, alienate him from White.

1837   Poe resigns from the *Messenger* in January and then moves his family to New York, where he unsuccessfully seeks employment. Maria Clemm manages a boarding house to help make ends meet. One tenant, bookman William Gowans, befriends Poe and initiates him into the world of antiquarian books.

1838   Poe moves his family to Philadelphia early in the year. Harpers publishes *The Narrative of Arthur Gordon Pym* in July. Late this year he contributes "Ligeia" and "The Psyche Zenobia" (later, "How to Write a Blackwood Article") to the Baltimore *American Museum*.

1839   Poe helps Thomas Wyatt compile *The Conchologist's First Book* and *A Synopsis of Natural History*. He becomes an editor of *Burton's Gentleman's Magazine*, to which he contributes most of its reviews and several tales including "The Conversation of Eiros and Charmion," "The Fall of the House of Usher," and "The Man That Was Used Up." "William Wilson" appears in *The Gift*. Lea and Blanchard publish Poe's first collection of short stories, *Tales of the Grotesque and Arabesque* in December at Philadelphia. Also in December, Poe begins contributing cryptographic puzzles and miscellaneous articles to *Alexander's Weekly Messenger*.

1840   Poe continues contributing puzzles and essays to *Alexander's*, and, besides his editorial writings, contributes to *Burton's* "Peter Pendulum" (later, "The Business Man"), "The Philosophy of Furniture," and "Sonnet – Silence." The serial, "The Journal of Julius Rodman," which had begun in the January issue of *Burton's*, ends unfinished after Burton discharges Poe, who had been making plans to found his own literary magazine, the *Penn Magazine*. Unable to generate sufficient support for his proposed magazine, Poe delays his plans. George R. Graham buys *Burton's* in November and unites it with *The Casket* to form *Graham's Magazine*,

to which Poe contributes "The Man of the Crowd"
in December.

1841   Poe accepts an editorial position with *Graham's*, to which he
also contributes several tales: "The Colloquy of Monos and
Una," "The Descent into the Maelström," "The Murders in the
Rue Morgue," and "Never Bet the Devil Your Head."

1842   "Life in Death" (later, "The Oval Portrait") and "The Masque
of the Red Death" appear in *Graham's*, yet Poe resigns from
the magazine partway through the year. "The Pit and the
Pendulum" appears in *The Gift* and the first two installments
of "The Mystery of Marie Rogêt" appear in Snowden's *Ladies'
Companion* the last two months of the year.

1843   "The Tell-Tale Heart" appears in *The Pioneer* in January,
and the final installment of "The Mystery of Marie Rogêt"
appears in the February *Ladies' Companion*. Poe arranges
with Philadelphia publisher Thomas C. Clarke to issue his ideal
magazine, now titled *The Stylus*, and Clarke publishes a lengthy
biographical essay on Poe in his *Saturday Museum*. Plans for
the magazine fall through, however. In March, Poe visits
Washington, DC, to seek a position with the Tyler
administration, yet he gets drunk and ruins his chances for the
job. In June "The Gold-Bug" wins a $100 prize in a literary
contest sponsored by the Philadelphia *Dollar Newspaper*.
The tale is widely reprinted and also dramatized on the
Philadelphia stage. In July William H. Graham issues *The Prose
Romances of Edgar A. Poe*, which contains "The Murders in
the Rue Morgue" and "The Man That Was Used Up," the first
and only installment of a planned, serialized collection of Poe's
stories. In November Poe delivers his first public lecture, "Poets
and Poetry of America," a means of income he would frequently
resort to during the remainder of his life.

1844   In April Poe and Virginia move to New York City, where his
"Balloon-Hoax" dupes New Yorkers into believing that the
Atlantic had been successfully crossed by balloon. In May and
June, Poe contributes the essay series, "Doings of Gotham," to
the *Columbia Spy*. In October he obtains employment with the
New York Evening Mirror. Tales published this year include
"The Literary Life of Thingum Bob, Esq.," "Mesmeric
Revelation," "The Oblong Box," "The Premature Burial,"
"The Purloined Letter," "The Spectacles," and "A Tale of
the Ragged Mountains."

1845   In January, "The Raven" appears in the January *Evening Mirror*, is an instant sensation, and brings Poe newfound popularity and critical acclaim, which prompt his inclusion in the prestigious series, "The Library of American Books," published by Wiley and Putnam. *Tales* appears as part of the series in July and *The Raven and Other Poems* in November. Early in the year, Poe begins contributing to the *Broadway Journal*, becomes its editor in July, and, on borrowed money, then becomes its proprietor. This year, Poe revises and republishes many of his earlier stories in the *Broadway Journal*. Original tales first published this year include "The Facts in the Case of M. Valdemar," "The Imp of the Perverse," "The Power of Words," "Some Secrets of the Magazine Prison-House," "Some Words with a Mummy," and "The System of Doctor Tarr and Professor Fether." The periodical battle Poe wages with Longfellow contributes to his notoriety.

1846   Poe ends publication of the *Broadway Journal* in January. Periodical publications this year include "The Cask of Amontillado"; "The Literati of New York City," a lively series which generates much controversy and additional notoriety; and "The Sphinx."

1847   Virginia dies 30 January, and Poe himself is beset with illness through much of the year. "Ulalume" appears in the *American Review* in December.

1848   In February, Poe delivers a lecture on "The Universe," which forms the basis of his cosmological treatise, *Eureka*, which Putnam publishes in June.

1849   Poe lectures much this year. His periodical publications include "Eldorado," "Hop-Frog," "Mellonta Tauta," "Von Kempelen and His Discovery," and "X-ing a Paragrab." Visiting Richmond, he becomes engaged to boyhood sweetheart Elmira Royster Shelton, now a widow. On 3 October, he is found semi-conscious and delirious in Baltimore. He dies on 7 October. "The Bells" and "Annabel Lee" appear posthumously before the year's end.

SHORT TITLES AND ABBREVIATIONS

CH	*Edgar Allan Poe: The Critical Heritage.* Ed. I. M. Walker. London: Routledge and Kegan Paul, 1986.
Collected Works (Mabbott)	*Collected Works of Edgar Allan Poe.* Ed. Thomas Ollive Mabbott. 3 vols. Cambridge: Belknap Press of Harvard University Press, 1969–1978.
Complete Works (Harrison)	*Complete Works of Edgar Allan Poe.* Ed. James A. Harrison. 17 vols. 1902. Reprinted, New York: AMS, 1965.
E&R	*Edgar Allan Poe: Essays and Reviews.* Ed. G. R. Thompson. New York: Library of America, 1984.
Letters	*The Letters of Edgar Allan Poe.* Ed. John Ward Ostrom. 1948. Reprinted, with supplement. 2 vols. New York: Gordian Press, 1966.
Log	Thomas, Dwight and David K. Jackson. *The Poe Log: A Documentary Life of Edgar Allan Poe 1809–1849.* Boston: G. K. Hall, 1987.
P&T	*Edgar Allan Poe: Poetry and Tales.* Ed. Patrick F. Quinn. New York: Library of America, 1984.
Recognition	*The Recognition of Edgar Allan Poe* Ed. Eric W. Carlson. Ann Arbor: University of Michigan Press, 1966.

KEVIN J. HAYES

Introduction

On 1 January 1875, William M. Cash, an Alexandria, Louisiana news carrier, had a special New Year's Day gift for the customers on his paper route: he presented each with *The Bells*, a handsome, eight-page pamphlet reprinting the well-known poem by Edgar Allan Poe. Louisiana newspaper subscribers were not the only people to receive copies of *The Bells* as presents during the 1870s. In Philadelphia, a china and glassware retailer issued a complimentary edition of the poem for its customers during Christmas time, 1872, and the week after Christmas, grocery boys in the employ of Philadelphia grocer, Mitchell and Fletcher, gave copies of *The Bells* to their customers as New Year's Day presents.[1] Since bells had been a commonplace holiday motif for centuries, perhaps it should come as no surprise that copies of *The Bells* were being distributed to Philadelphia grocery shoppers or Louisiana newspaper subscribers. Anyone who believed what they read in the literary periodicals of the day, however, would hardly find Poe's writings suitable material to pass through the hands of impressionable young news carriers and grocery boys.

While Poe had achieved a status in France equal to that of a great national author and, through his French reputation, was gaining much acceptance in other parts of Europe, his reputation among the literati in English-speaking nations was ambiguous. Many of the articles in the English-language press in 1875 conveyed animosity toward Poe. One characterized him as a madman and attempted to muster evidence in an unconvincing effort to verify the diagnosis in clinical terms.[2] Robert Louis Stevenson wrote one of the more balanced essays of the time for the New Year's issue of the widely-respected British literary weekly, *The Academy*. Stevenson expressed his conviction that Poe had "the true story-teller's instinct," related his appreciation of "The Cask of Amontillado" and "The Masque of the Red Death," yet deprecated several of Poe's other stories and critiqued his personal image. Before analyzing the tales, Stevenson observed, "I cannot find it in my heart to like either his portrait or his character; and though it is possible that we see him more or less refracted through the strange medium of his works, yet I do fancy that we can detect, alike in these, in his portrait, and in the facts of his life . . . a certain jarring note, a taint of something that we do not care to dwell upon or find a name for."[3]

To be sure, not everyone who was writing about Poe in English during the 1870s expressed such skepticism toward his works and his person. In the mid-1870s, Poe gained his greatest British admirer, John H. Ingram, who began defending Poe in print with a rousing defense in *Temple Bar* in 1874 and began publishing his multi-volume collected edition of Poe's works the same year. The first two volumes of the Ingram edition appeared in late 1874, and Stevenson's essay forms a review of these. Volumes three and four would appear in early 1875.

In short, by the time people rang in the New Year, 1875, three predominant attitudes toward Poe had emerged: popular acclaim, measured skepticism, and ardent enthusiasm. The copies of *The Bells* William Cash distributed to Louisiana newspaper subscribers indicate Poe's acceptance among the general public. Robert Louis Stevenson represents the skeptics, and Ingram, like Charles Baudelaire before him, was an ardent enthusiast. These three varying attitudes toward Poe prevailed into the twentieth century. Writing in the 1920s, Paul Elmer More assumed the skeptical position as he articulated the other two, identifying Poe as "chiefly the poet of unripe boys and unsound men," the unsound men, from More's viewpoint, being the ardent enthusiasts.[4] Like many skeptical professors of literature after him, More associated Poe with adolescence and refused to acknowledge the wide-ranging literary and aesthetic implications of his imaginative and critical writings.

These three basic attitudes toward Poe have persisted to the present day. In the United States, virtually all students read some Poe during their news-carrier years, and Poe, perhaps more than any other author taught in middle schools and high schools today, functions as a catalyst for teaching students the magic of reading. Most leave school with fond memories of reading Poe. While some do not reread Poe after leaving high school, many do. Those who read him with growing fondness over the course of their lives belong among the ardent enthusiasts. Those who choose the study of literature as their profession may take one of two different directions. They may, like many of the contributors to this present volume, become enthusiasts and devote much of their professional lives to the study of Poe's life and art or, alternatively, they may turn skeptic and question Poe's significance to literary history. *The Cambridge Companion to Poe* has been designed for those who are returning to Poe with a general desire to know more about the man and his work. Its purpose is to provide a general overview of his writings and to indicate some of their complexities. It might even help to turn potential skeptics into enthusiasts.

Prior to completing their individual chapters, contributors to the present volume were issued a challenge: to write chapters that would contain fundamental information for students returning to Poe for the first time since their youth as well as new information and ideas that would appeal to seasoned Poe scholars. The contributors rose to the challenge and accomplished their tasks admirably. Regardless of individual focus, each of the following chapters presents a combination of general overview and original insight. Taken together, this collection of essays offers a fresh view of Poe's life and work for the new century.

The image of Poe that emerges from the following chapters is, however, considerably different from the image of Poe people held in William Cash's time. As the nineteenth century gave way to the twentieth, Poe was known, first and foremost, as a poet. The list of books in the 1897 Sears catalog, for example, extended for dozens of pages and contained multiple editions of Poe's verse, but no editions of his short tales.[5] With the celebration of the centenary of Poe's birth in 1909, his short stories began to achieve renewed attention. Reflecting on the numerous centenary tributes that had appeared in the London press during the week of the centenary, Arnold Bennett, writing the following week, observed, "Last week we all admitted that Poe had understood the 'art of the short story.' (His name had not occurred to us before.)"[6] The trend that began with the centenary continued over the course of the century. Marie Bonaparte, in her groundbreaking study, *Edgar Poe, Étude Psychanalytique* (1933; translated as *The Life and Works of Edgar Allan Poe: A Psycho-Analytic Interpretation* [1949]), subsumed Poe's verse into the biographical portion of the study yet devoted separate chapters to nearly all of the major stories. Poe's verse continued to attract considerable attention through the mid century, however, for his rich symbolism and scrupulous attention to poetic form was especially appealing to the prevailing critical approach of the time, the New Criticism. As Structuralist critical approaches gave way to Post-Structuralism, however, readers began recognizing anew the importance of reading Poe in relation to his cultural milieu. Consequently, emphasis shifted to those works that could be analyzed in relation to their times. Furthermore, the still-burgeoning emphasis on criticism in literary studies has placed additional importance on Poe's large body of critical writings.

The *Cambridge Companion to Poe* reflects current attitudes toward Poe's work. Only one chapter specifically treats his poetry whereas a majority of the chapters take his fiction as their subject, and three concern his critical writings. While the individual chapters in this collection need not be read in any particular order, they have been arranged in such a way as to build upon one another. The first three chapters take Poe's life and critical writings as their subject. Chapter One, Kent Ljungquist's "The Poet as Critic," offers a good overview of Poe's criticism, yet in so doing simultaneously provides a basic outline of his life and literary career. In Chapter Two, "Poe and His Circle," Sandra Tomc, also taking Poe's life and critical writings as her subject, argues that Poe, like contemporaries N. P. Willis and Rufus Wilmot Griswold, deliberately cultivated sensationalism as a way of gaining notoriety and establishing his literary career. Rachel Polonsky, while treating Poe's connections with European aesthetic philosophy in Chapter Three, "Poe's Aesthetic Theory," devotes much attention to the fine humorous tale, "The Literary Life of Thingum Bob," and, in so doing, offers a challenging new interpretation of the story.

The middle portion of this volume, comprising Chapters Four through Nine, situates Poe's imaginative writings within several different modes of discourse to show how Poe both followed yet departed from a variety of literary approaches and genres. In Chapter Four, "Poe's Humor," Daniel Royot offers an appreciation of Poe's sense of humor and situates it within the long-standing traditions of American literary and folk humor. In Chapter Five, "Poe and the Gothic Tradition," Benjamin Franklin Fisher begins by placing Poe among Anglo-American Gothic novelists and then provides close readings of several of Poe's Gothic tales to show how he manipulated and challenged the conventions of Gothic fiction and horror. In Chapter Six, "Poe, Sensationalism, and Slavery," Teresa Goddu also considers Poe's use of horror yet complicates it by showing his indebtedness to the rhetoric of anti-slavery discourse. Those authors who argued against slavery recognized the value of horror as a rhetorical strategy. Poe, in turn, recognized the literary value of their descriptions of slavery. Goddu's chapter, though not intentionally, nicely ties together two strands of Poe's work advanced in earlier chapters, namely his interest in horror and his understanding of the value of sensationalism to literary discourse.

The next three chapters situate Poe's writings within other discursive practices. In Chapter Seven, "Extra! Extra! Poe Invents Science Fiction!" John Tresch evaluates the claim that Poe deserves recognition as the inventor of modern science fiction. While identifying precursors to science fiction in such earlier literary genres as utopian fiction, Tresch delineates Poe's significant contributions to the genre and shows how subsequent practitioners reflect Poe's influence. Similarly, Peter Thoms evaluates Poe's contributions to the detective story in Chapter Eight, "Poe's Dupin and the Power of Detection." While readers nowadays take the conventions of detective fiction for granted, they were unknown before Poe's three detective tales featuring his master-sleuth, C. Auguste Dupin. In Chapter Nine, "Poe's Feminine Ideal," Karen Weekes examines Poe's depiction of women in his verse and fiction and challenges the notion that any of Poe's fictional women represent his feminine ideal and instead sees Poe's female creations largely as intellectual manifestations of his ideas.

Chapters Ten through Twelve provide more in-depth discussions of four individual Poe works. In Chapter Ten, "A Confused Beginning: *The Narrative of Arthur Gordon Pym, of Nantucket*," Geoffrey Sanborn examines the only book-length novel Poe brought to completion, a work that has continued to intrigue and puzzle Poe enthusiasts since its initial publication. Sanborn sees the novel as a search for identity analogous to what many young men in the United States were experiencing during the 1830s. In "Poe's 'Constructive-ness' and 'The Fall of the House of Usher,'" Scott Peeples takes what might be called a Neo-Structuralist approach as he parallels the House of Usher with its story to emphasize Poe's literary craftsmanship. Chapter Twelve, "Two Verse Masterworks: 'The Raven,' and 'Ulalume,'" examines what many consider Poe's two finest poems. In the first half of the chapter, Richard Kopley describes the composition of "The Raven," analyzes its themes, and situates it within the culture of Poe's day and the popular culture of our own. In the second half of the chapter, I attempt to reconcile the topical references in "Ulalume" with its formal and thematic elements.

The final two chapters trace Poe's cultural influence from the end of his life to the present day. In earlier chapters, Tresch and Kopley touch upon modern popular culture reflecting Poe's influence, but Mark Neimeyer offers a detailed treatment of the subject in Chapter Thirteen, "Poe and Popular Culture." Examining a variety of popular media from cinema to comic books, Neimeyer shows how Poe's life, works, and image have become enmeshed within the mass culture of the United States and, indeed, the world. Elite culture, on the other hand, provides the subject for the fourteenth and final chapter, "One-Man Modernist," which analyzes what Poe meant to avant-garde art movements from the mid nineteenth through the twentieth centuries.

Most of the contributors to this volume were assigned general approaches to take yet not given any specific Poe works to address. The result has allowed *The Cambridge Companion to Poe* not only to reveal the depth and breadth of Poe's accomplishment but also to emphasize different aspects of Poe's work not normally emphasized in the scholarship. Take Poe's humor, for example. Poe has never fully received his due as a humorist, yet this volume, as it has evolved, places new emphasis on Poe's humor. Besides Royot's general treatment of the subject, several other contributions consider Poe's humorous tales and reveal their wide-ranging implications. Polonsky shows how two of Poe's humorous tales reflect his aesthetic theory. Fisher and Goddu show how Poe combined horror with humor. Tresch shows how Poe's sense of humor helped lead him to science fiction. Regardless of their different critical approaches, subjects, or ultimate conclusions, the following chapters offer professional and provocative interpretations that all of Poe's readers – whether popular reader, enthusiast, or skeptic – will appreciate.

NOTES

1. *National Union Catalog: Pre-1956 Imprints*, 754 vols. (London: Mansell, 1968–1981), nos. P0436278–P0436280.
2. "A Mad Man of Letters," *Scribner's Monthly* 10 (October 1875): 690–699.
3. Robert Louis Stevenson, "Literature," review of *The Works of Edgar Allan Poe*, ed. John H. Ingram, *Academy* 7 (2 January 1875): 1.
4. Paul Elmer More, *The Demon of the Absolute* (Princeton University Press, 1928), p. 86.
5. Sears, Roebuck and Company, *1897 Sears Roebuck Catalogue* (1897; reprinted, New York: Chelsea House, 1968).
6. [Arnold Bennett,] "Books and Persons," *New Age*, new ser. 4 (January 28 1909): 284.

I

KENT P. LJUNGQUIST

The poet as critic

Edgar Allan Poe, poet, short story writer, and critic, was a controversial figure in the publishing world of antebellum America. His ability to spark controversy stemmed not only from an image concocted by his contemporary detractors but from the sharp tone and pointed content of the critical articles he wrote during his lifetime. He worked as an editor and contributor to magazines in several American publishing venues, including Richmond, New York, and Philadelphia. His continuing ambition was to found and edit his own magazine, an outlet that would have granted him financial security and artistic control in what he deemed an antagonistic literary marketplace. Poe's challenge to moralistic strictures against literature, his confrontations with the New England literary establishment, and his caustic and satirical critical style won him many enemies. Some readers too easily identified Poe with a voice like that of his deranged or vindictive narrators, a tendency made plausible by the misrepresentations of the Reverend Rufus Griswold, his literary executor. Griswold, who launched his literary career with editorial work for periodicals like the *Boston Notion*, reacted defensively when Poe attacked figures in New England's literary establishment. In fact, the "general caustic severity" of his criticism was one factor in Griswold's damning obituary that launched the Poe Legend, a combination of half truths and outright fabrications about Poe's personal habits and conduct. Griswold's portrait, in which Poe's role as a critic was relegated to that of a "dissector of sentences," almost irrevocably damaged his reputation.[1]

Griswold omitted from his obituary the fact that Poe was born in Boston, a city which would later be the object of some of his most stinging attacks. His literary career began in the late 1820s and early 1830s, and at that time the American writers against whom he began to measure his talent included William Cullen Bryant (1794–1878), John Greenleaf Whittier (1807–1892), John Neal (1793–1865), and Henry Wadsworth Longfellow (1807–1882). Each of these authors had achieved some degree of prominence by the early 1830s, but none of them confined themselves to a single literary genre or isolated outlets of publication. If Bryant's poetry served as a model to aspiring men of letters of the 1830s, he also toiled as chief editor for the *New York Review and Athenaeum*, as an assistant editor of the *New York Evening Post*, and as a contributor to and reviewer of literary gift books and annuals. If Whittier achieved a degree of notoriety for a rustic American verse akin to what Robert Burns had produced for Scotland, his literary apprenticeship had included editorial stints for the *Boston Philanthropist*, the *American Manufacturer*, and the *New England Weekly Review*. Neal edited the *Yankee*, and in that periodical he adopted an aggressive critical style, particularly when addressing his twin hobby-horses of plagiarism and originality, soon to be obsessions of Poe. In the pages of the *Yankee*, Neal noted how much poetry of the period imitated that of Bryant. Conscious of such charges was Longfellow, whose apprentice verses appeared alongside Bryant's in the *United States Literary Gazette*. In the early 1830s, moreover, Longfellow, like Poe, turned from poetry to criticism in his "Defence of Poetry" (1832) and a companion piece, "Old English Romances" (1833).

Each of these writers demonstrated that poetic or artistic creation and the critical function could complement one another. Poe, in fact, would later claim that inferior poets would inevitably lapse into false critiques, or to put the matter more positively, that "a poet, who is indeed a poet, could not...fail of making a just critique" (*E&R*, 6). Perhaps more important, each of them was a New Englander, and their explicit objective was to sink literary roots into that region's soil. When Poe convinced the Bostonian Calvin Thomas to publish his first book, *Tamerlane and Other Poems* (1827), it appeared as a volume avowedly "by a Bostonian," a nod to a region that would be an obsessive part of Poe's critical consciousness throughout his career. When he published his second volume of poems, *Al Aaraaf, Tamerlane and Minor Poems* (1829), he was still under the spell of Lord Byron as a poetic model, an influence he would never completely shed.[2] The aspersions cast upon Byron by Bryant and Longfellow may have weaned New England writers from the allegedly noxious influence of the British author's verse. The last of Poe's early poetic collections, his *Poems: Second Edition* (1831), published in New York, contained the distinctive verses "To Helen" and "Israfel" as well as an initial critical statement, the "Letter to Mr. ——," an attack on derivative followers of the British Lake School reminiscent of Byron's in "English Bards and Scotch Reviewers" and *Don Juan*. In 1831, such an attack reminded American readers not just of Byron's criticisms but of strictures levelled against an "American Lake School," whose titular head was Bryant, also called the "American Wordsworth."[3] Whatever the case, the "Letter to Mr. ——," which was republished in revised form as "Letter to B——" in the *Southern Literary Messenger* (July 1836), constitutes Poe's first substantial statement on his poetics. It contains an initial statement on the aims of poetry as opposed to the objectives of science and other literary forms:

> A poem...is opposed to a work of science by having for its immediate object, pleasure, not truth; to romance by having, for its object an indefinite instead of a definite pleasure, being a poem only so far as this object is attained; romance presenting perceptible images with definite, poetry with indefinite sensations, to which end music is essential, since the comprehension of sweet sound is our most indefinite conception. Music, when combined with a pleasurable idea, is poetry; music without the idea is simply music; the idea without the music is prose from its very definitiveness. (*E&R*, 11)

As many scholars have noted, Poe derived his definition of poetry in part from Samuel Taylor Coleridge, praised in the essay for his "towering intellect" and "gigantic power." Such reverence is accorded to Coleridge at the expense of Wordsworth, who represents the view that the "end of poetry is, or should be, instruction." This alignment of poetry with moral instruction Poe labels a "heresy" of the Lake School, treated sometimes dismissively, sometimes playfully in the essay. The tone of flippancy and sarcasm applied to philosophic and aesthetic issues would be one of the hallmarks of Poe's criticism in later years. In bowing to the wisdom of men like Coleridge and Robert Southey, the wise critic need not be sober or reverential but must learn to laugh at "poetical theories so prosaically exemplified."

Whatever tone adopted by the critic, Poe felt that the poet should be predisposed toward indefinite images and sensations enhanced by music or sweet sound. Music could thus be a vehicle for the exploration of unearthly beauty, not to be confused with mere prettiness. As he wrote in "Letter to B—," poetry might render the "airy and fairy-like," but latent in its impact was "all that is hideous and unwieldy" (*E&R*, 7–11).

Poe once again acknowledged his debts to Coleridge in a review of Robert Montgomery Bird's novel, *Sheppard Lee* (*Southern Literary Messenger*, September 1836), one of his first significant critical statements on prose fiction. The main character in Bird's novel experiences metempsychosis (inhabiting the bodies of persons who had died), a plot device that Poe would use in "Ligeia" and "A Tale of the Ragged Mountains." In the review Poe seizes upon Bird's handling of the occult. Objecting to incredible or improbable elements in the narrative, Poe claims that unraveling a plot by awkwardly appealing to the supernatural constitutes an affront to artistic standards. This censure of Bird's idiosyncratic characters and extraordinary plot devices may seem like an early call for realism in fiction, but the review calls for more than minute attention to credible detail.

After scoring Bird's capricious exploitation of the "explained supernatural" – a technique he may have associated with the works of Washington Irving and Anne Radcliffe – Poe eschews "directness of expression" in narratives of improbable events. He states a preference for leaving "much to the imagination – in writing as if the author were firmly impressed with the truth, yet astonished at the immensity, of the wonder he relates, and for which, professedly, he neither claims credence – in minuteness of detail." Minute particulars, Poe suggests, have little bearing on the thrust of narrative fiction. A subtle author can exploit "the infinity of arts that give verisimilitude to a narration," and at the same time, he can leave a residue of wonder at events "not to be accounted for." Rather "than explaining away his incredibilities," the artist can give them vividness and character (*E&R*, 402–403). The review of *Sheppard Lee* anticipates other critical statements on the artful combination (what Poe would call "novel combinations") of verisimilitude and improbability in prose fiction. Twentieth-century critics have applied the principles enunciated in the review of *Sheppard Lee* to Poe's own works of supernatural or speculative fiction, including the longer narrative, *The Narrative of Arthur Gordon Pym* (1838).

If Bird failed to integrate fully the various threads of his narrative, poets, too, could be found wanting in their failure to achieve novel combinations. In an early review of Joseph Rodman Drake's *The Culprit Fay and Other Poems* and Fitz-Greene Halleck's *Alnwick Castle* (*Southern Literary Messenger*, April 1836), these two prominent New York poets appeared to lack the true poetical faculty in rendering natural scenery. Poe would acknowledge in a January 1837 review that Bryant occupied a secure and respected position among the American authors in general; by implication Bryant, a native New Englander, now clearly occupied a superior position among New York poets, easily surpassing the likes of Drake and Halleck. That status owed much to Bryant's "repeated reference to the beauty and majesty of nature." However ardent and loving his renderings of natural scenes and vistas, Bryant's poetic vision was limited to nature in its "moral" and "physical" manifestations. His verses may lack the "spiritual" or soul-stirring characteristics reserved for poets of the first rank. If Poe generally limited his remarks on Bryant to the poet's efficient handling of word choice, prosody, and versification – Bryant had delivered formal lectures on these subjects in the 1820s – he adopted a broader perspective in the "Drake-Halleck Review." He went beyond derision of the two poets to a fuller expression of his thoughts on ideal forms of beauty and the poetic sentiment. In particular, Poe takes great relish in ridiculing the sentimental endowment of natural objects with human significance. For example, he disparages the absurdity of Drake's fairies and fays talking to the "spirits of the waves," or "using a muscle shell for a boat," or donning such equipment as an "acorn helmet," "a turtle down plume," "a cloak of the wings of butterflies," or the "shield of a ladybug." Poe remarks on such a practice: "The truth is, that the only requisite for verse of this nature ... is a tolerable acquaintance with the qualities of the objects to be detailed, and a very moderate endowment of the Faculty of Comparison ... which is the chief constituent of Fancy or the power of combination. A thousand such lines may be composed without the least degree of the Poetic Sentiment, which is Ideality, Imagination, or the creative ability." Drake and other inferior poets engage in Comparison, a mechanical process aligned with fancy, which transfers objects from the human sphere to a natural setting. As in the "Letter to B—," flippancy and satire coexist with Poe's alignment of true poetry with an aspiration for the unearthly and mystical. Imagination, the true soul of poetry, springs from "the mystical," "the august," "the ideal" (*E&R*, 520–525). If it was impossible for Poe to read without laughing descriptions of a mechanically equipped fairy or sprite, he would later comment that humor and ideality could coexist. In a review of the New England poet John Brainard, he claimed that one "branch of humor ... blends so happily with the ideal, that from the union result some of the finest effects of legitimate poesy. We allude to what is termed 'archness' – a trait with which popular feeling, which is unfailingly poetic, has invested, for example, the whole character of the fairy" (*E&R*, 411).

Many of the concerns in the "Drake – Halleck Review" surface again in Poe's review of Thomas Moore's *Alciphron* (*Burton's Gentleman's Magazine*, January 1840). Previously Poe had relegated the fancy to a secondary status below the imagination. He was following Coleridge once again by claiming that the fancy combines while the imagination creates. Rather than sustaining this sharp distinction in the *Alciphron* review, he argued that the difference between fancy and imagination was a matter of degree: "The fancy as nearly creates as the imagination; and neither creates in any respect. All novel conceptions are merely unusual combinations." Manifesting his erudition by modifying Coleridgean categories, Poe turned his learning against American poets, and his test case was once again Drake's "The Culprit Fay," whose conception never rose above "mere fancy." In contrast to the mechanical comparisons found in Drake's poem, Shelley's poetry did not belabor physical properties or "moral sentiment." To beauty and ideality, Poe added a new ingredient derived from the German critic Augustus William Schlegel – what he termed "the mystic." Poe's first-hand knowledge of the German language was limited, and his citation of Schlegel presented a learned and cosmopolitan posture as he skewered American poets. Whatever the case, Poe argued that in place of a moralistic theme that might dominate a literary work – like a "transparent upper current of meaning" – the mystic functioned suggestively as an unobtrusive secondary element. Poe is intentionally vague in assigning moral value to this mystic undercurrent of meaning; rather than an overarching moral message, the mystic is similar to moving air or musical accompaniment. However imprecisely Poe defines this poetic desideratum, it is nevertheless a powerful element in what G. R. Thompson calls his supernalist aesthetics. Musical notes and earthly images can offer glimpses of "a far more ethereal beauty beyond" (*E&R*, 334–337).[4]

In his review of Bryant's *Poems*, Poe claimed that the poet faltered when he strained to find parallels between natural phenomena and the moral world. In such cases, Bryant's "mere didactics" lapsed into primitive expression (*E&R*, 441). When Poe turned his attention to Longfellow's *Ballads and Other Poems* in a short review in *Graham's Magazine* (March 1842), he likewise claimed that "his conception of the aims of poesy is all wrong" – that "his didactics are all out of place" (*E&R*, 682–683). A longer review of the *Ballads* the following month in *Graham's* elaborated on these ideas and discussed with greater specificity as well many of the issues mentioned in the review of *Alciphron*.

Several years before confronting Longfellow's poetry, Poe had written a brief review of his *Hyperion, A Romance* (*Burton's Gentleman's Magazine*, October 1839), thus beginning what would be a tumultuous five-year involvement with the New England author's works. *Hyperion* was in some ways the record of a European tour, but like other travel books Poe reviewed, it contained an unwelcome tendency toward random dispersion of detail. Longfellow lacked the successful combining power of the true artist, and Poe found *Hyperion* "without design, without shape, without beginning, middle, or end." Longfellow's inefficient mixture of heterogeneous elements caused Poe to ask, "what earthly object has his book accomplished? – what definite impression has it left?" (*E&R*, 670). Unity of "design," "impression," or "effect" would be important criteria when applied to the genres of fictional and nonfictional prose, and Poe would expand and reformulate his thoughts on the aesthetic unity of prose works when he later confronted the works by a former college classmate of Longfellow, Nathaniel Hawthorne.

Poetic originality became an even more central critical standard when Poe evaluated Longfellow's verses. Novelty, when the poet artfully combines existing forms of beauty, fulfills the aims of creativity. But particularly when the poet aspires to a beauty not found in earthly forms – when he thirsts for supernal beauty – are the primary aims of poetry met: "This burning thirst belongs to the *immortal* essence of man's nature. It is equally a consequence and an indication of man's perennial life. It is the desire of the moth for the star. It is not the mere appreciation of the beauty before us. It is a wild effort to reach the beauty above" (*E&R*, 686). Longfellow confounded the true aim of poetry with the demands of morality and truth. He erred in assuming that "the inculcation of a moral" was essential to poetry. Acknowledging a deep respect for truth, Poe suggested that a calm, unexcited disposition allowed the mind to discover the truth, a different mood from that which allowed access to the poetical. Aligning poetry with the faculty of taste, a mediating category that occupied a distinct position between the intellect and the moral sense, Poe refused to mix "the obstinate oils" of poetry, truth, and morality. One can discern in the Longfellow review the germ of Poe's evolving notion that aesthetic appreciation, rather than didactic purpose, was a chief poetic value. He would later give fuller expression to these ideas in "The Poetic Principle," noting that the aspiration for pure forms of beauty, embodied in the feminine ideal, reflect the spiritual yearnings of mortal human nature.

Poe's elevation of novelty and ideality as hallmarks of poetic genius, joined to his intensifying opposition to didactic verse, gave to his definition of poetic originality an avant-garde flavor in sharp contrast to Longfellow's more conservative position, outlined in essays in the late 1820s and early 1830s. Further contributing to Poe's increasing animus toward Longfellow, a January 1844 article in London's *Foreign Quarterly Review* excoriated American poets as either imitators or plagiarists. The article in the British periodical briefly called Poe an imitator of Tennyson (the British poet Longfellow imitated, or so Poe claimed), but it praised Longfellow because of his immersion in the European literary tradition. When Longfellow published a miscellaneous collection of poems called *The Waif*, all of Poe's tumultuous feelings toward the New England poetry establishment came to a head. Turning the tradition of New England moralism against that region's most celebrated poet, Poe detected a "moral taint" in *The Waif* in a brief note at the end of the second part of his review, which appeared in the *New York Evening Mirror* on 14 January 1845 (*E&R*, 702). Poe's criticisms of Longfellow extended back to his negative assessment of *Hyperion* in 1839, but up to this point, they were no more intense than those offered by other critics of the New England poet. Poe's note in the *Mirror* might today be viewed as what it was intended to be – a footnote in a longer column – had not other periodical editors and contributors also raised questions about Longfellow's originality and the contents of *The Waif*. Longfellow's New England friends, too, sprang to his defense, and the combative Poe sensed that a regional cabal had developed around Professor Longfellow, the most prominent of New England's literati and the darling of New York editors like Lewis Gaylord Clark. Outright accusations of plagiarism against Longfellow surfaced, and Poe conducted his own "little Longfellow war" on the subject in the pages of the *Broadway Journal*, the urban periodical for which he began to work in 1845. Various periodicals and anonymous correspondents entered the fray, and the names of almost all the most celebrated poets of the time (including Neal, Whittier, and Bryant) were brought into a bitter literary battle that raged in the popular press for several months. Toward the end of the controversy, the *Boston Post* would add to the fashionable word-play on Poe's name: "Poe, the critic, is within a t of being a poet."[5] Whether one views Poe's attacks on Longfellow as satirical, excessive, tasteless, or just, they contributed to his image as a slashing, vindictive critic. Influential editors like Griswold and Clark of the *Knickerbocker* were unforgiving in their assessments of Poe's critical judgments.[6]

Fresh from his "little war" over plagiarism with Longfellow, Poe returned to the city of his birth in October 1845 to speak before the Boston Lyceum. Poe's first public lecture had been a presentation on "American Poetry" before the William Wirt Institute in Philadelphia in November 1843, and he used this and subsequent lectures to refine his notions on the nature of poetry and to counter Griswold's attempt to establish an American poetic canon in his influential anthology, *The Poets and Poetry of America*. In Boston he prefaced his recitation with remarks against didactic verse, then read his long philosophical poem, "Al Aaraaf." At his audience's request, he finished his performance with a reading of "The Raven." In the wake of his attacks on Longfellow and his defenders, Poe became the object of ridicule among Boston editors, including Cornelia Walter of the *Boston Transcript* and Leander Streeter of the *Boston Star*. Poe responded to these criticisms in the *Broadway Journal* by claiming the "soft impeachment" of a hoax. "Al Aaraaf," he asserted, was a juvenile poem chosen for the occasion because he could not have been expected to produce a new, original poem for a Boston audience. With this slap at Longfellow's Boston and its appetite for derivative verses, he further insulted his Boston audience by claiming that he was drunk when he read "Al Aaraaf."

By appearing before the Boston Lyceum, Poe knew that he was participating in a respected New England cultural institution. He must have been familiar with the tradition of New England oratory, embodied in figures like Ralph Waldo Emerson. In all likelihood, he confounded this brand of New England eloquence with a high moral tone, a consistent, even obsessive object of attack in Poe's reviews that surfaced with special prominence in the year of 1845. Another object of attack was New England Transcendentalism, for he claimed to have chosen the abstruse "Al Aaraaf" for an audience of vague thinkers, that is, transcendentalists.[7]

In his satires, "How to Write a Blackwood Article" and "Never Bet the Devil Your Head," Poe used *reductio ad absurdum* to ridicule Transcendentalism. In assaulting Transcendentalism on stylistic grounds, he questioned the "Carlylisms," "Euphuisms," "Merry Andrewisms," and "metaphor-run mad" of this school of writing. Transcendental style, he argued, often lapsed into "obscurity for obscurity's sake" or "mysticism for mysticism's sake." Emerson, Carlyle, and the poet William Ellery Channing were scorned for their inability to distinguish obscurity of expression from expression of obscurity.

Poe attacked stylistic excesses, but his irreverence extended to the social philosophy of the Transcendentalists. Fashioning himself a member of the Virginia gentry, a social class to which he could only aspire, he objected to Transcendentalist views on abolition and reform. Adopting a hostile stance once again because of regional bias, he hardly discriminated among individual literary figures and social thinkers. He referred to Boston as the Frogpond or as headquarters of "the Humanity clique,"[8] and lumped together writers from this city with Transcendentalists and Socialists.

In the light of Poe's battles with New England authors in the mid-1840s, particularly on the issues of novelty and originality, one can easily detect a more caustic tone in his remarks on the fiction of Nathaniel Hawthorne if one examines respectively reviews of *Twice-Told Tales* in 1842 (*Graham's Magazine*) and in 1847 (*Godey's Lady's Book*). In *Graham's* Poe had claimed, "Mr. Hawthorne's distinctive trait is invention, creation, imagination, originality.... Mr. Hawthorne is original at all points." By 1847 Poe had clearly modified his position, "The fact is, that if Mr. Hawthorne were really original, he could not fail of making himself felt by the public. But the fact is, he is not original in any sense" (*E&R*, 579). Any reader familiar enough with the writing of the German fantasy writer Ludwig Tieck, Poe seemed to suggest, could hardly think Hawthorne original. Hawthorne's borrowings from Tieck had been widely noted during his lifetime, culminating in James Russell Lowell's famous lampoon of Hawthorne in "A Fable for Critics" (1848): "He's a John Bunyan Fouqué, a Puritan Tieck."[9] Poe had encountered reviews associating Hawthorne and Tieck, and may have wanted to deflect attention from his own perceived borrowings from Hawthorne. Just as Longfellow's exposure to German sources had been used as a weapon in the plagiarism war, Poe used the name of Tieck to question Hawthorne's originality. Criticizing Hawthorne's penchant for allegory – his allowing what should have been suggestive or unobtrusive to become dominant – Poe mixed this reservation about Hawthorne with his impatience with perceived stylistic peculiarities, supposedly absorbed from the Transcendentalists.

> He is peculiar and not original . . . Indeed, his spirit of 'metaphor-run mad' is clearly imbibed from the phalanx and phalantsery atmosphere in which he has been so long struggling for breath. . . . Let him mend his pen, get a bottle of visible ink, come out from the Old Manse, cut Mr. Alcott, hang (if possible) the editor of 'The Dial,' and throw out of the window to the pigs all his odd numbers of 'The North American Review.' (*E&R*, 574–588)

The phalanx to which Hawthorne belonged was the questionable utopian social experiment at Brook Farm. In drawing from the 1847 review important principles of short fiction, notably Poe's theory of single effect, literary historians have questioned the accuracy and the justness of these remarks. The experiment at Brook Farm was at the point of collapse, Hawthorne had left Concord's Old Manse, the *Dial* was extinct, and Emerson had embarked on a tour of England. Hyperbolic or irate, Poe's remarks on Hawthorne reflect his charged and hostile attitude toward New England Transcendentalism and its central figures. To the extent that an heroic or unitary vision of Transcendentalism has been questioned by social historians, however, his opinions on the movement remain pertinent.

Nearly all Poe's criticism on poetry and fiction was written for the magazines for which he toiled. Ever the creature of the periodical milieu, he could not help but be knowledgeable about the range and diversity of publishing outlets: the penny daily, the mammoth weekly, the cheap magazine, the literary monthly, the pamphlet, the pirated story, and the collection of fugitive pieces. Magazines like *Graham's*, for which he toiled in the 1840s, earned the label "namby-pamby," for their attempt to cater to a polite middle class audience. Occupying a decidedly different place on the publishing spectrum were periodicals that catered to the fast-paced lives and popular tastes of their readers. The most notorious of the penny papers was the *New York Sun*, edited by Richard Adams Locke (1800–1871). The *Sun* published sensational and fictitious stories in the guise of fact, and Locke's "Moon-Hoax" (August 1835), with its narrative of strange creatures and winged bipeds on the lunar surface, was one of the newspaper sensations of the 1830s. Sensing that Locke had ushered in a new and different age in commercial journalism, Poe commented: "the object of the journal professed to be that of 'supplying the public with the news of the day at so cheap a rate as to lie within the means of all.' The consequences of the scheme, in their influence on the whole newspaper business of the country, and through this business on the interests of the country at large, are probably beyond all calculation" (*E&R*, 1214).[10] This era of professional metropolitan journalism ushered in the commercialization of print. In an era of increased sensationalism in journalism editors might exploit colorful topics or appeal to the reader's sense of excitement or novelty by covering exotic journeys or developments in the sciences (or pseudosciences). Works of fiction imitated the techniques of journalism, and Poe was not above exploiting newspaper readers' appetites for extravagant claims presented in the guise of fact. His own "Balloon Hoax" (*Extra Sun*, 13 April 1844) was composed in the style of a "scoop" or "big story" periodical writing. If this story duped New Yorkers into believing that the Atlantic had been crossed in seventy-five hours, his "Facts in the Case of M. Valdemar," written in the wake of the Boston Lyceum fiasco, was a hoax on mesmerism, a fad he associated with the Party of Progress in Boston. The scientific tone and reportorial narration of these pieces contributed to their successes as hoaxes, and they show Poe's capacity to combine his skills as a fiction maker and working journalist.

Able to manipulate aspects of the periodical on which he was working, Poe used each publishing medium to wield his editorial pen, to function as a patron to women writers, or to engage in overt promotion of his own work. The author of "Some Secrets of the Magazine Prison House" and "X-ing a Paragrab," he experienced the low pay for "poor devil authors" as well as the editorial drudgery of preparing and editing copy. Of his variable successes in the American periodical milieu, the "Autography" was one venture that seemed to fulfill its promise. Developed in three installments in *Graham's Magazine* from November 1841 to January 1842, his plan was to accompany autograph signatures of the famous and obscure literati with comments on individual character, as suggested by relevant features of penmanship. Appended to each autograph was literary gossip that spiced the critical commentary on each author's writings. By February 1842, he was able to look back on the success of the series and its significant contributions in furthering the cause of *Graham's*: "Those articles have had a great run – have done wonders for the Journal."[11] The humor of the "Autography" might appear to be obvious: Poe would bring that most idiosyncratic feature of an individual author, an example of writing from his own hand, into the impersonal world of print. He would use the stylistic features of others, sometimes stressing personal peculiarity or idiosyncrasy, for the purposes of promoting himself and his own journal. His assemblage of autographs, spread out over three installments, would constitute a gathering together of America's literary lions, but would also include a number of asses. If some sensitive readers of the series took in "sober earnest...what everybody else understood to be at least half meant in jest,"[12] Poe could savor some of the best jokes in the series. The names of famous writers, tied to their autographs, would pique readers' attention and increase circulation. The series allowed him some irresponsible fun at the expense of authors he disliked and flattery for those he favored. In a prelude to the *Graham's* series (*Southern Literary Messenger*, 1836), he could even treat the authors as "puppets," putting words in the mouths of individual authors. Halleck, for example, is called upon to claim that a work he had never seen on a general subject could be nothing but original:

> Your poem on 'Things in General,' I have not had the pleasure of seeing. I have not, however, the least doubt of its – of its – that is to say, of its extreme delicacy of sentiment, and highly original style of thinking – to say nothing at present of that – of that extraordinary and felicitous manner of expression which so particularly characterizes all that – that I have seen of your writings. I shall endeavor, sir, to procure your Poem, and anticipate much pleasure in its perusal.[13]

If the 1836 "Autography" had a fictional setting, the *Graham's* series appears on the surface to be more factual and critical, but Poe's semi-serious or facetious tone, established in his early years as an editor, is once again in evidence. Whatever the case, the plan for the "Autography," adapted in "The Literati of New York City," provided the stimulus for a full-scale survey of American authors. (Among the New England authors skewered in the 1836 "Autography" were John Neal and William Ellery Channing while Longfellow, Oliver Wendell Holmes, Charles Sprague, Bryant, Whittier, and others appeared in the 1841–1842 series.) One can only lament that this ambitious project (possibly bearing the title *The Living Writers of America*), like his plan to own and edit his own magazine, was never fulfilled since it would have provided more comprehensive insight into Poe's critical practices and their application to the American literary scene.

Today the student has recourse to Poe's criticism in nicely edited collections,[14] but as the previous discussion shows, nearly all these pieces were written in his role as an editor or reviewer for the individual periodicals for which he toiled. Despite the diversity of publishing outlets and their occasional nature, these pieces reflect a remarkably coherent, self-conscious view of poetry and the creative process. In composing "The Philosophy of Composition" (1846) after writing "The Raven," he joined an original poem and a rationale for its creation in artful combination. He countered the Romantic assumption that the poet works in a "fine frenzy" of pure inspiration. Offering a painstakingly deliberate account of the stages of composition of his most celebrated work, he demonstrated that the poet was of necessity a critic and underscored the corollary principle that the critical process was creative. Whatever sleight of hand or bravado are used in his highly rational rehearsal of the steps followed by the practicing poet, the essay is noteworthy for the central role of "effect," the conscious choice of an emotional atmosphere that takes primacy over incident, character, and versification. In this essay and in "The Poetic Principle" (1850), he refined ideas previously presented in a review of Longfellow's *Ballads and Other Poems* (1842). He also offered his famous pronouncement that "the death of a beautiful woman is the purest of all poetical themes." Once again stressing the emotional effect of the literary text on the reader, Poe claimed that poetry works to achieve "elevation of soul," an emotional transport that could not be long sustained. Thus, he further asserted that "a long poem is a contradiction in terms" (*E&R*, 19). Because of his insistence that a poem's affective impact was enhanced by music or "sweet sound," Poe devoted considerable attention to techniques of versification, as both "The Philosophy of Composition" and "Rationale of Verse" (1848) indicate.

Whatever the origins of Poe's artistic practices and critical principles – probably a combination of English and German sources (Coleridge, the Common Sense philosophers, A. W. Schlegel, perhaps Kant and Schiller)[15] – his influence has been immense. His reviews of Hawthorne mark him as the first significant theorist of the modern short story. Approaching the tale as a painter or a landscape architect might deal with his craft, Poe discusses the importance of "design," the accommodation of heterogeneous elements into a "unity of effect or impression." Indeed his notion that the brevity of the short story could concentrate "the immense force derivable from totality" is a principle overt or latent in many twentieth-century examples of the form. Later writers may not have emulated his more pronounced Gothic effects, but writers as diverse as Robert Louis Stevenson, Jorge Luis Borges, and Vladimir Nabokov have used Poe's stories as pretexts for their own fictional experiments. His influence on theories of poetry has been less powerful although his celebration of pure forms of beauty and his opposition to the "heresy of the didactic" laid a foundation for champions of aestheticism and Symbolism. His citation and close reading of key passages from works he reviewed suggest some affinity with formalist criticism. These various strands of influence – affirming that a work of art is a rational construct – suggest an image of Poe as a conscious craftsman far different from that of his nineteenth-century detractors.

NOTES

1. Rufus Wilmot Griswold, "Death of Edgar Allan Poe," *New York Daily Tribune*, 9 October 1849; reprinted in *Recognition*, pp. 31, 35.
2. Scholarship on the Byron–Poe connection is extensive, much of it synthesized in Katrina Bachinger, *The Multi-Man Genre and Poe's Byrons* (Salzburg: Institut

Für Anglistik and Amerikanistik, 1987) and her *Edgar Allan Poe's Biographies of Byron* (Lewiston, NY: Edwin Mellen Press, 1994). See also Kent P. Ljungquist, "Howitt's 'Byronian Rambles' and the Picturesque Setting of 'The Fall of the House of Usher,'" *ESQ* 33 (1987): 224–236.

3. For discussion of Poe's critical theories within the context of viewpoints expressed by Bryant and Longfellow, see Kenneth A. Hovey, "Critical Provincialism: Poe's Poetic Principle in Antebellum Context," *American Quarterly* 39 (1987): 341–354.

4. See G. R. Thompson, *Circumscribed Eden of Dreams: Dreamvision and Nightmare in Poe's Early Poetry* (Baltimore: Edgar Allan Poe Society, 1984), and Thomas S. Hansen, and Burton R. Pollin, *The German Face of Edgar Allan Poe: A Study of Literary References in His Works* (Columbia, SC: Camden House, 1995).

5. "All Sorts of Paragraphs," *Boston Post*, 1 May 1845, p. 1.

6. See Sidney P. Moss, *Poe's Literary Battles: The Critic in the Context of His Literary Milieu* (Durham: Duke University Press, 1963); Burton R. Pollin, "Poe as the Author of the 'Outis' Letter and 'The Bird of the Dream,'" *Poe Studies* 20 (1987): 10–15; Kent P. Ljungquist and Buford Jones, "The Identity of Outis: A Further Chapter in the Poe – Longfellow War," *American Literature* 60 (1988): 402–415; and Ljungquist, "The 'Little War' and Longfellow's Dilemma: New Documents in the Plagiarism Controversy of 1845," *Resources for American Literary Study* 23 (1997): 28–59.

7. See Ljungquist, "Poe's 'Al Aaraaf' and the Boston Lyceum: Contributions to Primary and Secondary Bibliography," *Victorian Periodicals Review* 28 (1995): 199–216.

8. Burton R. Pollin, "The Living Writers of America: A Manuscript by Edgar Allan Poe," *Studies in the American Renaissance, 1991*, ed. Joel Myerson (Charlottesville: University Press of Virginia, 1991), p. 165.

9. James Russell Lowell, "A Fable for Critics," in *Literary Criticism of James Russell Lowell*, ed. Herbert F. Smith (Lincoln: University of Nebraska Press, 1969), p. 189.

10. For Poe's responses to the economics of the book and periodical trade, see Terence Whalen, *Edgar Allan Poe and the Masses: The Political Economy of Literature in Antebellum America* (Princeton University Press, 1999).

11. Poe to Frederick W. Thomas, 3 February 1842, in *Letters*, 1: 192–193.

12. "Mr. Poe's 'Autography,'" *Philadelphia Public Ledger and Daily Transcript*, 23 December 1841, p. 2.

13. *Collected Works* (Mabbott), 2: 269. For an informative discussion of "Autography" within the context of Poe's humorous strategies, see Donald Barlow Stauffer, *The Merry Mood: Poe's Uses of Humor* (Baltimore: Edgar Allan Poe Society of Baltimore, 1981), pp. 15–17.

14. In addition to *E&R*, which is not complete, see *Literary Criticism of Edgar Allan Poe*, ed. Robert L. Hough (Lincoln: University of Nebraska Press, 1965), and *Selections from the Critical Writings of Edgar Allan Poe*, ed. F. C. Prescott (1909; reprinted, Staten Island: Gordian Press, 1981).

15. See Rachel Polonsky, "Poe's Aesthetic Theory," in Chapter Three.

2

SANDRA TOMC

Poe and his circle

The obituary notices following Poe's death in 1849 struggled to make sense of what fellow-authors felt was the central contradiction of his life: that he was one of the country's preeminent literary "geniuses" yet he had lived a life of misery and privation. Overwhelmingly, Poe's contemporaries were forced to conclude that his peculiar personality was responsible for his lack of professional success. Many, like fellow-author Nathaniel Parker Willis, felt that Poe's particular habits and talents as a writer foreclosed the possibility of material reward: "Mr Poe wrote with fastidious difficulty, and in a style too much above the popular level to be well paid." George R. Graham agreed: "[T]he very organization of a mind such as that of Poe – the very tension and tone of his exquisitely strung nerves . . . utterly unfitted him for the rude jostlings and fierce competitorship of trade." Henry Beck Hirst felt it was Poe's refusal to join the critical status quo that made his failure inevitable: "Poe was no time server, and as a critic he could not, and would not *lie*. [Λ]s a consequence, he made enemies, – like carping muck-worms in the barnyards, of literature . . . But their number was legion – and he was only one." Finally, in a particularly memorable version of this theme, Rufus Griswold portrayed Poe as a madman incapable of functioning within the "numberless complexities of the social world": "He walked the streets, in madness or melancholy, with lips moving in indistinct curses, or with eyes upturned in passionate prayers . . . and all night, with drenched garments and arms wildly beating the wind and rain, he would speak as if to spirits that at such time only could be evoked by him from that Aidenn close by whose portals his disturbed soul sought to forget the ills to which his constitution subjected him" (*CH*, 311, 382–383, 316, 299–300).

Poe's "disturbed soul," responsible in these accounts for his alienation from a mainstream literary and "social world," remains a powerful explanatory device in modern assessments of his professional life and works. On one hand, Poe's "peculiarity" has justified his absence from most twentieth-century accounts of American literature, which have largely accepted Vernon

Parrington's decision that the "problem of Poe, fascinating as it is, lies quite outside the main current of American thought."[1] On the other, Poe's "disturbed soul" accounts for his extraordinary presence in twentieth-century elaborations of psychoanalytic theory. It was Marie Bonaparte's analysis of Poe's tales as scripts of his psychic disturbance that inspired Jacques Lacan's famous seminar on the "The Purloined Letter" and finally typified Poe, in his very peculiarity and alienation, as a subject of "'timeless' psychoanalytic themes."[2] Addressing themselves to these two literary-historical and psychoanalytic traditions, which exclude and include Poe for the same reasons, many recent scholars have tried to dispel the idea of Poe as a disturbed and alienated outcast and to rethink him instead as a subject of specific antebellum social and cultural forces. Terence Whalen argues that "Far from being the wild offspring of an autonomous or diseased mind, Poe's tales were . . . the rational products of social labor, imagined and executed in the workshop of American capitalism."[3]

The present essay contributes to these attempts to reimagine Poe in the context of his society and culture, but at the same time I have no wish to ignore or jettison Poe's "disturbed soul" as somehow incidental to his place in "the workshop of American capitalism." Poe's contemporaries were quick to blame what they saw as his particular eccentricities for his failure as a professional author, but obscured in contemporary and modern accounts of Poe's alienation is the extent to which a rhetoric of social and psychic dysfunction circulated generally in antebellum critical and authorial formulations, describing and vilifying not just Poe but dozens of his fellow-authors, including the authors of his obituary notices. At its simplest level, the antebellum rhetoric of dysfunction described fairly accurately the individuals who took up professional authorship in the absence of other means of financial support at a period when writers were paid poverty wages. But at another level the rhetoric of dysfunction mediated and conditioned material relations within literary "trade" that perpetuated itself through what might be called the peculiar behavior competitive capitalism required. Looking at Poe and other authors of his generation with similar career trajectories and economic means, I want to underline the extent to which his personal peculiarities, far from being incidental or antithetical to his career, played dynamically with a literary industry that embraced and cultivated dysfunction as a condition of authorial productivity and repute.

When Poe turned to professional authorship in the mid 1830s he selected a career almost guaranteed not to issue in what antebellum society judged to be pecuniary or professional success.[4] Although the United States was experiencing the early stages of an explosion in the production and traffic of print materials, comparable in scope to the late twentieth-century digital revolution, several factors ensured that American authors were not among those who profited from the increased demand for their wares. The lack of international copyright legislation meant American publishers could freely pirate popular British works without remunerating their authors, which made them reluctant to invest capital in writers at home. American writers were thus in the position of either paying for publication themselves or sell manuscripts outright and forego royalties. This undercutting of domestic authors was abetted by the continued dominance of the myth, if not the actuality, of the avocational author – the "gentleman scribbler" who penned *belles lettres* in his idle hours. Although this period witnessed the emergence of a new breed of writers, bohemian sons and daughters of middle class families and educated printer's apprentices who together would eventually gel into a class of white-collar professionals, there remained enough individuals happy to churn out poetry, fiction, and essays for little or no money remained to keep the myth of the gentleman scribbler alive and standards of remuneration for all except writers of renown extremely low.

Virtually the only avenue open to writers without capital or some alternative source of income was magazine work. Here again, the chances for pecuniary success were low. Although periodicals like *Graham's* were paying their most famous contributors up to $50.00 for a poem in the early 1840s, the standard rate of pay until late in the decade remained $1.00 per page. Since magazine contents were not copyrighted, writers could see their contributions stolen and reprinted in dozens of other magazines across the continent, swelling the subscription lists of rival journals, without realizing another penny for their work. Those who sought a regular income as writers had few options but to take on editorial work, a grueling, feverish labor that in most cases paid subsistence wages. By one estimate, Poe received $624.00 annually as editor of *The Southern Literary Messenger*, in addition to which his employer paid him $1.60 per page for the poems, reviews, and short stories he contributed. This income did not place him above the equivalent of the 1981 national poverty level.[5]

Given these conditions, who was attracted to professional authorship? No one of much worth, according to James Fenimore Cooper. "Talent is sure of too many avenues to wealth and honors in America," Cooper regretfully noted in *Notions of the Americans*, "to seek, unnecessarily, an unknown and hazardous path [of authorship]."[6] Authorship offered rewards, to be sure. At a period when *belles lettres* were entangled on the one hand with an ideal of genteel leisure – an ideal fortified by the number of genteel individuals still willing to produce literature in their idle hours – and on the other with Byronic glamour, authorship held out the seductive, if not always materially tangible, rewards of prestige and fame. The lack of immediate financial stability, however, meant that vocational authorship tended to attract a specific kind of person. It appealed to the socially disenfranchised, persons of genteel education and limited means who sought in authorship a social luster to which they otherwise had little access; it appealed to the socially ambitious individuals of "middling" or lower class status, who longed for the sheen of fashion and prestige; and it appealed, more broadly, to those who would not or could not conform to the standards of normality described for their particular family and class. The ranks of professional authorship, in short, tended to be made up of outsiders, individuals who were judged by their society (and often by themselves) to be marginal or inadequate and who sought in authorship some form of success and consolation.[7]

According to most modern critics and biographers, Poe belonged mainly to the category of the dispossessed. The orphaned son of actors, he was raised in Richmond, Virginia in the prosperous household of his merchant foster father, John Allan.[8] Never quite admitted into the fold of Allan family legitimacy (although Poe was their only child, the Allans made no move to adopt him legally), Poe never quite lost a sense of his own orphaned status. Like other sons of wealthy southern merchants, Poe was taught, as he put it, to "aspire to eminence in public life,"[9] to which he added a rather desperate desire to please and impress his foster father. But whether because of temperament or circumstances, Poe's tendency throughout early adulthood was to mix his aspirations and his desire to please with choices that reaffirmed his alienation. By the time he decided upon authorship as his sole career at the age of twenty-six, he had behind him a record of failures, debts, family quarrels, and unconventional romantic attachments. Poe assured Allan, "I feel that within me which will make me fulfil your highest wishes and only beg you to suspend your judgement until you hear *of* me again."[10] But a thwarted career at the University of Virginia, a brief stint in the US Army, and then a briefer career at West Point, unenthusiastically financed by Allan, issued in neither public eminence nor the more quotidian goal of Allan's approval. Allan died without bequeathing his foster son a penny of his considerable fortune. Poe, suffering from bouts of severe depression and even suicidal, crowned this final bitter token of his dispossession by falling desperately in love with his thirteen-year-old cousin, Virginia Clemm, whom he secretly married in the same year.

Poe had been publishing poetry throughout this period, primarily at his own considerable expense. Although these volumes went largely unnoticed and remained largely unsold, Poe's reason for producing them was of a piece with his quest for eminence and approval. As he told Allan when he asked his support of $100.00 for the publication of yet another volume: "At my time of life there is much in being *before the eye of the world* – if once noticed I can easily cut out a path to reputation."[11] Even so, it was only when all hope of a legacy from John Allan vanished that Poe thought seriously about making a living as a writer. Successively orphaned, rejected, disowned, and disinherited, Poe, in Kenneth Silverman's opinion, came to professional writing with "a sense of deficiency in himself and of envy toward others he thought more adequate."[12]

Many of Poe's contemporaries entered professional authorship with similar ambitions and records of failure, exile, emotional instability, and unconventional sexual or romantic choices. Although one could look at any number of Poe's friends and employers – William Burton, for example, proprietor of *Burton's Gentleman's Magazine*, a bigamist and former itinerant actor of what one contemporary called the "vulgar indecent" variety[13] – I want to focus here on two of Poe's memorialists, Nathaniel Parker Willis and Rufus Wilmot Griswold. I choose these writers for several reasons. Like Poe, they came to authorship without connections or other sources of income; they all engaged in similar work, editing journals and writing short fiction, poetry, and criticism; they all appealed to the same audience, educated, middle-brow readers in search of taste and the occasional scandal; and they all achieved the zenith of their fame at about the same time, in the mid-1840s. All three, in addition, knew each other fairly well and moved in the same social circles. Poe worked for Willis as a subeditor on the *Weekly Mirror*, and it was Willis who first published "The Raven." Griswold not only moved in the same circles as Poe but curiously shadowed him, anthologizing Poe in *Poets and Poetry of America*, replacing him as editor of *Graham's*, supplanting Poe in Frances Osgood's affections, and then emerging as his literary executor and purveyor of his defamation after Poe's death. Although from different backgrounds, all three shared similar "peculiarities," including a history of social and familial exile and feelings of envy and deficiency.

Nathaniel Parker Willis, the son of a staunchly Puritan Boston printer, distinguished himself early by his inability to live according to the standards of the institutions he found himself confronting.[14] A student at Yale in the 1820s, Willis abandoned his father's hopes that he would follow in the paternal footsteps and pursued life in the fashionable society of Boston instead. Willis's theater-going, champagne drinking, and flamboyant dandyish clothes infuriated members of his church, and in 1829, in the first of a series of exiles, he was excommunicated. Having abandoned the codes of the church, however, Willis proved equally incapable of abiding by those of the society he had chosen instead. Perennially in debt and not shy about advertising his sexual exploits with seamstresses, wealthy married women, and mistresses of other men, Willis was finally driven from Boston in disgrace, reviled throughout the city for his "dissipations" and having, in his own words, not "a sou in the world beyond what my pen brings me" and "a world of envy and slander at my back."[15] Although not, like Poe, inclined to depression, Willis shared with Poe a keen sense of his own inadequacy and despite his disgrace in Boston yearned for a place in what he called "high life," clinging to a literary career as his only means of achieving it.

Rufus Griswold had far less auspicious origins than either Poe or Willis. One of fourteen children born to a farmer in the backwoods of Vermont, Griswold, an "unruly," "restless" child,[16] left home at the age of fifteen when both school and his brother's shop proved too confining. Griswold was introduced to literature as well as to "emotional abandon and freedom"[17] through an intense, probably romantic relationship with another writer, George C. Foster, with whom Griswold lived until he was seventeen. Disengaging himself from what had become yet another confining circumstance, Griswold took to transience, probably apprenticing as a printer at some point and eventually finding work on a Syracuse newspaper. A self-described "solitary soul wandering through the world, a homeless, joyless outcast,"[18] Griswold shared with Poe a tendency to depression and morbidity. Upon the death of his wife, Griswold, who would dub Poe a "madman," was so overcome with grief that in what he called "a fit of madness" he went to the vault where his wife had already been interred for forty days and "turned aside the drapery that hid her face. . . . I kissed for the last time her cold, black forehead – I cut off locks of her beautiful hair, damp with the death dews, and sunk down in senseless agony beside the ruin of all that was dearest in the world. In the evening, a friend from the city . . . found me there, my face still resting on her own, and my body as lifeless and cold as that before me."[19] But if Griswold had Poe's "exquisitely strung nerves," he had Willis's ambition and drive. He pursued letters for the stated purpose of "elevating those excluded from an aristocracy of learning"[20] and conceived of himself as America's great disseminator of *belles lettres* to the masses.

To the extent that professional authorship attracted individuals who were deemed by their society, and generally by themselves, to be socially marginal and psychically and sexually peculiar, personal dysfunction was not, as the tradition of Poe scholarship paints it, aberrant or incidental to the wage system of literary production but a systemic part of it, an outcome of paltry salaries, unpleasant working conditions, and promises of prestige. Nor did this system render a writer's peculiarities any more incidental in the subsequent pursuit of professional success. Although Poe, Willis, and Griswold turned to authorship in the hopes of earning glamour, eminence, and, perhaps most elusive of all, money, the circumstances in which they worked did not lend themselves to the easy attainment of these goals, for the same system that attracted the "talentless" offered few ways of transcending that category. To be awarded high rates of remuneration or to get financial backers for one's own literary ventures, required, as Poe understood, getting "before the eye of the world," becoming known, that is, for an identifiable body of work. But in the competition for reputation those writers who depended on their literary wages for a living, especially editors, were at a distinct disadvantage. Working as much as fifteen hours a day and expending all their intellect and creativity on the routine production of copy or the tiresome labour of "cutting-and-pasting" from other journals, editors, Poe explained, had "no time on [their] hands" and could themselves "write nothing worth reading."[21] The still-prevalent convention of publishing magazine pieces anonymously only added to the difficulty of producing a recognizable literary corpus and public identity. Professional writers, furthermore, competed not only with each other for popular favor and critical renown but with a flood of pirated British writers and a domestic lettered elite who had no need of immediate rewards and could afford to pursue writing at greater leisure. Amateur "scribblers" could produce commodious works – novels, translations, histories. Professional writers, bereft of time, generally lacking the education of their amateur counterparts, and unable to finance the publication of books independently, were forced to opt for literature specific to the magazines: social commentary, reviews, short fiction – literature that in the popular estimate of the day was meant to be consumed immediately and forgotten promptly.

The wage-dependent writers who succeeded in this inhospitable system generally did so not by drawing attention to their scattered and unidentifiable aesthetic talents but by drawing attention to themselves, by cultivating sensationalism, scandal, and notoriety – by trafficking, that is, the peculiar and outrageous features of their own personalities. Although the sensational self was a relatively new commodity in the 1830s, its currency was enabled both by the development of an ideology of individualism, with its celebration of the properties of idiosyncracy and iconoclasm, and by the related rise of sentimental culture over these same years, which encouraged personal display and self-revelation as categories of enjoyment and consumption. Thus while the rhetoric of dysfunction in one sense merely described wage-dependent authors, it also featured centrally in the terms of their self-fashioning, public image, and success. Poe's antisocial peculiarities, both as individual and author, especially his mean-spirited criticism and regular assaults on Longfellow, need to be understood in this context. Like Willis, from whom he seems to have taken his model of personality exploitation, Poe coined his own flaws and deficiencies – his envy, animosity, and alienation – in the production of a public self whose enormous currency lay precisely in its antisocial character.

The acquisition of literary fame via the display and cultivation of personal oddity was a trail blazed by Willis in the late 1820s and early 1830s.[22] Willis's earliest magazine venture, *The American Monthly Magazine*, was notable for establishing its editor as a foppish voluptuary, a figure then recently popularized by Bulwer-Lytton's *Pelham* but considered decadent and even dangerous by Boston's staid literary establishment, the more so because it seemed a public extension of Willis's private inclinations. Such, at least, was the opinion of conservative Boston journalists, who dubbed Willis "lewd Natty" and warned readers to sequester their daughters from the "indelicacies" of his poetry.[23] Partly because of Willis's knack for parlaying his indecent private life into his public self, *The American Monthly Magazine* was a hit, boasting a readership of about 700 and fixing an equation between personal dysfunction, scandal, and success that would mark the next and most important phase of Willis's career. Having worn out his welcome in Boston, he traveled to Europe in 1831 as foreign correspondent for *The New York Mirror*. With his eye on a life among the "fashionable," Willis, posing as an *attaché*, insinuated himself into the circle of Lady Blessington, one of London's leading hostesses, and hobnobbed at her home with all the "lions" of literary Britain: Bulwer-Lytton, Thomas Moore, Benjamin D'Israeli, the Count D'Orsay. Partly out of ignorance, partly, it would seem, out of the same habitual rebelliousness that made him such an irritant to Proper Boston, Willis wrote the *Mirror* some extremely unflattering descriptions of his new friends. When these were leaked to the British public by the Tory press, the Blessington circle was mortified, and Willis, again disgraced, found himself flayed in journals on both sides of the Atlantic. Far from damaging Willis's professional career, however, his disgrace in London, which highlighted not only his raciness and daring but his clumsiness among his social betters, gave him more than ever a kind of salacious caché. His letters to the *Mirror* were reprinted in over 500 American newspapers and periodicals. During the next decade Willis parleyed his infamy and social blunders into the most commercially successful literary career of the era, becoming the first professional author in the US to make a reasonable living by the efforts of his pen alone.

Poe apparently took his cue from Willis. Evidence suggests that he submitted one of his earliest poems ("Fairy-Land") to Willis's *American Monthly Magazine* and was rudely rejected.[24] He was preoccupied enough with Willis to satirize him in "The Duc D'Omlette" (1832) and "Lion-izing" (1835).[25] While "Lion-izing" mocks the new culture of celebrity that had recently (and in Poe's opinion groundlessly) made Willis so stellar a commodity, Poe seems to have taken to heart the lesson Willis taught and began to shape himself professionally in a similar mold. Writing T. H. White, the *Messenger's* proprietor who was then considering him for the position of editor, Poe assured White that though "Berenice" approached the very "verge of bad taste," this was exactly what magazine readers wanted. Poe went on to stress the emerging links between sensationalism and reputation. Regardless of the "cant of the day," Poe argued, no one cares for simplicity. It little mattered whether articles such as "Berenice" were in bad taste, he argued that readers avidly seek such tales. These are "the articles that find their way into other periodicals . . . and in this manner, taking hold upon the public mind, they augment the reputation of the source where they originated."[26]

Like Willis, who capitalized on what conventional antebellum society considered his failings and abnormalities – sexual indecency, foppery, a lack of respect for his betters – Poe achieved his early reputation not only by trafficking in "bad taste" but, more generally, by proffering his dispossession and alienation as features of his public self. Positioning himself overtly as an outsider, a sort of arrogant and autonomous literary orphan severed from the implicitly familial organization of what he called "cliques," Poe launched an assault on the existing literary establishment in a series of reviews virtually unprecedented for their cruel and vituperative candor. Not coincidentally, perhaps, Poe's first major attack was aimed at the *New York Mirror*, with which Willis was affiliated. In a review of *Norman Leslie*, a novel by Theodore S. Fay, one of the *Mirror's* editors, Poe denounced a system of promotion enabling Fay to celebrate his own anonymous publication in the pages of his own journal: "Well! – here we have it! This is *the* book – *the* book *par excellence* – the book bepuffed, beplastered, and be-*Mirrored*: the book 'attributed to' Mr. Blank, and 'said to be from the pen' of Mr. Asterisk . . . *Norman Leslie*, gentle reader . . . is, after all, written by nobody in the world but Theodore S. Fay, and Theodore S. Fay is nobody in the world but 'one of the Editors of the New York Mirror'" (*E&R*, 540). Having exposed Fay as the author of his own congratulatory announcements, Poe poured scorn on the novel itself: "As regards Mr Fay's *style*, it is unworthy of a school-boy. The 'Editor of the New York Mirror' has either never seen an edition of Murray's Grammar, or he has been a-Willising so long as to have forgotten his vernacular language" (*E&R*, 547).

Poe's mention of Willis, however derisive, suggests the extent to which the review had its context in the exploitation of personality Willis typified. And Poe reaped a similar reward. Barely noticed for the poems he had previously published, Poe now found himself and the *Messenger* lauded in periodicals North and South. "Eschewing all species of puffery," said the *Pennsylvanian*, "the *Messenger* goes to work upon several of the most popular novels of the day, and hacks and hews with a remorselessness and an evident enjoyment of the business, which is as rare as it is amusing." Poe himself was called an author of "distinguished merit," "the best of all our young writers," "a gentleman of brilliant genius and endowments" (*CH*, 83, 85, 86, 87). Although the traditional view of Poe is that he sabotaged his professional career through a personal, dysfunctional animosity to the era's powerful literary and publishing coteries, Poe's professional success was in the first place contingent upon that animosity – and upon the connotations of dysfunction that went with it. If the *Norman Leslie* review had the extremely salutary effect of bringing Poe "before the eye of the world," it did so on the terms that the review itself dictated, in the sense that Poe was almost unanimously figured thereafter, whether in approval or approbation, as an eccentric and antisocial outsider.

Not unexpectedly, the counterattacks launched by the *Mirror* and its friends cast Poe's vaunted idiosyncracy in a decidedly negative light, characterizing Poe not just as an outsider but as a misfit. Willis Gaylord Clark, editor of the *Philadelphia Gazette*, noted that the *Messenger*'s critical department, despite its professed "impartiality and discernment" was "decidedly *quacky*," and its "eccentric sternness in criticism, without the power to back one's suit withal . . . merits the strongest reprehension." Colonel William L. Stone of the *New York Commercial Advertiser*, similarly stressed Poe's wilfully alien, adversarial position: "The duty of the critic is to act as judge, not as enemy, of the writer whom he reviews; a distinction of which the Zoilus of the Messenger seems not to be aware. . . . The critic of the Messenger has been eulogized for his scorching and scarifying abilities and he thinks it incumbent upon him to keep up his reputation in that line, by sneers, sarcasm, and downright abuse."[27] The eccentricity stressed by the *Mirror*'s allies was equally underlined in the notices that complimented and lauded Poe, though in this case his "eccentric sternness" was held out as a positive characteristic. The *Pennsylvanian* felt Poe's criticisms were "a relief to the dull monotony of praise which rolls smooth in the wake of every new book," and that "a roughness which savors of honesty and independence is welcome." Echoing Poe's opinions regarding what attracts the "eye of the world," the *Charlottesville Jeffersonian* told readers that although passages in Poe's review of *Norman Leslie* "are in bad taste," the piece "is amusing and will be read." The *Richmond Compiler* complimented Poe on his "great dexterity and power" as a critic, adding, "He exposes the imbecility and rottenness of our *ad captandum* popular literature, with the hand of a master. The public I believe was much delighted with the admirable scalping of *Norman Leslie*." Not content with stressing Poe's eccentricity, the *New Yorker* more emphatically endowed him with the racialized alterity suggested in the metaphor of "scalping": "The Southern Editor has quite too savage a way of pouncing upon unlucky wights . . . like the Indian, who cannot realize that an enemy is conquered till he is scalped. . . . We think the *Messenger* often quite too severe . . . but still able and ingenious" (*CH*, 83, 85, 87, 90).

Like Willis and Poe, Griswold achieved early success by coining his personal and social alienation. But Griswold, who would figure so sensationally in Poe's posthumous history, is an interesting figure in the sense that, born ten years later than Willis, his self-fashioning had its source not only in his own personal foibles but in the discourse of scandalous celebrity writers like Poe and Willis had already established. Whereas Willis and Poe, for all their feelings of inadequacy, could both boast of a gentleman's education, Griswold's alienation was a product of his low birth and lack of formal schooling. And perhaps because he was, so to speak, invisible within the patrician norms of literary culture, Griswold's fashioning of himself as a public personality had less to do with highlighting any definitive personal characteristics of his own than with developing a kind of protean lack of identity in the service of promoting his famous contemporaries. This promotion, as with Poe and Willis, had an intimate as well as public dimension: Griswold's self-diminution in the presence of his literary betters was manifested personally in his relative lack of interest in the progress of his own career compared to his avid interest in the careers of his contemporaries, whose volumes and mementos he collected with geekish fervor. Oliver Wendell Holmes said of him, "What a curious creature Griswold is! He seems to be a kind of naturalist whose subjects are authors, whose memory is a perfect fauna of all flying and creeping things that feed on ink" (*CH*, 41). Appropriately, Griswold achieved fame as a purveyor of fame. He first made a name for himself shamelessly pirating British and French novels for cheap distribution. This commerce in overseas reputations rehearsed the terms of Griswold's more lasting and loftier fame as the era's supreme anthologist of American writers, inaugurated with his widely influential *The Poets and Poetry of America* and extended through a long series of anthologies, annuals, and edited collections. Like Poe and Willis, Griswold had a public reputation founded upon and ultimately inseparable from his personal idiosyncrasies. He was known as a "mountebank" and "curiosity," a "diminutive thing," in the words of *The Town* (*CH*, 98, 41, 98). He was identified less with any talents of his own than with the pure conveyance of publicity, as *The Town* implied when it parodied Griswold's plans for yet another anthology: "The Reverend Dr. Ridiculous W. Grizwold is in town superintending the publication of his great work, 'The Advertisers and the Advertisements of America.' . . . The volume is to be illustrated by a bouquet of heads, done in brass, of those who have acquired fame in this high branch of scholastic composition" (*CH*, 100).

To what extent the exploitation of personality on the part of any of these writers was initially conscious or intentional is difficult to know. Writing his sketch of Willis for "The Literati of New York City," Poe himself expressed uncertainty about the role intentionality played in the production of celebrity. He thought it probable that Willis "only acted in accordance with his physical temperament; but be this as it may, his personal greatly advanced, if it did not altogether establish his literary fame" (*E&R*, 1124). And yet conscious manipulation of reputation, if negligible at first, tended to grow: once ventured into the public arena and rewarded with attention, "physical temperament" became a commodity to be cultivated and ventured again. Poe, for example, in his biography of himself for the *Philadelphia Saturday Museum*, not only gave himself respectable birth but peppered the piece with exaggerations and lies intended to stress his decadent alienation: he had lived a wild and dissipated life at the University of Virginia; he had got into mysterious "difficulties" in Russia (he had never been to Russia) from which he had to be extricated by the American consul.

Although flayed by Poe in the 1830s, Willis seems to have taken the abuse less as a personal affront than as a species of rhetoric that promoted both their careers. When Poe, who by this time had become Willis's friend, wrote him in 1845 asking if Willis would reply to an insult published by Charles Briggs, Willis answered, certainly not, "A reply from *me* to Mr. Briggs would make the man," and summarized, "Notoriety is glory in this transition state of our half-bak'd country."[28] Willis, in addition, did little to discourage Poe's virulent criticism of other writers, including Longfellow, upon whom Poe launched his first extended attack while in Willis's employ on the *Mirror*. Although many Poe scholars cite what became known as the Longfellow War as a mark of Poe's "bizarre" and self-destructive aberrance,[29] Willis took the attack as business as usual in the business of notoriety. Writing to Longfellow's friend Charles Sumner to dismiss the incident, Willis concluded, "Tomorrow's paper will contain Hillard's reply, and then I shall leave him & Poe to do a *joust* together in my pages, which of course will serve Longfellow in the end."[30] "[M]y policy," he told Sumner in a follow-up letter, "is always to *fan up* any smothered discontent, and give it the chance of contradiction. I *always* beg men who come with literary whispers against *me* to get them *into print* forth with, where I can meet them." Although Willis was finally pressured by Longfellow's friends into distancing himself from Poe, he suggested to Sumner that he not only approved of Poe's attacks but encouraged them: "Another thing – I mean to let Poe make a feature of his own in the Mirror, and be recognized as the author of criticisms there, and I am obliged, (to have anything good from him) to give him somewhat free play. Tell Longfellow he shall never suffer 'in the long run' from me or mine."[31]

Yet if writers like Poe, Willis, and Griswold consciously cultivated and capitalized on their own peculiarities, the rhetoric of dysfunction in which they trafficked also had an energy that exceeded authorial intention and circled back to determine a writer's behaviour and choices in ways not always within his conscious control. While I do not wish to return this argument to the psychological models usually summoned to account for what finally emerged as Poe's self-destructive behaviour as an author, I do want to emphasize the extent to which certain psychological structures and attendant patterns of behaviour were encouraged by a market system that made personal failings a condition of celebrity and success. Although Poe, Willis, and Griswold had all turned to authorship in the hopes of rising above their feelings of worthlessness, trading in notoriety proved the wrong way of going about it. As the literary market of the 1840s grew increasingly dependent on the traffic in personalities for sales, competition, and profit, it not only continued to attract peculiar individuals and to encourage their self-exploitation, it generated what might be called a whole culture of authorial dysfunction. The dynamic relationship of this culture both to competitive practices among writers and to an emerging capitalist publishing system made it extremely difficult for writers to escape or circumvent the dysfunctional identities responsible for their success as competitive, commercial properties. The result was that writers ended up internalizing – or rather reinternalizing – as a principle of behaviour the worthlessness that designated their commercial and competitive worth; they behaved in ways that reaffirmed their inadequacy. Not only the disastrous latter part of Poe's career, but the careers of Willis and Griswold display the workings of this process, for all three writers compulsively replayed their inadequacies until they ruined their professional chances and thus cemented their "talentless" status once and for all. In doing so, however, they did not compromise their value to the market. Although the tendency in Poe scholarship is to attribute his professional failure to psychic peculiarities that rendered him "unfit" for the demands of the popular market, Poe's value to this market was, as ever, contingent upon his record of failure and defeat.

Much as their self-exploitation enabled Poe, Willis, and Griswold to bubble to the surface of a system that otherwise encouraged submergence, it also inveigled them in a circuit of competition that by the mid-1840s had itself been reshaped by the pressure put on writers to trade in personalities. Standards of remuneration and the chances for fame remained as low as ever, and precisely for these reasons the business of notoriety, fed as much by desperate and ambitious writers as by a growing public thirst for intimate revelation, boomed. The debasement of writers, accordingly, ballooned into a culture in itself whose internal dynamics of competition had a reciprocal relationship to the larger publishing economy. As more and more writers discovered the promotional virtues of effrontery, hostility, and self-display, they collectively authorized newly personalized modes of aggression among themselves. Personal attack and insult, considered daring when Poe had used them in the mid-1830s, were, by the mid-1840s, a standard currency of literary interaction.[32] Much as Willis's letters argue for the gentlemanly dimensions of the business of notoriety, the overall effect of strategies of self-promotion that involved not only coining one's own eccentricities but publicly harping on the flaws and weaknesses of one's competitors, was to generate competitive tactics that, far from being gentlemanly, were all the more brutal for obviating distinctions between the professional and personal. Open and bitter feuds among writers not only raged in the periodicals of the 1840s, but reverberated unwholesomely in writers' psychic lives and spilled easily into private encounters, manifesting themselves in fierce enmities, vendettas, egregious professional favoritism, parlor gossip, threatened duels, and even, on occasion, outright physical abuse. This charged, volatile culture of mutual and self-abasement, which issued from conditions in the market, in turn fed the market system, helping to fuel an aggressive, laissez-faire publishing economy – called by contemporaries "cheap and nasty" – that flourished throughout the 1840s, not least because wage-earning writers, still being undercut by publishers, foreign imports, and domestic amateurs, were now undercutting each other.

Many writers were aware of the dubious gains to be had from participating in a culture of insult and self-abasement that only aggravated existing feelings of low self-worth and in many cases positively damaged professional opportunities. But entering this culture was much easier than leaving it. An economy that depended for its vitality on displays of dysfunction tended to reproduce, regardless of a writer's intentions or well-being, the reputation that sustained his market value, whether as a commercial property whose scandalous displays drummed up sales or as an embattled competitor among other writers. Thus although at some point in their careers Poe, Willis, and Griswold recoiled from a public reputation premised on the constant reiteration of their shortcomings they all found that they were unable to escape the public selves initially responsible for their market success. When Willis, for example, upon his marriage in 1835, sought to leave behind his reputation for amorous dalliance, he found that the popular press refused to drop the matter – and kept refusing for the next twenty years. Blameless though his private behavior became, Willis was routinely flayed for his supposed sexual escapades until well into the 1850s, when he was finally too sick and feeble to make the accusations plausible.[33] Whereas Willis was not allowed to escape his reputation for sexual license, Griswold was not allowed to escape his for the mechanical delivery of other authors' distinctions. Stung by a review (possibly penned by Poe) that accused him of being deficient as a linguist, Griswold suddenly offered himself to the public in that learned guise as a translator of the French poet, Béranger. The response of his long-time friend Horace Greeley, himself a veteran of editorial trenches, was not to encourage Griswold in his cultivation of the French language (a gentleman's pursuit), but to put him in his rightful place as a literary worker: "I want to thrash you for the way you have done Beranger.... Gris, you *must* not get up works so jobbingly. You will never get above journeyman's wages unless you amend."[34] And Poe, similarly, was not allowed to escape his reputation for ruthless animosity toward the era's powerful literary coteries. When Poe's New York *Literati* series for *Godey's* appeared shortly after Poe's extended assaults on Longfellow and his Boston "clique" – assaults which had earned Poe the distinction of being virtually unemployable – Margaret Fuller scornfully accused him of not being nearly venomous enough. "People were looking for a furious unbottling... of prussic acid. But instead of these biting, withering and scorching elements, what was our astonishment to find only a few slender streams of sugar house molasses.... As to the independence for which we have heard Mr. Poe commended, we certainly have never seen so small amount of that commodity in a literary review as is contained in his 'honest opinions.'"[35]

This subordination of the writer to his own market value was equally accomplished by writers themselves. Among the many things that link Poe, Willis, and Griswold is their seemingly compulsive re-performance of their flaws and defects, often in defiance of their reluctance to do so and to the detriment of their own best interests. Such behaviour inhered in the logic of a commercial success premised on personal abasement. While Poe, Willis, and Griswold had all turned to authorship in the hopes of stanching their feelings of inferiority, and while all presumably envisioned, as Poe said, that "hour... when I may come forth with a certainty of success,"[36] the "certainty of success" in this system was an ever-receding horizon. Not only involved in consciously peddling their flaws but constantly reconfronting them in their professional relationships and in the publicity that elaborated their fame, these writers were barred from experiencing the transcendence of inferiority that success promised. Since success for them was only available on the terms of their currency as dysfunctional personalities, they obsessively pursued success – they pursued an experience of achievement – through the repeated performance of their flaws, a performance distinguished by its irrational lack of regard for immediate professional and personal well-being and by its redelivery of the writer to the terms of his competitive value.

Thus Willis, who was privately pained and bewildered by the accusations of sexual misconduct that hounded him, nonetheless repeatedly handed the press fodder for these attacks – not by actually engaging in indecorous behaviour but, more irrationally, by arousing a suspicion that he did. Once he took the odd step of publishing the love letters (fan mail) sent him by a besotted female reader. Another time, in the midst of Bishop Onderdonk's trial for sexually harassing his parishioners, Willis, precisely at a moment when he should have kept quiet, came out on the side of the Bishop.[37] The same was true for Griswold. Although aggrieved by his reputation as a "jobber," Griswold could not stop himself from doing "jobs." In the mood of depression following his wife's death, he planned or put together so many compilations that his friend, James T. Fields, fearing for Griswold's literary respectability, made a special trip from Boston to Philadelphia "to suggest . . . the propriety of checking" his "publishing ambition rather than urging the horses onward."[38] Even Griswold's acceptance of the role of literary executor for Poe, which has puzzled biographers of both writers given not only the hostility and mistrust between them but Griswold's subsequent declarations of distaste for the task, is of a piece with his frequently compulsive assumption of the editorial role.

Similar acts of compulsion typified the latter half of Poe's career, which illustrates with particular acuity the logic of the hollow triumph, with its demonstrations of inadequacy in the ceaseless pursuit of success. Poe's assaults on Longfellow for plagiarism, for example, which apparently began as a publicity stunt, initially had precisely that effect. Celebrated nationally for "The Raven," Poe was even more talked about for daring to attack America's premier poet.[39] But as if this very success, predicated on his animosity toward Boston's haute literary cliques, only refreshed Poe's feeling of being excluded from what he called "the adventitious influence . . . of social position" Longfellow enjoyed,[40] and it impelled him to more extended and intense displays of the hostility and marginality that, in founding his fame, promised his eventual triumph. Like Griswold, consequently, who could not stop doing "jobs," Poe could not stop writing about Longfellow. Accordingly, as Poe's fame grew without ever producing the "certainty of success" that his celebrity at once promised and foreclosed, Poe was driven to increasingly violent acts of aggression and self-isolation, like his humiliating performance of his own insufficiency at the Boston Lyceum, or his obsessive, hostile denunciations of Boston in the wake of the opprobrium that followed. The growing violence of Poe's avowals of his alienation reached a crescendo when Poe, accused (probably wrongfully) by some of the women poets in his circle of a gross lack of gentlemanly tact, declared to the New York literati that he suffered from episodes of insanity.[41]

And perhaps by this point Poe's description of himself had a certain accuracy, for there is no question of the damage that this compulsive rehearsal of their deficiencies inflicted on writers. In Poe's case, the repeated performance of his animosity and alienation fueled the sense of his own worthlessness, fed his tendencies toward depression and alcoholism, and intensified hostility in his professional relationships, all of which combined to make him anathema to potential employers. Indeed, the very terms of Poe's success, premised as they were on his alienation from prevailing literary authorities, clinched his professional demise. Nor was Poe alone in stifling his own potential as a writer. Unhampered by the performance of hostility Poe's fame mandated, Griswold and Willis fared far better than Poe in their negotiation of professional opportunity. But for whatever professional success they achieved, Griswold and Willis engineered a professional self-sabotage similar in spirit, if not in scale, to Poe's.

Although Griswold existed in a constant state of anxiety about his own editorial shabbiness and lived "sick with fear" that his books would be read by "those who know how such [books] should be made,"[42] he never got over his "cheap and nasty" productivity. He cherished the dream of transcending his editorial role and authoring a hefty, respectable history, but despite his relative affluence in the 1850s he was so obsessed with editing that he waited until he was almost dead from tuberculosis to produce his magnum opus and then ended up writing "in haste" and "carelessness" with little "thought of the graces of composition."[43] Dead at the age of 42, Griswold not surprisingly left his contemporaries with the impression that he was "deficient" in "absolute talent and ripe scholarship."[44] Although Willis achieved a fame and financial success that far surpassed that of Griswold or Poe, reportedly earning in the late 1840s somewhere in the area of $10,000 a year, he could not leave well enough alone. Long after Willis might have rested on his laurels, he kept himself in the public eye, compulsively re-performing his blunders until he finally immolated himself permanently by his ill-conceived coverage of the Civil War as a high society event. "Pitilessly overworked," as he put it, to the end, Willis, like Poe, died in poverty, remembered by the next generation of writers, if he was remembered at all, as a case of "arrested development."[45]

But if these acts of self-abasement were psychologically and professionally damaging to writers, if they demolished self-esteem and sabotaged professional achievement, they energized the 1840s market system as a whole. Each time Willis proffered a reference to some sexual issue the resulting explosion of public outrage, however painful to him personally, charged his celebrity, punched up sales, galvanized enemies and set in motion a cycle of "jousting," of retaliation, anger, and one-up-man-ship that Willis himself, ironically, understood was immeasurably healthy for the "trade." It is important to stress, moreover, that demoralized, downtrodden, and impoverished individuals were not simply the accidental dross of this system; they were absolutely crucial to it. Their compulsive pursuit of an unattainable success turned them into compulsively productive workers, like Griswold, who turned out anthology after anthology with the regularity of a machine, or Willis, who had the habits of a workaholic and had to be sedated on his deathbed to be stopped from going to his office.[46] And not just their compulsiveness but their sense of worthlessness was a positive, productive attribute in the machinery of laissez-faire publishing. If Poe was unable to profit personally from his reputation, his reputation itself, at the very moment of his own deepest misery and impoverishment, had never been so flagrantly profitable a commodity. Capitalizing on the appealing combination of Poe's sensational reputation and his ostensible worthlessness both to himself and to potential employers, Louis Godey, the proprietor of the popular *Godey's Lady's Book*, hired Poe for the comparatively cheap price of $172 to pen a series of "opinions" of the New York literati. The series, *because* of Poe's reputation for vitriol – because, that is, of the very conditions that rendered Poe unemployable – was so wildly popular that, in Godey's words, "the May edition was exhausted before the first of May, and we have had requests for hundreds from Boston and New York, which we could not supply."[47] And even dead Poe continued to feed this system. In yet another self-destructive gesture, Griswold, in his edition of Poe's works, advertised himself as Poe's detractor, a move that resulted in yet more jousting and violent denunciation and that ensured, even as it demoralized Griswold, that the dead Poe retained his competitive edge.

It is no wonder, then, that Poe's contemporaries struggled so earnestly upon his death in 1849 to understand the contradictions of his career, its seemingly senseless conflation of genius and public debasement, of success and poverty, of arduous self-promotion and inexplicable self-sabotage. Nor is it any wonder, given that Poe's memorialists, were, like Poe, produced by even as they themselves produced the system and conditions of market competition, that they subsumed the troubling paradoxes of his career by conjuring yet again the figure of Poe's dysfunction – of alienation, hostility, and even madness – that had formed the axis of Poe's own professional self-fashioning. Doubtless struggling with similar contradictions in their own careers, Poe's memorialists summoned an obfuscatory logic that enshrined as it discreetly authorized the exploitation of mental and aesthetic labor under the sign of a glamorous alienation from class commercialism. It was Poe's "genius," his contemporaries concluded, perhaps with themselves in mind, that exempted him from decent wages and proper respect. It is a final irony of Poe's career that his compulsive assumption of the role of embattled, half-mad "genius," a role that cost him self-esteem, his comfort, and arguably his sanity, continues to anchor his reputation today, feeding simultaneously high scholarly and popular culture systems that perhaps no less than the antebellum literary field obscure the causal links between psychic and social peculiarity and commercial productivity, between worthlessness and profit.

NOTES

1. Vernon Louis Parrington, *Main Currents in American Thought: An Interpretation of American Literature from the Beginning to 1920*, 3 vols. (New York: Harcourt, Brace and World), 2: 58.
2. Shawn Rosenheim and Stephen Rachman, "Introduction," *The American Face of Edgar Allan Poe*, ed. Rosenheim and Rachman (Baltimore: Johns Hopkins University Press, 1995), p. xi.
3. Terence Whalen, *Edgar Allan Poe and the Masses: The Political Economy of Literature in Antebellum America* (Princeton University Press, 1999), p. 9.
4. The numerous accounts of antebellum publishing and professional authorship include William Charvat, *Literary Publishing in America, 1790–1850* (Philadelphia: University of Pennsylvania Press, 1959) and *The Profession of Authorship in America, 1800–1870: The Papers of William Charvat*, ed. Matthew J. Broccoli (Columbus: Ohio State University Press, 1968); and John Tebbel, *Between Covers: The Rise and Transformation of Book Publishing in America* (New York: Oxford University Press, 1987).
5. John Ward Ostrom, "Edgar A. Poe: His Income as Literary Entrepreneur," *Poe Studies* 15 (June 1982): 2, 1.
6. Qtd. in Sidney P. Moss, *Poe's Literary Battles: The Critic in the Context of His Literary Milieu* (Durham, NC: Duke University Press, 1963), p. 5n2.
7. Although I refer to men and women, it was almost exclusively men in the 1830s and 1840s who ventured into professional authorship without alternative sources of financial support – hence my use of the masculine pronoun throughout this essay. It should also be noted that by and large those writers who lived solely on the income from their literary endeavors were from lower or working class backgrounds. Writers from more genteel backgrounds often relied simultaneously on the money they made from writing and on other, often meager or sporadic sources of income, such as patronage appointments, small inheritances, and familial support.
8. Biographical information on Poe comes mainly from Kenneth Silverman, *Edgar A. Poe: Mournful and Never-Ending Remembrance* (New York: HarperCollins, 1991).
9. Poe to John Allan, 19 March 1827, in *Letters*, 1: 7.
10. Poe to John Allan, 1 December 1828, in *Letters*, 1: 10.
11. Poe to John Allan, 29 May 1829, in *Letters*, 1: 20.
12. Silverman, *Edgar A. Poe*, p. 72.
13. Silverman, *Edgar A. Poe*, p. 142.
14. General biographical information on Willis is from Henry A. Beers, *Nathaniel Parker Willis* (Boston: Houghton Mifflin, 1890), and Thomas N. Baker, *Sentiment and Celebrity: Nathaniel Parker Willis and the Trials of Literary Fame* (New York: Oxford University Press, 1999).

15. Qtd. in Beers, *Willis*, p. 140.
16. Joy Bayless, *Rufus Wilmot Griswold: Poe's Literary Executor* (Nashville: Vanderbilt University Press, 1943), p. 7.
17. Bayless, *Rufus Wilmot Griswold*, p. 9.
18. Bayless, *Rufus Wilmot Griswold*, p. 11.
19. Bayless, *Rufus Wilmot Griswold*, p. 66.
20. Qtd. in Bayless, *Rufus Wilmot Griswold*, p. 17.
21. Qtd. in Silverman, *Edgar A. Poe*, p. 109. Also from Silverman are the hours Poe worked on *The Broadway Journal*, p. 245. These hours were by no means unusual. The endless hours of work involved in editing are a standard subject of complaint among antebellum editors. Griswold reported at one point (1846), "I now work fourteen hours a day (which is more than they do in the mines)" (qtd. in Bayless, *Rufus Wilmot Griswold*, p. 114).
22. As Michael Allen suggests, these writers also drew on the cult of personality popularized in British magazines. See *Poe and the British Magazine Tradition* (New York: Oxford University Press, 1969).
23. Qtd. in Baker, *Sentiment*, pp. 48, 47.
24. See Baker, *Sentiment*, p. 46, and Silverman, *Edgar A. Poe*, pp. 53–54.
25. Kenneth L. Daughrity, "Poe's 'Quiz on Willis,'" *American Literature* 5 (March 1933): 55–62.
26. Poe to T. H. White, 30 April 1835, in *Letters*, 1: 57–58.
27. Qtd. in Moss, *Poe's Literary Battles*, pp. 45, 46.
28. Nathaniel Parker Willis to Edgar Allan Poe, 1845?, *Complete Works* (Harrison), 17: 206.
29. See, for example, J. Gerald Kennedy, "The Violence of Melancholy: Poe Against Himself," *American Literary History* 8 (1996): 536.
30. Nathaniel Parker Willis to Charles Sumner, shelf mark bMS Am 1.9 [16? January 1845], published by permission of the Houghton Library, Harvard University.
31. "Nathaniel Parker Willis to Charles Sumner," shelf mark bMS Am 1.9 [27? January 1845], published by permission of the Houghton Library, Harvard University.
32. I know of no study that addresses as a phenomenon in itself what I am calling the culture of dysfunction, though there are studies that consider the separate battles between cliques and individuals. See, for example, Perry Miller's account of the battle between the Knickerbocker circle and nativist writers in *The Raven and the Whale: The War of Words and Wits in the Era of Poe and Melville* (New York: Harcourt, Brace & World, 1956). Many arguments among writers had a political or sectional cast, but these categories do not by any means encompass the sheer range of the disputes. It should be noted, also, that wage-earning writers were not the only ones to participate in the culture of insult, but unable to retreat to other professions or sources of income, those authors who depended primarily on the market for their livelihood were forced to inhabit this culture in a way that amateurs were not.
33. For the attack on Willis, see Sandra Tomc, "An Idle Industry: Nathaniel Parker Willis and the Workings of Literary Leisure," *American Quarterly* 49 (1997): 780–805.

34. "Horace Greeley to Rufus Griswold," 13 November 1843, in *Passages From the Correspondence and Other Papers of Rufus W. Griswold*, ed. William M. Griswold (Cambridge, MA: W. M. Griswold, 1898), pp. 146–147.

35. Qtd. in Moss, *Poe's Literary Battles*, pp. 224–225. Poe, Willis and Griswold were not the only writers unable to escape the terms of their initial success. Perry Miller, *Raven*, p. 47, speaking of Charles Briggs and Herman Melville, notes that each was "cursed . . . with an initial success from the shadow of which he could never escape."

36. Qtd. in Silverman, *Edgar A. Poe*, p. 232.

37. See Baker, *Sentiment*, pp. 128, 123.

38. James T. Fields to Rufus Griswold, 13 September 1844, in *Passages*, p. 159.

39. Silverman, *Edgar A. Poe*, p. 250.

40. Qtd. in Silverman, *Edgar A. Poe*, p. 254. In a compelling reading of the Longfellow War, Meredith McGill, "Poe, Literary Nationalism, and Authorial Identity," *American Face*, p. 294, locates the source of Poe's argument with Longfellow not just in the latter's wealth and literary influence but in the "maddeningly empowered use of anonymity as a literary device" that these advantages, in Poe's mind, enabled.

41. Moss, *Poe's Literary Battles*, p. 221.

42. Qtd. in Bayless, *Griswold*, p. 117.

43. Rufus Wilmot Griswold, *The Republican Court; Or, American Society in the Days of Washington* (New York: D. Appleton, 1854), p. iii.

44. From an untitled memoir (evidently late nineteenth-century), reprinted in *Passages*, p. 37.

45. Willis is quoted in Beers, *Willis*, p. 349. The account of Willis's "arrested development" is from Edward F. Hayward, "Nathaniel Parker Willis," *Atlantic Monthly* 54 (1884): 213.

46. Willis's compulsive work habits are treated at length in Tomc, "Idle Industry."

47. Quoted in Ostrom, "Literary Entrepreneur," p. 5. Also from Ostrom is Poe's payment for the "Literati."

3

RACHEL POLONSKY

Poe's aesthetic theory

The word "aesthetic" and its cognates have clung to the name of Edgar Allan Poe. A handful of his more resonant statements about poetic art have found a place within histories of "aesthetic theory,"[1] and he has formed a permanent posthumous association with the late-nineteenth century cultural movement or mode of sensibility known as "aestheticism." On the strength of a scattering of suggestive lines from his critical prose, posterity has assured Poe an early, in some accounts freakishly early, position in the genealogy of the various doctrines grouped together under the label "Art for Art's sake."[2]

The word "aesthetic" was still working its way into the English language in Poe's lifetime. It had first come into use as a technical term in Germany in 1750, in the title of A. T. Baumgarten's treatise, *Aesthetica*, which attempted to set out a philosophically-grounded theory of taste; it later furnished Immanuel Kant with the basic concept for an inquiry into the philosophy of art in his *Critique of Aesthetic Judgment* (1790). Kant refined and systematized ideas about art that had been germinating since the beginning of the eighteenth century, and defined "aesthetic judgment," the faculty of taste, as peculiar and specific, disinterested, universal, and distinct from the pleasures of the senses or practical morality. The work of art, in Kantian theory, pleases for its own sake.

In 1798, "aesthetic" was invoked in an article in the *Monthly Review* as part of "a dialect peculiar to Professor Kant."[3] By 1821, the word was no longer peculiar to Kant, though still, for English speakers, peculiar. Coleridge, of whom Kant had, by his own admission, taken philosophical "possession of him as with a giant's hand,"[4] expressed regret that he could not "find a more familiar word than aesthetic, for works of taste and criticism."[5] In the 1830s and 1840s, when Poe was writing his "works of taste and criticism," "aesthetic" was defined by one popular encyclopedia as "the designation given by German writers to a branch of philosophical inquiry, the object of which is a philosophical theory of the beautiful." It was, however, still not regarded as "an established English word," and was met with skepticism and impatience by English-speaking commentators, one of whom dismissed it as a "silly pedantic term...one of the metaphysical and useless additions to nomenclature in the arts in which the German writers abound."[6]

The word "aesthetic" does not occur in Poe's literary, critical, or theoretical writings. As we shall see, Poe was more likely to poke fun at than to resort to the unwieldy and vaporous philosophical ideas and terms that flooded the critical language in the early nineteenth century and entranced, among others, Poe's Transcendentalist contemporary Ralph Waldo Emerson. However, the German philosophical discourse of aesthetics – which had moved discussions of art and beauty onto new ground – provides a looming backdrop to all that Poe has to say about the writer's work. Until the end of the eighteenth century, literary theory had traditionally been modelled on the comparatively manageable terms of ancient rhetoric established in treatises such as Aristotle's *Poetics* and Horace's *Ars Poetica*; it was essentially a matter of telling artists how to accomplish the task of teaching and delighting their audiences, either with their imitations of what is, or with their improving conceptions of what "may be, and should be."[7] In the early nineteenth century, the English Romantic poets reversed the mimetic model of creativity, and turned their attention from the work of art to the poet's own creative process, defining art as the communication of the inner processes of the poet's imagination or soul onto the images of the external world. Art's ultimate effects are beyond technical analysis, a communication to the receiver of indefinable excitements and intensities originating in the "soul" of the artist. A new vocabulary, and a new level of philosophical complexity and quasi-theological obscurity were introduced into the language of criticism in the generation preceding Poe. This raised new questions about what is intelligible and susceptible to theoretical solution. Poe was inevitably and inextricably caught up in such questions.

While not a direct descendant of Romantic criticism, Poe draws at will on its conceptual vocabulary, its rhetoric, and its metaphors, most strikingly in the lecture "The Poetic Principle" – written at the end of his life and often regarded as a summary of his thinking about aesthetic questions – in which his most striking "aestheticist" apothegms appear. In "The Philosophy of Composition," however, Poe discards the Romantic organic metaphors for poetry which envisages artistic creation as a process of spontaneous growth, and redirects critical attention onto technique, to art as a clever illusion which the artist controls like a mathematical or mechanical problem. Poe's imagination was constantly drawn towards elaborate technical systems and deft scientific tricks that promise to solve the mysteries of existence. Mechanical inventions – and theories that work like mechanical inventions – are the components of the fantasy world of his tales: home-made balloons that will ascend as high as the moon; techniques of mesmerism that will take us to the other side of death; ratiocinative and intuitive intelligences, like Monsieur Dupin's, that will unravel any mystery. In his criticism Poe frequently resorts to phrenological explanations of human imaginative and intellectual powers, interrupting a discussion of Coleridge's writing, for example, with comments about the shape of his forehead (*E&R*, 512). He made money on the side deciphering cryptographic puzzles in the pages of the popular press. His last creative efforts were spent on *Eureka*, no less than an attempt at an explanation of everything, whose title boldly invokes the exultant "I have it!" of Archimedes. There was, however, no scientific formula available that would crack Poe's critical problem and satisfactorily account for the origins and effects of the work of art.

In this discussion I will consider what Coleridge would have called Poe's "works of taste and criticism" as the coordinates of a fundamentally uncoordinated body of aesthetic theory which ultimately turns away from the possibility of theorizing about art. I shall examine the language of these essays, their rhetorical and metaphorical devices, and the stance they adopt in relation to the critic's audience, the reading public. Rather than attempting to puzzle out some underlying internal logic, I shall draw attention to their incoherences, eccentricities – or, to use a word Poe himself favored, their perversities – as well as to their moments of modest good sense. Poe was interested in intellectual games and hoaxes: with this in view, I will cross the boundaries of genre and consider his critical essays alongside two of his less well known satires of literary life. These satires make farce out of the language of aesthetic theory, transforming it into nothing more exalted than a counterfeit currency in a literary world of greed and pretence. They demonstrate both the extent to which Poe, always yearning for the key that will solve the puzzles of existence, nonetheless found ludicrous and unmanageable the tools for critical understanding that his generation had inherited from the newly-emerged tradition of aesthetic theorizing, and how remote criticism was from the rational science of his fantasies.

Poe's aesthetic writings had an effect arguably disproportionate to their coherence or originality. Surveying Poe's theoretical arguments about art, commentators generally restrict their references to isolated sentences or paragraphs taken from a few literary critical reviews and short treatises which, when read as wholes, lack the coherence and rhetorical force of their more resonant parts. This fact is oddly consistent with Poe's own poetics, which stipulate that "suggestiveness" and "indefinitiveness" of meaning are preferable to rigorous sense and coherence of subject matter (*E&R*, 133). Poe's aesthetic theory is perhaps more remarkable for its effect than for its substance; more intriguing by virtue of its reception than for its content. When near the end of his career he put into print those polished phrases, "the heresy of *The Didactic*" and the "poem *per se* . . . written solely for the poem's sake" (*E&R*, 75–76), Poe was not the first to have distilled the axioms of eighteenth-century German aesthetics into neat formulations or to have reproduced in neat and memorable apothegms the Kantian definition of the work of art as possessing the quality of purposiveness without purpose. In this respect, Poe occupies a position some way along a diverse lineage of names which includes Benjamin Constant ("L'art pour l'art, sans but, car tout but dénature l'art." ["Art for art's sake, with no purpose, for any purpose perverts art."])[8]; Victor Cousin, ("Il faut . . . de l'art pour l'art . . . le beau ne peut etre la voie ni de l'utile, ni du bien, ni du saint; il ne conduit qu'a lui-meme." ["We must have . . . art for art's sake . . . the beautiful cannot be the way to what is useful, or to what is good, or to what is holy; it leads only to itself."])[9], and which leads through Gautier, Baudelaire, Mallarmé, Valéry, T. S. Eliot, A. C. Bradley, the American New Critics and many others, all of whom made similar statements and founded poetic and critical practices upon them. Poe is a crucial link in this chain. T. S. Eliot claims in his essay "From Poe to Valéry" (written almost exactly a century after Poe's death) that there is a "tradition" of thinking about poetry that genuinely originates with Poe, a tradition which Eliot regards as "the most interesting development of poetic consciousness anywhere in that . . . hundred years" (*Recognition*, 219).

Eliot found that he had to look at Poe's work through the eyes of his French admirers, taking "a distant view of it as a whole" rather than making any attempt to analyze his individual writings in detail. He regarded Poe as a puzzle, a "stumbling block" to the "judicial critic" (*Recognition*, 205). Unlike the cryptographic teasers that Poe prided himself on being able to decipher for the delight of the reading public, the mystery of his effect as an aesthetic theorist does not readily admit of a solution. Harold Bloom confessed to finding Poe's renown as a literary critic and theorist unaccountable: a mysterious French "myth." Adapting Oscar Wilde's "aestheticist" epigram, Bloom concluded that Valéry "saw his impression of Poe clearly, and he saw Poe's essays as in themselves they really were not."[10] For Eliot, however, it did not fundamentally matter what Poe's essays were or were not, whether "The Philosophy of Composition" was "a hoax, or a piece of self-deception, or a more or less accurate record of Poe's calculations." What mattered was the effect of these illusions: namely, the introspective critical method that Poe's essay "suggested to Valéry" (*Recognition*, 218).

The strange effects of the written word, the caprices of literary fame, and the confusions that proliferate around a writer's name even within his own lifetime were not unfamiliar material for concern, reflection, or laughter in Poe's world. Coleridge, whose critical writings provided Poe with material for the elaboration of his own poetics, had begun his *Biographia Literaria* (1817) announcing, as the reason for troubling the reader with his "exculpation," his own surprising celebrity and his dismay at the illusions generated by his writings: "It has been my lot to have had my name introduced both in conversation, and in print, more frequently than I find it easy to explain...Most often it has been connected with some charge which I could not acknowledge, or some principle which I had never entertained."[11] For Eliot, "entertaining" principles was some way short of holding sincere convictions; he remarked of Poe that "all of his ideas seem to be *entertained* rather than believed" (*Recognition*, 213). If indeed Poe merely entertained ideas, it was also his lot, as a literary journalist engaged in a constant struggle with extreme poverty, to have to "entertain" with his ideas, to please with his principles. Baudelaire caught this aspect of Poe when he applied to him the word "juggler," "almost as praise," insisting that Poe was no less noble or great a writer when he played the role of "caricaturist" or "practical joker" than in his most "rigorous analysis" or his "most ravishing and beautiful conceptions."[12] Baudelaire regarded "The Philosophy of Composition" more as "hoax" than "self-deception"; that is, more as an entertainment, a kind of extrovert display for a general public, than as "critical introspection." In Baudelaire's eyes, Poe's hoax had the serious purpose of making the "people of the world" see the "labor demanded by that *objet de luxe* called 'Poetry.'"[13]

"Look at *me!*" Baudelaire would have Poe's essay say, "how I labored – how I toiled – how I wrote!" (*P&T*, 786). In fact these words are taken from the last lines of Poe's spoof "biographia literaria," a short satire entitled (with, undoubtedly, an eye on Coleridge) "The Literary Life of Thingum Bob Esq." The "how" in these lines works in two ways: in the sense of "how much," and in the reference to the techniques he brought to bear in writing; "how" he pulled off his effects. Thingum Bob, a literary charlatan, ends his account of his literary ascent with a public display of himself in the act of writing, a throwing-open of the study door: "You should have seen me – you *should*. I leaned to the right. I leaned to the left. I sat forward. I sat backward. I sat upon end, I sat *tete baissée*...bowing my head close to the alabaster page. And, through all, I – *wrote*" (*P&T*, 786). This minor "grotesque" appeared in the *Southern Literary Messenger* in December 1844, the month before the first publication of "The Raven," the poem that brought Poe sudden fame, and which provides the subject-matter for his own general invitation to the spectacle of himself in the act of writing, "The Philosophy of Composition." This minor story works as a kind of satirical mirror to Poe's famous account of how a poet makes a poem.

It is worth noting here that Poe took satire seriously as a genre and thought it underrepresented and worth promoting in his own country. In his 1849 review of James Russell Lowell's *Fable for Critics,* he expressed doubt that the lack of satire in America was, as some had suggested, the effect of a democratic society with an absence of suitable aristocratic targets for mockery. Conceding that the reading and writing classes in America could not easily be distinguished from one another, Poe nonetheless argued for the possibility, indeed the usefulness, of self-satire. The "namby-pambyism" of American letters was due more to lack of literary skill than to lack of worthy material, an effect of the "general want ... of that minute *polish*" and "natural sarcastic power" (*E&R,* 815) that satire demands of a writer. "The Literary Life of Thingum Bob Esq." is a satire both of the mercenary rough-and-tumble of the American literary periodicals and of the semi-mystical lexicon of Romantic aesthetics that had saturated American literary discourse. As such, it is also a polished and sarcastic piece of self-satire. For, as we shall see, Poe did not just resent the mass market in poetry and literary criticism, he was also part of it; the periodical press guaranteed him his livelihood. At the same time, at the level of thought, Poe was as beholden to and caught up in Romantic aesthetic discourse as he was resistant to it.

"The Literary Life of Thingum Bob Esq." is the monologue of a charlatan, a critic and poet made famous by an "Ode on 'The Oil-of-Bob,'" a poem in praise of an advertising jingle for a grooming oil invented by Thingum Bob's own father, a merchant-barber in the prosperous city of Smug. His "bequest to posterity" begins in precisely the manner in which Coleridge had introduced his *Biographia,* with an account of "tottering first steps" on the "high road to the pinnacle of human renown":

> My name, indeed, has been so long and so constantly before the public eye, that I am not only willing to admit the naturalness of the interest which it has everywhere excited, but ready to satisfy the extreme curiosity which it has inspired. In fact, it is no more than the duty of him who achieves greatness to leave behind him, in his ascent, such landmarks as may guide others to be great.   (*P&T,* 766)

Where Coleridge had begun his *Biographia* describing his early poetic successes and failures, and how a "very severe"[14] schoolmaster had moulded his tastes, Thingum Bob describes how he began his writing life with a little unsuccessful experimental plagiarism which served to reveal to him the nature of the literary game played by the periodicals. Having cut and pasted excerpts from a few "unknown or forgotten volumes" by Dante, Homer, Shakespeare, and Milton that he had discovered amid "the rubbish of an old book-stall, in a very remote corner of the town" and consequently been thoroughly drubbed by the anonymous critics in the *Hum-Drum*, the *Lollipop*, and the *Rowdy-Dow*, he decides to fall back upon honesty and to prosecute the "entirely original" winning ode (*P&T*, 768), which, when combined with a few crafty critical strategies, secures him the "immortality" of fame, riches, and sweet revenge on his erstwhile critics in the form of monopoly ownership and editorship of a single periodical with vast circulation, merging all the magazines that had once condemned him.

In the course of his story, all Thingum Bob's rivals and detractors evaporate, and he is left alone to write, having concluded that "that indescribable something men will persist in terming 'genius' is but *diligence* after all" (*P&T*, 786). Genius is the same indefinable "something" that Coleridge had taken care to distinguish from mere "talent" in the *Biographia Literaria*.[15] The transformation here of "genius" into a commodity, a word that turns into a strategy for financial power, brings the aesthetic discourse of Kant and Coleridge directly into the field of Poe's satire. In Romantic theory, one cannot "guide others to be great" as Thingum Bob promises to do. Words like "genius" function to define artistic activity as intrinsically beyond rules, systems, generalizations, or any possibility of technical demonstration. Kant had decreed in *The Critique of Judgment* that "of all the arts poetry (which owes its origins almost entirely to genius and will least be guided by precept or example) maintains the first rank."[16] For Coleridge, the phenomenon of "genius" has important implications for reading as well as for writing. Just as an *ars poetica* – a "how-to" manual to the art of writing poetry of the sort that had circulated in Western culture since antiquity – becomes unthinkable within the Romantic conception of poetic "genius," so ultimately does a manual of how to read poetry. "Taste" cannot be the prerogative of a wide reading public; it is, for Coleridge, the "prerogative of poetic genius" alone to "distinguish by parental instinct its proper offspring from the changelings, which the gnomes of vanity or the fairies of fashion may have laid in its cradle or called by its names. Could a rule be given from *without*, poetry would cease to be poetry, and sink into a mechanical art."[17] In other words, it takes a poetic genius to know a poetic genius.

Thingum Bob's monologue is a fantasy of literary control; by sheer cunning and craft, diligence and style, the aspiring writer manages to overcome all obstacles in his path and guarantee himself literary immortality on his own terms. Literary success is a matter of getting the knack of writing, and getting on with it. Sarcastically adumbrating crucial aspects of the poetics of "The Philosophy of Composition," Thingum Bob's final boasting flourish is to add, "What I wrote it is unnecessary to say. The *style!* – that was the thing" (*P&T*, 786). Poe's self-satire here seems to anticipate Eliot, who was to criticize "The Raven" in precisely these terms, accusing Poe of indifference to content in his pursuit of style; in Poe's work, he wrote, "the subject is little, the treatment is everything" (*Recognition*, 218).

In "The Philosophy of Composition," Poe puts aside the Romantic language of genius and inspiration (though, as we will see, he will return to it in "The Poetic Principle"). He treats poetry as a mechanical device which is nonetheless committed to having an "effect" on those irreducible non-mechanical attributes of human being (heart, intellect, and soul) by representing, like a skilled actor on the stage, those similarly non-mechanical emotional phenomena (sorrow, despair, love, loss, and beauty). This is a piece-by-piece discarding of the post-Kantian Romantic illusion of poetry and of the activity of the poet, an unmasking of the labor and the trickery upon which its suggestive charms depend, pointedly addressed to a wide public. In this respect, it differs from treatises like Coleridge's *Biographia Literaria*, which tend, because the Romantic aesthetic places art beyond the reach of precept, to be obscure about their intended readership. Poe invites the public into his study, and works into the texture of his aesthetic theory his acute awareness of the breadth and diversity of that reading public, and of the exigencies faced by the working writer, producer of the poetic *objet de luxe*.

The "necessity" of pleasing this combined "popular" and "critical" audience is the occasion of the poem, Poe indicates in a disclaimer which paradoxically draws attention to the set of external circumstances which it purports to exclude as irrelevant to the analysis of the poem, but which, as we have seen, precisely, directly, dictates its length and other aspects of its formal structure. "The Philosophy of Composition," while insisting that the work of art, "the poem per se," should be considered without reference to external factors, is genially explicit about the external circumstances of its own composition. The idea for the essay, Poe indicates, was more a magazine editor's businesslike sense of the possibilities of journalistic skill and what might interest his readership than any obscure afflatus: "I have often thought how interesting a magazine paper might be written" which would reveal "the processes by which any one of his [the writer's] compositions attained its ultimate point of completion" (*E&R*, 14). The aesthetic principles codified in Poe's essay can also be seen as arising, at least in part, from his working circumstances; poetic form responds to the exigencies of time and space in a world of work. Though he would have it that the poem took shape "with the precision and rigid consequence of a mathematical problem," "unity of impression" derives less from some universal, mathematical measure of possible "excitement" or "ecstasy" in the experience of reading than from the "length of one sitting" before "the affairs of the world interfere" (*E&R*, 15). The concepts of "connoisseurship" and "virtuosity" which had arisen in late eighteenth century Europe, when the leisured life of the aristocracy was becoming available to an increasing number of people, and are bound up with the Kantian emphasis on art-as-such, hover in the background to Poe's comments about time. How long does the writer have to perfect his craft? How much time does the reader have for contemplation of the poem before the "affairs of the world" distract? By rhetorical deftness, Poe constructs the semblance of a logical syllogism or mathematical solution for what are, in fact, pragmatic businesslike judgments. He implies that the ideal length of a poem can be conclusively deduced by holding in view some unspecified "degree" of excitement which is, as though geometrically precise, "not above the popular, while not below the critical taste." He talks of the "ordinary induction" to which he resorted in order to produce something as unquantifiable as "artistic piquancy." He refers to his mathematical calculations of the "utmost conceivable amount of sorrow and despair." As though he were the mathematician and inventor Archimedes, he uses the mechanical metaphor of a "pivot on which the whole structure might turn" (*E&R*, 16–20).

Baudelaire's entertainment metaphors – Poe the "jongleur," the "farceur" – are apt to the realities of Poe's life as well as to the aesthetics of "The Philosophy of Composition." He was the orphaned child of actors who had travelled from town to town, entertaining audiences across America. Vivid and well-informed theatrical metaphors, analogies, and up-to-date thespian jargon guide the argument and the rhetoric of the "Philosophy of Composition." In his "Exordium to Critical Notices" (1842), an essay in which he pleads for a principled and independent American literary criticism, he had described "the world at large" as "the only proper stage for the literary *histrio*" (*E&R*, 1027). Returning to this theatrical metaphor at the beginning of "The Philosophy of Composition," he describes "the properties of the literary histrio" which the poets who prefer to have it "understood that they compose by a species of fine frenzy – an ecstatic intuition" – would "shudder" at letting the public see. "Properties" here has the narrow sense of "stage properties," rather than the wider meaning of "general characteristics": "the wheels and pinions – the tackle for scene-shifting – the step-ladders and demon-traps – the cock's feathers, the red paint and the black patches" (*E&R*, 14). Poe's stylish metaphor runs away with itself here and obscures with visual color the preceding description of the labor and pain of the creative process, the battle-ground between impulse and craft that is literary work. Throughout, theatrical metaphors run beneath the linguistic surface of the essay. Take, for example, that rich word "point" which occurs several times in the first paragraphs to mark out the co-ordinates in the shape and design of the poem ("the tone at all points"; "its ultimate point of completion"; "no one point in its composition" [*E&R*, 13–14]) before it is tuned into a precise and, in Poe's time, up-to-date theatrical designation: "in carefully thinking over all the usual artistic effects – or more properly points, in the theatrical sense – I did not fail to perceive immediately that none had been so universally employed as that of the *refrain*" (*E&R*, 17). The *Oxford English Dictionary* gives, as one of the many meanings of the word "point": "*Theatr.* A gesture, vocal inflection, or some other piece of theatrical technique used to underline a climactic moment in a speech, rôle, or situation; a moment so underlined. Usu. used with the implication that the integrity of the performance as a whole is being subordinated to the desire for immediate applause."[18] Its first recorded use is 1822. With this parenthesis ("or more properly points, in the theatrical sense"), Poe tunes up the meaning of the word "effect" to give it a narrow technical sense.

"Effect" is the single most important word in this essay, recurring with insistent regularity throughout, sometimes more than once within a single sentence. The "consideration of an *effect*" (*E&R*, 13), Poe tells us, is the starting point of composition. Considerations of effect dictate the choice of locale which itself appears to conform to the exigencies of the stage, an interior space framed by a proscenium arch: "it has always appeared to me that a close circumscription of space is absolutely necessary to the effect of insulated incident: it has the force to frame a picture" (*E&R*, 21). Poetic originality itself as presented in this essay is no more than "novelty of effect," an "obvious and so easily attainable a source of interest" which the poet must keep "always in view" (*E&R*, 13); another method, in other words, of pleasing the public. Indeed, every creative choice the poet makes is made "for effect," rather than to satisfy some transcendent inner compulsion of his enraptured soul. What Eliot would regard as poetic "self-consciousness" is more a matter of the poet's acute awareness of how he appears in the eyes of others, of the effect he is having on the public stage of literature – "the literary histrio" – than of solitary self-watching of the kind in which Eliot perceived Valéry to be theoretically occupied.

"Effect" is, indeed, a keyword in Poe's theoretical work as a whole. It recurs throughout his critical writings. He writes praisingly of Tennyson's "Lady of Shallott," that the poet has achieved "a suggestive indefinitiveness of meaning" that brings about "a definitiveness of vague and therefore of spiritual effect" (*E&R*, 1331). Beauty itself, he asserts in "The Philosophy of Composition," in a tacit move from the object of perception to the perceiver's stance that mirrors Kantian aesthetics, is "not a quality, as is supposed, but an effect... [an] intense and pure elevation of soul – not of intellect" (*E&R*, 16). "Soul" which responds to "beauty" is distinguished from "intellect" here in order to manoeuvre "beauty" out of the grasp of the intelligence, to make it unintelligible. Likewise, if the word "effect" provides a key to poetry for Poe, it is not a key that will unlock mysteries, but rather one that will shut the door fast on them. The word "effect" serves to foreclose theoretical speculation and sometimes to dismiss any attempt at critical analysis as futile. His "Marginalia" in praise of the "vague and . . . spiritual effect" of "The Lady of Shallott" begins by asking why "some people fatigue themselves in attempts to unravel such fantasy pieces." To account critically for great poetry is as impossible as unweaving the *ventum textilem* (*E&R*, 1331). In short, Poe's assertions about poetry rest rhetorically on the word "effect"; but the cause of the effect remains, for theoretical purposes, obscure.

What, then, is the role of the critic in the "literary *histrio*"? Poe, always a working critic, was certainly seldom lost for words; indeed, as a writer paid by the line, he would have been lost without them. He published innumerable critical reviews and notices in the course of his literary career, though he wrote with a surer pen and a clearer sense of purpose when sarcastically panning the barely literate maunderings of a Theodore S. Fay, or flirtatiously promoting the "fervid and fanciful" verses of Lydia M. Child, than when faced with the "poetic genius" of Tennyson (*E&R*, 1198). For all this, he cannot finally decide what criticism should be; at times, as we saw in his reading of Tennyson, he seems to doubt that rational discussion of aesthetic material is possible at all. In Poe's approach to criticism, we observe contradictory impulses that parallel those we have noted in his discussions of creative work. On the one hand, Poe makes a great show in his critical writings of wanting to clear a space for "truth" in aesthetic discourse, of distinguishing criticism from the intrusive clamour of other kinds of writing. "Truth," he writes, is an "unadulterated air" which the "universal corruption and rigmarole" of the world of writing make it impossible to breathe. Criticism, he urges elsewhere, is a "circle of thought" that needs to be "marked out from amid the jarring and tumultuous chaos of human intelligence" (*E&R*, 509). He hesitates to call criticism a "science" – "shall we so term it?" he asks in a telling parenthesis in his "Exordium to Critical Notices" – but is not satisfied by the notion that aesthetic judgment may come down to no more than "opinion." Though he is sure that critical judgments should be about the work "as such" and that the "critic has really nothing to do" with the "opinions of the work," he cannot convince himself that even when the work of criticism is neither "an essay, nor an oration, nor a chapter in history nor a philosophical speculation, nor a prose-poem, nor an art novel, nor a dialogue," it is, by that token, any less an opinion, any closer to a mathematical truth (*E&R*, 1027–1032).

In "The Literary Life of Thingum Bob, Esq.," Poe satirizes the impurity of critical discourse, as well as the notion that criticism might be all a matter of system or technique. In the course of his successful "literary life," Thingum Bob had found it expedient to play the critic, putting on the guise of Thomas Hawk ("tomahawk" was one of Poe's own critical aliases), "scalping" and "brow-beating" the "herd of poor-devil authors," which task he found "a far less onerous occupation than poeticizing: for [he] went upon *system* altogether, and thus it was easy to do the thing thoroughly and well" (*P&T*, 781–782). In a comic adumbration of the formalism of "The Philosophy of Composition," Thingum Bob describes the knack of critical practice. Criticism is essentially a culinary business: a cutting-and-pasting which involves taking cheap editions of the works of William Cobbett and Lord Brougham (contemporary figures in British politics) and a couple of manuals of "Slang" and "The Art of Snubbing," slicing them up, serving the pieces, placing them in "a large tin pepper-castor," adding to them the books to be reviewed (also carefully shredded and sifted) and dusting the whole mixture out onto a piece of foolscap, anointed "with the white of a gander's egg ... where it stuck" (*P&T*, 782). The results are then published to general acclaim in the same journals of "profound sagacity ... well known for the deliberate gravity of [their] literary decisions" that had once spurned Thingum Bob's plagiarisms from the greatest poets in the Western tradition as "a medley of incoherent and ungrammatical bombast" (*P&T*, 770).

"The Literary Life of Thingum Bob, Esq." is itself a kind of systematic shredding, shaking-up, and satirical reassembling of the essential and circumstantial elements of a literary critical life in mid nineteenth-century America: fame, tradition, originality, rivalry, plagiarism, reputation, pseudonymous or anonymous criticism, the circulation of periodicals, philosophical ideas, politics, lies, tricks, editorial power, and the freelancer's insatiable yearning for "speedy insertion and prompt pay" (*P&T*, 768). The ingredients in critical discourse, as it is represented in Poe's "grotesque," are the quasi-theological terms of Romantic aesthetics – "imagination," "inspiration," "genius," "soul," "heart," "sublimity," "pathos," and "POESY" – all stirred into a verbal stock composed of words taken from the cut-and-thrust world of the magazines: "twattle," "trash," "rant," "drivel," "braggadocio," "penny-a-liner," "balderdash," and "cant."

Quite how "jarring and tumultuous" Poe found contemporary aesthetic discourse can also be judged from his satire "How to Write a Blackwood Article" (1838), where a punning play on the suggestive likeness between the words "cant" and "Kant" supplies Poe with an obvious, though significant, joke (*P&T*, 279) (which will recur in the "Mellonta Tauta," the monologue of a certain punning Pundita). This story pastes the single word "flummery" onto all the formulaic pseudo-profundities of what passes for contemporary "fine writing." Psyche Zenobia (also known as Suky Snobbs), an aspiring writer of tales of grisly death and premature burial much like Poe's own tales of horror, is instructed in the art of critical prose by the editor of a literary periodical. His instructions again adopt the mechanical terms of a recipe: how to "spice" an article with "little scraps of learning or bel-espritism"; how to "use big words"; the importance of saying "something about objectivity and subjectivity" – those terms borrowed from Friedrich Schlegel that Coleridge had heaved into the English language in the *Biographia Literaria*; the importance of adding learned footnotes and a "good spicing of the decidedly unintelligible." This discourse, for all its references to books with titles like "*Metaphyische Anfangsgrunde de Naturwissenschaft*" and "*Kritik der reinem Vernunft*," must never actually say anything; it must restrict itself to the "vague" and "indefinitive": "hint everything," the editor tells the young hopeful, "assert nothing" (*PT*, 280–283). Poe seems to turn the satire on himself again: "the style! – that was the thing."

In "The Poetic Principle," a lecture delivered in a public hall in 1848 to an audience of over 2,000, Poe adopts a critical position founded upon an explicitly Kantian insistence on the distinctness of the aesthetic "faculty." The world of the mind is divided among "Pure Intellect, Taste, and the Moral Sense." Poe uses this simplified Kantian philosophy of mind to head off the need for any attempt to make the aesthetic intelligible or susceptible to theoretical understanding: "He must be theory-mad beyond redemption who ... shall still persist in attempting to reconcile the obstinate waters of Poetry and Truth" (*E&R*, 76). The "aesthetic" can only be defined, not in the "truth" terms which require "severity" of language, simplicity, precision, and terseness, but rather through an "efflorescence of language" (*E&R*, 76), by a showy piling on of poetic metaphors. Poetry is "elevating excitement" of the "soul" (*E&R*, 71). Poe told his audience, which included the current object of his romantic affections, Helen Whitman, that poetry is a sign of "a thirst unquenchable ... the desire of the moth for the star" (*E&R*, 77), or perhaps like his earliest fictional hero Hans Pfaall's similarly misproportioned balloon-journey into space to escape his debts and his wife, "a wild effort to reach the Beauty above us" (*E&R*, 77). Here again, we find Poe's argument carried along by suggestion and indefinitiveness, and the poet playing to the crowd for maximum effect. Poe still wants to have it both ways, however, and continues to use mathematical metaphors, talking of the "value of the poem being in the ratio of [its] elevating excitement"(*E&R*, 71). Likewise the impossibility of a long poem is asserted in terms of mathematical proof: "it follows from all this that the ultimate, aggregate, or absolute effect of even the best epic under the sun, is a nullity: – and this is precisely the fact" (*E&R*, 72). Working against the grain of all this efflorescence and mathematical masquerading, however, is a straight-talking call for a practical criticism that is not "theory-mad," but which will attend diligently and pragmatically to poetic material. The rhetorical terms of the first paragraphs of "The Poetic Principle" are frank, untheoretical, and provisional. Poe begins by describing the design of the essay as neither "thorough" nor "profound," but rather a "random" presentation "for consideration" of the poems which "best suit" his own taste (*E&R*, 71). In relation to his views on ideal poetic length, he simply asks to be permitted "a few words in regard to a somewhat peculiar principle, which, whether rightfully or wrongfully, has always had its influence in my own critical estimate" (*E&R*, 71). The critical judgments that appear at the end of the poem, on a series of love poems calculated to woo Helen Whitman, who was seated in the front row of Poe's vast audience, are cast in Coleridgean terms of "imagination" and "fancy." His comments on the poetry of Thomas Moore end with a perversely abbreviated flourish which captures in a sentence the eccentricity and unevenness of Poe's powers as a literary critic: "In the compass of the English language I can call to mind no poem more profoundly – more weirdly imaginative, in the best sense, than the lines commencing – 'I would I were by that dim lake,' . . . I regret that I am unable to remember them"(*E&R*, 85). He leads his audience to a ringing theatrical "point," but fails to make any other kind; his performance lacks the integrity and force of reasoned argument, and even the grace of simple demonstration.

Whatever his strengths and weaknesses as a critic, there were moments in the course of his writings about the creation and appreciation of poetry when Poe could imagine criticism as complex and demanding work founded on simple, flexible, principles. When asking himself, in an early review, how we should discuss and evaluate poetry and its effects, he puts aside for a moment all his stage properties that had provided his criticism with its effects – the mathematical metaphors, the mystical flights and metaphysical categories, the diluted Kantian philosophy of mind, the local and intellectual animosities, even the art-for-art's sake exclusion of all considerations external to the "poem as such" – and says simply, "to this end we have many aids – in observation, in experience, in ethical analysis, and in the dictates of common sense" (*E&R*, 511). In the midst of the often opaque theorizing of the *Biographia Literaria*, Coleridge had coined the simple term "practical criticism"[19]; in the midst of all the "flummery" of his own critical discourse and the "corruption and rigmarole" of the world he worked in, Poe was able, for a moment, to imagine just how practical criticism might be.

NOTES

1. See, for example, Katharine Everett Gilbert and Helmut Kuhn, *A History of Aesthetics* (London: Thames and Hudson, 1939).
2. See Kevin J. Hayes, "One-Man Modernist," below.
3. *Oxford English Dictionary*, ed. J. A. Simpson and E. S. C. Weiner, 2d ed., 20 vols. (Oxford: Clarendon Press, 1989), 1: 206.
4. Samuel Taylor Coleridge, *Biographia Literaria: or, Biographical Sketches of My Literary Life and Opinions*, ed. James Engell and W. Jackson Bate, 2 vols. (Princeton University Press, 1983), 1: 153.
5. *Oxford English Dictionary*, 1: 206.
6. *Oxford English Dictionary*, 1: 206.
7. Sir Philip Sidney, "An Apology for Poetry," *Elizabethan Critical Essays*, ed. G. Gregory Smith, 2 vols. (Oxford University Press, 1904), 1: 159.
8. Benjamin Constant, *Journal Intime*, ed. D. Melegari (Paris: Albin Michel, 1925), p. 8.
9. Victor Cousin, *Cours de Philosophie Professé à la Faculté des Lettres Pendant l'Année 1818 sur le Fondement des Idées du Vrai, du Beau et du Bien* (Paris: Hachette, 1836), p. 224.
10. Harold Bloom, "Introduction," *Edgar Allan Poe: Modern Critical Views*, ed. Harold Bloom (New York: Chelsea House, 1985), p. 13.
11. Coleridge, *Biographia Literaria*, 1: 5.
12. Charles Baudelaire, "Notes Nouvelles sur Edgar Poe," *Oeuvres Complètes*, ed. Marcel A. Ruff (Paris: Seuil, 1968), p. 347.
13. Baudelaire, *Oeuvres Complètes*, p. 356.
14. Coleridge, *Biographia Literaria*, 1: 8.
15. Coleridge, *Biographia Literaria*, 1: 224.
16. Immanuel Kant, "Critique of Aesthetical Judgment" in *Philosophies of Art and Beauty: Selected Readings in Aesthetics from Plato to Heidegger*, eds. Albert Hofstadter and Richard Kuhns (University of Chicago Press, 1964), p. 327.
17. Coleridge, *Biographia Literaria*, 2: 83.
18. *Oxford English Dictionary*, 11: 1130.
19. Coleridge, *Biographia Literaria*, 2: 19.

4

DANIEL ROYOT

Poe's humor

Sphinx or hoax? Aside from the *poète maudit*, the satanic dandy revered by Baudelaire, and the alleged dope-ridden neurotic gratifying public tastes with the morbid paraphernalia of his Gothic tales, Poe was also a born humorist equally inspired by parody and self-mockery. In an anti-romantic vein so common among the popular humorists of his time, he enjoyed applying his acumen to deride the outpourings of emotions too often surging from mediocre fiction and poetry. Through a mysterious alchemy, humor was at least for him a short-lived euphoric response apt to exorcise the fiendish visions harassing his mind. This Janus figure seemed to view the world in two opposite directions, yet sometimes provided a dual perspective to reconcile extremes paradoxically. In his *Anthologie de l'Humour Noir*, André Breton held that the contradiction between the acclaimed poet of "The Raven" and the wretched drunkard, was itself humorous since it implied an open conflict involving logical lucidity at odds with the vapors of liquor.[1] Plagued with his physical insufficiencies and mental strains, Poe was able, however, to overcome his sense of alienation and filter the agonizing material he stumbled over in his private life and literary career, thus intermittently giving himself narcissistic comfort through an economy of expenditure in feeling, as Freud later defined the process. Facing the bleak consequences of his recurrent failures, Poe derived a new power in his own eyes by wryly manipulating images and re-evaluating conventional role-models to disclose imposture. Poe's abhorrence of the didactic prompted him to enlist his reader as an accomplice. Nudged toward laughter through the medium of satiric irony or sheer extravagance, the latter was expected to be tickled out of conformity. In the mean time Poe's hoaxes and explorations of the ludicrous were intended to slough off European trappings and undermine the cultural hegemony of smug New England pundits. His sense of the absurd could hopefully liberate his reader from the cultural pressures tailoring his imagination, while his manifold paradoxes were applied in myriad ways to voice his subversive attitudes. Both an acrobat walking a tightrope over a nightmarish abyss, and a jester whose histrionics were poised between horror and laughter, Poe resorted to comedy and satire to survive haunting predicaments. Granted that he may have been taken too seriously by critics eager to tear off the veil from his short fiction and to reveal his quintessential mournfulness, anyone attempting to exhume the funny bone from his tales at all costs would run the risk of overreaching himself.

The persona: voices and masks of the American Grotesque

In Poe's Baltimore, "windies" about the swashbucklers of the southwestern canebrakes had accustomed the public to the demigods of the wilderness such as Davy Crockett and Mike Fink. Those yarns consisted of stringing incongruities and absurdities together in a digressive manner. The *conteur* cracked jokes with a straight face while his monologue unraveled along spiralling anecdotes. Poe's review of Augustus Baldwin Longstreet's *Georgia Scenes* for the *Southern Literary Messenger* in 1836 pays homage to such a realistic presentation of folklife in native humor. The hyperbolic tall tale was in fact a frame story frequently staging a gentlemanly narrator playing the part of a shrewd observer of men and manners in the backwoods. He would set a distance between himself and the protagonist who gradually appeared as a big liar. But in some other cases the punchline of the yarn belied the narrator's first impressions. In "Georgia Theatrics," the gentleman's ears "are assailed by loud, profane and boisterous voices, proceeding apparently, from a large company of raggamuffins" (*E&R*, 779). The brutal fisticuffs which he overhears turns out to be no brawl at all but the dramatic staging of heroic fantasies by a boy impersonating fighting ring-tailed roarers. Also recorded by Poe "The Fight" evokes practical jokes such as eye-gouging and gander-pulling, the combatants senselessly becoming friends again at the end. "The Horse Swap" derides the rascality of tricksters who find it good to be shifty by concealing the many defects of a hack. While such narratives were challenging gentility with chaotic, iconoclastic images, the narrator usually stood aloof from the burlesque *dramatis personae* and retained his credibility. Familiar with this interplay of hyperbole and understatement Poe soon capitalized on southern lore as exemplified in "The Gold Bug." The ironic epigraph suggests the lethal dangers of the South Carolina island, rather than the treasure trove of the American wilderness which is ready for William Legrand's taking:

> What ho! What ho! this fellow is dancing mad!
> He has been bitten by the Tarantula.
> *All in the Wrong* (*P&T*, 560)

In the narrative, Poe gives a twist to folk humor since the scarabeus is no bugbear but a clue to Captain Kidd's cache. Whereas Mike Fink shot off a black's heel whenever he disliked its shape, it is Jupiter's task to flog his master when he happens to lose his mind, thereby also reversing the myth of Robinson Crusoe and Friday.

From behind the comic masks contrived by Poe, versatile, discordant voices express contradictions between appearance and reality. Successive impersonations enacted in the tales may suggest a whole range of idiosyncrasies. Among such metamorphic personae emerge for instance the devious, unreliable narrator, the clever witness adopting an innocent pose, the mad scientist and the victimized scapegoat. Poe's plurivocal mode of discourse and provocative masquerading are as much indebted to Pope, Dryden, and Swift as to antebellum regional humor. Problematic views of his comic spirit should therefore consider the comedies and satires as a palimpsest with popular and classical material engraved in an elaborate literary creation transcending crude hoaxes and trivial yarnspinning. Poe's insistence on the single effect to be achieved in a short story as expressed in his notice of Hawthorne's *Twice-Told Tales* (1842) might seem to run counter to the free-wheeling narrative in native American humor. Yet the ironic coexistence of operators and protagonists in conflict, or incongruously juxtaposing contradictory interpretations of the same object, is well in keeping with the endless process of pirouetting and whirling in the *Tales of the Grotesque*.

As the sources of the Folio Club indicate, Poe was attentive to the emergence of sectional humor. In New England cockalarum heroes had grown even more popular than the Yankee doodle with the rise of Jacksonian democracy. Regional eccentrics became national figures with political fables about the rise and fall of the common man after Seba Smith created the character of Jack Downing in 1830. The sharp traders were early examples of the confidence man in a turbulent society. The country bumpkin who peddled notions in his native Maine was promoted by the Down East humorist to the function of special adviser of Old Hickory in mock letters satirizing his entourage. Poe liked the humorist in Seba Smith but later ridiculed his epic in verse *Powhatan*: "The simple truth is that Mr. Downing never committed a greater mistake in his life than when he fancied himself a poet, even in the ninety-ninth degree" (*E&R*, 922). John Neal, editor of *The Yankee*, was likewise bent on evaluating Down East typology in his wild, erratic style, once back from Baltimore to his native Portland in the early 1820s. A member of the Delphian Club nicknamed Jehu O'Cataract by 1816, Neal was later targeted by Poe in "Diddling Considered as One of the Exact Sciences," a tale of the Folio Club first entitled "Raising the Wind," and specifically intended to caricature roguish Yankee cupidity through an incipient specimen of the confidence man to be later exploited by Melville. In a tone reminiscent of naturalist Buffon listing the features of newly discovered species, the narrator identifies the behavior of the swaggering "diddler" who epitomizes slyness and braggadocio. In the second part of the tale, he is shown transmuted into a hateful swindler who outwits credulous citizens. Poe's satire is general rather than individual. The indictment of Yankee inventiveness for betraying the ideal of utilitarianism may have been lost on the reader, especially in the allusion to Jeremy Bentham whose secretary happened to be Neal in 1825.[2] When Poe cynically writes "Your diddler is audacious. – He is a bold man," (*P&T*, 608) he has in mind Neal's cowardly refusal of a duel in Baltimore on account of his Quaker faith. Throughout the tale, Poe's rhetoric of irony is based on dead-pan statements rationalizing attitudes so far likened to crude rural mores. The teller adopts various poses, such as that of the pedantic historian in: "The origin of the diddler is referrible to the infancy of the Human race" (*P&T*, 609). Elsewhere he mingles sophisticated and homespun imagery with anticlimactic effects: "A diddler may thus be regarded as a banker *in petto* – a "financial operation," as a diddle at Brobdignag. The one is to the other, as Homer to "Flaccus" – as a Mastodon to a mouse – as the tail of a comet to that of a pig" (*P&T*, 608).

The final part of Poe's tale duplicates standard Yankee tricks in an anecdote about cheating Philistine America. While the minutiae of realistic details, including the transcript of an announcement, lends verisimilitude to the fraud, humorous enjoyment blunts the satiric edge of the fable which altogether makes fun of both trickster and victim, being only mildly committed to harsh denunciations of social evils.

Poe is clearly indebted to the tradition of the comic frame story. In many tales a character is introduced in the opening scene to tell about remarkable events. The author pretends to be part of the audience, claiming that he has merely recorded the teller's own words. The yarn may not be about the raconteur but he is the one who searches for the extraordinary and tests the limits of the possible. He seeks to prove that the adventure or experience told exceeds all expectations. Such is the case in "The Devil in the Belfry," a story of witchcraft with the connotations of a truculent Breughel painting: "No one who knows me will doubt that the duty thus self-imposed will be executed to the best of my ability, with all that rigid impartiality; all that cautious examination into facts, and diligent collation of authorities, which should ever distinguish him who aspires to the title of historian" (*P&T*, 298).

Yet the narrator of Poe's tales is hardly ever expected to be as reliable as he promises. He magnifies the fantasy with realistic details and real happenings with fantasy. When the tale is allegedly autobiographical he manipulates appearances to make invention coincide with observation. In the narrative, the weird may have to emerge from the familiar to be credible. The intrusion of the fantastic does not antagonize the reader if he admits that extraordinary events are possible in a universe not necessarily remote in space or time, but whose configuration is without the scope of the mind. A hoax is all the more successful as its author is skillful enough to maintain the wilful suspension of disbelief. When the truth is revealed, the mock event is enjoyed as pure fun. The success of such a story depends on the narrator's sustained ambiguity. The reader will innocently take the narrative at its face value, until he discovers evidence that he has been deluded. Like his fellow southerners Poe could not fail to test the gullibility of newcomers and greenhorns with such a ritual of initiation as illustrated in the folksong *The Arkansas Traveler*. Sometimes Poe even satirized his reader's assumptions through a pose that only the most clever discerned. In "The MS. Found in a Bottle" Poe loves to recreate and celebrate the way human fancy receives and combines the real and the fantastic so that they are blurred in the hyperbolic evocation: "From billows a thousand times more stupendous than any I have ever seen, we glide away with the facility of the arrowy sea-gull; and the colossal waters rear their heads above us like demons of the deep, but like demons confined to simple threats, and forbidden to destroy" (*P&T*, 197).

Yet the narrator thinks himself devoid of imagination and simply seems to record events faithfully, ready as he seems for an accurate transcript of the Apocalypse. On the contrary, the utterly unreliable narrator of "Why the Little Frenchman Wears his Hand in a Sling" is clearly identified by his colloquial Irish dialect speech. Comic mimesis is thus achieved through a deviant phraseology which enhances the discordance of a boastful teller also disqualified as a vain, self-styled lady-killer. In other instances, the narrator's inadequate interpretations also serve Poe's Socratic irony by proving facts so far unnoticed. Such is the case with the short-sighted narrator of "The Spectacles." He falls for and marries an eighty-two-year-old lady who later happens to be his great, great grandmother. Far from blinding himself like Oedipus, the parodic double of Hypolites staunchly depends on poor glasses. His absurd neoplatonic faith in love at first sight is corroborated by repetitive references to "ethical magnetism" and other romantic ravings. His flaw actually results from curbing the world to his myopic logic, which in fact causes sequences of disasters whose graphic evocation has the burlesque vitality of a wild goose chase.

Hoaxes and masquerades

Poe's humor debunks the illusions of the mystical and the vagaries of philosophical idealism as developed by the Transcendentalists whom he labels

"Frogpondians" after the pond on Boston Common. His invention of spurious events and conversely his ruses of elaborate detection are directed against the falsity of literary hegemony and scientific pretensions. He stubbornly values his derisive art as an eye-opener meant to awaken his reader's skepticism, his taste for mystification being a clue to his overriding irony. The hoax ranges from the conspicuously farcical to the pseudo-scientific. In "The Thousand-and-Second Tale of Scheherazade," he lampoons encyclopedic knowledge by quoting the famous volume "Tellmenow Isitsöornot." Affecting to use scientific methods in "Maelzel's Chess-Player," he finally admits that analysis is inconclusive and relies on chance. So does Legrand elaborate ratiocination in "The Gold Bug." "Thou Art The Man" also exemplifies the epistemological function of irony. Charles Goodfellow is a criminal mystifier who speaks like Anthony over Caesar's body in Shakespeare's *Julius Caesar* (III, 2, 80 ff.) to deceive the crowd, but fatally betrays himself. The intrusion of dramatic irony through Old Charley's slip when alluding to "the heir of the worthy gentleman" does not fully dispel ambiguities, so far as the omniscient narrator has withheld information and partially misled the reader into both literal meaning and nonsense. Now he conducts his own counterinvestigation on the death of Shuttleworth who incidentally shifts from life to death and back – "Old Charley" is himself tricked to his downfall by means of a whalebone, a mechanical device contrived to give the appearance of life to the corpse of Shuttleworth and operate a slapstick *deus ex machina*.

Foreshadowing P. T. Barnum, Poe delighted in mystification. "The Balloon Hoax" is a text of fiction expected to be read as an authentic document about real facts. The prologue constitutes a *verbatim* record of Poe's announcement in *The New York Sun* on 13 April 1844, about the first transatlantic crossing of a flying machine. The subsequent narrative enlarges upon the astounding deed by combining technicalities with bird's eye views of the landscapes in an apocryphal journal of the flight. The rapturous delight of the crew annihilates the threat of the waters below, especially when elemental forces are subdued by human inventiveness. As far as the exhilarating adventure smacks of the Emersonian spiritual ambition to reach for a star, at least metaphorically, the "double entendre" slyly associates the overstated enunciation with implicit ironic deflation.

"The Unparalleled Adventure of One Hans Pfaall" amounts to a tall tale version of the then popular myth of the man in the moon. It is discomfiture rather than exhilarating success that awaits Poe's clown astronaut. As he ascends to the dead planet, the balloon is attracted by its gravity and collapses instead of smoothly alighting. Ultimately, "the dark and hideous mysteries which lie in the outer regions of the moon" (*P&T*, 994) are strangely reminiscent of the American desert described by explorers of the Great Plains in the earlier part of the nineteenth century.

Shifting from the cosmos to the cruel sea, "MS. Found in a Bottle" first recalls travel narratives by accumulating precise observations substantiating the validity of one Solomon Seadrift's log, before the protagonist caught in a storm is hurled with irresistible violence upon the rigging of a phantom ship (*P&T*, 194). Then only the inveterate naive reader would not realize that Poe is pulling his leg. For a time the frenzied actor-narrator on his flying trapeze is the reverse replica of Sam Patch, the jumping folk-hero who in 1829 dived to his death in the Genesee Falls. But Solomon is finally engulfed into "the bowels of the earth" (199) and crosses the threshold to the unknown, following his epic struggle with the monstrous forces of the ocean. The voyage of discovery turns out to be a Grotesque trip into the absurd. Like Aladdin's lamp the bottle has revealed secrets from the depths but forever remains as incredible as magic.

Poe's pandemonium: satires and caricatures

A conjurer whose sleight-of-hand triggers off laughter by subverting conventions, Poe is also as attentive to graphic effects as a cartoonist. His caricatures reflect the studied distance he establishes between his wilful distortions and his perceptions of reality. His sense of indirection enables him to vent his aggressiveness without openly degrading his models. As previously exemplified in the distinction between voice and mask, Poe's Janus figure is expressed in the functions of *eiron* and *alazon*. The former manipulates an unstable reality, feigns blindness, practices a false naivety, and uses his wits as a weapon. The *alazon* is the clown who cultivates illusion and never quite realizes he has been in error. In Poe's parodies and pastiches ironic contrasts are drawn between matter and manner, subject and object. Reshuffling human types, he substitutes drunken sailors for aristocrats to spoof Disraeli's *Vivian Gray* in "King Pest." The mock-heroic antics of the common run of humanity emulating the elite, coexists with the burlesque treatment of upper society. As a matter of fact, Poe spares no humbug on the American scene.

In "The Duc De L'Omelette," European nobility is evoked in the portrait of an epicurean Duke expiring in a paroxysm of disgust upon seeing an ortolan deprived of its feathers ("déshabillé de ses plumes"). After awakening in the presence of the Devil, he refuses to strip and engages Satan in a game of cards. He escapes after winning and returns to his ortolans. Poe's satire is double edged. Not only does it lampoon French decadent noblemen reveling in regal fantasies, but also the American initiators of a transatlantic culture fascinated with the lustre of exotic romance and snobbishly striving to be proficient in high-flown French.

Despite its mysterious oriental setting "Four Beasts in One – or the Homo-Cameleopard" is a biting political fable destined to enlighten fellow citizens. The King of Antioch disguises himself as a giraffe to be worshipped by his dumb subjects on the streets. But he is overthrown by lions, tigers, and leopards who recover their dignity after punishing brutal, dishonorable humans. An allegory of Jacksonian democracy, Poe's tale addresses the issues of propaganda and mob rule. In 1833, Seba Smith already had Jack Downing keep behind Andrew Jackson to help him respond to enthusiastic crowds. As the White House confidante says: "I reached my arm round under his and shook him for about a half hour as tight as I could spring."[3] At the same time Davy Crockett himself angrily applied the metaphors of royalty to the President, while political cartoonists showed Jackson in robe and crown as King Andrew and caricatured both his regal vanity and the servile adulation of his followers. Though Poe's and Seba Smith's Horatian satire avoid invective against the imperial presidency they do not spare the dumb masses.

A potential candidate to the White House, the heroic Indian fighter, General Winfield Scott is burlesqued in the hoax "The Man that was Used Up" (1839). Under the name of Brevet Brigadier General A. B. C. Smith, who defeated the Kickapoos and Bugaboos, Poe's protagonist has been left with a mangled body now cleverly mended so that artificial limbs and organs have apparently permitted a perfect return to normality. But secretly he is nothing more than "an odd looking bundle of something" inadvertently kicked out of the way by the narrator. The surrealistic rendering of the general's condition relieves the situation of its more immediate terrors. The body is trivialized when seen as a puppet composed of detachable spare parts. The prosthetic devices substituting for natural morphology question man's vital, organic unity. Superimposed medical engineering could predictably induce a nervous voyeuristic smile. But now seen as a dehumanized machine, General Smith cannot easily claim hero worship and least of all run for president. Therefore grim humor subsides into gruesome burlesque.

Ten years later, Winfield Scott was upbraided by James Russell Lowell in the *Biglow Papers* as a blood-sucker during the Mexican War.[4] But the Massachusetts volunteer Birdofreedum Sawin who had lost an arm, a leg, an eye and his mind on the Mexican battlefields, wanted to run for president, meanwhile complaining that his wooden leg could not assimilate the amount of liquor that his body consumed in large quantities.

Poe also revels in unmasking political schemers by resorting to an archaic observer whose judgments often echo Gulliver's evaluations of Lilliput.

"Some Words with a Mummy" brings back to life the mummy of Count Allamistakeo, in fact a truth-speaker resurrected from a remote past with an electric charge. Although Rip Van Winkle's slumber does not compare in duration to the Ancient Egyptian's, both characters awaken to the disappointing avatars of American democracy on which the uncommitted survivor of Pharaonic civilization passes sour strictures. With the uncontested privilege of seniority, Allamistakeo remembers the uprising of thirteen Egyptian provinces and the resulting despotism of a state ruled by the mob.

Poe's satirical allegory is allusive and only cheers on disillusioned readers. By refusing to compromise with shoddy political behavior, he keeps his ethical standards from being lowered but remains vigilant through the humorous exposure of charlatans, half-way between hostility and tolerance. The same distrust of politicians is echoed in Washington Irving's *Knickerbocker History of New York* by the evocation of peaceful pipe-smoking Dutch colonists suddenly in the grip of compulsive utopian fallacies.

Turning to the social scene, Poe also shows the normal lapse into the absurd in "The System of Doctor Tarr and Professor Fether." An innovative French asylum expected to grant more freedom to its inmates is ultimately run by lunatics who have tarred, feathered, and locked their keepers while the imaginative practitioner Doctor Maillard is driven demented. The ingenuous narrator who visits the place is only mildly surprised at the antics of madmen masquerading as sane individuals. One crows vociferously, another flaps his arms like wings and all demonstrate wild eccentricities. Ironically the naive visitor fears the keepers who strive to free themselves, while trusting his wrong assumptions and refusing the truth based on glaring evidence. Foolishly backing up sophisticated French experts who promote a so-called "soothing system," the narrator luckily survives the pandemonium but does not acquire the capacity to distinguish between common sense and madness.

Throughout the humorous tales, Poe's cultural geography explores specimens of the dominant literary fauna. "Lionizing" is an allegory of exhibitionism and megalomania about mediocre writers promoted to the status of the lionized *literati*. The narrator who earned a reputation from his treatise on nosology shoots off the nose of a rival who in his turn becomes idolized in fashionable circles. Like Diogenes in his barrel, Poe holds a lantern to discover a true man of letters among plagiarists, servile imitators, transcendentalist apostles of spiritual regeneration, inky ladies drowning their pages under lachrymose effusion, and puffing addicts to sentimentalism. Poe sarcastically substantiates his opinions in an article on Theodore S. Fay, editor of the *New York Mirror* and author of *Norman Leslie: A Tale of the Present Times* (1835), a melodrama about an innocent girl in the clutches of an Italian seducer of "mean extraction, but of great beauty and talent." Poe does not hesitate to enlist a Frontier demigod to make his case: "Alas! Mr. Davy Crokett, – Mr. Davy Crockett, alas! Thou art beaten hollow – thou art defunct, and undone! Thou has indeed succeeded in grinning a squirrel from a tree, but it surpassed even thine extraordinary ability to smile a lady into a fainting fit!" (*E&R*, 541).

Another Poesque fable about the press bears on parochial controversies. "X-ing a Paragrab" stages two competing newspapers in the city of Nopolis far "out West." A dyspeptic renegade from New England, Mr. Touch-and-go Bullet-head has just founded the *Tea-Pot* to challenge John Smith (sic), the embattled owner of the *Gazette*. The first onslaught of the former is expressed in blunt interjections mostly using words with the letter o. Responding with an aggravated proportion of the same vowel, John Smith ironically points to the circular reasoning of a Yankee carried off by sounds instead of pondering over meaning. Stung to the quick, the vehement editor of the *Tea Pot* counter-attacks with a long draft in which not a single word is without an o. The rhetorical skirmish is transmuted into a mock-heroic Shakespearian historical play. John Smith is denounced by the Down East intruder as a "frog, come out of a Concord bog." (*P&T*, 920). When setting to print the hand-written piece, the printer's devil finds an empty box when he reaches for the prized letter. Suspecting a *Gazette* spy of the theft, the resourceful young devil replaces o with the superabundant X. The cryptic text is deemed "mystical and cabalistical" (922) by a populace ready to lynch Touch-and-Go Bullet-head but soon subdued by the lure of the so-called "hieroglyphics" now omnipresent in local phraseology. The last word belongs to the young printer's devil who states that the XXX ale drinking, wild Down Easter simply never belonged before vanishing from the scene. The raging nonsensical controversy has been centered around typesetting, and form has prevailed over meaning. For the narrator Orestes Augustus Brownson's transcendentalist casuistry might have proved that Yankee Touch-and-Go Bullet-head was not irascible, thus suggesting the power of rhetoric among the Frogpondians and their total reliance on words and signs at the expense of shrewd thinking.

In a similar vein, "The Literary Life of Thingum Bob, Esq." is an allegory of authorial humbug told in the first person by the son of barber Thomas Bob who stipends the editor of the *Gad-Fly* for an ode entitled "Only Genuine Oil-of-Bob." The "genius of the stanzas" soon recognizes his son's "divine afflatus" and launches his literary career. Trusting classical works rather than his own inspiration, Thingum sends excerpts from Dante and Shakespeare, signed "Oppdeldoc," to magazine editors who soon reject the lines they think written by mad men or idiots. In the mean time they publish the egregious trash of contributors who fawn on them. The raging quarrels over "ignorant ravings" induces Thingum to compose a two-liner:

> To pen an Ode upon the "Oil-of-Bob
> Is all sorts of a job"
> (Signed,)
>
> Snob (*P&T*, 772)

As related by the persona, the battle of books erupting after the publication of his piece by the *Lollipop* boosts the sales to half a million copies and earns Thingum an editorial job to slander other writers. He now tears off pages from Cobbett's *Complete Works* and shreds them into a sieve before pasting them together for publication. Thingum is even shamelessly induced to browbeat his father in a style reminiscent of practical jokes. He ends up as editor of the *Goosetherumfoodle* after several mergers. The nonsensical reversal of values is performed by Thingum's preposterous ordering of words and ideas. His soaring hyperboles are equally self-defeating as he unconsciously exposes himself and believes in his own lies. Being a fool among knaves gives him a false sense of reality but as opposed to Don Quixote, he is foolish without dignity while competing for celebrity.

Probably the most biting castigation of Transcendentalist misconception and idealization of the dogged facts of life is "Never Bet the Devil Your Head," a riddle progressively leaking its secrets. The belated association of Dammit with dogs suddenly brings into light the full significance of diverse incidents, as if the text was suddenly deciphered. The truth has been hidden from the reader long enough for the very last sentences to cause an anticlimactic burst of laughter after Dammit has jumped to his death upon the injunction of an old gentleman who might well be a Frogpondian: "I bedewed his grave with my tears, worked a bar sinister on his family escutcheon, and, for the general expenses of his funeral, sent in my very moderate bill to the transcendentalists. The scoundrels refused to pay it, so I had Mr. Dammit dug up at once, and sold him for dog's meat" (*P&T*, 467).

Learning that Dammit will be sold as dog's meat calls attention to an illusion entertained since the beginning of the tale. The butt of the fable is the Transcendantalist postulation of secret essence before even considering the object concerned. The rhetorical device allowing the construction of meaning in advance of observation artificially postulates abstract notions without ever putting them to the test of experience. When faced with a thought-provoking mystery the narrator defines it as "queer" and grants himself time to scrutinize Dammit's strange behavior. On the contrary, the Transcendentalists and Idealists would readily resort to sublime notions reflecting their philosophy and call Dammit "mystic" (Coleridge), "pantheistic" (Kant), "twistical"

(Carlyle) and "hyperquizzitistical" (Emerson) (*P&T*, 461). This tautological method of reasoning is further upbraided in *Eureka*: "There are people, I am aware, who busying themselves in attempts at the unattainable, acquire very easily, by dint of the jargon they emit, among those thinkers-that-they-think with whom darkness and depth are synonymous, a kind of cuttlefish reputation for profundity: but the finest quality of thought is self cognizance" (*P&T*, 1275).

Humor, violence, and horror

Toying with taboos and enjoying transgression were linked in Poe's mind to his capacity to endure suffering and remain poker faced. For Aristotle comic mimesis implied no pain or damage. But whose pain or damage did Aristotle have in mind? Characters experience comic pains that produce a hilarious effect in the tales, whether from physical aggression in "Loss of Breath" or mental torture in "A Predicament." Poe's black humor is a form of bravado designed to articulate genuine fears and partly allay such fears. Its violence even sometimes invites readers to enjoy the feel of killing and mutilating. Fanciful though this comic spirit may be, it entertains no illusion. It is nurtured on anguish but seeking to evade pain through chaos, remains a shared experience as opposed to satanic laughter that chills the listener to the bones. Paraphrasing the Freudian *acte manqué* the term *peur manquée*" (failed fear) might define Poe's humor, excessive and unreal as it often is.

As in Voltaire's *Candide* and Rabelais's *Pantagruel and Gargantua*, there is in the tales of humor a dual ambiguous view of violence. After the Lisbon earthquake, Candide is bewildered, aghast, bleeding, and throbbing but there is no sustained emotional weight in the narrative. In "King Pest," the crowd of ludicrous characters is bound to submit to some well deserved disaster while the reader remains detached from their destiny. Two drunken sailors find their way into the forbidden "stronghold of the pestilence," a wine cellar peopled with degenerate merrymakers drinking from skulls. As in John Gay's *The Beggar's Opera* (1728) the underworld freaks ape aristocratic decorum while King Pest, whose hideously lofty forehead looks like a crown of flesh, holds a human thigh bone in his hand. Mayhem is made a cause of enjoyment through frantic saturnalia.

Poe's manifold parodies of Gothic themes create an odd pleasure in disorientation, laughter thus amounting to the recognition of the insubstantiality of the threat that had previously been frightening. Screaming may even coincide with laughing as in the Grand Guignol theater. Poe is fascinated by boundaries, especially the limit between life and death, and dilutes the passage from the one to the other, enabling characters to talk from across an anaesthetized world. First published under the title "A Decided Loss" in 1832, then reprinted in the *Southern Literary Messenger* (1835) and later as one of the *Tales of the Grotesque* (1839), "Loss of Breath" is "A Tale neither in nor out of Blackwood" as its subtitle indicates. Following a mock-heroic prologue, the bombastic tone of the opening lines contrasts with the incoherence of the subject. The Dickensian designation of the protagonist as Mr. Lackobreath, himself confronted with his rival Mr. Windenough, sets the mood for an apocalyptic though burlesque spectacle of multiple mutilations symbolically likened to castration. Paradoxes crop up as the absurd prevails and the world has gone topsy-turvy once the protagonist has said: "Anaxagoras, it will be remembered, maintained that snow is black, and this I have found to be the case," (*P&T*, 153). So far as the phrase "loss of breath" has first been taken literally, Poe humorously capitalizes on the identification of breath with an object. Bouncing off like a disjointed puppet, the victimized first-person narrator is subjected to dissection, torture, and hanging. Horror is defused by the disjunction between the individual and his consciousness. Such graphic incidents create a surreal atmosphere, anesthetizing the harshest reality and assuming unexpected dimensions. After the narrator-actor has snatched the breath first caught by his rival, now entombed like himself, the farcical happy ending miraculously abolishes chaos with the recovery of speech.

Psyche Zenobia grapples with the Edinburgh literary wilderness in "A Predicament," inserted in "How to Write a Blackwood Article." The ambitious, brainless Bluestocking is in fact the burlesque female counterpart of Lackobreath. Blackwood even lets loose a dog at the soul-searching "Queen of Hearts" whose lofty ideals have to meet the requirements of a sensational ordeal. Psyche loses her dog, her black servant, and her life after her exhilarating contemplation of transcendental spiritual space from above a steeple. Once her head has been sliced off by a clock hand, it still takes a sniff from a box, regardless of the logical link expected between cause and consequence. Her last words being "I have done," at least Psyche's utmost literary achievement coincides with her last moment. The rhythm of the story is discontinuous, syncopated, bordering on the kaleidoscopic, but though untrue the plot has real effects.

In "The Facts in the Case of M. Valdemar," the narrator declares himself under pressure to reveal a mesmeric experiment he carried on M. Valdemar who indirectly identified the former as "My Dear P—, " in a personal letter (*P&T*, 834). Obviously on the defensive the narrator states that the reports have been grossly exaggerated, also adding that the cataleptic patient exclaimed: "I say to you I am dead" being all the while a very talkative corpse. Eager to give gruesome details about the body eventually rotting away and letting out a liquid mass of putridity, the doctor, whether candid or mad, admits that his account will be deemed incredible. He delivers a frightening diagnosis of the ills of the still living M. Valdemar in an impressive terminology including "ossified lung," "purulent tubercles," "aneurism of the aorta." In a negative review of *The Partisan* (1835) by William Gilmore Simms (*E&R*, 891–905), Poe had objected to the use of cruel and ghastly descriptions, but in the case of Mr. Valdemar the cumulative, short-lived effect of the medical report is so absurd that it alters the previously lurid aspect of the scene and becomes a gore extravaganza.

Conclusion

The ritual denouement of Poe's comedies remains ambiguous. Taking for granted that a happy ending is implicitly conditional, he hastens to lower the curtain so that the spectator may not think twice about the plot. His humor appropriates the most unexpected impulses in his shaggy-dog stories for the purpose of creating a kind of anarchic, Dionysian euphoria. He introduces absurdities to remove the crust of exclusive meaning and create a paroxystic experience. Relying on indirection and comic masks, James Russell Lowell alternated jocular entertainment with incisive irony in his native New England, but his humor remained consistently didactic. As he declared: "If I put on the cap and bells and made myself one of the court-fools of King Demos, it was less to make his majesty laugh than to win a passage to his royal ears for certain serious things which I had deeply at heart. I say this because there is no imputation that could be more galling to any man's self-respect than that of being a mere jester."[5]

Poe's humor has no such ethical overtones. It is an imitation of sacrificial expulsion by resorting alternately to the scapegoat and the buffoon. As Rene Girard points out, the demon that used to cross over from hell to harass humans in ancient mythologies was progressively transfigured into a comic denizen.[6] In the course of history, ancestral terror has gradually been changed into farcical profanity and aggressiveness into merrymaking. So do the tales allowing Poe a comic relief by staging the absurd contradictions of a Janus figure impersonating both the clown and the genial transgressor who challenge dogma and induce a cheerful nihilism.

NOTES

1. André Breton, *Anthologie de l'Humour Noir*, (Paris: Sagittaire, 1940).
2. Benjamin Lease, *That Wild Fellow John Neal and the American Literary Revolution* (University of Chicago Press, 1972), p. 65.

3. Seba Smith, *The Life and Writings of Major Jack Downing of Downingville* (Boston: Lilly, Wait, Colman and Holden, 1833), pp. 213–214.
4. James Russell Lowell, *The Biglow Papers, First Series (1848): A Critical Edition*, ed. Thomas Wortham (DeKalb: Northern Illinois University Press, 1977), p. 78.
5. James Russell Lowell, *The Writings of James Russell Lowell in Prose and Poetry: Riverside Edition* 10 vols. (Boston: Houghton Mifflin, 1890), 7: 57.
6. René Girard, *La Violence et le Sacré* (Paris: Hachette, 1998).

5

BENJAMIN F. FISHER

Poe and the Gothic tradition

Few would hazard a challenge to long-standing opinions that Poe was a master of the Gothic horror tale, although many might not as readily be aware that he did not invent Gothic fiction. When he began to attract widespread attention by publishing several macabre tales in the *Southern Literary Messenger* in early 1835, critics sounded negative notes concerning his "Germanism," a synonym for Gothicism, just as they deplored his wasting talents on what they deemed had become an outmoded type of fiction. Such caveats, as well as many offered over the course of the century succeeding his death, notwithstanding Poe's Gothic tales, are what have typically attracted greatest numbers of readers, and that allurement is wholly understandable. A descent from such British milestones in literary Gothicism as Horace Walpole's *The Castle of Otranto* (1764), William Beckford's *Vathek* (1786), W. H. Ireland's *The Abbess* (1798), or Sir Walter Scott's *The Bride of Lammermoor* (1819) is evident in Poe's writings. In his own day the brief tale of terror, familiarly known to the Anglo-American readership as the signature for fiction in the popular *Blackwood's Edinburgh Magazine*, served as Poe's, and other Americans', model, time and again, although his accomplishments in the short story far surpassed what now often reads like so much dross in the pages of the celebrated Scottish and other contemporaneous literary magazines from the first half of the nineteenth century. Well into his literary career, in his second review of Nathaniel Hawthorne's *Twice-Told Tales*, Poe alluded to the fine "*tales of effect* [to be found] in the earlier numbers of Blackwood [which were] relished by every man of genius" (*E&R*, 573). In his mind such effect, or unity of impression, was inevitably coupled with "terror, or passion, or horror." In a later review of Hawthorne, Poe cited as praiseworthy specimens of American tale writing William Gilmore Simms's "Grayling; or, Murder Will Out," Washington Irving's *Tales of a Traveller*, and Charles Wilkins Webber's "Jack Long; or, The Shot in the Eye," along with many of those by Hawthorne (*E&R*, 586–587) – all in the Gothic mode – albeit he took Hawthorne to task for a too heavy-handed allegorical vein in many of his stories. Poe also spoke of Hawthorne's tales, in general, as analogous to those of the German author, Ludwig Tieck, whose tales number among the highlights of German Gothicism.

I

One might well ask at this juncture: "Just what is Gothic tradition?" Such a query has been answered rather glibly, by some, and it may well require some elaboration of less witty propensities. A remark by Donald E. Westlake, present-day detective fiction aficionado, exemplifies the former attitude; to him, a Gothic "is a story about a girl who gets a house."[1] Although many Gothic works do involve just such a story – witness Ann Radcliffe's *The Mysteries of Udolpho*, Charlotte Brontë's *Jane Eyre*, or a host of twentieth-century paperback Gothic novels with covers showing a young girl against the backdrop of a great house looming nearby, one good example being Sandra Brown's romance novel, *Slow Heat in Heaven* (1988) – other elements often carry as great, or greater, significance. Not every Gothic story takes place in a house (or haunted castle), a house is not necessarily a primary consideration in many first rate exemplars of the tradition, nor does a girl figure as *the* character throughout Gothic fiction.

The term "Gothic," admittedly, originated in a confluence of history and architecture. The Goths were a northern Germanic European people whose ways and beliefs differed largely from those of Greco-Roman Classical civilization farther south. To the southern outlook, the Goths were wholly uncivilized and barbarous. When the initiation of architecture that departed radically from the low, heavily-arched forms in "Romanesque" pervasive darkness consequent upon the inability to construct large windows because they would have weakened the stonework, such newer buildings, chiefly the great cathedrals that arose all over northwestern Europe and the British Isles from the eleventh century onward, provided structures which permitted far more light to illuminate the interiors. Employment of vaulted (pointed) arches within and of huge "flying buttresses" for support outside, gave to these vast, tall cathedrals an appearance of a winged bird or a growing plant. What was essential to architectural soundness was often deemed "grotesque" by those who beheld the tangible forms. Gothic cathedrals speedily make one aware of an innate desire to look upward, and they convey senses of great space. Even with far more lighting than Romanesque buildings afforded, a sense of considerable shadowiness or obscurity is inescapable when one enters Gothic buildings or their cloisters. To those who objected that such tall structures were often adorned with what the extremely practical mind saw as inessential decorations, the response was that these buildings were, after all, symbols of human attempts to glorify God, and that His eye could see what mere human vision could not.

Great cathedrals that have changed little since the middle ages still dot Continental Europe. In Great Britain, however, once Henry VIII decided that allegiance to the Pope in Rome was no longer necessary and, as a concomitant, that much in the way of cathedrals, abbeys, monasteries, convents, and, often, churches of far lesser status, would contribute substantially to the wealth of the Crown, many Gothic buildings fell into ruins because they were no longer maintained. In addition to the symbolism in the ruined architecture, the British mind came to associate a downright immorality with some of the thinking and practices in Roman Catholicism. For example, once Henry's decrees for creating the Anglican Church became operable, ties between Roman Catholicism and Continental European political class structures seemed dangerous. Moreover, celibate clergy, especially monks and nuns, eventually came to be anathema in British eyes. The clergy contributed in another way to Gothic tradition. The hooded, flowing robes worn by many members of ecclesiastical orders dovetailed precisely with stereotypical conceptions of ghosts in bedsheets, and, amidst the strange visionary responses otherwise created by Gothic architecture's combination of vastness and obscurities, they offered plausible models for supernatural beings. Another off-center assumption about Catholic practices concerned live burial as punishment for clerical recalcitrance. Since paranoias about actual premature burials persisted well into the early years of the twentieth century, here was a motif with compelling outreach to many readers.

Little wonder, then, that ruined architecture from "medieval" times merged with tyrannical and profligate conduct by members of the ruling classes throughout much of Europe, to produce Horace Walpole's intriguing Gothic novel, *The Castle of Otranto* (1764). In this brief novel appear, if in crude, pioneering fashion, hallmarks of what in many ways has continued to inform Gothic literature up to our own times. To epitomize, the basic Gothic plot entails vicious pursuit of innocence/innocents for purposes of power, lust, money, at times singly, at others collectively. Issues of identity and power, often relating to family situations of lineage or marriages (which in their turn might affect history, and which in later Gothic works often were centered in smaller numbers of characters, ultimately to operate within the consciousness of just one character), along with sexuality and gender considerations, came to hold greater importance than the eerie settings that provided mysterious backdrops for equally mysterious speeches and actions in previous Gothic works. Military situations or others involving social unrest likewise contributed recurrent themes, devolving, no doubt, from like features in Renaissance drama, principally that of the revenge tragedy stamp.

Such substance enhanced emotional uncertainties and disturbances among the characters, and created scenes in which life and death draw close, whether in actual battle or in some non-military combat and trauma in which opposing characters lead readers to think of wins and losses. Supernaturalism was also significant in Walpole's novel. A gigantic supernatural helmet crushed Manfred's son, Conrad, before he could marry. A figure in an ancestral portrait became animated. In the hands of his literary descendants, supernatural trappings were often taken to incredible lengths. Once the Germans adapted British Gothicism into their own imaginative literature during the later eighteenth and early nineteenth centuries, they were reputed by Anglo-American readers and critics to have carried natural and supernatural horrors to even greater extremes. Thus, the notion of all things German as barbarous reared its head once again, and one frequently encounters the epithet "German" as a term of disapprobation from the 1790s on through Poe's time. Furthermore, supernatural powers were often ascribed to medical doctors and scientists or pseudo-scientists.

What finally emerged as a mainstay in Gothic works, architectural setting or not, was an atmosphere conducive to anxieties in the protagonist and, depending on the situation in the story, among other characters in general. The literal haunted castle, cathedral, monastery was often transformed into some natural setting conducive to unrest and fears, or, in yet another kind of development, to a haunted mind which required no castle or frowning mansion to stimulate terrors, the corridors of the psyche sufficing to engender such a frisson. Mary Shelley's *Frankenstein*, for example, drew repeatedly on landscapes to throw into high relief the emotional explosions that occur throughout the novel. American authors, understandably, had no castles, abbeys, or cloisters in the near proximity that European authors had, and thus American Gothics tended to foreground other varieties of tangibles. Hawthorne in *The Scarlet Letter* (1850) focused first on the forbidding jail so important to life in seventeenth-century Boston, shifted to the scaffold, and then made landscapes reflect the lights and shadows in human life and character. In his tales he effected similar shifts. In "Young Goodman Brown," for example, action moved from colonial Salem to the frightening forest that so bedeviled the journeying Goodman Brown; or the weird lime kiln that formed the scene in "Ethan Brand," or the kaleidoscopic scenes wherein natural setting mirrored human emotions in "Alice Doane's Appeal." Melville took Gothicism onto the seas in many of his books, and *Moby-Dick* (1851) owed much to Gothic tradition in matters of characterization of Ahab, Ishmael, and Moby-Dick himself, as well as in its handling of superstitions and of settings like the *Pequod*, an aqua-Gothic haunted castle, if ever there was one, or the mysterious oceans, whose depths hinted of mystery and the unknown.

To address other important topics, we see that sexual themes in *The Castle of Otranto* had been linked with violence, brutality and death, often leading to parricide and, in the case of Prince Manfred, the protagonist, near incest. Such themes were intensified in many later Gothic works, so readers hostile to Gothicism have charged that they are little better than pornography. Many Gothic villains are possessed of a startlingly piercing eye, which functions symbolically in phallic terms in its ability to penetrate its victims' innermost secrets. That feature links with the Evil Eye in folklore, which has powerfully magic, hypnotic effects. If pornographic texture is to be found easily in Gothic tradition, so is another popular-culture element, namely, humor. Many readers of Walpole's novel find that the hyperbolic language and high-pitched emotions verge so strongly toward the ridiculous as to suggest a strong comic impulse indicative of his satirizing the melodramatic qualities potential in horrifics.

Since Walpole himself claimed that the impulse for this book came to him in a dream, and since dreams take us into territories of non-rationality, the argument for comedy (which is premised on the non-rational) in *The Castle of Otranto* cannot be overlooked. An even greater infusion of satire, many believe, characterizes William Beckford's Oriental Gothic novel, *Vathek* (1786). Whatever the status of humor in these works, a strong tendency to lampoon what readers could interpret as intentional or unintentional comedy in Gothic writings, entered and has continued to be vital in Gothic tradition. The satiric sections in Jane Austen's *Northanger Abbey*, published in 1818, but written a decade earlier, when the British Gothic fad had reached a high point, have often been revisited by literary scholars, although that novel is but one among many hits at the rage for a non-critical devouring of Gothics. Such eagerness for thrills caused many writers, just as eager to turn a profit, to serve out horrors that became ever more sleazy. The numerous "penny dreadfuls" and "bloods" that were aimed at a public who would not question any plausibility in what they read, as long as it contained their desired stimuli of melodramatics.

Well before Poe's debut on the literary scene in the 1820s and 1830s, then, and continuing long after his death in 1849, blendings of horror and humor enlivened Gothic productions. Such "sportive Gothic," as one critic has called many of Washington Irving's handlings of supernaturalism, appealed to many American writers and readers, Poe included. Spoofs or "quizzes" of Gothicism abounded in the Anglo-American literary world of this era. A related consideration, and this one in existence almost before a steady stream of creative writings came from the pens of Americans who undertook authorship, was a desire to create a literature that would manifest the nationalistic trends infusing American life. Such thinking led many

Americans to deplore what they deemed the inferiorities of Old World literature in the face of the cultural milieu on the new continent. Literary Gothicism thus drew recurrent fire in critical sections of American literary magazines, such barbs darted in hopes of encouraging aspirant American writers to shy away from a seemingly decadent mode. William Dunlap, for one, who had spearheaded American theater and dramatic movements in northeastern cities, turned his hand, late in life to fashion several Gothic tales, albeit in "It Might Have Been Better, It Might Have Been Worse," a magazine tale of the early 1830s, he used up Gothic superstition emanating from misunderstandings among the characters, who all too quickly assumed that strange occurrences originated in supernatural rather than ordinary circumstances. An even more interesting case of this nature occurs in the works of James Kirke Paulding. In his stances as critic, notably in "National Literature" (1820, expanded in 1835), he praised the realism he perceived in then current American life; in his fiction, he often employed Gothic trappings, only to reveal that a healthy realism could eventuate triumphant at their expense. A number of Paulding's comic Gothic tales are set in the Near East, as if to suggest that weird fantasies are, overall, unAmerican. One tale, however, "Cobus Yerks," originally published in the *Atlantic Souvenir* for 1828, which has an American cast much in the manner of Irving's "The Legend of Sleepy Hollow," recounts the torments arising from Cobus's (Jacob's) being pursued by a presumed spectral dog, concluding, however, with the revelation that any "otherworldliness" stemmed from Cobus's drunkenness.

American Gothic works tend to transform European architecture into American landscape as material for intriguing hauntings. Dunlap and his friend, Charles Brockden Brown, exemplify such early transformations, and they may be considered the founders of American literary Gothicism. Several Dunlap plays are the first preeminent Gothic works by an American author. Commencing with *Leicester* (1794) and *Fontainville Abbey* (1795), an adaptation of Mrs. Radcliffe's novel, *The Romance of the Forest*, Dunlap promoted the American scene in his far more renowned play, *André* (1798), which features the American Revolution and its inherent anxieties as background against which André's tragedy and its accompanying emotional traumas are enacted.[2] Brown's novels, *Wieland, Ormond, Arthur Mervyn*, and *Edgar Huntly*, all published as the eighteenth century concluded, embody Gothic horrors, but those horrors prove to have bases in human psychology rather than in the presumed supernatural horrors that create the Wieland family's upheavals. In *Arthur Mervyn*, a yellow fever epidemic furnishes grim situations that harrow character's psyches with as much intensity as any ghostly presence might. Dunlap's and Brown's Gothic works contain none of the humorous undercurrents that infiltrate those by some of the other Americans mentioned above, but, in all, a prevalent tendency to depend less on the supernaturalism of European Gothic tradition and to employ more psychological substance is evident. Granted, some Americans continued to draw upon what we might define as "straight" supernaturalism to enhance their Gothic productions, as is the case with John Greenleaf Whittier's *Supernaturalism of New England* (1831), expanded into *Legends of New England* (1847), William Austin's famous short story, which domesticated into American literature the legend of the Flying Dutchman, "Peter Rugg, the Missing Man," published first in 1824, and often reprinted, or some of the other dramatists, as well as many now forgotten writers, whose wares grew tedious because of cardboard characters in improbable situations, fashioned merely as thrills for thrills' sake.

2

Poe's greatest literary achievement was his renovation of the terror tale from what had been its principal intent, to entertain by means of "curdling the blood," to use a widely current phrase of the times, into what have been recognized as some of the most sophisticated creations in psychological fiction in the English language. He realized at the outset of his career that Gothicism was eminently compatible with psychological plausibility in literature, and he worked out such designs in combination repeatedly throughout his literary career. His first strong yearning, however, was to be a poet, and he returned to the writing of poetry during his career, albeit, after he had brought out three slim volumes of poems between 1827 and 1831 yet secured no profit, he foresaw that he could not gain sufficient financial recompense from that genre to maintain himself. Understandably, from one who looked to the poems of Byron, Shelley, and Coleridge as his own poetic models, Poe's verse reveals unmistakable Gothic characteristics. *Tamerlane*, for example, centers on the dying confession of the titular protagonist to a Roman Catholic priest – a literal impossibility, but one of those anachronisms that course through many earlier Gothic works, in which the "medieval" or – to cite another strain readily assimilated into the emerging tradition – "Oriental" Gothic, characters speak the English language of a much later period, not to mention that they also embody the moral outlooks of a later historical era rather than what might more plausibly be their different national or ethnic outlook. Tamerlane's memories reveal his imperious, volatile nature: "And, I believe, the winged strife/And tumult of the headlong air/Have nestled in my very hair" (*P&T*, 25). He adds that heaven and hell war in his emotions, and thus this passage, later supplemented by allusions to Eblis, betrays Poe's debts to Beckford's *Vathek*, wherein Eblis and hearts set afire are given prominence.

Typical of many Gothic characters, Tamerlane suffers effects of a blighted love affair with a maiden who was far superior to him in her abilities to love (he subsumed his own capacities for love in his will to political and military power), and well before his dying hour he has wearied of what the world has brought to him: might tinged with deep loneliness. Thus he stands as forerunner not only to other characters in Poe's poems, notably the speaker in the early "Dreams," another angst-ridden, disconsolate protagonist, and those in poems like "The Lake—To—," "Lenore," "To One in Paradise," "Dream-Land," "The Raven," "Ulalume," "Annabel Lee," or "For Annie" (this last being atypical in that the protagonist–speaker's torments have vanished, though what they seemed to be is vividly depicted). Tamerlane also adumbrates the protagonists in Poe's fiction. The weird settings in some of the poems – "The Haunted Palace," "The City in the Sea," "The Sleeper," "The Coliseum," "Dream-Land," "The Raven," and "Ulalume" – likewise evince Poe's familiarity with the foreboding remoteness and mystery which had well before his time become commonplaces in Gothic tradition.

Most of Poe's tales devolve from Gothic tradition. When he turned from the creation of poetry as his literary mainstay to the writing of fiction, he naturally wanted to produce what would sell. What had been selling well, despite any grumblings from reviewers, was Gothic fiction, so to that mode Poe turned with an eagerness that eventually led him into some amazing pathways. Poe's preparation for creating fiction that would appeal to the marketplace made him aware of the highs and lows in Gothicism, so much so that, like other American writers, he quickly fledged his wings as a fiction writer by attempting a book that, had it appeared, would doubtless have inspired a far different image of Poe than that which for so long stood: a drunken, drug-ridden, debauching necrophiliac creature whose own morality, or lack thereof, filtered into his writings.

"Tales of the Folio Club" featured monthly meetings of a group of pretentious litterateurs, who followed a supper replete with ample alcohol by readings and critiques of their own endeavors in fiction. The club members were modeled upon then well-known authors of popular fiction, each to read a story composed in his recognized manner, and debates over its merits and demerits would ensue. Also each renowned writer would feature as the first-person narrator in his own tale. No publisher would risk the uncertain returns from so subtle a project, so Poe ultimately dismantled the book and published the tales individually in newspapers and magazines. Thenceforth, although his contemporaries recognized satire and parody in these early tales, nobody has ever wholly concurred as to their implications. Poe's ceaseless revisions compounded this confusion because what may have read as comedy within the Folio Club arrangement might be read, with equal validity, as intense seriousness in another context. Debates over what is serious, what comic, in Poe's fiction continue to the present day.

One striking example of this multiplicity is offered by Poe's first published tale, "Metzengerstein," filled with terror-fraught escapades in remote Hungary: family feuds and resultant revenges; a family curse; a supernaturally animated tapestry rather than a haunted portrait; a supernatural, fiery-colored gigantic horse (the reincarnation or metempsychosis of old Count Berlifitzing into his favorite kind of animal to wreak his revenge), which destroys young Metzengerstein in a sensational conclusion when horse bears rider up the many spiraling staircases of the latter's burning palace, to leave behind the smoke image of a great horse. Frederick had apparently torched old Berlifitzing's stables, causing the old man's death. Frederick's own increasing isolation, terror, and demise bear out the curse – that the Berlifitzings would triumph over the Metzengersteins.

This tale reads almost as if it were an encyclopedia of "German" supernatural horrors. Nevertheless, for an apprentice work, which might readily betray its models, it demonstrates its author's sophistication. The stacatto effects in the prose attain onomatopoeic heights. The "stupendous and magnificent battlements of the Palace Metzengerstein," for instance, "were discovered crackling and rocking their very foundation under the influence of a dense and livid mass of ungovernable fire" (*P&T*, 141). We can almost hear the hissing and see the flames rising. Poe's attentiveness to unity of impression or effect as the mainspring of artistry in short stories is in evidence, too. The Latin motto, which translates as "Living I was your plague – dying I will be your death," leads convincingly into the opening of the tale: "Horror and fatality have been stalking abroad in all ages" (*P&T*, 134). Horror and fatality, along with the beliefs in metempsychosis, or transmigration of souls, which are quickly solidified as primary themes, heightened by the curse on the Metzengersteins, are rounded off deftly in the close of the tale. The rapid succession of scenes, along with the increasing mysteriousness that each displays, adds to the elements of angst and fatality that hover closely around Frederick.

In Poe's Folio Club scheme, so he wrote at one point, the critical commentaries were to function as much as or more so than the tales themselves as vehicles for mirth.[3] Thus "Metzengerstein" may not have required any submerged comedy to stand among the Folio Club tales in sixth place, read by "Mr. Horrible Dictu, with white eyelashes, who had graduated at Gottingen" (*P&T*, 132), conveying lurid German supernatural horror. By the time of this reading, the club members were probably affected by gluttony and drunkenness, and therefore their evaluations rather than the texture of the piece itself may have created pretentious "criticism," which would come naturally from the "Junto of Dunderheadism" that the Folio Club was (*P&T*, 131).

What they might have understood and, more likely, what they would have misunderstood about "Metzengerstein" might well have been laughable.

Whatever the quantity of the "Germanic" within "Metzengerstein," it remains an important barometer to Poe's subsequent achievements in Gothic fiction. The supernatural horse adumbrates the near otherworldly qualities of the cats in "The Black Cat," published ten years later. The emotionally overwrought protagonist characterized in Frederick also heads a line of similar characters in Poe's fiction. Frederick's unrestrained evil, which extends to death-dealing acts, recurs in many more Poe protagonists, as does his weltering in guilt, remorse, and confusion, which prompt him to bombastic speeches and violent actions. Frederick's overwrought state of mind threads its way among Poe's later first-person narrators as they take center stage in the tales, in his assuredly Gothic novel, *The Narrative of Arthur Gordon Pym* (1838), and in many of his poems, most notably "The Raven" and "Ulalume," which might be called Gothic stories in verse. Moreover, Frederick's fate – resulting from his efforts to subdue the great horse, an animal symbolic of revenge and its evil consequences – harks back to Coleridge's ancient mariner, to C. B. Brown's Wieland, to Mary Shelley's Dr. Frankenstein and other overreaching Faust-like characters from Renaissance revenge tragedy and classical mythology, and it anticipates such works as *Moby-Dick* and, looking into twentieth-century manifestations, the King Kong, Godzilla, Dracula, and Jurassic Park films.

"MS. Found in a Bottle," as told by Mr. Solomon Seadrift, a name that undercuts the wisdom of biblical Solomon as it makes the narrator suited to tell a "drifty" story, may be read as one, among several, drunkards' tales told in the Folio Club. The narrator asks us to give credence, as he seems to, to mounting horrors that stretch probability to its limit. Should we take at face value his ostensibly calm outlook, such that, as he is assaulted by natural and then supernatural phenomena, he cooly writes in his diary until he realizes that death is near? Finally, in just as orderly a procedure, he inserts his manuscript into an empty bottle, corks it and tosses it to the tempestuous waves as he is about to go down with the ship. Or should we query the nature of the bottle whence comes this manuscript? Poe's original motto for this tale was "A wet sheet and a flowing sea," a line of verse from Alan Cunningham. In nineteenth century slang, one did not have to be *three* sheets to the wind to be intoxicated; *one* would do. Along with the narrator's "imbibing" of "shadows," until his soul became a "ruin" (another old colloquialism for poor-quality gin), should we wonder that we may be near some very subtle wordplay on Poe's part, especially since language of intoxication characterizes the state of most Folio Club members? The dream elements permeating this domestication of the Flying Dutchman legend more than tepidly suggest good causes for some of the incredibility, although we may sense that the storyteller's "imbibing" emptied the bottle into which his manuscript went. Once again, though, Poe has wrought an artful tale, in which perimeters of the natural and supernatural, or the sober and the mirthful, to hold forth the truth-versus-fiction theme in deft fashion.

The initial popularity of "MS. Found" as the prize tale in a Baltimore newspaper contest, may have come about because the judges' indecisiveness concerning just which of the several tales submitted by Poe could have led them to favor a sea story during the time when Baltimore was far better known as a port city than it is today. Furthermore, nautical tales of stirring adventure on the high seas were much in favor in the 1830s, chiefly because Sir Walter Scott's, James Fenimore Cooper's, and Frederick Marryat's sea fiction had won vast audiences and found many imitators. This tale has been frequently reprinted, and its reprintings have by no means been confined to selections of Poe's works, but have been anthologized in collections of adventure, mystery, fantasy, and sea stories.

Another ambiguous tale, "The Assignation," features non-supernatural Gothicism. Here the effects of the narrator's adventures literally and figuratively assault his vision, making it Gothic. As he beholds the sensational rescue of a drowning baby by a mysterious stranger, who has dived from a dark window directly facing that of the beautiful young Marchesa Aphrodite (he is her lover, perhaps the father of her child), and the puzzling remark of the lady that follows, he perceives and suggests a mere physical assignation of this captivating pair. Mirrorings of several types, visual and emotional, tangible and intangible, coalesce with the narrator's befuddlement, so he misunderstands the essence of love that bonds the Marchesa and the stranger. These motifs are reinforced when, early next morning, the narrator visits the stranger's apartments, there to be overwhelmed, first, by his dizzying journey up great staircases to reach the inner chambers, and, once within, by the incongruous assemblage of art objects collected by his host. He is dizzied in more ways than one. All the while a sense of something's being amiss, of emotions teetering on the edge of life and death, of potential violence counterpointed by the seeming relaxation of his host, contributes an aura of mystery that is enhanced by a viewing of the lifesize and lifelike portrait of the Marchesa, whose likeness, with the addition of wings, suggestive of her Psyche role in her relationship with the more physical-seeming stranger, is illuminated by the same kind of dazzling light that had visually and emotionally affected the narrator on the previous night. Both the stranger and his beloved are made analogous to what were in Poe's time admired as ultimates in statuary art, Canova's Venus and the Belvidere Apollo – a pair doubtless driven by passions beyond mundane imagination. The stranger-lover, modeled upon Lord Byron, has attempted to mitigate his frustrations in love by collecting artwork, which, however, is incongruous, as if to symbolize the imperfections caused when only the physical side of human nature is emphasized. Thus he and his beloved look to another world, on the far side of the grave, to consummate their genuine, spiritual love. That is, having sated themselves sexually, they commit suicide (death of an individual self to establish a new unified self) in hopes of uniting their souls. This vein of thought the earthy, sensual narrator cannot fathom, thus the events leading up to, and including, the lovers' deaths, are beyond his comprehension, save as he can recount them in sensational story terms. Delightful irony sounds in his closing remark: "a consciousness of the entire and terrible truth flashed suddenly over my soul" (*P&T*, 211). Has the whole truth of what he has observed suddenly come to him, or is his notion of entirety bounded by the usual meaning of "assignation"?

The bulk of the tale is set in the stranger's dwelling, Poe's adroit modification of the haunted castle from earlier Gothicism. The stranger's "castle" is indeed "haunted," but the haunting is grounded in human psychology instead of vengeful specters, scary noises, and dilapidated architecture. The art collection is startling, as art objects tend to be in Gothic works, and the emphasis on interiority urges us to consider the psychological depths in the tale. The narrator's mind may incline toward interpreting situations in sexual terms, but that same mind is capable of evoking interesting symbolic fiction. Yet another psychological twist devolves from the statue motifs; time-honored folklore posits that any human who falls in love with a statue, or with a supernatural being, is doomed to unhappiness, often leading to death for one or both lovers. Specifically, the theme of a young man betrothed to a statue underlies this tale, and readers alert to this folk superstition might find satisfaction in Poe's treatment of this theme.

"The Assignation," originally entitled "The Visionary," figured in the Folio Club context of humor and horror being misconstrued by an intoxicated audience. Not surprisingly, Poe's handling of a portion of the late Lord Byron's romantic life (he and his Italian lover did not commit suicide; he died in the war for Greek independence, and she long outlived him), is cast in story-book, fantasy form, as we learn in the opening paragraphs of the tale. The cream of this jest is that the well-known Romantic poet and biographer of Byron, Thomas Moore, would obviously have been detected in the guise of Mr. Convolvulus Gondola, the Folio Club reader-narrator of this tale. Moore's reputation encompassed eroticism and a predilection for alcohol. To have a drunken Tom Moore face the passionate in Byron's life would indeed have amused many readers in Poe's day because Moore's biography was attacked by those who found his presentation inaccurate. The amazed, and amazing "visions" of both stranger-lover and narrator may, in part, emanate from alcohol, as is borne out by the erratic thinking of the latter and that in the former as he contemplates death before and after drinking from the poisoned goblet. The attention to the type of wine consumed, the wordplay on Thomas Moore – Thomas More, who, legend had it, laughed on his way to execution, and the additional bit of comedy in the stranger's chafing his guest for drunkenness, heightened by wordplay on alcohol as the host's "tone of voice dropped to the very spirit of cordiality" in apologizing for his own laughter at his visitor's expense (*P&T*, 205): all are calculated to test a reader's acumen, although the accompanying aura of uneasiness and mystery from unknown causes upholds the surface Gothic frisson.

From these beginnings, in which the incoherence of alcoholics' fumblings to express themselves, in tandem with their perceptions, which may plausibly be irrational and tend to envisioning of violence, brutality, sex, confusion in the face of the unknown or, at least, the not immediately apprehendable, Poe went on to craft what are far more subtle renderings of Gothic art. Tales like "The Fall of the House of Usher," "The Pit and the Pendulum," the detective, or, as Poe preferred, "ratiocinative" tales, "The Tell-Tale Heart," "The Black Cat," "The Masque of the Red Death," "The System of Dr. Tarr and Professor Fether": all of these are founded solidly on Gothic tradition. Poe's modifications of the Gothic, however, imbue these fictions with great art. Poe divined how he could manipulate conventions of Gothicism to create fine psychological fiction. Responding to the disapproving charges of "Germanism" targeting some of his early tales – "Berenice," "Morella," "Usher" – Poe stated in the "Preface" to his first collection of fiction, *Tales of the Grotesque and Arabesque* (1839): "If in many of my productions terror has been the thesis, I maintain that terror is not of Germany, but of the soul, – that I have deduced this terror only from its legitimate sources, and urged it only to its legitimate results" (*P&T*, 129). Such terror finds excellent symbols in the spiraling staircases and the downward spirals into ocean depths or mouldering subcellars of ruinous mansions and abbeys, or their equivalents. Many of his characters' movements from place to place lead to actual or figurative vertigo or bewilderment. Many of the buildings or even individual rooms may symbolize the interiors of human heads, i.e., minds. Poe found in Gothic tradition the very kinds of settings and characters that, transformed in his imagination, would contribute wonderful symbolism to psychologically plausible narratives of multiple outreach.

"The Pit and the Pendulum," for example, harbors many of these legitimate terrors, none supernatural in origin, although at times the narrator-protagonist's tormented consciousness may make him and readers temporarily think that supernaturalism is at work. The narrator-victim's confinement in the pit may signal his like descent into his own inner self. This tale has many sources in popular horror tales from *Blackwood's* and other like periodical publications, to C. B. Brown's *Edgar Huntly*, to historical materials on the Inquisition.[4] These foundations have perhaps accounted for the tale's continuing popularity. The symbolism may also continue to touch readers' own innermost emotional chords (fear of the dark, fear of torture and pain, fear of starvation, fear of the unknown, fear of death), and this factor may promote a recurrent fascination for such reading. Richard Wilbur stated that, for him, Poe's probings of psychic states, "transitions between those states, and the possible meanings and implications that such states might have[,]" plus his employment of dream structures are, along with his obviously well considered diction, what constitute Poe's greatness. This greatness is exemplified in his tales, no matter how odd their language may initially seem. Doubtless, Wilbur's response matches those of many other readers as to what is so compelling about Poe's tales.[5]

Once the Inquisition judges have pronounced the narrator's death sentence, his swoons and fantasies regarding their moving lips transform from the thinnest lines to "writh[ing] with a deadly locution," predicate, for him, no mercy. Just so the candles shift from conveying angelic charity to "meaningless spectres with heads of flame" (*P&T*, 491). The descent, as he is borne to his prison, seems as endless as it is confounding, and the madness that befalls him is akin to that of countless other victims in Gothic tradition, but with this difference, that he is journeying into the heart of his own dark inner depths. His later gropings to determine size and shape of his cell symbolize a tormented soul's explorations of its every dimension, during which sight and sound verge on the meaningless. The depth of despair into which he has been plunged is minuscule in comparison with the depth of the pit – a fine renovation of the live-burial motif.

"The Pit and the Pendulum" and other tales in the Poe canon have striking resemblances to present-day psychological experiments that restrict normal sensory activities; the result: hallucination. The narrator in Poe's tale regales us with hallucinatory sensations as he proceeds through his nightmare. No matter what the physical stimulus, the experience is predominantly emotional. In that satire upon popular terror fiction, "How to Write a Blackwood Article," Poe insinuated a bit of utter truth, so far as his own aims and methods are concerned, when Mr. Blackwood, seasoned publisher of terror tales, advises: "Sensations are the great things after all" (*P&T*, 281). In Poe's fiction sensations and things become well nigh interchangeable, and in "The Pit and the Pendulum" they very artistically intermingle.

Two much admired tales, "The Black Cat" and "The Tell-Tale Heart," both appeal in terms of their Gothicism. In the former, as in "Metzengerstein," animal and human characteristics are reversed as the narrator who, whatever his disclaimers, reveals, bit by bit (to create a buildup of suspense), that he is indeed quite sadistic and maniacal – or animalistic – while the cats seem to become quite human. Alcohol complicates his nature, although there is none of the comedy in this alcoholic's story as there had been in the Folio Club narratives. His torturing and hanging of his first cat prove his cruelty, and the conflagration that destroys his home, leaving him to mull the significance of the cat relief on one undestroyed wall, recalls a similar weird display in "Metzengerstein." His rationalizing of this circumstance only plunges him into deeper irrationality (who would throw a dead cat at a sleeper to rouse him!). When a new cat appears on the scene, one reminiscent of the dead Pluto, the distinct white spot on its breast, to the narrator, comes more and more to look like a gallows. The narrator now reveals that evil impulses have mastered him, and within a short time he comes to abhor this second cat as strongly as he had its predecessor, intends to kill it with an axe, but, by mere chance – so he says – he murders his wife when she deflects the blow. He walls up the corpse in the cellar, and, as the cat has vanished, he assumes that he is freed from this tormentor. When the police come to investigate and, having discovered nothing amiss, are about to depart, what the narrator has described as the spirit of perverseness motivates him to tap the wall, whence a terrifying howl sounds. The wall is opened, the corpse revealed, with the cat atop its head, and so the narrator has conducted a near live burial. The cat represents the man's non-rational nature, a fitting bit of symbolism for this animal because of long cherished folk beliefs about the cat as familiar to those who are evil. The narrator's inadvertent temporary burial of the cat along with his intentional burial of his wife's corpse may imply that the narrator has walled up, or, in psychological terms, repressed the feminine, nurturing elements in his psyche. He moves from a kindly, mild frame of mind and actions to increasing personal isolation and violent hostility toward others. "The Black Cat" may, in its inclusion of masculine and feminine traits as parts of an integrated self (what Poe's Dupin in "The Purloined Letter" distinguishes in his distinguishing the mathematician from poet, or the intellectual from the imaginative being) show an advance over the man – only in "The Pit and the Pendulum," and an alignment with "Berenice," "Morella," "The Assignation," "Ligeia," "The Fall of the House of Usher," "The Oval Portrait," and "Eleonora" – the group generally designated Poe's tales about women. One might say that in "The Black Cat," as in several of the others, the narrator is bested by an avenging woman whom he has wronged. But this wife remains dead; there is no actual supernaturalism to thicken the plot; and it is the very alive cat that brings about the denouement. Here, then is another Poesque modification of Gothicism.

"The Tell-Tale Heart" similarly centers on the effects of a guilty conscience, that of the narrator, who has murdered the old man with whom he lives. Setting out to prove his sanity, this narrator, well before his story ends, convinces us that he is indeed mad. He is a clear-cut descendant from Gothic characters whose nerves furnish the platform on which they live. The detailed care in planning the old man's death, the ascription of the narrator's motives having stemmed from the appearance of the victim's eye, and the tense buildup to the actual murder, as the killer watches and listens, (his actions, mirrored in the old man's responses, which are laden with anxiety and forebodings): all reveal the narrator's derangement. He calls his madness "over acuteness of the senses" (*P&T*, 557); ironically, his over-acute sensitivity leads to his arrest. When he thinks he can hear the beating of the dead man's heart, which drives him over the brink, what our narrator actually experiences is the urgings of his own guilty conscience gone mad. Since the tale centers on seeing and hearing, both senses located in the head, Poe, by means of these organs' sensations, again prompts readers to focus on the human head, and, more specifically, on the human mind. Heart and mind are often used interchangeably to signify emotions, and emotions pointedly signify in this story. The title itself may embody an irony; although the narrator tries to establish the rationalism in his madness, he is nevertheless betrayed by his "heart," that is, his emotions. Those emotions are, appropriately, contextualized in his head's aching and his ears' ringing. Thus sound and sense meld here as we more typically think of them melding in a poem.

Psychological states, most often those with a suggestion of dream informing them, are major elements in Poe's Gothic tales. To glance at another species of his work, we may find these very states well structured in "The Murders in the Rue Morgue" and the other Dupin tales, despite some readers' distinguishing Poe's detective fiction from his other on grounds of simpler diction in the former, as well as the detection process itself, and that the situations in the detective tales are not so fantastic as those we find elsewhere in Poe's fiction. Nearly all of Poe's tales, however, may be categorized as crime stories, whether the crime be against another or against the self. Furthermore, this first ratiocinative tale actually suggests a lurid Gothic: atrocious murders in a supposedly locked room, odd "language," lack of ordinary human motive, clues pointing toward a supernatural agency at work. Dupin's leading the narrator, his dimwit companion, through the steps in the crime builds toward a case for supernaturalism. This possibility is finally deflated in the revelation that an orangutan, trying to imitate its master shaving, turns savage and kills the two women in what had not at the time he entered been a locked room. The murders are improbable but not impossible, and so here, as in other tales, are hoax underpinnings; what seems to be supernaturalism eventually harks back to the explained supernaturalism often employed by some other authors. Poe's narrator tries to throw off readers with his claim that he is not "detailing any mystery, or penning any romance" (*P&T*, 402), a claim analogous to those arguing for truth and reality in "MS. Found," "William Wilson," "The Black Cat," or "The System of Dr. Tarr and Professor Fether" – and just as suspect. In a tale wherein the police arrest a man named Le Bon (the good), who is cleared by a sleuth named Dupin – in which, pronounced as someone with a southern background as Poe had might have spelled, to "English" it, as Duping, we may not overlook touches of comedy as provisions of relief from horrible brutality.

Another tale with emphatic Gothic surfaces, "The Masque of the Red Death," transpires in a recast haunted abbey, penetrated by a nefarious "villain," who kills all who have sought refuge there. The abbey, however, very much resembles the interior of a human head, and, given the reiterated allusions to blood and time, what symbolizes the plague raging without may in reality be normal attributes of human life, which cannot be eluded, even by the inhabitants of Prince Prospero's dream world – delusive though that world is – and who themselves are dreams. If the "Red Death" mummer is so frightening to them, he is so because they fear realities of time and death, symbolized by blood, which, as concerns ordinary life, is temporal. The colors red and black may represent life, particularly as it is maintained through sexuality, and concluded in death, as it is represented by the awesome ebony clock. The clock, too, reminds the dreamers of time, a fearful experience for them. That the tale closes in the scarlet and black chamber, its color scheme recalling the story of Rahab the harlot's scarlet cord, which saves her and her family from the death (i.e., blackness) meted out to the other citizens of Jericho, reiterates the promotion-termination-of-life that structures the cycle. Prospero is a Gothic villain, one of those who upsets the normal order of life, and who would envision death as a plague. He and his followers vainly combat an "antagonist" who, to them, would be terrifying, but who, to more realistic minds, would be a grim, but essential, part of life.[6]

"The Fall of the House of Usher" probably measures as one of Poe's greatest achievements in the short story, and it has admitted many approaches. The tale offers an anxiety-ridden narrator–protagonist, a haunted mansion tenanted by haunted siblings – who eventually come to "haunt" the storyteller – a mysterious doctor, whose intents seem to be nefarious, plus a veritable gallery of Gothic properties: bewildering corridors, eerie chambers, a terrifying poem that descends from the interspersed "songs" in many Gothic novels (with this difference; Usher's poem dovetails with the additional discordant sounds heard in the tale instead of providing a bit of relief), a picture that is animated in its inanimation, a large serving out of supernaturalism or seeming supernaturalism, mystifying illness of a perishing frail one, distorted thought and sense perceptions that disturb Usher and the narrator, live burial and the horrifying return of the interred, the deaths of both Usher siblings, collapse of the mansion, and the lasting effects of these horrors upon the narrator. All these, and much more, are dramatized with model concision.

Not accidentally does Poe give us a tale of disintegrating bodies, but, more important, disintegrating psyches as well, which he frames with a mansion that looks like a human head. Granted, that "head" is grotesque in its corporeal appearance, but once again Poe directs our closer attention to what lies inside. The opening of the story seems to take place outdoors, but what is the precise geographical location of "a singularly dreary tract of country" traversed by the narrator on horseback (*P&T*, 317)? I submit that even at this initial stage Poe is establishing a geography of the imagination. At the House of Usher the narrator "found myself," a loaded phrase which in context with the variations on "house," helps to establish a psychological emphasis within the tale, no matter what outward Gothic trappings lie at the surface. In what does this self consist? Very quickly, attention is drawn toward the building proper, which is "melancholy," a "mansion of gloom," so thinks the onlooker. Ironically, although he presents himself as a rational, orderly friend capable of coping with Roderick Usher's negative fantasies, this narrator's vocabulary is strikingly Gothic in its implications, as is evident in the quotations above. In thinking about how a "mere different arrangement of the particulars of the scene, of the details of the picture" (*P&T*, 317–318) would alter his responses, he looks down into the tarn beside the house, only to sustain an even greater "shudder" at the image seen there – which, of course, includes that of his own face. The bleakness of the house, its "vacant eye-like windows," the rank weeds and pale trunks of decayed trees nearby, mirror his own countenance and thus his own mindset. Were this head of his – which resembles the mansion in appearance, and thus occasions his emotional unrest, because what he sees appalls him – to look different, were it not so melancholy (a word which, in Poe's day, implied both physical and mental illness), he might be of a more pleasant frame of mind.

His horse being stabled by a servant, the narrator's proceeding ever farther within is fraught with rising anxieties because of the valet's "stealthy step" and the "low cunning and perplexity" of the family doctor, who "accosted me with trepidation" as he exited (*P&T*, 320). Two questions immediately emerge: (1) Are these other persons so sinister as they appear to the narrator, or is this additional Gothic vocabulary expressive of his own fragile psyche? (2) Does his ultimately leaving behind horse, servants, and doctor symbolize his departure from everyday normalcy and scientific rationality? He never again sees either horse or other persons, once he enters the presence of the Usher twins, and so a "yes" reply to the second question seems to be logical.

Roderick Usher may, on one hand, descend from the terrifying Gothic villain in his treatment of Madeline; he may have committed incest with her, and then – in a fit of guilt and remorse as she sickens, with an admixture, nonetheless, of power mania – he buries her alive. Roderick as artist figure may suggest that he feels no bounds of ordinary human love or decency. He is, however, a "sick" artist in that his poem is horrifying, his music weird, his own situation mirrored in the blankness of his painting (which is nevertheless frightening), and his choice of readings bizarre. None of his accomplishments or interests soothe him; in fact their appearances seem to punctuate increases in the debilitation of his psycho-physical state. Madeline remains a shadowy figure when she first appears, rightly so, no doubt. The Usher twins represent the states of the narrator's own physical-emotional constitution. That they are ill indicates that all is not well with the visitor's soul and, perhaps, given his repulsion when he beholds his own image in the tarn, his body either.

The narrator is more closely tied to the Usher "house," in all its manifestations, than he consciously admits. Roderick is an artist figure gone mad in this drama inside a house that symbolizes a head (ergo, its emphasis on the mind). His burying or repressing the other part of his self, exemplified by Madeline, to whom he is inextricably bound, is an attempt by the deranged imaginative portion of a self to put down the physical, earthy, sexual elements without which no self can be integrated or functional in positive ways. Madeline's name, which may mean "Magdalen," "lady of the house," and "tower of strength," has sexual implications, the last meaning creating a deft irony in its phallicness. In depicting the Madeline-Roderick relationship, Poe may have drawn on vampire lore, as is suggested by the last volume cited among Usher's favorite readings. The ritual in this one was used to ward off vampires.[7] This segment of the plot acts as a mirror to the narrator in relation to his own well being, and since what he witnesses leads into decay and death, no wonder he is terrified. Madeline's avenging return results in the deaths of the Usher twins, Roderick indeed dying from very fear of fear itself, which, he remarked earlier, would bring about his death. The narrator flees as the house cracks and sinks into the tarn, but the events in which he has participated influence him so much that he cannot choose but tell the story. Naturally he would be driven to emotional states bordering on madness in experiencing a welter of horrors within his own being. The fissure in the mansion's stonework mirrors the split between the Usher twins, and, since they share characteristics, physical and emotional, with the narrator, he, too, is severally fissured. Like many of Poe's other narrators, he has a confessional reaction, and that motivates his matchless telling of a story of a "fall," but this fall is one of psychic disintegration that anticipates correlations between emotional stress and organic illness which have occupied much scientific thinking generations later.

Gothicism figures significantly in many more of Poe's fictions and poems. The readings offered above are representative of the modifications to which he subjected Gothic tradition. From Poe's tales and poems, often through some pathways as serpentine or spiraling as those to be found in "Usher," "Masque," "Metzengerstein," "The Assignation," and "Tarr and Fether" (which in part may parody, under the guise of reality-madness paradigms. the Gothic effects in "Usher," "Masque," and "Murders"),[8] Poe's Gothicism casts shadows over many later works in fantasy, science, and detective fiction – not to mention the numerous "modern Gothics" that continue to pour forth – just as it enters the work of Edith Wharton, William Faulkner, Eudora Welty, Flannery O'Connor, Hart Crane, Stephen King, and much else.

NOTES

1. Quoted by Bill Pronzini, *Gun in Cheek* (New York: Coward, McCann and Geoghegan, 1982), p. 199. For a good treatment of literary Gothicism, see Devendra P. Varma's *The Gothic Flame* (London: Arthur Barker, 1957).
2. See my "William Dunlap, American Gothic Dramatist," *Transactions of the Samuel Johnson Society of the Northwest* 17 (1988): 167–190.
3. Poe to Harrison Hall, 2 September 1836, in *Letters*, 1: 103–104.
4. *Collected Works* (Mabbott), 2: 678–680, 697–700. I also suggest another source, W. H. Ireland's Gothic novel, *The Abbess* (1798), published in England and Baltimore. A prisoner endures tortures of the mind as he carefully explores his cell, finding that the walls portray terrifying fantastic shapes. See my introduction to *The Abbess* (New York: Arno Press, 1974) 1: xxiii–xv, as well as 3: 7–8, and 4: 24–25.
5. Richard Wilbur, *Conversations with Richard Wilbur*, ed. William Butts (Jackson: University Press of Mississippi, 1990), pp. 151–152; Wilbur, "The House of Poe," in *Recognition*, pp. 255–277.
6. Joseph Patrick Roppolo, "Meaning and 'The Masque of the Red Death,'" *Tulane Studies in English* 13 (1963): 59–69.
7. Lyle H. Kendall, "The Vampire Motif in 'The Fall of the House of Usher,'" *College English* 24 (1963): 450–453; and James O. Bailey, "What Happens in 'The Fall of the House of Usher'?" *American Literature* 35 (1964): 445–466.
8. See my "Poe's 'Tarr and Fether': Hoaxing in the Blackwood Mode," in *The Naiad Voice: on Poe's Satiric Hoaxing*, ed. Dennis W. Eddings (Port Washington, NY: Associated Faculty Press, 1983), pp. 136–147.

6

TERESA A. GODDU

Poe, sensationalism, and slavery

Defending "Berenice," in a letter to Thomas White, Poe confesses that the tale's "subject is by far too horrible" yet asserts that the "history of all Magazines shows plainly that those which have attained celebrity were indebted for it to articles *similar in nature – to Berenice*." This nature consists of "the ludicrous heightened into the grotesque: the fearful coloured into the horrible: the witty exaggerated into the burlesque: the singular wrought out into the strange and mystical." Poe justifies such work: to "be appreciated you must be *read*, and these things are invariably sought after with avidity." While Poe couches his economic interest within assertions about originality and careful style and also by noting that "some very high names valued themselves *principally* upon this species of literature," he concludes the letter by stating that the marketplace rather than the critic is the final arbiter: "The effect – if any – " he writes, "will be estimated better by the circulation of the Magazine than by any comments upon its contents."[1] Elevating economic success over good taste, Poe demonstrates early in his career his desire to master the literary marketplace and his awareness that manipulating its conventions offered the key to such mastery.

In this chapter, I investigate Poe's exploitation of a particular segment of the sensationalized literary marketplace: the scene of slavery and the demonized and sentimentalized racial images accompanying it. As Karen Halttunen has shown in her work on murder narratives and the cult of sensibility, sensationalism permeated Anglo-American culture in the early nineteenth century. The sensationalism of the American penny press, captivity narratives, dime novels, historical accounts of the Inquisition, and exposés on mental institutions and prisons "appealed to a popular voyeuristic taste for scenarios of suffering."[2] If, as Halttunen concludes, the "flogging scene" lies at the core of this sensationalistic culture, then slavery serves as a significant social context for the discourse of sensationalism. From the accounts of Nat Turner's insurrection (1831) to Moses Roper's slave narrative of repeated floggings (1838) and Theodore Weld's compendium of horrors, *American Slavery As It Is* (1839), slavery was conventionally figured in sensationalistic terms. According to Weld, the "facts and testimony as to the actual condition of the Slaves" could "thrill the land with Horror."[3]

While the facts of slavery were themselves "terrible and almost incredible," as Frederick Douglass states in *My Bondage and My Freedom* (1855), depictions of slavery were shaped to meet the demands of the literary marketplace.[4] Douglass, for instance, opens his 1845 *Narrative* with the conventional scene of flogging (his Aunt Hester's whipping), and sensationalizes this spectacle by deploying the conventions of sexualized cruelty that his readers would expect: "Before he [the slavemaster] commenced whipping Aunt Hester, he . . . stripped her from neck to waist, leaving her neck, shoulders, and back, entirely naked. . . . She now stood fair for his infernal purpose."[5] In his advertisement to *The Confessions of Nat Turner*, Thomas Gray exploits the public's fear and curiosity by stimulating their emotions with the "awful" lesson of the "diabolical" Turner, his "fiendish band," and their "dreadful conspiracy" in order to ensure the text's wide circulation and his own profit.[6] Choosing to base his arguments in *American Slavery As It Is* on excessively horrible facts rather than foundational principles, Weld also relies on a more heightened rhetoric to arouse his jaded readers. Weld is advised to reject certain testimony "not because the facts are not well authenticated but because those which are merely *horrid* must give place to those which are absolutely *diabolical*. . . . Such facts are *now* demanded. . . . They will now serve as the . . . needed stimulus exciting to prompt and vigorous action."[7] The huge circulation of *American Slavery As It Is* – it sold 100,000 copies in the first year and was the national best seller of 1839 – as well as the general popularity of the slave narrative, demonstrates that the sensationalistic discourse of slavery sold.[8]

Ever aware of market trends, Poe capitalized on the conventions of slavery in his sensationalist fiction. Poe's tales respond to a literary market culture that traded on the terror of slavery. Poe utilized the conventions deployed by pro- and anti-slavery proponents alike to sell his own tales. By situating Poe's tales in relation to the literary marketplace rather than Poe's particular psychology, I want to shift the critical debate about Poe and slavery from a discussion of Poe's politics (whether he was proslavery) to an analysis of the specific print culture in which his tales operated and the cultural conventions they employ.[9] In doing so, I hope not only to reframe the relationship between Poe's tales and the context of slavery, but also to illuminate broader configurations of the antebellum literary marketplace. For, by titillating and terrifying, caricaturing and critiquing, Poe's tales of sensation simultaneously exploit their culture's conventions of slavery and race and expose them as market productions.

I

Before turning to an examination of particular tales of sensation – "How to Write a Blackwood Article," "A Predicament," "The Pit and the Pendulum," "Hop-Frog" – in relation to the discursive conventions of slavery, I first want to give a fuller account of the literary marketplace that Poe operated within and out of which his sensationalistic fiction emerged. As an editor of periodicals located in different publishing centers – *The Southern Literary Messenger* (Richmond), *Burton's Gentleman's Magazine* and *Graham's Magazine* (Philadelphia), *The Broadway Journal* (New York), as a writer who published in periodicals ranging from ladies' magazines to the penny press, and as a reviewer of many American and British authors, Poe operated within a wide-ranging print culture.[10] He would have become familiar with the sensationalized discourse of slavery through any number of sources. For instance, Poe had access to newspaper accounts of Nat Turner's insurrection if not Gray's *Confessions* or Samuel Warner's *Narrative of the Tragical Scene* (1831), which also describes Turner's "massacre" as a "scene horrid in the extreme"; he would also have known Thomas Dew's *Review of the Debate in the Virginia Legislature* (1832), which discusses the "ghastly horrors of the Southampton tragedy."[11] Newspapers from *The Liberator* (3 September 1831) to *The Richmond Enquirer* (30 August 1831) reported on the insurrection in sensationalistic terms: the former describes itself as "horror-struck at the late tidings"; the latter calls Turner's band "banditti" and "horrible...monsters."[12] Even if Poe did not read *American Slavery As It Is*, he would have been familiar with its conventions since many of the cruelties were compiled from advertisements in southern newspapers. Under headings such as "Tortures, By Iron Collars, Chains, Fetters, Handcuffs, etc" or "Brandings, Maimings, Gun-Shot Wounds, etc" *American Slavery As It Is* catalogues slavery's atrocities through the slaveholder's own testimony.[13] Besides his familiarity with sensationalized accounts of slavery from the daily papers, Poe read selections from *American Slavery As It Is* in Charles Dickens' *American Notes* (1842) which reprinted unattributed excerpts from the tract in its section on slavery.[14]

Proslavery tracts, such as James Kirke Paulding's *Slavery in the United States* and William Drayton's *The South Vindicated From the Treason of Fanaticism of the Northern Abolitionists*, both reviewed in the *Southern Literary Messenger* (April 1836) while Poe was editor and written by authors with whom Poe had personal connections, employ the discourse of sensationalism even as they accuse abolitionists of fanaticism. Paulding, for instance, opposes the "fictitious horrors with which slavery has been invested in the United States" with sensational descriptions of the barbarism perpetrated on slaves in Africa.[15] Drayton's discourse on the evils of abolitionism is more excessive. He imagines liberated slaves as "fiends let loose upon the earth" over whose "midnight conflagration, and the noon-tide massacre – scenes of lust, cruelty, and horror... the arch fiend himself might sicken"; he depicts abolitionists as "capable of any act, however, atrocious; they would dip their hands in human gore, and then, with their crimson fingers, turn over the leaves of the Bible to find a sanction for the deed."[16] In an effort to dispute them, these texts reiterate antislavery's arguments and its rhetorical techniques; they adapt the same discourse of sensationalism that they condemn. Indeed, the flood of antislavery publications – books, tracts, periodicals – into the South during the 1830s forced proslavery to respond to antislavery's specific discursive strategies.[17]

The cross-fertilization of pro- and antislavery discourse and the use of sensationalist discourse on both sides meant that Poe's location in both southern and northern publishing centers yielded him access to this discourse irrespective of his political position. More importantly, the sensationalized discourse of slavery circulated in mainstream print culture as well. In 1840, *Graham's Magazine*, for instance, published "The Slaver," which describes the "awful spectacle" of a sinking slave ship and its "hideous" corpses that float by "almost fiend-like in the gloom."[18] British periodicals, reprinted and circulated in the United States, included tales of sensation side by side with essays on colonial slavery and reviews of books describing New World slavery.[19] The British periodicals often recited a litany of slavery's terrors and tortures in their articles on colonial slavery.[20] In February 1831, for example, *Blackwood's* published a venomous review of Mary Prince's slave narrative. The review not only rails against the "hideous falsehoods and misrepresentations which are advanced against the colonists by their enemies" but also reprints substantial excerpts from Prince's narrative. In the course of cross-examining Prince's "pretended history," Macqueen further disseminates its depictions of floggings and other forms of physical torture as well as its implication of sexual abuse.[21] Because periodicals regularly reviewed and recirculated works that sensationalized slavery, Poe's intimate knowledge of periodical culture well acquainted him with this discourse.[22]

Since the sensationalized discourse of slavery circulated widely within transatlantic print culture, Poe would have been familiar with its generic conventions and its audience appeal. Besides sensationalizing slavery these conventions gothicized race, often demonizing slaves as monsters and fiends. Hence, as H. L. Malchow argues, we must not only be attentive to the ways in which race and slavery inform sensational discourse, but also to the ways in which sensational language is deployed to mark racial and cultural difference.[23] By turning to an examinination of how Poe both appropriates and parodies the conventions of sensationalism in his tales, I show how he exploits and deconstructs cultural formations of race and slavery. Moreover, I argue that his sensationalist fiction not only redeploys discursive conventions of race and slavery, but also acknowledges its dependency upon culturally constituted meanings for its shocking effects.

2

In seeing race and slavery as central to Poe's sensationalism, I take my cue from Poe's linked tales, "How to Write a Blackwood Article" and "A Predicament," first published in the *American Museum* (November 1838) under the titles "Psyche Zenobia" and "The Scythe of Time" and later republished in *Tales of the Grotesque and Arabesque* (1839) and *The Broadway Journal* (1845). The first provides a "how-to manual" on constructing a sensationalistic *Blackwood's* tale while spoofing the magazine's style; the second presents itself as an "article of the genuine *Blackwood* stamp" (*P&T*, 279). As Michael Allen has shown, Poe was indebted to *Blackwood's* for his sensational style as well as his understanding of how to write serious literature and still attract a popular audience. An elite British magazine that also had wide circulation, *Blackwood's* mixed esoteric articles with sensationalist fiction and literary gossip.[24] By presenting a burlesque of *Blackwood's* style in these two tales, Poe unveils the mystifications inherent in its aesthetic. As Kenneth Dauber argues of Poe's burlesques in general, Poe exaggerates *Blackwood's* assumptions in order to expose them.[25] The first tale discloses the role conventions play within *Blackwood's* to sell class status, and the subsequent tale reveals how the tale of sensation depends on slavery and its racialized images for its commercial viability.

In the first, "How to Write a Blackwood Article," the Signora Psyche Zenobia, eager to "introduce a better style of thinking and writing" to her literary society, seeks advice from Mr. Blackwood on how to compose in the *Blackwood* mode (*P&T*, 279). He informs her of the value of sensations: "Should you ever be drowned or hung, be sure and make note of your sensations – they will be worth to you ten guineas a sheet" (*P&T*, 341). Psyche Zenobia learns that the proper sensational subject (getting baked in an oven, stuck fast in a chimney, or choked to death by a chicken bone) and manner of narration (metaphysical, transcendental) can earn her a literary reputation and make her money. A high style coupled with a sensational subject makes *Blackwood's* marketable. The sensational story, full of "taste" and "terror," "*The Dead Alive*," is a "capital thing!"; "*Confessions of an Opium-eater*" has plenty of "fire and fury" and a "good spicing of the decidedly unintelligible" (*P&T*, 281). Throughout the tale, Poe discloses the elitism that marks the *Blackwood's* model as a market effect; class status serves as the literary capital used to sell the magazine.

Mr. Blackwood's revelation that *Confessions* was not written by Coleridge but by Blackwood's pet baboon Juniper "over a rummer of Hollands and water" underscores the way in which *Blackwood's* good taste is a market ploy: it was a "nice bit of flummery, and went down the throats of the people delightfully," Mr. Blackwood claims (*P&T*, 281). This passage also depicts the author as enslaved to the very marketplace he manipulates. By substituting Coleridge for DeQuincy and DeQuincy in turn for a drunken baboon, Poe not only plays off the guessing game that circulated around the authorship of DeQuincy's *Confessions*, but also deflates the author's status from gentleman to that of slave. The author's representation as a "baboon" denotes the author's enslavement, given the racial association between monkeys and "blackness" in the nineteenth century.[26] Depicted as the publisher's pet, who is addicted to gin, the author is made dependent on the publisher and a slave to the insatiable demands of the literary marketplace. Reducing the author to an alcoholic baboon and literalizing the language of taste – tales are described as being dished or spiced up or easily ingested – "How to Write a Blackwood Article" materializes and hence deflates the mystifications of *Blackwood's* style. Such materializations and other rhetorical tricks in turn highlight the conventionality of its style and its operations within the literary marketplace.

The comedy of "How to Write a Blackwood Article," then, arises from its self-conscious transformations of the literary marketplace's conventions, especially its conversion of the crass and commercial into the tasteful and erudite and back again. The name Psyche Zenobia spiritualizes the "vulgar corruption" of the narrator's true patronym, Suky Snobbs, and elevates her class status to that of her namesake, Queen Zenobia. However, Zenobia's literal understanding of her name – she concludes that Psyche's meaning as "a butterfly" refers to her garish multi-colored dress – undermines her attempt to spiritualize it. Dr. Moneypenny, Zenobia's literary patron and market advisor, as his name suggests, might advise Zenobia to spell "'cant' with a capital K," but Zenobia does not understand the jest inherent in such a transposition: "but I know better," she states seriously. Zenobia's failure to understand the figurative gestures of the *Blackwood's* style and the conventionality on which they rely makes her the butt of Dr. Moneypenny's jokes and creates the comic effects of the two tales. Unlike Dr. Moneypenny, who can simultaneously elevate his style and expose the absurdity of such mystifications, Zenobia is unable to perform or to understand such maneuvers: "for my life I can't see what he means" she states (P&T, 278–279). Zenobia's material nature and her blindness, which are literalized in "A Predicament" when she becomes all body with the loss of her eyes and then her head, make her the perfect narrator for Poe's aim: to uncover the market manipulations that the conventions of Blackwood's style attempt to mask. Zenobia unwittingly demystifies the ideological conventions that Mr. Blackwood and Dr. Moneypenny would have their readers buy into. Moreover, in using a rare female narrator to create an obvious distance between his own persona and that of his narrator, Poe simultaneously flaunts the conventions of the marketplace and exposes his own technique. While this exposure comes at the woman writer's expense, it enables Poe – like the two-part structure of his tale – to make his own mastery of the marketplace visible.

If the first story, "How to Write a Blackwood Article," foregrounds the conventionality of the tale of sensation, the second story, "A Predicament," highlights the ways slavery and its attendant racialized images circulate as central sensationalistic conventions. In "A Predicament," her attempt at a sensational story, Zenobia sets out to find an adventure in the streets of Edinburgh with her companions, her "negro-servant Pompey" and her "little lap-dog Diana." The trio ascend the tall steeple of a Gothic cathedral; once inside, Zenobia climbs upon Pompey's shoulders to view, through the small aperture in the dial plate of a gigantic clock, the sublime scenery below. In her romantic reverie, she disregards Pompey's request that "he could stand it no longer, and requested that [she] would be so kind as to come down" and, as a result, has her head caught in the descending hand of the clock. Pompey, his feelings hurt from their quarrel, and Diana, having been told to sit in the corner, disregard her cries for help; Zenobia then recounts her sensations as her eyes fall out and roll into the gutter and as her head is slowly severed from her body. Able to function as a mere body, Zenobia descends from her elevation only to witness Pompey flee in horror and to discover Diana eaten by a rat (P&T, 287, 293).

This tale works on many levels: as a critique of common sense philosophy (as Bruce Weiner shows) or of romanticism since time cuts short Zenobia's sublime experience and as a spoof of transcendentalism's "second sight."[27] I am interested, however, in how the figure of Pompey operates to reveal that the discourse of sensationalism relies on slavery for its terrifying effects and that the racialized images sensationalism deploys are market productions. Just as Zenobia must stand upon Pompey's shoulders in order to have access to her sensational experience, her story depends upon his conventionalized roles as a sentimentalized suitor and as a dehumanized dunce for its dramatic (and Poe's comic) effects. By foregrounding this figure of "blackness" in a tale overtly announced as tailor-made for the literary marketplace, Poe signals the central role race and slavery play in the cultural discourse of sensationalism.

Significantly, this figure of "blackness" goes unmentioned both by critics who examine the tale and by those who investigate the issue of race in Poe's work more generally. These linked tales, when discussed at all, are viewed in terms of their ingenious doubling construction, their relation to *Blackwood's* formula, their philosophical critique, or their critique of sensationalism.[28] Except for Toni Morrison's and Terence Whalen's brief remarks, I know of no other critics who address Pompey as a figure of "blackness."[29] Pompey's absence within the critical discourse signals the challenge he poses to the conventional reading of Poe's sensationalism as being devoid of social significance. Pompey, like his more overt counterpart, Hop-Frog, signals the social implications tied to slavery that lie at the heart of Poe's sensationalism.

Pompey also poses a challenge to the conventional assessment of Poe's deployment of racial stereotype as racist. Toni Morrison sees Pompey's "mute and judgmental" reaction to the "antics of his mistress" as an exception to Poe's usual technique of "othering": Pompey is an "unmanageable" slip in Poe's overall strategy to "secure his characters' (and his readers') identity."[30] Given the ways in which Poe's tales of doubling dislodge identity and reveal its instability, Pompey proves to be less the exception to Poe's technique than its exemplum. In having Pompey's namesake in "The Man That Was Used Up" look into the Brigadier-General's mouth with "the knowing air of a horse-jockey" before replacing his teeth, Poe reduces the General to a horse and discloses that "whiteness" depends upon "blackness" for its identity (*P&T*, 316). Rather than representing an "unmanageable slip," Pompey is paradigmatic of the ways in which Poe exploits racial stereotype even as he exposes its construction. In Jonathan Elmer's words, Poe "remains, inextricably, both analyst and symptom."[31] Through the figure of Pompey in "A Predicament," Poe makes visible the workings of a sensationalist aesthetic that depends on slavery and racialized images for its effects even as he traffics in that aesthetic to meet market demands.

Pompey's relation to the literary marketplace is evident in his portrayal as both commodity and convention: "He was clad with a striking simplicity. His sole garments were a stock of nine inches in height, and a nearly-new drab overcoat which had formerly been in the service of the tall, stately, and illustrious Dr. Moneypenny" (*P&T*, 289). Naked, except for Dr. Moneypenny's overcoat and a neckcloth wrapped around his neck, Pompey is cloaked as capital. The stock and the overcoat mock Pompey's ill-fitting aristocratic pretensions: since the coat is too large for him, he must hold it up out of the dirt with both hands. They also underscore his service to the "stock" conventions of the marketplace. The juxtaposition between the overcoat's "nearly-new" drabness and its being "well cut" and "made well" reveals its dual function: to signify the marketplace's well-worn conventions as well as their continued commercial success. Like the pair of "tailor's-shears" Mr. Blackwood uses to cut and paste *Blackwood's* articles from other sources and the scraps of learning he dresses up to "look quite as fresh as ever," Pompey is outfitted to meet the demands of the marketplace (*P&T*, 280–289). He is not inherently simple; rather he is "clad with a striking simplicity," a stereotype tailored for a marketplace where, as Poe states in his letter about "Berenice," "simplicity is the cant of the day." Indeed, Pompey's buffoonishness – he stumbles and falls at one point in an act that Zenobia states was inevitable – is manufactured from his tripping over the trailing skirt of Moneypenny's overcoat. Dressed in Dr. Moneypenny's over-sized overcoat, then, Pompey embodies the commercial viability of the ill-fitting racist images that Zenobia, and Poe, capitalize on in the telling of their tales.

Zenobia may assure Pompey that she will be "considerate and bear as lightly as possible upon his shoulders," but she exploits his conventional stock for all she can (*P&T*, 292). Like Poe's own possible source, Pompey Ducklegs in Paulding's *Westward Ho!* (1832), Zenobia's initial description of Pompey illustrates her use of racial stereotype: "He was three feet in height (I like to be particular) and about seventy, or perhaps eighty, years of age. He had bow-legs and was corpulent. His mouth should not be called small, nor his ears short . . . Nature had endowed him with no neck, and had placed his ankles (as usual with that race) in the middle of the upper portion of the feet" (*P&T*, 289).[32] While this passage employs racial stereotype, it also underscores its conventionality. The particularity of her account of his height is immediately undermined by her uncertainty about his age; her use of the conditional "should not be called" as well as her parenthetical aside "as usual with that race" signals her adherence to already scripted literary devices – that blacks have big mouths, large ears, and oddly placed ankles. Zenobia's insistence that "nature" endows Pompey with no neck is contradicted by the stock he wears around his neck. The stock's placement around Pompey's neck associates it with the iron collar slaves were forced to wear, which signified their status as commodities; the odd image of Pompey's ankles, another location for chains, also suggests that Pompey's bodily deformities are produced by slavery rather than an essential aspect of his race.[33] Zenobia's characterization of his teeth and eyes also unveils the constructedness of stock conventions: like Paulding's "Pompey the Little," whose "black face presented a beautiful contrast to the ivory teeth,"[34] Pompey's teeth "were like pearl, and his large full eyes were deliciously white" (*P&T*, 289).

Zenobia's description of Pompey's "whiteness" as "delicious" reveals the ways in which racial stereotype functions to mediate unspeakable desires. Pompey's pearly teeth and his large full eyes are the signifiers of Zenobia's increasingly apparent sexual attraction to him. Zenobia may attempt to follow the proper conventions of racial caricature in her narration, but her inability to deploy them figuratively results in exposing their construction and hidden investments.

Throughout Zenobia's story, Poe exploits racial convention even as he discloses its assumptions. His use of the generic slave name Pompey, for instance, signifies the character's conventional status. Besides Paulding's *Westward Ho!* Pompey is a slave name in Robert Bird's *Sheppard Lee* (1836), and it occurs in an advertisement quoted in Dickens' *Notes*. Naming two other characters Pompey – the "negro valet" in "The Man That Was Used Up" (1839) and the dog in "The Business Man" (1840) – Poe underscores the figure's conventionality. Like the Brigadier-General in "The Man That Was Used Up," whose stately demeanor consists of cobbled together body parts, Poe's characters consist of a collage of conventions. Poe's reiteration of racist stereotypes, like his reuse of Pompey's name, foregrounds the conventionality of these stereotypes and unmasks their assumptions. By associating Pompey with a dog in each of the three stories (he is associated with Zenobia's lap-dog Diana, is derisively called a dog by the Brigadier-General, and literally becomes a dog in "The Business Man"), Poe unveils his culture's racial codes – its conventional dehumanization of the slave. Like Pompey in "The Man That Was Used Up," who constructs the General out of "capital" parts, Poe understands how these racial conventions garner him capital.

Within "A Predicament," Poe employs conventional sentimental images of the master/slave relationship while also unveiling the mystifications inherent in that ideology. Allied with the poodle, Diana, Pompey is depicted as one of Zenobia's "two humble but faithful companions." Diana's five inch height and "blue riband tied fashionably around her neck" parallels Pompey's physical description (*P&T*, 288). This doubling underscores Pompey's role as property since nineteenth-century English law "viewed animals simply as the property of human owners," as well as his servitude since dogs were often "described in terms that suggested human servants" and "epitomized the appropriate relationship between masters and subordinates."[35] Zenobia's strikingly similar introductions of each of her companions, however, converts her ownership of each into love: "Diana, my poodle! sweetest of creatures!" is echoed in "Pompey, my negro! – sweet Pompey!" (*P&T*, 288). Just as Diana's and Pompey's collars are transformed from signifiers of enslavement into fashion items, their servitude is expressed through the language of aristocratic politesse and sympathetic friendship.

"Leaning upon the arm of the gallant Pompey," Zenobia is "attended at a respectable distance by Diana"; Diana is the "darling of her heart" while Pompey is depicted as her "faithful friend" (*P&T*, 289, 296, 292). Pompey's dehumanization is disguised by Zenobia's sentimental attachment to her pets. This story, like "The Black Cat" (1843), plays off the cultural convention of viewing slaves as animals and the master/slave relationship as akin to that of a master to a pet.[36]

Poe's exaggeration of Zenobia's attachment to Pompey, however, turns sentiment's fictions inside out, making them obscene. Just as the dependence of master on servant, as signified by Zenobia's reliance on Pompey's arm for support, is made fully visible when she places her full weight on his shoulders and literalizes how her elevated status depends on the strength of his body, so too is her sympathetic affection for Pompey revealed to be based on illicit passion rather than chaste devotion. Pompey is described not only as a "gallant" attendant but also as a lover: Zenobia states, "I thought of Pompey! – alas, I thought of love!" and their fights are presented as a lover's quarrel. Concerned with the "false *steps*" she has taken and may take again with Pompey, Zenobia forces herself to abandon his arm, which she leaned on "in all the confidence of early affection," and to become more cautious. Pompey, however, actualizes her false step when in reaching for her hand he trips and falls forward, his head "striking [her] full in the – in the breast" and precipitating their fall "upon the hard, filthy, and detestable floor of the belfry" (*P&T*, 289–291). Here the "pure" love of pets is sexualized and materialized: Pompey's head is in Zenobia's breast (or as the dash before breast and his three foot height implies, her lap) as they fall entwined onto the filthy floor. The comic effect of this image unveils its serious critique: the idealized fictions that disguise the ultimately unruly economic dependencies inherent in the system of slavery can fail, leaving master as well as slave dehumanized and in the dirt. As Joan Dayan states of Poe's fictions, "lurking in every effusion of ennobling love is the terror of literal dehumanization."[37] While this terror is less obvious in "A Predicament" than in some of Poe's other tales because of its comic tone, its threat remains. In this passage, the threat is ultimately located in miscegenation which the sensational's disregard for boundaries underscores.

The neat hierarchy of power, structured through race and species, set up at the beginning of the tale collapses by its end. The "sweet" Pompey turns "cruel" when he refuses to come to Zenobia's aid due to his hurt feelings. The lack of proper sympathy here justifies rebellion. Moreover, hidden in Pompey's polite entreaty that "he could stand it no longer, and requested that she [Zenobia] would be so kind as to come down" lies the threat of revolt. Pompey, like many of Poe's figures of "blackness," hides within his subjugated demeanor an insurrectionary potential. His early description as "humble *but* faithful" foreshadows the possibility of revolt: his lower class status is a threat to his faithfulness rather than its complement. Moreover, he may look at Zenobia "piteously with his large eyes" after she tears out his hair in revenge for their fall on the belfry floor, but his hair remains "alive" standing on "end with indignation" "far beyond [Zenobia's] grasp." The transformation of Mr. Blackwood's "savage" bull-dogs that threaten to eat Zenobia alive at the end of "How to Write a Blackwood Article" into Diana's "injured innocence" at the beginning of "A Predicament" also warns that within every sweet lap-dog lurks a wild beast. The final "horrible" image of Zenobia's "beloved puppy" having been "cruelly devoured" by a monstrous rat, which re-enacts the fate that Zenobia escapes at the end of "How to Write a Blackwood Article," further underscores the potential for hierarchies to reverse. The animals – the dog and the rat – play out with less politeness the same power struggle as the humans: the rats, like Pompey, are cruel. Once again the sensational deflates the discourse of sentiment as Zenobia's "little angel" Diana is reduced to the "picked bones" that symbolize her use-value as food (*P&T*, 287–296).

If Diana's death underscores the tale's critique of sentimental conventions to elide the power dynamic that lies at the heart of all relationships, especially those associated with property, Pompey's final image in the tale suggests sensationalism's dependence on "blackness" as a register for its effects. Unsure of what Pompey saw "so *very* peculiar" in her appearance, the decapitated Zenobia states, "The fellow opened his mouth from ear to ear, and shut his two eyes as if he were endeavoring to crack nuts between the lids. Finally, throwing off his overcoat, he made one spring for the staircase and disappeared" (*P&T*, 296). While Zenobia's description plays off the racial caricature of black fright, her own lack of sensations – her objective view of her own severed body – critiques the voyeurism of Poe's readers who remain safely distant from the material reality that produces the aesthetic of sensationalism. Like Nu-Nu's fear and Pym's numbness at the end of *The Narrative of Arthur Gordon Pym*, Pompey displays the terror that Zenobia remains disconnected from. As with many of his tales, Poe embodies the horror and terror of the sensational in the image of "blackness." "A Predicament," however, reveals that the "blackness" of Poe's sensationalism is not just metaphysical but social: located in the black body of slavery.

Pompey's final exit from the tale, after throwing off Dr. Moneypenny's overcoat, points to the ways in which "blackness" is a marketplace commodity. Once the figure of "blackness" is no longer commodified through conventions, he is no longer visible. "Blackness" exists only in relation to the market conventions that cloak it. "A Predicament," then, schematizes the mechanics of Poe's sensationalism by showing it to be bound up with "blackness" and aware of its market investments. Through Pompey, Poe exposes the workings of the sensational aesthetic and reveals himself to be a cogent interpreter of the marketplace. However, despite his mastery of the market, his tales remain dependent on it for their effects. Without the racial stereotypes and sensationalized images from slavery that make up the stock of his literary capital, Poe would end up, as Zenobia does, bankrupt. Having lost her signifiers of class status and her conventional companions, Zenobia is reduced to nothing and must end her tale: "Dogless, niggerless, headless, what *now* remains for the unhappy Signora Psyche Zenobia? Alas – nothing! I have done" (*P&T*, 297). Once her conventions become unveiled – her gallant servant starkly unmasked as a "nigger" – Zenobia loses the ability to produce her tale. In the tale's final lines, Poe may expose the contemptuous racial codes upon which Zenobia's story rests, but he continues to circulate their conventions.

3

In the remainder of this chapter, I want to explore how Poe deploys the sensational discourse of slavery that he outlines in "A Predicament" in another tale written in the *Blackwood* mode, "The Pit and the Pendulum" (1842). Taking seriously Poe's claim in his preface to *Tales of the Grotesque and Arabesque* – that he has deduced "terror only from its legitimate sources, and urged it only to its legitimate results" (*P&T*, 129) – I turn to examine how Poe utilizes scenes of torture from the sensationalized discourse of slavery to create this tale's terrifying effects. Whereas "How to Write a Blackwood Article" and "A Predicament" schematize and parody the conventions of sensationalism, "The Pit and the Pendulum" deploys them. The tale is a serious rewriting of "A Predicament": the clock tower becomes a dungeon, replete with carnivorous rats and a scythe of time poised to cut through the narrator's chest rather than his neck. The specific figure of "blackness" here becomes generalized to the darkness itself, "the blackness of darkness" (*P&T*, 492) that oppresses and stifles the narrator. "Blackness" serves as the visible signifier of the narrator's unnameable horror and unspeakable suffering; it mediates and registers the tale's terrifying effects. While this story has many sources, like the *Blackwood's* stories "The Iron Shroud" (1830) and "The Man in the Bell" (1821), and has been read as being a "universal fable of man's condition,"[38] it also trades on the terrors of slavery – the horrors of "blackness" – to achieve its thrilling effects.

Poe's general portrait of the pit as a "dungeon," a "tomb," or a "hell" plus his specific invocation of the Inquisition depend upon the discourse of slavery for its culturally resonant effects (*P&T*, 494, 499). While Harriet Jacobs's description of slavery in her narrative *Incidents in the Life of A Slave Girl* (1861) as a "deep, and dark, and foul...pit of abominations" peopled by "fiends who bear the shape of men" whose "secrets...are concealed like those of the Inquisition" is perhaps the best counterpart to Poe's pit, despite its historical belatedness, similar descriptions of slavery as a dungeon, hell, or pit and parallels between slavery and the Inquisition circulated in the 1830s.[39] In his antislavery tract, *Picture of Slavery in the United States of America* (1834), George Bourne describes slavery as a "bottomless pit," compares slave quarters to "the dungeons of the Popish Inquisition," and argues that the plantation contains the "infernal secrets of the kidnapper's prison-houses."[40] The *Narrative of James Williams* (1838), whose validity prompted much debate, identifies slavery as a "reign of terror" and the "secrets of the prison-house" with "the Inquisitors of Goa and Madrid" who "never disclosed the peculiar atrocities of their 'hall of horrors.'"[41] A witness in Theodore Weld's *American Slavery As It Is* argues that the slave's condition is *"second only to the wretched creatures in Hell"*.[42] Alternately, the pro-slavery tract, *The South Vindicated from the Treason and Fanaticism of the Northern Abolitionists*, borrows the language of the Inquisition to describe abolitionists, conspirators who meet around "the bubbling cauldron of abolition...filled with its pestilential material, and the fire beneath kindled by the breath of the fanatics."[43] Since both pro- and antislavery utilized the sensational images of the Inquisition to make their arguments, Poe's invocation of the Inquisition in "The Pit and the Pendulum" also contains a more specific reference to slavery.

The tale's connection to the context of slavery becomes clearer in its particular scenes of horror and atrocious cruelty. George Bourne calls slavery "the climax of cruelty."[44] The narrator's purposefully slow and seemingly never-ending torture, as signified by the scythe of time that gradually descends from the ceiling, resembles that of the slave whose body was submitted to "daily, hourly, ceaseless torture" and who was "MURDER[ED]...BY PIECE-MEAL" so as not to destroy his capability for labor.[45] The prison's metallic wall, "barriers of iron" hemming in the narrator and heated to "sear" his "writhing body," symbolize the narrator's confinement in terms specific to slavery: the chains of iron that imprison slaves as well as the iron brand that signifies their body's status as property (*P&T*, 503, 505). The narrator's torture on the rack by the scythe of time and the rats also corresponds to a flogging scene: the scythe threatens to cross and cut into the secured body like a whip; the rats, who look at the narrator as prey and who swarm over him and devour his bandage, approximate the custom of leaving a flogged body for carrion to devour alive.[46] The narrator's revelation that his freedom is a false one since he remains "in the grasp of the Inquisition" emphasizes his extreme imprisonment: "Free! – I had but escaped death in one form of agony, to be delivered unto worse death in some other" (*P&T*, 503). Like Charles Ball who argues in his narrative, *Slavery in the United States* that from "the despotism of the master, there is scarcely any conceivable limit, and for its cruelty there is no refuge,"[47] the narrator focuses on his torturers' arbitrary power and the limitless nature of their abuse.

Just as the story's rhetoric of crime and judgment can be traced to the discourse of slavery – Ball, for instance, calls slavery a "DAMNING CRIME" – so too does its rhetoric of the unspeakable and its images of limitlessness depend upon the indescribable horrors of the peculiar institution. As Angelina Grimké states in her personal testimony, "the sufferings of the slaves are not only innumerable, but they are *indescribable* . . . it mocks all power of language."[48] Sensationalism, as Weld argues throughout *American Slavery As It Is*, was the only discourse that could capture the "cruel barbarities" of slavery that were "more terrific, if possible, than death itself."[49] Slavery's unspeakable nature – it is both indescribable and incredible, below and beyond language – is reiterated in the tale's attempt to depict states of "seeming nothingness" and extreme horror. The narrator's attempt to measure his dungeon – to find the "limits of the limitless" – symbolizes his attempt to name the unnameable (*P&T*, 492–493). The circular pit, which lies at the center of his prison, is at once the physical manifestation of slavery and a representation of its indescribable nature. Poe's tale, then, not only draws upon slavery's litany of tortures but also upon its sensationalist discourse of unspeakable horror to achieve its terrifying effects.

While Poe does not unveil the workings of his sensationalism in "The Pit and the Pendulum" as he does in the "*Blackwood*" parodies, he does underscore how his sensational discourse relies upon cultural conventions for its effect. Throughout the tale, the narrator views his own situation through the lens of previous narratives. The narrator states: "there came thronging upon my recollection a thousand vague rumors of the horrors of Toledo. Of the dungeons there had been strange things narrated – fables I had always deemed them – but yet strange, and too ghastly to repeat, save in a whisper." These reflections not only emphasize the strange and unspeakable nature of his experience, but also reveal the ways in which his experience is mediated by conventions: "the death just avoided, was of that very character which I had regarded as fabulous and frivolous in the tales respecting the Inquisition." Rumors and readings about the Inquisition structure his response to his situation: he steps "with all the careful distrust with which certain antique narratives had inspired me" and cannot "forget what [he] had read of these pits." The way the narrator's experience is mediated through convention is also evident in the description of the chamber which has walls "overspread and disfigured" by "figures of fiends in aspects of menace, with skeleton forms, and other more really fearful images." The chamber proffers representations of the horrors along with the horrors themselves; the narrator first experiences the pendulum as a "pictured image... such as we see on antique clocks" rather than an actual instrument of torture; moreover, when the walls heat up, giving a "richer tint of crimson" to the "pictured horrors of blood" already on their walls, they only further actualize the hell that the narrator has already been experiencing (*P&T*, 494–498, 504). Throughout the story, then, Poe presents horror as already conventionalized. The reader, like the narrator, experiences the tale's terror through images and discourse already circulating.

"The Pit and the Pendulum" depicts horror as not only conventionalized but also commercialized. The tale's epigraph places the conventions of terror that it exploits within the realm of the marketplace. The Latin epigraph – which translates "Here the wicked mob, unappeased, long cherished a hatred of innocent blood. Now that the fatherland is saved, and the cave of death demolished; where grim death has been, life and health appear" – is followed by the phrase: "*Quatrain composed for the gates of a market to be erected upon the site of the Jacobin Club House at Paris*" (*P&T*, 1394, 491). The site of terror and torture is transformed into a marketplace. Terror is turned into a quotation that graces the gates of commerce, consumed now by the mass marketplace rather than enacted by the wicked mob. As the story demonstrates through the red, glaring eyes of the rats who make the narrator their "prey," the terrifying portraits whose "[d]emon eyes" glare at the narrator in "a thousand directions," and his constant sense of being watched, the narrator's suffering becomes a consumable artifact for a voyeuristic audience (*P&T*, 502, 504). Once again, Poe exposes the literary marketplace's taste for sensational scenes of horror even as his tale exploits that appetite for its own commercial success.

4

As I have been arguing throughout this chapter, Poe trades on the discourse of slavery to manufacture the terror of his tales and to make them sell even as he reveals the conventions he appropriates to be market productions. He is complicit with the literary marketplace even as he critiques it. One of his final tales, "Hop-Frog" (1849), makes his simultaneous mastery of and enslavement to the literary marketplace clear. On one hand, "Hop-Frog" presents a stinging critique of how the literary marketplace turns the author into a slave to the audience's voracious appetite for sensationalized horror.

On the other, it shows the author's mastery of convention. In figuring the literary marketplace as the site of slavery, the tale elides the very different subject positions of author and slave. Poe's appropriation of the figure of the slave as a means to explore his fiction's commodification in the literary marketplace is no less problematic than his use of slavery's sensationalism to sell his tales. In neither case does Poe's critique of the literary marketplace outweigh his adherence to its conventions.

"Hop-Frog," a parodic simulacrum of the murdering Ourang-Outang in "The Murders in the Rue Morgue" (1841), begins by symbolizing the author not as that of the mastering detective, but as the jester, abused, misshapen, and armed only with convention and audience expectations. Depicted in terms of the racial stereotypes of "blackness" – a "monkey" – as well as of enslavement – he is a "captive" who has been "forcibly carried" from some "barbarous region" – Hop-Frog represents the author as slave. Made to drink wine, Hop-Frog resembles Blackwood's baboon, Juniper: both represent the author as the property of the marketplace and as a slave to its desires. The king, described as a "capital figure," and his ministers, portrayed as fat, signify the "gourmandizing public"[50] – we "want characters – *characters*, man – something novel," the king demands – as well as the master whom the author/slave must serve: the king abuses both Hop Frog and his female companion, Trippetta (*P&T*, 900–901). Moreover, through the destruction of the king, the author's revenge on his crass audience is symbolized as a slave revolt. He is the embodiment of the insurrectionary figure of "blackness."

In giving the king the pageant he demands, Hop-Frog manipulates the conventions of the marketplace to enact his revenge. He frees himself from his captive status by captivating his audience with his jest; he literally and metaphorically holds the keys that imprison his audience in the ballroom. Hop-Frog's jest simultaneously performs the conventions of sensationalism and exposes their investments: that sensationalism depends upon slavery for its effects, that it embodies terror in the form of "blackness," and that it appeals to its audience's voyeurism. Promising the king a pageant that will produce a tremendous "*effect*" that will frighten the ladies, Hop-Frog utilizes the conventions of racial stereotype by dressing the king and his ministers as savage apes and by chaining them together in order to enact the "excellent sport" of his country. This "sport" turns out to be a lynching. The ourang-outangs are hoisted "violently" on a chain into the air and suspended there; they are then lit on fire by Hop-Frog until they become a "fetid, blackened, hideous, and indistinguishable mass." This scene mirrors the violence regularly inflicted on slaves. In transforming the staging of this violence into a materialization of it, Hop-Frog's jest unveils the everyday horror that lies beneath the sensational image and, in doing so, it implicates its audience. The king and his ministers register the terror by becoming a mass of blackness; the spectators who begin by laughing at the "predicament of the apes" are rendered "horror-stricken" and powerless (*P&T*, 904–908). The comic effects of Zenobia's predicament are transformed into a stinging indictment of voyeurism.

By literalizing the conventional representation of the sensational, Hop-Frog subverts his audience's expectation even as he plays to it. His jest proclaims a mastery of sensationalism's conventions and enables his escape from the marketplace. By reversing the hierarchy of power – he climbs on top of the king's back (a reverse image of Zenobia standing on Pompey's shoulders) – and by displacing the horror of "blackness" from his own body to those of his audience, Hop-Frog escapes his own terrifying commodification: "The cripple hurled his torch at them, clambered leisurely to the ceiling, and disappeared through the skylight." Instead of symbolizing his slave status, his gait now signifies his leisure. Hop-Frog's freedom, however, is only an imaginative projection: "it is supposed that" he and Trippetta "escape[d] to their own country: for neither was seen again" (*P&T*, 908). Like Pompey, Hop-Frog cannot be imagined outside the marketplace that enslaves him.

This imaginative limit is compulsively repeated in Poe's tales. Each of the stories I have examined end with a scene of liberation: Pompey's flight from Zenobia, the narrator's rescue from the pit, Hop-Frog's escape through the ceiling. These scenes, however, are only gestured toward, never represented; in marking the story's end, they signify the limits of representation. Poe's tales that compulsively reiterate the market's conventions cannot imagine themselves outside its boundary. Poe may be able to demonstrate his mastery of the marketplace, but never his freedom from it; he may expose its workings but he relies on its effects. Figuring the author through the figure of "blackness," Poe symbolizes his enslavement to the marketplace. Like Hop-Frog, he serves the marketplace even as he subverts it. His liberation from the marketplace is only an imaginative projection – his mastery just another market effect.

NOTES

I wish to thank J. Gerald Kennedy for asking me to think about "How to Write a Blackwood Article" and "A Predicament" and for his detailed comments on an earlier version of this essay and Mark Schoenfield for his insightful reading.

1. Poe to T. H. White, 30 April 1835, in *Letters*, 1: 57–58.
2. Karen Halttunen, "Humanitarianism and the Pornography of Pain in Anglo-American Culture," *American Historical Review* 100 (April 1995): 313, 334.
3. Theodore Dwight Weld to Gerrit Smith, 28 November 1838, in *Letters of Theodore Dwight Weld, Angelina Grimké, and Sarah Grimké*, eds. Gilbert

H. Barnes and Dwight L. Dumond, 2 vols. (New York: Appleton-Century, 1934), 2: 717.

4. Frederick Douglass, *My Bondage and My Freedom*, ed. William L. Andrews (Urbana: University of Illinois Press, 1987), p. 3.

5. Frederick Douglass, *Narrative of the Life of Frederick Douglass, an American Slave*, ed. Houston A. Baker, Jr. (New York: Penguin, 1982), p. 52.

6. Thomas R. Gray, *The Confessions of Nat Turner*, ed. Kenneth S. Greenberg (Boston: Bedford Books, 1996), pp. 40–41. As Greenberg argues in his introduction, p. 8, Gray was in desperate financial straits when he arranged to tell Turner's story; *Confessions* sold well (40,000–50,000 copies) and was reprinted twice.

7. Sereno W. Streeter and Mary W. Streeter to Theodore Dwight Weld, 26 December 1838, in *Letters of Theodore Dwight Weld*, 2: 733.

8. See Charles W. Nichols, "Who Read the Slave Narratives?" *Phylon* 20 (1959): 149–162, and William L. Andrews, *To Tell a Free Story: The First Century of Afro-American Autobiography, 1760–1865* (Urbana: University of Illinois Press, 1986) for publication information on slave narratives.

9. See my *Gothic America* (New York: Columbia University Press, 1997), pp. 73–80, for a longer discussion of the problem of positioning Poe as a proslavery southerner. See Terence Whalen, *Edgar Allan Poe and the Masses* (Princeton University Press, 1999), pp. 111–46, for an analysis of Poe's political position and racial views.

10. For the fullest discussion of Poe and contemporary print culture, see Kevin J. Hayes, *Poe and the Printed Word* (New York: Cambridge University Press, 2000).

11. Samuel Warner, *Authentic and Impartial Narrative of the Tragical Scene which Was Witnessed in Southampton County (Virginia) on Monday the 22d of August Last, When Fifty-Five of Its Inhabitants (Mostly Women and Children) were Inhumanly Massacred by the Blacks!* ([New York:] for Warner and West, 1831), p. 5; Thomas R. Dew, *Review of the Debate in the Virginia Legislature of 1831 and 1832* (1832; reprinted, Westport, CT: Negro Universities Press, 1970), p. 6.

12. Gray, *Confessions*, pp. 71, 67.

13. Theodore Dwight Weld, ed., *American Slavery As It Is: Testimony of a Thousand Witnesses* (1839; reprinted, New York: Arno, 1968), pp. 72, 77.

14. Charles Dickens, *American Notes for General Circulation* (Leipzig: Tauchnitz, 1842), pp. 281–297. Poe met Dickens in Philadelphia in 1842 during his tour of the United States. Joan Dayan, "Poe, Persons, and Property," *American Literary History* 11 (Fall 1999): 406–407, argues that "The Pit and the Pendulum" and "The System of Doctor Tarr and Professor Fether" are based on Dickens' description of the Eastern Penitentiary.

15. James Kirke Paulding, *Slavery in the United States* (1836; reprinted, New York: Negro Universities Press, 1968), p. 229.

16. William Drayton, *The South Vindicated from the Treason of Fanaticism of the Northern Abolitionists* (Philadelphia: H. Manly, 1836), pp. 246–247, 15.

17. See W. Sherman Savage, *Controversy over the Distribution of Abolition Literature* ([Washington, DC: Association for the Study of Negro Life and History, 1938), for a fuller discussion of how antislavery flooded the South with their tracts.

18. "The Slaver," *Graham's Magazine* 17 (October 1840): 148.

19. See Michael Allen, *Poe and the British Magazine Tradition* (New York: Oxford University Press, 1969) for a discussion of the influence British periodicals had on Poe.
20. See, for instance, James Macqueen, "The British Colonies," *Blackwood's Magazine* 29 (February 1831): 186–213; [Henry Malden,] "Review of Four Essays on Colonial Slavery," *Edinburgh Review* 55 (April 1832): 156–157.
21. James Macqueen, "The Colonial Empire of Great Britain," *Blackwood's Magazine* 30 (November 1831): 744.
22. *The Southern Literary Messenger*, for instance, reviewed works critical of slavery such as Harriet Martineau's *Society in America* (3 [November 1837]: 641–657), and noticed other antislavery texts, including Lydia Maria Childs, *Appeal in Favor of That Class of Americans Called Africans* (1 [July 1835]: 651).
23. H. L. Malchow, *Gothic Images of Race in Nineteenth-Century Britain* (Stanford University Press, 1996), 7.
24. Allen, *Poe and the British Magazine Tradition*, 23.
25. Kenneth Dauber, *The Idea of Authorship in America: Democratic Poetics from Franklin to Melville* (Madison: University of Wisconsin Press, 1990), p. 135.
26. See Malchow, *Gothic Images of Race*, pp. 32–33, and Nancy Harrowitz, "Criminality and Poe's Orangutan: The Question of Race in Detection" in *Agonistics: Arenas of Creative Contest*, ed. Janet Lungstrum and Elizabeth Sauer (Albany: State University of New York Press, 1997), pp. 177–195, for readings of this racial conflation.
27. Bruce Weiner, "Poe and the *Blackwood's* Tale of Sensation" in *Poe and His Times*, ed. Benjamin Franklin Fisher (Baltimore: Edgar Allan Poe Society, 1990), pp. 46–65.
28. Burton R. Pollin, "Poe's Tale of Psyche Zenobia: A Reading of Humor and Ingenious Construction" in *Papers on Poe*, ed. Richard Veler (Springfield, Ohio: Chantry Music Press, 1972), pp. 92–103; Allen, *Poe and the British Magazine Tradition*; Weiner, "Poe and the *Blackwood's* Tale of Sensation"; David Reynolds, *Beneath the American Renaissance: The Subversive Imagination in the Age of Emerson and Melville* (New York: Knopf, 1988), pp. 238–239.
29. Toni Morrison, *Playing in the Dark: Whiteness and the Literary Imagination* (Cambridge, MA: Harvard University Press, 1992), 58; Terence Whalen, *Poe and the Masses*, pp. 140–141, finds Pompey indicates Poe's "wariness toward slavery."
30. Morrison, *Playing*, p. 58.
31. Jonathan Elmer, *Reading at the Social Limit: Affect, Mass Culture, and Edgar Allan Poe* (Stanford University Press, 1995), p. 11.
32. J. K. Paulding, *Westward Ho!* (New York: Harper, 1832), pp. 28–29, nicknames Uncle Pompey "Pompey Ducklegs" because "of a pair of little bandy drumsticks, by the aid of which he waddled along after the fashion of that amphibious bird."
33. Moses Roper, *A Narrative of the Adventures and Escape of Moses Roper From American Slavery* (1838; reprinted, New York: Negro Universities Press, 1970), p. 48, for instance, describes not only having an "iron collar around his neck" but also "irons on his feet." Dickens, *American Notes*, p. 286, describes slaves with irons around their ankles and necks.
34. Paulding, *Westward Ho!*, p. 29.

35. Harriet Ritvo, *The Animal Estate: The English and Other Creatures in the Victorian Age* (Cambridge, MA: Harvard University Press, 1987), pp. 2, 18, 20.

36. Lesley Ginsberg, "Slavery and the Gothic Horror of Poe's 'The Black Cat'" in *American Gothic: New Interventions in a National Narrative*, ed. Robert K Martin and Eric Savoy (Iowa City: University of Iowa Press, 1998), pp. 99–128.

37. Joan Dayan, "Amorous Bondage: Poe, Ladies, Slaves," in *The American Face of Edgar Allan Poe*, ed. Shawn Rosenheim and Stephen Rachman (Baltimore: Johns Hopkins University Press, 1995), p. 192.

38. Weiner, "Poe and the *Blackwood's* Tale of Sensation," p. 57.

39. Harriet Jacobs, *Incidents in the Life of a Slave Girl*, ed. Jean Fagan Yellin (Cambridge, MA: Harvard University Press, 1987), pp. 2, 27, 35.

40. George Bourne, *Picture of Slavery in the United States of America* (Middletown, CT: Edwin Hunt, 1834), pp. 97, 151, 124.

41. *Narrative of James Williams*, in *The Anti-Slavery Examiner*, no. 6 (1836–1840; reprinted, Westport, Conn.: Negro Universities Press, 1970), p. 2.

42. Weld, *American Slavery As It Is*, p. 61.

43. Drayton, *The South Vindicated*, pp. 158–159.

44. Bourne, *Picture of Slavery*, p. 33.

45. Weld, *American Slavery As It Is*, pp. 57, 34.

46. See, for example, Charles Ball, *Slavery in the United States: A Narrative of the Life and Adventures of Charles Ball, A Black Man* (1837; reprinted, New York: Negro Universities Press, 1969), pp. 256–257, who describes one such flogging.

47. Ball, *Slavery*, p. iv.

48. Ball, *Slavery*, p. 5; Weld, *American Slavery As It Is*, p. 57.

49. Weld, *American Slavery As It Is*, p. 21.

50. John Bryant, "Poe's Ape of UnReason: Humor, Ritual, and Culture," *Nineteenth-Century Literature* 51 (1996): 45.

7

JOHN TRESCH

Extra! Extra! Poe invents science fiction!

1. Special edition from the past

NEW YORK CITY, April 13, 1844 – In an unprecedented feat of human ingenuity and artistic audacity, Mr. Edgar Allan Poe of Fordham today reported a purely *imaginary* feat of science and technology as a *fait accompli*, creating a near-riot outside the offices of *The New York Sun*. The stir was caused by citizens who sought to purchase a special edition containing the fallacious report of a hot air balloon's crossing of the Atlantic. By making facts of physical philosophy the basis and central concern of an adventure tale, Mr. Poe has invented *science fiction*. The *seriousness* and *high-mindedness* of this fictional mode will soon undoubtedly allow it to take its place among the most highly esteemed and prestigious genres of literature.

Countless unsuspecting readers were duped by Poe's report, which claimed the paper's front page with the large-type headline, "Astounding News! By Express Via Norfolk! Signal Triumph!" The article described in minute and technically plausible detail the flying apparatus allegedly invented and flown by well-known aviator Mr. Monck Mason. In all instances the author of the report was careful to explain the principles of aeronautics, meteorology, navigation and mechanics upon which the unexpected phenomena observed by his protagonists relied.

Mr. Poe, who will be known to the reader as the most beloved of our native poets and literary fabricators, has already earned for himself an untarnishable posterity through his ethereal and ideal poetry, his creation *ex nihilo* of detective fiction, and his *scientifically rigorous* literary criticism, and is everywhere acknowledged to have set American literature on its feet once and for all. One feels that artistic and speculative advances of the widest possible variety and of a truly *general* and *cosmical* significance cannot be far behind.

2. Invention, discovery, or hoax?

The suspicion of a hoax frequently hovers over Poe's treatments of science and reason. It therefore seems appropriate to begin an article on

Poe's relationship to science fiction with a "factual report" of dubious veracity.

I will leave it to other chapters in this volume to reveal the "facts in the case" of Poe's reputation during his lifetime and after, as well as the fortunes of the other genres and forms he helped spawn. I should point out, however, that most reports of the public stir and sensation caused by the fictitious news report now called "The Balloon Hoax" are suspiciously linked to Poe himself.[1]

Moreover, the title of the present article is something of an *enhancement* of the role Poe plays in most histories of science fiction. In the first part of this chapter I will suggest that Poe did not so much *invent* science fiction as *discover* it in an existing tradition, reshaping it for his own ends and adapting it to the forms of rhetoric, images of truth, and technologies reigning in his day. But as suggested by the nearness in his epistemology between fact and hoax and between truth and imagination, for Poe, it is a short step – or *leap* – from discovery to invention.

We will then examine the *mechanics of displacement* in Poe's writings. His speculative fictions arose from the encounter with new sciences and technologies that were stretching and surpassing the boundaries of the world. The logic of astonishment in his tales – not only those now classed as "science fiction" – suggests an understanding of reason and technology as ways of worldmaking, as reality-stabilizing machines. A discussion of the most visible sciences of the first half of the nineteenth century will lead to a consideration of Poe's skeptical epistemology, focusing on the necessarily *debunking* aspect of science in relation to itself: the claims and practices that support the current image of reality may eventually be shown to be nothing but a more or less well-coordinated *hoax*. To borrow the conceit of "The Philosophy of Composition," for Poe, science, technology, and other techniques of verisimilitude are the tools that set the stage of the world, framing and manipulating reality's spectacle.

Poe's fictional responses to science reflect back upon his own "rational" theories of literature; he understood language, logic, and rhetoric as *technologies*. The last part of this article will argue that Poe's reflexivity about the media of communication make him a central precursor for developments in the science fiction of the twentieth century, suggesting connections between Poe's work and fiction, film, and music of recent decades. I aim to convince the reader of the vitality and relevance of Poe's science fiction, obsessed as it is with transport beyond the limits of reason and knowledge – both for what it proposes as the subject of art and for what it suggests about the place of science and technology in our constantly changing world.

3. Poe and the futures of the past

The claim that Poe invented the genre that would become science fiction is based not on "The Balloon Hoax" but on "The Unparalleled Adventures of One Hans Phaall" (1835). Although framed by a comical, grotesque introduction, the tale fastidiously recorded plausible conjectures about the visible and atmospheric conditions that would be experienced by a vessel travelling from the earth to the moon. A comparable "Moon Hoax" penned by Richard Adams Locke – Poe's editor at the *Sun* in 1844 – had appeared in June 1835, three weeks *after* "Phaall." Because of the greater notoriety of Locke's series of reports of observations of life on the moon, allegedly gathered by John Herschel's powerful new telescope in South Africa, Poe later insisted upon his priority to Locke and to other reports about life on the moon: "In 'Hans Pfaall' the design is original, inasmuch as regards an attempt at *verisimilitude*, in the application of scientific principles (so far as the whimsical nature of the subject would permit,) to the actual passage between the earth and the moon" (*P&T*, 1001). Some have disputed his claim by pointing out the numerous precedents for his speculative fictions, in religious traditions of prophecy and revelation, in political philosophy dating back to Plato's *Republic*, and in critical and satirical versions of the "earthly paradise" developed in More's *Utopia* or in Rabelais' *Gargantua and Pantagruel*. Poe's detractors have also noted the speculative extensions of contemporary technologies on the floating Isle of Laputa in Swift's *Gulliver's Travels*, and the imaginary and comical voyages to the moon recounted in the seventeenth century by Cyrano de Bergerac. In the early nineteenth century, works of E. T. A. Hoffman and Mary Shelley, in which the Gothic encountered the new feats of chemistry and mechanics, offered more recent precedents.

In the 1930s, Hugo Gernsback, whose journal *Amazing Stories* is generally accepted as founding the pulp science fiction market in the United States, returned attention to the American roots of a genre that had come to be associated with European intellectuals – H. G. Wells and Jules Verne to be sure, as well as Ralph Bellamy, William Morris, H. Rider Haggard, George Bernard Shaw, Samuel Butler, Gabriel Tarde, and Villiers de l'Isle-Adam. Gernsback wrote:

> By 'scientifiction' I mean the Jules Verne, H. G. Wells and Edgar Allan Poe type of story – a charming romance intermingled with scientific fact and prophetic vision . . . Not only do these amazing tales make tremendously interesting reading – they are always instructive . . . They supply knowledge . . . in a very palatable form . . . New inventions pictured for us in the scientifiction of today are not at all impossible of realisation tomorrow.[2]

Later science fiction authors have sought to mark their distance from the "gee-whiz" quality of *Amazing Stories*, associated as much with the gleaming future of rounded edges, low-resistance tailfins and teardrop shapes of the "streamline" design movement featured on its covers as with its optimistic ideology of progress through the efforts of the individual boy-inventor.[3] Ironically, some critics have used Poe's "vulgar" interest in machines as a case for excluding him from "high literature," while others have sought to qualify his membership to the canon of science fiction on the basis of an insufficient "cognitive" content, a predominance of themes appropriate to horror or fantasy, or an inappropriate technophobia. Others acknowledge him as a founder of science fiction, but in a form that, like the image of science fiction offered by Gernsback, is hopelessly *passé*.[4]

Following the superb introduction and notes to Harold Beaver's *Science Fiction of Edgar Allan Poe*, it seems unnecessary to argue the case for Poe's inclusion in the canon of science fiction any further. As for his status as "pioneer" of the genre, at the very least we can be sure that with the rigorous attention to detail aiming at logically consistent verisimilitude that Poe applied in "Phaall," "The Balloon Hoax," and other tales, Poe prepared the way for the speculative fictions of the century to follow; we will later argue that Poe set the precedent for modes of science fiction that came into their own in the second half of the twentieth century.

4. Machines of displacement

The term "pioneer" suggests travel in uncharted lands, like the land explorations in the abortive *Journal of Julius Rodman* and those on sea to the south and the sublime in *The Narrative of Arthur Gordon Pym*. Just as Hans Phaall's adventures are "unparalleled" because they escape the coordinate system of the earth (much like the "Purloined Letter" escapes the grid of the police), the tales of Poe that are readily classifiable as science fiction frequently take as their focus a vessel or machine that allows for displacement "off the map."

We have mentioned the devices that permitted the unprecedented voyages by air in "The Balloon Hoax" and "Hans Phaall." Ships for travelling by sea are of course present in "MS. Found in a Bottle," in which a man who suffers from a "common error of this age," that is, of referring occurrences to the principles of "physical philosophy," an error which fails to prepare him for the encounter with the gigantic ship that arrives out of the mists with aged wanderers consulting ancient mathematical devices. "Descent into the Maelstrom" contains a ship broken into bits off the Norwegian coast; caught in the vortex of the whirlpool, the narrator observes that a barrel descends less quickly than other objects. The barrel to which he attaches himself is the token of the abstract thought that allowed him to stay afloat, much like the embodiment of reason found in "Maelzel's Chess-Player" and Babbage's calculating engine. Like a ship, reason is a tool, a device that allows one to get from one place to another, or, when one is being swept by an irresistible flow, to stay in one place.

The devices featured in the above tales produce movement by air, by sea, and by thought. The series of tales dealing with mesmeric phenomena deal with movement in the fluid medium of the electric or magnetic ether, into regions hitherto uncharted; the regular mesmeric pass by which trance states were induced joins these accounts of hypnotic research to the recurrent imagery of clock and pendula in "A Predicament," "The Angel of the Odd," and of course, "The Pit and the Pendulum." Furthermore, at the time, a mesmerized patient was compared to an automaton, one claimed by a state somewhere beyond active, conscious life and complete cessation of vitality.[5] "A Tale of the Ragged Mountains" relates the experience of spirit travel or metempsychosis of a mesmerized patient, while "Mesmeric Revelation" and "The Facts in the Case of M. Valdemar" follow a mesmeric suspension of life into the regions of death; whether intended as a hoax or not, the latter tale was taken by many as a factual report. By focusing on the mechanical device that induces the mesmerized state, these tales prolong the "unparalleled voyages" above. In the spirit colloquies, these regions are reached by death (in the case of "Eiros and Charmion," a death brought by a fiery comet colliding with a dystopian earth polluted by a spiritually corrupt humanity), itself a voyage mechanized in the coffin-contraptions of "The Premature Burial" and "Thou Art the Man."[6]

The "charming romance(s) intermingled with scientific fact and prophetic vision" found in Poe as well as in such luminaries of the late nineteenth century and early twentieth as Wells and Verne share with the "romance" popularized by Walter Scott the centrality of voyages, but divert their attention to the *instruments of displacement*. Verne retold "Hans Phaall" as *From the Earth to the Moon* and "The Balloon Hoax" in *Around the World in Eighty Days*, while taking off from where *The Narrative of Arthur Gordon Pym* left off with *The Ice Sphinx*. Moreover, the tale that has been identified as the prototype for the bulk of twentieth century science-fiction, H. G. Wells' "The Time Machine," finds a precedent in two tales of Poe.

In Poe the imaginary voyage of earlier utopias and earthly paradises begins to take place not in space but in time. "Some Words with a Mummy" shows the embalmed corpse of the pharaoh Allamistakeo reanimated by the application of galvanic fluid, a time machine powered by the same electric, magnetic, and *spiritual* mechanism as mesmerism. "Mellonta Tauta" contains a letter written from the future (found floating in a bottle on the Sea of Darkness), on board the great balloon ship, the *Skylark*. But unlike the triumphant vision of man's creative powers that Shelley, poet of "Ode to a Skylark," imagined in *Prometheus Unbound*, the future described by the correspondent is one in which humans' onward-marching technology has not protected the individual from becoming expendable cannon fodder, disposable balloon ballast.

Poe's devices of travel from one world to another parallel advances in the sciences and technologies of the second quarter of the nineteenth century that were altering the parameters of time, space, and matter. His compulsive interest in the gadgetry of science and industry was not that of an awestruck amateur; rather, schooled in mechanical engineering at West Point with the best scientific education available in his country, and steeped, as his "Notes on Arts and Science" show, in contemporary reports of discoveries and innovations, his interest in instrumentation and the *technological* bent of his understanding of science were shared by contemporary scientists. Improvements in instrumentation were the ways by which sciences *moved forward*, extending the reach of human perceptions and allowing them, as a later expression had it, "to boldly go where no man has gone before."

5. Space ships, time machines, and electric rays; or, nineteenth century science

Poe repeatedly describes the encounter between worlds. The "MS. Found in a Bottle" (like the time capsule discovered in "Mellonta Taunta," a machine for transmitting a message across time), in which the pedantic reasonableness of the narrator, the level-headed, calculating utilitarian in "Peter Pendulum" or "Diddling Considered as One of the Exact Sciences," yields progressively to an alternate regime of knowledge, as suggested by the aged alchemists upon the ghost ship *Discovery*. Such encounters took place day to day in this period, which has been identified as that of a "second scientific revolution."

For the new science of geology, time travel was an everyday affair; mapping the successive strata uncovered by the gashes cut into the earth for new rail lines allowed a glimpse into the earth's secret history. Poe's *Conchologist's First Book*, a slightly hurried rewrite that is not without its innovations, was a popular text for the amateur classifier of shells, natural records of deep geological time; a comparable scheme of classification with its temporal implications later established by Darwin's Bulldog and Aldous' father, Thomas Huxley, would furnish the structural underpinnings for Wells' *Time Machine*.[7] Extrapolations from fossil evidence led to narratives of the creation and progress of the earth and universe including

J. P. Nichol's *Architecture of the Heavens*, a major source for Poe's *Eureka*, itself another conceptual time machine. Similarly, the decipherment of the Rosetta Stone allowed a glimpse of Ancient Egypt much as did the time machine that reanimated "Allamistakeo." By extending the reach of human perception into the past, the temporal framework of the present was stretched. Comparably, the development of networks of worldwide time-keeping in such centers as the Paris observatory, Greenwich, and, eventually, the Smithsonian Institute in DC aimed to bring about a standard time, a single clock which would tick at the same rate for the entire globe.

The same observatories that were *reshaping time* were coordinating efforts to *remake space*. New lenses and modes of analysis of light penetrated more deeply into the details of the extraterrestrial region, heightening the detail of aspects of the firmament hitherto understood as nebulous. The extension of networks of time-keeping and meteorology was aided by the electric telegraph, which by the 1840s traversed many regions of the European and American Continents. Preparing these global networks were the voyages of astronomers and natural historians like Alexander von Humboldt (to whom *Eureka* is dedicated). New techniques of representation – maps, tableaux, and especially *panoramas* – brought visible data from around the globe together for immediate and synoptic comparison. Furthermore, just as voyages were remapping the continents, the oceans, and the routes to the Poles, the air suddenly became inhabitable by humans with the balloons featured so prominently in Poe's tales; these were small-scale mobile laboratories. The assembly and comparison of the data from these journeys extended the reach and gaze of humans further than ever before, literally around the globe. Everyday life was being overhauled, due to the much-celebrated "annihilation of time and space" brought by new forms of communication: the transport of goods, people, and information by rail, steamboat, postal system, and telegraph. The limits of the world were stretched as the tools by which the world was accessed and perceived were changed.

Along with time and space, *matter* was undergoing major changes in this period. The old assumptions of Newtonian physics of an orderly clockwork universe of points and forces were giving way in favor of a search for new devices to investigate the movement of fluids – ether, light, electricity and magnetism, heat – from one place to another. This was a physics of intermediate regions or *milieux*; it relied upon improvements in instruments of observation and experiment – media – to create its effects. The magnetic amulets and passes in Poe's mesmeric tales were descended from comparable devices used by Mesmer himself; although frequently subjected to criticism, many still understood hypnotism according to the same principles as those of ordinary magnetic lodestones, the electric batteries developed by Volta, and the "vital fluids" studied by Galvani. In the 1820s, Oersted arrived at a simple experimental apparatus that showed that magnetism could be converted into electricity, phenomena elaborated in France by Arago (who plays a bit part in Poe's alchemical hoax, "Von Kempelen's Experiment") and in England by Faraday. Studies of light, electricity, and magnetism continued to rely upon the concept of the *ether*, the "imponderable" fluid medium whose nature was obscure but whose theoretical utility made it indispensable. Following *naturphilosophie*, research in various fields shared the horizon of the search for a single, modifiable substance or fluid underlying matter and phenomena like light and electricity. These investigations in physics were linked to ongoing research in the spectacular new science of chemistry.

In Poe's time, a revelation of the mysteries of matter and spirit seemed to be right around the corner. His tales, like the sciences of his time, focused on devices for exploring space, time, and matter. The *encounter between incommensurable worlds*, in which the assumptions of what counts as "logical" must give way in the light of new experience was as central to his fiction as to the age in which it appeared. Like Poe's unparalleled protagonists, the arts and sciences were crossing and redrawing the parameters of the world.[8]

6. Poetically engineering a new nature

The notion of scientific progress necessarily undercuts the claims of science itself. Considered historically, any fact is just a hoax that is believed until it is debunked. Technologies that Poe's texts describe are metaphors for encounters between different conceptual, experimental, and communicational *techniques of worldmaking*.[9] The tools of science, like the machinery of reason and the "leap" of the artist, are devices for crossing the gap between the current approximations of the structure of the universe and the cosmic truth that may lie behind it; a new world replaces the old.

In order to get a sense of Poe's epistemology, imagine two machines of different scales. The largest one, the macromachine, is the universe as a whole, approximated in the "beautiful truths" of *Eureka*, whose outlines are sketched by imaginative leaps akin to those taken by the great speculators Kepler and Laplace. In this machine, all elements are perfectly adapted to each other; each cause is seamlessly coupled with each effect. This is the cosmos of the Stoics, the great whole that escapes us in all but its most general traits and most minute particulars. Now, the second machine, the micromachine, is any of the tools that humans construct and use to make themselves at home in the cosmos – houses, boats, steam engines, agricultural techniques, telescopes, writing. The smaller machines are *imperfect* since they are made by finite and fallible intelligences; they can only approximate the order of the macromachine. The difference between God's creation, the macromachine, and the human-made, micromachines that engage it (with varying degrees of adaptation) is that unlike human creations, as Poe memorably puts it, "the plots of God are perfect," with all of their elements mutually adapted.

Human endeavor thus can be understood as an always-incomplete attempt to bridge a gap between two regions, between the tentative human order and the necessarily elusive order of the cosmos. Like the narrator of "MS. Found in a Bottle" who states that "the Pyrrhonism of my opinions has at all times rendered me notorious" (*P&T*, 189), Poe is fundamentally a *skeptic* about human knowledge. What currently passes for "reality" or "the world" is an imperfect tissue of conjectures and practices patched together as a makeshift version of the wider, ungraspable cosmos. The fabric of reality is an enormous hoax held together by endless smaller hoaxes.[10] Poe repeatedly mocked the notion that the creeping and crawling of induction and deduction were the only means of arriving at the truth – of crossing the *intermediary zone* between human intelligence and the divine; these methods were only suited to "Mill-horses," intellects out of step with steam and electricity. Instead one must travel this distance by means of the *leap* of imagination. Further, he argued against J. S. Mill's attempt to reduce the world to a single logical order, proposing: "That a tree can be both a tree and not a tree, is an idea which the angels, or the devils, may entertain." Between the order of the cosmos and human representations of it lies a vast distance that can never be completely bridged; two trees, one in the order of human logic, and one in the order of the divine logos may be at once the same tree while separated by the distance between human finitude and the infinity of God. Partially bridging this gap we find human technologies that structure the relation between humans and the cosmos in specific ways; these are the *media* that shape and reshape the world.

Writing, reason, and other technologies are thus the tools we use to cross the intermediate zone between man and God. "The Domain of Arnheim" tells of the narrator's friend Ellison, who, in possession of unlimited wealth and ambition aspired to create an incomparable work of art. He builds a landscape garden where "the art intervolved is made to assume the air of an intermediate or secondary nature – a nature which is not God, nor an emanation from God, but which still is nature in the sense of the handiwork of the angels that hover between man and God" (*P&T*, 863–864). The narrator's tour through the mazy crystal canyons of Ellison's creation, with its beds of flower-blossoms resembling "a panoramic cataract of rubies, sapphires, opals and golden onyxes, rolling silently out of the sky" (*P&T*, 867), suggests a fairy-tale hallucination engineered into three dimensions. In the space between man and God appears an angelic art, a *new nature*.

Ellison's consummate realization of artistic creation is elsewhere understood in terms borrowed from contemporary physics. Poe identifies the luminiferous ether as "the great medium of creation," whose "awful *nature*" he associates with "the various phaenomena of electricity, heat, light, magnetism; and more – of vitality, consciousness and thought – in a word, spirituality" (*P&T*, 1352). Because of the perfect mutual adaptation of the universe, described in *Eureka*, every physical phenomenon is connected directly or indirectly with the whole of existence. Every word uttered, therefore, creates a vibration in the ether whose effect is everywhere felt and retained. In "The Power of Words," a disembodied consciousness engenders a wild star whose "brilliant flowers *are* the dearest of all unfulfilled dreams," and whose "raging volcanoes *are* the passions of the most turbulent and unhallowed of hearts" (*P&T*, 825). Words, written or spoken, convert thoughts into vibrations; the poet alters and recreates the world.

As suggested by the Greek term *techne rhetorike*, a text is an instrument constructed for a purpose. "The Rationale of Verse" expresses the aim of a poem as *unity*, in which all parts work together towards the production of a single, ideal effect. A text becomes more effective – and thus more ideal – as it approaches this perfect, or divine, adaptation. Since, in *Eureka*, an increase in complexity necessarily produces an increase in electricity, it follows that a poet capable of approximating the ideal, or an author who made nearly perfect plots, would grow to resemble the spirits of Poe's colloquies. Like in the "Domain of Arnheim," he would create an angelic and supremely *effective* art; the artist himself would become an altered, intermediate being, something like alien, or an *electric angel*.

As Poe's notion of God as a constructor of worlds and author of the cosmic text suggests, in his epistemology, writing and technology – both human and divine – are united as modes of creation. Taking elements of the present world (discovery) and joining them in new ways (invention), the artist leaps into unknown dimensions of the cosmos. From the point of view of the present, the report of his discoveries may seem to be a *hoax*. Yet these leaps into the regions beyond – in space, time, matter and thought – lay down rails for the world of the future. Different technologies or media are different means of structuring such leaps; the pathways they stabilize become the new worlds we share.

7. Navigating the new media order

The machine that is central to Poe's reflection on the power of words is the text. The means by which texts were constructed, formatted, and distributed was undergoing a transformation in his day, one of which he was uniquely conscious. Poe was one of the rare authors who had direct contact with the process by which written words were transformed into printed words. Throughout his career he worked in all aspects of the magazine trade, not merely as author of tales and poems but as editor, anonymous writer of features and reviews, and as typesetter. Words, sentences, and stories were assembled, following a skilled and repetitive technique, from replicable, standardized, and interchangeable parts.

Advances in printing technology, specifically the emergence of the steam press, stereotyping, anastatic printing, and improved paper production, allowed the quarterlies, weeklies, and the new dailies to proliferate. By the time Poe worked in his first editorial office in the early 1830s, regional and national journals had become an obligatory point of passage for the dissemination of knowledge of all kinds and were the main route for bringing news, commentary, and political views to the physically dispersed public. Like Balzac in France and Dickens in England, Poe in the USA was one of a new generation of authors whose works reached their primary audience through journals.[11]

Accordingly, Poe fitted his art to the new medium, honing the theory and practice of the short story to a fine edge. He intensified the impact of his tales by restricting them to the length that could be read in a single sitting, striving for maximum unity, and not hesitating to deploy the grotesque and shocking as ways of capturing and holding the attention. In parallel with the new daguerreotype, about which he wrote on multiple occasions, he sought to perfect linguistic techniques that could convey settings, actions, characters, and moods with a maximum of precision. The theory of poetry he advanced in "The Philosophy of Composition" – in which the first and most important consideration is *unity of effect* – is the literal description of a search for *increased technical efficiency* in a new mode of production. Like the scientists of his time who endeavored to construct new instruments and experimental mechanisms in order to create more robust and varied phenomena, Poe mastered a new media regime and exploited its potentials for producing *sensations*. As the self-conscious inheritor of the Ciceronian tradition of the orator as master of all tools of effective speech, flexible enough to adapt to any case and all circumstances, Poe understood the material basis of communication as another aspect of the technology of rhetoric.[12]

For Poe, words were indissociable from the fact of mechanical mediation by the printing press; the "ideas" in his texts were material objects, designed to bring about material transformations. The plans for his ideal literary magazine, *The Stylus*, emphasize that "Literature" requires a concrete network of readers and producers, as well as the links that join them. The *Stylus* – an iron instrument that draws lines – aimed at writing a literary nation into existence, creating the critical condition for the recognition of his work. In his "science fiction," Poe did not simply give paradigmatic form to a new literary genre; he showed how to exploit a reconfigured discursive network in the relationship between authors, readers, production, and distribution of texts. His refinement of the short story of sensation – targeted at a doubled audience of easily-manipulated masses and appreciative critics – did not just establish a new set of styles and themes, but set a *formal* and *practical* precedent upon which the specialized audiences created by the editors and publishers of the science fiction pulps could build.[13]

8. Strange loops (1): writing

During and after the Second World War, new potentials of human control and invention made possible a new scale of chaos and destruction. Following Gernsback's visions of a golden age of individualistic invention and technocratic administration, science fiction began catching up to Poe's often bleak vision of human future, expressing its fears about the technologies of the present in tales of an age to come. The pessimistic, dystopian turn taken by science fiction as the ravages of unchecked production and social engineering appeared in both such "literary" efforts as Orwell's *1984*, Huxley's *Brave New World*, and Yevgeni Zamyatin's *We*, as well as in more comfortably genre-specific works like those of Arthur C. Clarke, Clifford Simak, and Poe devotees Isaac Asimov and Ray Bradbury.[14]

Instead of discussing these practitioners from science fiction's "golden age," however, I'll develop an alternative conception of the genre by concentrating on one of its central strands. The works of science fiction whose affinity to Poe I wish to bring out here are not content simply to depict a full-blown alternative reality. Instead they take the status of reality in general as a permanent question, and postpone a final response by focusing on the variable tools, including those of language and symbolic construction, by which worlds are made and unmade. In this section, the key precursor for Poe's work is no longer Jonathan Swift and his Lemuel Gulliver but Lawrence Sterne and his *Tristram Shandy*.

Poe delights in pulling the rug out from under his characters – bringing that which was buried back up to the surface and undermining the assumptions upon which they thought they could stand. Stanley Cavell identifies the "Imp of the Perverse" as a skeptical satire of the Cartesian *cogito*: the philosopher's claim to know that or what he thinks is fragile indeed, and may at any moment be overturned by the unknown forces within the human mind.[15] Poe also delights in subjecting his readers to such reversals, in the juxtaposition of worlds – including the juxtaposition of the world of the text with the real world to which it ambiguously refers. Poe is undoubtedly an important reference for such "metafictional" authors as Borges, Calvino, Nabokov, John Barth, and Paul Auster. The preface to *Pym* establishes the theme of a constant distancing of the self, of the sliver between the text and the world Foucault pries open in discussions of *Don Quixote*, and of the works of René Magritte, surrealist explorer of the paradoxes of recursivity. Self-estrangement and doubling are the central issues of "William Wilson," and, in connection with techniques of representation, of "The Oval Portrait." The perverse effects of the mixing of logical levels – the crossing of a text's hierarchy of worlds (texts within texts within the world itself considered a text) in unexpected ways – is a recurrent (and recursive) trait of Poe's writings.

Yet for Poe, this reflexivity surpasses the merely psychological and linguistic. Poe did not just reinvent a genre, but reordered the material matrix of his texts' delivery as means of altering the world, in much the same way as the sciences and technology reordering themselves shift the parameters of the real. Accordingly, it is those science fiction authors who are interested in the media – technologies of representation, communication, and transportation – that will have the greatest affinities with this fundamental aspect of Poe's works, instead of the "scientifiction" authors lauded by Gernsback, or those "metafictions" whose fundamental trope is language. The claim that the world is shaped by language and symbol is meaningless without a grasp of the concrete reality of words and language and an understanding of the other tools that establish the concrete and conceptual parameters of what counts as "real." A text can be considered in parallel to a telescope, a microscope, a clock, or a network of transportation as a relatively stable medium that shapes and regulates the relationship between two comparatively fluid entities. Printed words establish a relation between sender and receiver, and between receiver and the world perceived. Poe's texts reworked the "veil of the soul," as he put it, through which the reader perceived his world. The machines of displacement they feature are metaphors for the displacement worked by the text and by the other new technologies reshaping the contemporary environment.[16]

Poe-like pathological mixing of reality levels and jumps between them mark the work of many of the most interesting canonically science-fictional authors of the 1960s and 1970s, in which reflection about the medium of communication is constantly at play. The recurrent anthropological themes of Ursula K. Le Guin's novels – in which the rituals, habitat, practices, biological constraints and technologies of fictional "cultures" are imagined with great richness – recall the juxtaposition of worlds that ran through Poe's works, as well as the culture shock one encounters upon opening a text that the skilful writer may choose either to heighten or assuage. The power that stories have to hold societies together is a theme that recurs in her own stories, one taken to uncanny extreme in the psychiatric patient of *The Lathe of Heaven*, who appears, via his encounter with his shrink, to be reweaving the fabric of reality both within and beyond the psychiatric office.

Stanislaw Lem as well explores the plasticity of the real on an alien planet in *Solaris* (beautifully adapted for cinema by Tarkovskii, whose *Stalker* treads similar ground), while his *Futurological Congress* has the reader grasping for some point of stability as the narrative and its world leap through a convoluted architecture of successive realities following the release of a toxin in the hotel where the title's congress for the imagining of the future is held. As Poe put it in the close of his "Balloon Hoax": "What magnificent events may ensue, it would be useless now to think of determining" (*P&T*, 755); the unexpected leaps of technological change and the world shifts they bring about (including the generalization of models of logical hierarchy that have passed from number theory to computer science via corporate structuring and planning to all aspects of everyday life) make futurology a permanently unsettling business.

Philip K. Dick is perhaps the master of the reality jump and of the twisted interpenetration of levels of the real. His media of alteration include Madison Avenue advertising, psychosis, lots of drugs, counterfactual histories, divine invasions, and alien possessions. *The Three Stigmata of Palmer Eldritch* combines theological reflections and a biting critique of contemporary corporations, a tale of dreary life on space colonies enlivened only by radio emissions from a corporate satellite and a cult surrounding a drug-enhanced role-playing game, Perky Pat, with an eerie resemblance both to the sickly sweet fairy tales of advertising and to the "special consensus" that has, since the development of the specialized audiences of the pulps, held networks of science fiction fans together. Palmer Eldritch is the business magnate who is the vessel for an alien lifeform that invades the sacrament of the Perky Pat game, seizes the reality of the player (and the reader), and drags it through a vertiginous corkscrew of incomplete worlds.

The theme of alien invasion runs through the works of William Burroughs. As direct descendant of the founder of the Burroughs adding machine corporation, it is little surprise that the war of the worlds related in centripetal fragments in his *Nova Express* concerns a battle over technologies of communication. A race of anthropomorphic reptiles from Venus controls weapons that record and replay images, controlling Earth by subjecting the population to a relentless addictive cinema of hallucinations. The narrative of this novella, like that of *Naked Lunch*, is rendered notoriously obscure by the use of the "cut-up" method of composition, in which the paper upon which Burroughs typed the story was chopped into fragments of varying sizes and reassembled. This method – recalling the link between typesetting and cryptography in Poe – refigures the image of the world as a system of indefinitely de- and re-composable bits of information being presented by Norbert Wiener and his MIT allies during the early cybernetic age, as well as the noise that increases the more information is conveyed. The constant jumps in level of reference in Burroughs' writing – passages from satire to fantasy to quasi-factual reporting to confessional without warning – suggest, as Marshall McLuhan put it, "a non-stop express of innovation that cannot be endured indefinitely," the succession of overlapping and contradictory sensory environments (TV, computer, airplane, nuclear bomb) being introduced in the "electric age."[17]

9. Strange loops (slight return): radio, film, feedback

Such a reflexive play on the technologies of communication is, of course, possible in media other than writing. Like Poe, Orson Welles was a consummate performer and impresario; furthermore, the subject of Welles' works is frequently the pathological splitting of the self, an uncertainty about the relation between image and reality, and the productive and destructive impact of new technologies. The structural reflexivity of one of his works may epitomize the genre of science fiction: Though it would be a stretch to claim all of his works as science fiction, his breakthrough broadcast of a radio-play version of H. G. Wells' *War of the Worlds* on 30 October 1938, shares Poe's reflexivity about the medium of communication. In *Citizen Kane* (which begins and ends in a Xanadu whose name is taken from the same "Kubla Khan" that inspired "The Domain of Arnheim"), cinema envelops and constantly asserts its alterity and superiority to print; in *War of the Worlds*, however, the potentials of the relatively new network of radio were stretched to depict the non-existent technologies of the invaders. This media event exemplifies a recurrent structure of science fiction, one identifiable in the exploitation of the daily journal in the depiction of transatlantic travel that occurs in "The Balloon Hoax," Melies' early cinematic depiction of space flight in *Voyage to the Moon*, and the drag-racing star ships fabricated out of digital imagery in George Lucas' *Star Wars: Episode One*. These works' depiction of imagined technologies of the future reflect surreptitiously upon the power of a new medium in the present to fabricate consensus about what the "real world" is.

In film, Stanley Kubrick comes to mind as a recent, frequently science-fictional director with significant subterranean connections to Poe. We can note his speculative excursion in collaboration with Arthur C. Clarke in

2001: A Space Odyssey (echoing *Pym* in its narrative self-consciousness and its sublimely open-ended conclusion), the roundabout link via Nabokov's novel between *Lolita* and "Annabel Lee," the gothic tale of mental dissolution and haunting that recapitulates "The Black Cat" in *The Shining*, and the shrill apocalyptic satire of *Dr. Strangelove*. However, the director-auteur who may best realize Poe's understanding of science and science fiction as developed here is David Cronenberg. His *Dead Zone* (based on a story by Stephen King, like Kubrick's *Shining*) opens with a recitation of "The Raven" and deals with the dissolution of a man of exaggerated sensitivity who is haunted by a lost love and troubled by telepathic visions of the past, the present (à la "Tale of the Ragged Mountains"), and of regions beyond death ("Mr. Valdemar"). The self-destructive twins of *Dead Ringers* recall Poe's various doppelgangers with boundary issues, while *Videodrome*, *The Fly*, and *Scanners* meditate upon lifelike machines, the interpenetration between image and reality, and technologies that recreate nature. His recent film, *eXistenZ*, while exploring the implications of virtual reality, eschews the use of digital effects, suggesting that already with cinema (and other more ancient media or modes of structuring relationships between entities, such as religion, politics, drugs, and love) one is already dealing with a technology that dangerously intermingles art and life, producing "reality bleed-through effects." Similar themes organize his adaptation of *Naked Lunch*, in which the Burroughs character, William Lee, receives guidance through the mental / material Interzone via his contact / cockroach / typewriter. Lee sports the blank expression and almost parodically straight-laced attire of the film noir hero, what Burroughs called "banker drag"; this mode of self-presentation, like Magritte's men in bowler hats, is the twentieth-century update of Poe's fastidiously matter-of-fact narrators whose excessive emphasis on their own reasonableness and ordinariness is a foil for the shudders that traverse their reality.

It is no coincidence that many of the artists who combine a Poe-like reflection on technologies of communication as worldmaking devices with the presentation of "science fictional" scenarios frequently make use of mind altering substances as plot devices, and otherwise, as Poe notoriously also did. A drug, like other of Poe's mechanisms of displacement, is a medium that alters perceptions and shifts the parameters of the user's world. Perhaps because of the reports of alcoholism and opiate dependency that surround Poe, he has been a crypto-reference for various strands of "experimental" popular music from the 1960s onward. While Byron seems to be the main prototype for Jimi Hendrix's flamboyant persona and Georgian ruffles, his frequent journeys to outer space ("EXP," "Third Stone from the Sun"), identification with aliens, and excursions undersea and to the poles ("1983: A Merman

I Should Turn To Be"), lock *Electric Ladyland*'s "Burning of the Midnight Lamp" into place as a retelling of "The Raven." One could say that what Poe did with the steam press, steel type, the magazine short story, laudanum, and romanticism, Hendrix did with FM radio, electronic amplification, the long-playing album, LSD, and the blues. The psychedelic African-American man/outsider as extra-terrestrial (or electric angel) re-appears in George Clinton's Parliament-Funkadelic, and in such rap as the Ultramagnetic MC's and Dr. Octagon. In the year 2000, the theatrical designer Robert Wilson staged an homage to Poe's life and works in Hamburg and Paris with music by Lou Reed; the overdetermined genealogy connecting these two to the author of "The Bells" includes Wilson's collaboration with Baltimorean Phillip Glass on the minimalist / conceptual / sci-fi "Einstein on the Beach" and Reed's Baudelairean self-styling within Andy Warhol's Factory of art production as the poet of modern depravity and "Heroin," as well as his successive transformations under the guidance of Martian dandy David Bowie. Aficionados and sufferers of progressive rock have also been blessed and cursed by interpretations of Poe's works by Peter Hammill, Prism, and *Dark Side of the Moon* producer Allan Parsons.

To return to the written word, one of the major recent developments in the science fiction writing of the last two decades is "cyberpunk," whose pages are filled with new drugs, technology, alien intelligences, and a reconstructed, dystopian nature. The secret plottings of multinational corporations, the obsessive search for secure technologies of information storage and the means of violating them, and the marketing of genetic and viral engineering that pattern the vividly imagined worlds of William Gibson in *Neuromancer* and *Count Zero* seemed like interesting conceits when they appeared in the early eighties; they now are matters of course. Gibson – along with Thomas Pynchon and Jeff Noon, affiliated authors we can only note in passing – shares Poe's paranoid understanding of reality as a complex and possibly senseless conspiracy in which various human and nonhuman agencies struggle to define what counts as real.

In his early short story, "The Gernsback Continuum" in *Burning Chrome*, Gibson's protagonist experiences the streamlined utopias of the pulp science fiction of the 1930s as a nightmare scenario; he concludes that the current chaos is preferable to the monotone perfection that *Amazing Stories'* "scientifiction" promised.[18] Though clearly a central influence upon the gadget- and progress-centered science fiction of the late nineteenth century and early nineteenth century, Poe's reflections on science place him beyond the Gernsback Continuum, linking him instead to central concerns in current investigations of the relationships between art, humanity, and technoscience. Today as much as in the early nineteenth century, certain questions cannot be avoided: What role do humans and their creations play in the shaping and reshaping of their world, and at what point have our efforts at mastery gone too far?

10. A last jest

The science and technology of Poe's age extended the experience of time, space, and matter, and showed that these seemingly immutable underpinnings of the world were open to change through human intervention. The obsession with technology that characterizes science fiction permeates Poe's writing inside and out, in its plot devices and its physicality, in its critical principles and its themes. His tales are acutely aware of their material basis, the historically-specific techniques upon which they rely to bring about the effect of verisimilitude. His works of literary criticism present a *science of fiction* that mirrors his investigations of the *fictions of science* we have sketched here.

Poe not only opened and redirected many lines of formal and conceptual development in speculative fiction, but added a grimmer, more anxious note to reflections on the future, demonstrating a canny awareness of the Faustian bargain to which our culture subjected itself when it put its faith in science's progress-through-destruction alone. His texts describe a set of unsettling machines whose function is to shift reality; his texts themselves are exemplary members of this set.

In this article, Poe has been presented as the definitive author of the steam, electric, electronic and nuclear ages, as the inventor of science fiction and metafiction, and as the patron saint of social constructivism, psychedelia, funk (via the Mothership Connection), punk (via the Velvet Underground) and cyberpunk (via the Mona Lisa Overdrive). Before accepting all of these claims, the reader may wish to bear in mind the following caveat, transmitted to us – in a bottle – by an ancient Cretan:

All statements about Poe are false, *including this one.*

NOTES

1. See Doris Falk, "Thomas Low Nichols, Poe, and the 'Balloon Hoax,'" *Poe Studies* 5 (1972): 48–49.
2. Quoted in Damien Broderick, *Reading by Starlight: Postmodern Science Fiction* (London: Routledge, 1995), p. 7. Gernsback's definition of the genre has of course been contested; John Clute and Peter Nicholls, *The Encyclopedia of Science Fiction* (London: Orbit, 1993), lists over twenty rival definitions. The present article accepts the selection made in Harold Beaver, ed., *Science Fiction of Edgar*

Allan Poe (London: Penguin, 1976) as a core grouping of Poe's science fiction, while sympathetic with David Ketterer, *New Worlds for Old: The Apocalyptic Imagination, Science Fiction, and American Literature* (Garden City: Anchor Press, 1974), that nearly all of Poe's tales may be considered at least marginally science fictional.

3. See Andrew Ross, "Getting Out of the Gernsback Continuum," *Critical Inquiry* 17 (Winter 1991): 411–433.

4. Among the histories of science fiction that contest or qualify the inclusion of Poe's writings within the genre see Kingsley Amis, *New Maps of Hell* (London: Four Square, 1963); Paul K. Alkon, *Science Fiction Before 1900: Imagination Discovers Technology* (New York: Maxwell Macmillan, 1997); H. Bruce Franklin, *Future Perfect: American Science Fiction of the Nineteenth Century*, rev. ed. (New York: Oxford University Press, 1978); and Darko Suvin, *Metamorphoses of Science Fiction: On the Poetics and History of a Literary Genre* (New Haven: Yale University Press, 1979).

5. See Alison Winter, *Mesmerized!* (University of Chicago Press, 1998).

6. Discussing the lush interiors of "The Visionary," "Ligeia," and "The Fall of the House of Usher," Ketterer, *New Worlds for Old*, p. 66, argues that Poe's rooms often serve as machines for transport to an "arabesque" or "intermediate" realm. Henri Justin, *Poe dans le Champ de la Vertige: Des Contes à Eurêka, l'Elaboration des Figures de l'Espace* (Paris: Klincksieck, 1991), likewise follows the motif of the "construction of the chamber" in several of Poe's works, linking it to the maelstrom and the "heart divine" of *Eureka*.

7. Suvin, *Metamorphoses of Science Fiction*, p. 228.

8. Recent cultural histories of sciences of this time include David P. Miller and Peter Hans Reill, eds., *Visions of Empire: Voyages, Botany, and Representations of Nature* (New York: Cambridge University Press, 1996); Martin Rudwick, *The Great Devonian Controversy: The Shaping of Scientific Knowledge among Gentlemanly Specialists* (University of Chicago Press, 1985); Michel Serres, *Hermes: Literature, Science, Philosophy*, ed. Josué V. Harari and David F. Bell (Baltimore: Johns Hopkins University Press, 1982); Tom Standage, *The Victorian Internet: The Remarkable Story of the Telegraph and the Nineteenth Century's On-Line Pioneers* (New York: Walker, 1998); John Tresch, "Mechanical Romanticism: Engineers of the Artificial Paradise," PhD Thesis, Cambridge University, 2001.

9. On comparable notions in epistemology, see Nelson Goodman, *Ways of Worldmaking* (Bloomington, IN: Hackett, 1978); Ian Hacking, *The Social Construction of What?* (Cambridge, MA: Harvard University Press, 1999); Gaston Bachelard, *The New Scientific Spirit* (Boston: Beacon Press, 1984).

10. On Poe's hoaxes, Ketterer, *New Worlds for Old*, p. 54, writes, "Because all the grotesque tales are directed toward the demonstration that reality is a lie, a tale involving an act of chicanery should be seen in an analogical relationship to the illusory reality that man inhabits." See also Daniel Hoffman, *Poe Poe Poe Poe Poe Poe Poe* (1972; reprinted, Baton Rouge: Louisiana University Press, 1998).

11. See Kevin J. Hayes, *Poe and the Printed Word* (New York: Cambridge University Press, 2000).

12. See Marshall McLuhan, "Edgar Poe's Tradition," *Sewanee Review* 52 (January 1944): 24–33.

13. See Ross, "Getting Out,"; Sam Moskowitz, *Explorers of the Infinite: Shapers of Science Fiction* (New York: World, 1963).

14. See Brian W. Aldiss and David Wingrove, *Trillion Year Spree* (London: Gollancz, 1986); Dieter Wuckel and Bruce Cassiday, *The Illustrated History of Science Fiction* (New York: Ungar, 1989).

15. Stanley Cavell, "Being Odd, Getting Even (Descartes, Emerson, Poe)," in *The American Face of Edgar Allan Poe*, ed. Shawn Rosenheim and Stephen Rachman (Baltimore: John Hopkins University Press, 1995), 3–36.

16. See Michael Williams, *A World of Words: Language and Displacement in the Fiction of Edgar Allan Poe* (Durham: Duke University Press, 1988); the issue is pursued in Terence Whalen's *Edgar Allan Poe and the Masses: The Political Economy of Literature in Antebellum America* (Princeton University Press, 1999). For those familiar with Gaston Bachelard's epistemology, it may be helpful to describe Poe's theory and practice of language as a *phenomenotechniques of writing*.

17. Marshall McLuhan, "Notes on Burroughs", *Nation* 199 (28 December 1964): 517–518.

18. Ross, "Getting Out," 411.

8

PETER THOMS

Poe's Dupin and the power of detection

Edgar Allan Poe is commonly regarded as the father of detective fiction. In the three stories that feature his amateur investigator C. Auguste Dupin – "The Murders in the Rue Morgue" (1841), "The Mystery of Marie Rogêt" (1842–43), and "The Purloined Letter" (1844) – Poe invented the detective story,[1] a narrative whose "primary interest," as A. E. Murch writes, "lies in the methodical discovery, by rational means, of the exact circumstances of a mysterious event or series of events."[2] Chronicling a search for explanation and solution, such fiction typically unfolds as a kind of puzzle or game, a place of play and pleasure for both detective and reader. The popularity of the stories of Poe and his successors partly derives from this intense engagement with the text where, in the scrutinizing of evidence and the interpreting of clues, the reader becomes a detective and the detective a reader. Moreover, a detective like Dupin also becomes an author, who figuratively writes the hidden story of the crime. As a story that dramatizes the construction of a story,[3] replacing the unintelligibility of mystery with explanation, detective fiction emphasizes the potential comforts of narrative: the apparent provision of order, of meaning, of a metaphoric map in time (with beginning, middle, and end) that seems to tell us where we are.

Yet even as Poe fashions the ritual of reassurance that is crucial to the genre's popular appeal, he also deftly undercuts that experience. Just as Poe's stories seem to construct the detective as a figure of order, they also critique that figure, subverting the opposition between detective and criminal and challenging the investigator's innocent or objective viewpoint of the world. Ultimately, Poe's detective fiction pushes its readers away from the proffered answers and towards a renewed investigation of mystery. Indeed, to uncover Dupin's worldly motives for detection is to question the legitimacy of his solutions. To consider the detective as a force of surveillance is to glimpse how such supervisory acts of control help to produce the transgressive behavior of those seeking to elude control. To examine Dupin's authorial management of his case and its characters is both to sense his oppressive power and to perceive how this apparent agent of order privileges narrative moments of disorder, shock, and disorienting sensation. At the end of each story, the criminal responsible for the ostensible mystery may be exposed and thus metaphorically vanquished, but the shadowy Dupin, an even more powerful and manipulative figure, remains.

The textual imagery of the Dupin stories highlights the self-consciousness of the new genre – how its chronicle of detection is a story of reading and writing. The readerly dimension appears most obviously in the way detection in "The Murders in the Rue Morgue" and "The Mystery of Marie Rogêt" involves the study of newspapers; in addition, Dupin and the narrator consult a text by Cuvier in the former story and "a full report" from the Prefecture in the latter. Even when the armchair detective ventures to the scene of the crime in the Rue Morgue, he remains a reader, "examining the whole neighborhood, as well as the house, with a minuteness of attention for which [the narrator] could see no possible object." A similar act of reading occurs in "The Purloined Letter," when the reader Dupin visits the Minister's hotel wearing green spectacles, "under cover of which [he] cautiously and thoroughly surveyed the apartment" (*P&T*, 511, 413, 695).

Early in Poe's first detective story, "The Murders in the Rue Morgue," the narrator describes his initial encounter with Dupin "at an obscure library in the Rue Montmartre, where the accident of our both being in search of the same very rare and very remarkable volume brought us into closer communion" (*P&T*, 400). Here the search for an elusive text becomes a metaphor for detection, suggesting how the investigator is not only a reader but also a figurative writer seeking possession of a hidden story. That story (wrought by the criminal) is gradually uncovered by Dupin, whose authorial power is signaled by the way his voice, in each tale, takes over the narration (begun by his storytelling friend), filling the disturbing space of mystery with explanation. In "The Murders in the Rue Morgue," Dupin alludes to his linguistic prowess by suggesting how the complete story can be fashioned from a few fragments: "Upon these two words ['*mon Dieu!*']...I have mainly built my hopes of a full solution of the riddle" (*P&T*, 424). The same story illustrates his skill with words as he pens the advertisement, a tactic that, in luring the sailor to Dupin's home, suggests his narrative control over the characters in his case. Dupin's management of the action, however, is most brilliantly rendered in "The Purloined Letter," where the detective contrives several crucial scenes. He designs the sensational moment when the letter is handed over to the Prefect, a narrative turn that stuns G—, Dupin's companion, and, of course, the reader. He also controls his first visit to Minister D— by recognizing the performance of the criminal, who was "pretending to be in the last extremity of *ennui*"; by overmatching that act with his own pretense of arriving "by accident," of suffering from "weak eyes," and of being "intent only upon the conversation of [his] host" (*P&T*, 695); and by thus subjecting the criminal to his own plan of carefully scrutinizing the apartment.[4] When Dupin (whose name reflects his acts of duping) returns the following morning to retrieve a snuff-box that he purposely left behind, his manipulation continues: the Minister is distracted by the disturbance Dupin has engineered in the street below, and Dupin pockets the purloined letter, leaving behind a facsimile. Thus the criminal, who imprisons the royal lady in his plot of blackmail and who, by anticipating the moves of the police, effectively absorbs them into his own counterplot, becomes ensnared in the more encompassing designs of Dupin. As the authorial detective foresees, "being unaware that the letter is not in his possession, [the Minister] will proceed with his exactions as if it was. Thus will he inevitably commit himself, at once, to his political destruction" (*P&T*, 697).

In these stories about the making of stories, the criminal is the antagonist, who in making mystery obstructs the formation of a rounded narrative, and the detective is the hero, who in a skilled act of reading and writing uncovers what happened and devises the completed narrative of explanation. Dupin defeats the criminal, reducing him to a character inhabiting the detective's plot, and comforts us, seeming to validate our enterprise of reading as he guides us to a position of understanding. In "The Storyteller," Walter Benjamin argues that readers, who are caught in the midst of their own shapeless lives, seek solace in the novel, which offers the vicarious experience of a life that is completed by a literal death or a metaphoric one (the novel comes to its close): "What draws the reader to the novel is the hope of warming his shivering life with a death he reads about."[5] What draws the reader to detective fiction and particularly to the investigation of murder is, on the surface, a different impulse; in stories like "The Murders in the Rue Morgue" and "The Mystery of Marie Rogêt" death is not the end point that is sought in the quest for meaning but a mysterious question, an unsettling effect that compels the reader to search backward for the cause, for the narrative's beginnings. Of course, what links both acts of reading is the desire for a completed narrative structure of beginning, middle, and end, a mapping of time that momentarily seems to satisfy our need to be situated. Perhaps more dramatically than most narratives, detective fiction exploits the anxiety inherent in the basic human question: Why am I where I am? In the narrative formula Poe develops, the writer begins by disorienting the reader, fanning our uncertainty and fear with the inexplicable presence of a body or bodies, and then proceeds to soothe our distress by locating the subject or subjects in an explanatory context. The discovery of the corpse of a woman "floating in the Seine" (*P&T*, 509), seemingly in the midst of nothing, in "The Mystery of Marie Rogêt," inspires the need to place her: to give her a local habitation, a name, and finally a history that explains her death. Similarly, the locked-room mystery of the Rue Morgue presents the mysterious body of Mademoiselle L'Espanaye (a victim jammed upward into a chimney in a sealed room), raises the existential question of how she got there and turns to Dupin for an answer.

By placing the victim, attaching her to a narrative chain that accounts for her demise, Dupin reveals his ability to read the mysterious space of the city. Potentially a refuge, where the guilty can conceal themselves within the crowd,[6] the city reveals its secrets to Dupin, who proclaims "that most men, in respect to himself, wore windows in their bosoms" (*P&T*, 401). Dupin supports that claim by frequently entering into the minds of others and adopting their perspectives: he demonstrates a knowledge of the thoughts of both the narrator and the sailor in "The Murders in the Rue Morgue"; he assumes the voice of the victim and the character of her "murderer" in "The Mystery of Marie Rogêt"; and he perceives the reasoning of the Minister in "The Purloined Letter" (*P&T*, 401–404, 425–426, 538, 552, 693). Nothing or no one, it seems, can escape the vigilant eye of the detective as he surveys the city's bewildering expanse and plots its confusing particulars as a narrative path. Yet – and of course – the ostensible mysteries of detective fiction and the psychological comforts it offers are rather superficial. The investigator may seem to eradicate the explicit mystery that detective fiction offers, but he nevertheless leaves in its stead the disconcerting story of transgression; he may seem to rescue the isolated and problematical body by placing it into a narrative context, but that uncovered plot is, for example, no divine pattern but the work of the criminal. Perhaps even more bothersome is the character of the detective who would lead us out of the labyrinth of complexity. Poe's Dupin, who assumes an oppressive power in trespassing upon the private lives of others and in explaining the community to itself, is not the criminal's opposite but a tainted figure who is entangled in the very world he seeks to explicate.

Initially, the tales seem to construct Dupin as an unbiased observer, whose objectivity is guaranteed by his apparent aloofness from the social world in which crime occurs. In the early pages of "The Murders in the Rue Morgue," the narrator portrays Dupin as a reclusive figure from an "illustrious family" who, "by a variety of untoward events, had been reduced to such poverty that the energy of his character succumbed beneath it, and he ceased to bestir himself in the world, or to care for the retrieval of his fortunes." A victim rather than a manipulator of events, Dupin seems peculiarly without worldly power or concerns; as the narrator remarks, he and Dupin escape to "a time-eaten and grotesque mansion . . . in a retired and desolate portion of the Faubourg St. Germain," where their "seclusion was perfect" (*P&T*, 400–401), and they devote themselves to the life of the mind. Yet even as Dupin's physical and mental abstraction suggests that he stands outside society and thereby accurately observes its affairs, other details subvert that impression. Despite the narrator's claim that "it had been many years since Dupin had ceased to know or be known in Paris" (*P&T*, 401), the recluse is surprisingly well connected, knowing not only the Prefect of Police but also Le Bon (the unjustly accused in "The Murders in the Rue Morgue") and Minister D— (the criminal in "The Purloined Letter"). Indeed, as the stories unfold, Dupin emerges as a worldly detective who is driven by a variety of motives: to repay "a service" performed by Le Bon; to exact personal revenge on Minister D— for "an evil turn"; to pursue his "political prepossessions" by acting "as a partisan of the lady" in the same story (*P&T*, 412, 697–698). Additionally, Dupin seeks to obtain the egoistic pleasure that derives from defeating both the rival detectives (the Prefect G— and the speculating newspaper reporters in "Marie Rogêt") and the criminals, and to impress his power on the characters contained in his case, including those who are stunned and thus nervously weakened by the sensational narrative revelations that he devises. In "The Purloined Letter" and "The Mystery of Marie Rogêt," Dupin also works for the significant monetary reward that G— offers, a motive that is strongly voiced in the latter story when the detective links his "labor" to the reward that is offered only "for the conviction of [Marie's] assassin, or assassins"; as Dupin informs the narrator, "For our own purpose [the reward], therefore, if not for the purpose of justice, it is indispensable that our first step should be the determination of the identity of the corpse with the Marie Rogêt who is missing" (*P&T*, 520).

An examination of motive in the three Dupin stories reveals a curious contrast between the extent to which the detective's work is personally motivated and the extent to which the so-called crimes seem unmotivated or accidental. Usually the reader of detective fiction seeks to uncover the intention behind the crime, but this switching of motive from ostensible criminal to detective suggests that the real mystery lies elsewhere and that we should examine the act of investigation itself. In "The Murders in the Rue Morgue," for example, the title reflects the incorrect assumptions of journalists and police, for as Dupin argues nothing unnatural – or beyond the bounds – has occurred; the killings are the work of an orangutan which, in Poe's fictional version of Cuvier,[7] is merely being true to "the wild ferocity" of its nature. Although Dupin assures the sailor – "You have done nothing which you could have avoided – nothing, certainly, which renders you culpable" – we might suspect the detective's strategy of re-establishing society's innocence so completely that no one or no thing is declared guilty. Given the power of deciding what to include in and what to exclude from his narrative of explanation, Dupin overlooks (and thus, in a sense, endorses) the money-making motive of the sailor whose "ultimate design...to sell" the orangutan frames the story of bloodshed (*P&T*, 424, 428). The killings become merely an unlucky interlude within a successful financial venture that remains unquestioned; as we learn in the conclusion, the orangutan "was subsequently caught by the owner himself, who obtained for it a very large sum at the *Jardin des Plantes*" (*P&T*, 431). Admittedly, Dupin's concealment of a story of moral crime is partly a reflection of the limited scope of the detective's enterprise which, after all, focuses on legal offenses. But Dupin's reticence also suggests a desire to shield his own behavior: to examine the legitimacy of the sailor's project and, more particularly, his cruel domination of the orangutan would be to raise uneasy questions about the detective's own employment of power.

In a story that begins by describing how Dupin and the narrator become recluses in protecting their privacy and where the ostensible crime occurs as a violation of the personal space of the home, threats to personal autonomy would seem to demand special attention. But Dupin, in a solution that rewrites the presumed crime as a mere accident, seems to evade the issue, to cover over the way in which the orangutan's invasion of the residence of the L'Espanayes parallels the sailor's "excursion of pleasure" into "the interior" of Borneo (the home of the orangutan), which in turn parallels the detective's own pleasurable intrusions into the minds of those he investigates (*P&T*, 428). Dupin's boast – "that most men, in respect to himself, wore windows in their bosoms" (*P&T*, 401) – suggestively aligns his trespassing upon private (psychological) space with the orangutan's more visible and physically violent expression of power as it passes through a literal window. Thus Dupin's ability to read the city's inhabitants, to occupy their minds and perspectives, reflects not only his brilliance as a detective but also the threat he poses to others' independence. His nightly rambles, in which he "seek[s], amid the wild lights and shadows of the populous city, that infinity of mental excitement which quiet observation can afford," function as miniature versions of his official cases, in which he attempts to satisfy more fully his appetite for "intimate knowledge" and the power and authority it accords (*P&T*, 401). By luring the sailor to his chamber, locking the door, and arming himself with a pistol, Dupin takes physical possession of the sailor; but by extorting his confession, his secret story, the authorial Dupin also assumes proprietorship of this individual, who now functions as his character. In constructing his case, Dupin extends the bounds of his authority and of his narrative: he can tell the story of his companion, of the sailor, even of his rival G—, whom Dupin, in the language of usurping territory, defeats "in his own castle" (*P&T*, 431).

To read Dupin's solutions is to consider the power the detective wields in representing both others and himself. Indeed, Dupin's self-representation is contingent on his characterization of others: he is insightful and powerful, they are not; and in "The Murders in the Rue Morgue," he is innocent just as they are. By obscuring the sailor's mistreatment of the orangutan – as he captures it, removes it from its habitat, imprisons it in Paris, and attempts to subdue it with a whip – Dupin obscures his own oppressive use of power. What the sailor's confession suggests and what Dupin seems reluctant to highlight is the connection between power and violence. Dupin might depict the horrific killings as an accident, but Poe's tale suggests otherwise, linking the animal's deeds back to the actions of the sailor, who denies the individual space and thus autonomy of the orangutan. By constructing his association with the animal as a relationship (like Dupin's) between the dominator and the dominated, the sailor establishes the conditions for tension and inevitably violence:

> Returning home from some sailors' frolic on the night, or rather in the morning of the murder, he found the beast occupying his own bed-room, into which it had broken from a closet adjoining, where it had been, as was thought, securely confined. Razor in hand, and fully lathered, it was sitting before a looking-glass, attempting the operation of shaving, in which it had no doubt previously watched its master through the key-hole of the closet.
>
> (*P&T*, 428–429)

The sailor's attempt to define the place of the orangutan by confining it to a "closet" excites the resistance of that animal, which takes over the private space of the sailor's bedroom and assumes his activity of shaving. Momentarily displaced by the orangutan, the sailor struggles to regain mastery by producing his whip, and the animal flees pursued by its *owner*. Given the sailor's controlling conduct, the consequence – the orangutan's invasion of the L'Espanayes' home – should not be surprising: the orangutan seeks to evade the reimposition of the sailor's power; deprived of a home of its own, it seeks an available refuge; as an animal of "wild ferocity, and . . . imitative propensities" – a disturbing conjunction that implies that the former trait depends on the latter – the orangutan displays that violent disregard for personal boundaries exhibited by "its master." In other words, although Dupin declares that the sailor is "innocent of the atrocities in the Rue Morgue" (*P&T*, 424, 428), the sailor bears some responsibility, a truth that Dupin hopes to conceal in crafting his solution and, implicitly, a favorable representation of himself.

By exposing the motives of the detective, the Dupin stories undermine the authority of their solutions and invite the reader to reinvestigate the complexities of mystery. The two stories that follow "The Murders in the Rue Morgue" continue to develop the contrast between the strong motives of the detective and the apparent lack of motive in the hidden story of the crime. In "The Mystery of Marie Rogêt" Poe, in the guise of Dupin, confronted the *real* mystery of Mary Rogers; indeed, Poe expressed his belief that he had "*indicated the assassin* in a manner which will give renewed impetus to investigation."[8] But, as is now well known, Poe's solution, which would, it seems, designate the "'man of dark complexion'" as the murderer, was apparently overturned by a later development in the case (*P&T*, 551). Before the third and final instalment of "The Mystery of Marie Rogêt" was printed in the *Ladies' Companion*, a report of the deathbed confession of Mrs. Loss (the Madame Deluc of Poe's story) appeared in the New York *Tribune* of 18 November 1842:

> On the Sunday of Miss Rogers [sic] disappearance [Mary] came to [Mrs. Loss's] house from this city in company with a young physician who undertook to procure for her a premature delivery. – While in the hands of her physician she died and a consultation was then held as to the disposal of her body. It was finally taken at night by the son of Mrs. Loss and sunk in the river where it was found.[9]

In *Poe the Detective: The Curious Circumstances behind "The Mystery of Marie Roget"*, John Walsh suggests that Poe, facing "the strong probability that Mary Rogers had died in an abortion attempt," arranged for the postponement of the final instalment of the mystery from the January "to the February issue [of 1843] so that changes could be made in it." Walsh also illustrates how Poe, in revising the story for inclusion in his *Tales* (1845), "made fifteen small, almost undetectable changes in the story, all of which definitely accommodate the possibility of an abortion death at the inn of Madame Deluc...and then he added detailed footnotes so that it would appear he had been entirely correct from the start!"[10]

The details surrounding the story's publication and revision reveal a fascinating intersection between the fictional and the real as the manipulative tendencies of the character Dupin seem to pervade his author's cunning efforts to contrive a solution reflecting his brilliance. The vague conclusion of the tale fails to attribute motives for the killing of the fictional Marie, just as the apparent conclusion of the real mystery portrays a similarly motiveless death: Mary dies by accident. But the exploitation of each death is strongly motivated, indicating the writer-detective's desire for income and acclaim. Poe and Dupin – the sustained parallelism the story develops encourages us to confuse the two – attempt to defeat rival detectives represented by the (real and fictional) reporters, and thus establish their own superiority by uncovering the logical failings of the published speculation and by suggesting that reporters write with the motive of creating excitement and selling newspapers: "We should bear in mind that, in general, it is the object of our newspapers rather to create a sensation – to make a point – than to further the cause of truth" (*P&T*, 521). But are Dupin and Poe free of such worldly motives? As we have seen, Dupin clearly explains to his companion that he works for the reward offered by the Prefect. Moreover, the professional writer Poe (in constant need of money) seems not averse to profiting from the case and its sensational content; indeed, as he attempts to market his story to George Roberts's *Notion*, he does not forget to mention that the events upon which the story is based "created so vast an excitement, some months ago, in New-York."[11]

In the world of detective fiction, the investigator is the one character who usually profits from a crime. Typically, the criminal is caught and the victim suffers, but the investigator flourishes, acquiring (as the example of Dupin illustrates) pleasure from the hunt and both egotistical and financial gratification from the solution. Finding the solution means uncovering and thus gaining control of the hidden story of the crime, a position of power that the detective exploits with particular effectiveness in "The Purloined Letter." The reader of this tale might, however, be initially perplexed by the apparent absence of a hidden story; after all, from the story's beginning we know the identity of the thief and how he stole the letter. But what remains concealed is the letter itself, a document of crucial importance representing the narrative of the royal lady's illicit affair. Indeed, in the Minister's and Dupin's struggle to possess this letter, this hidden story of transgression, "The Purloined Letter" brilliantly dramatizes the contest for narrative control that underpins detective fiction.

Once again the hidden story seems lacking in motive; as an overflowing of desire, the secret relationship is reminiscent of the uncontrolled and unintended passion between furtive lovers that seems to lie behind the *crime* in "The Mystery of Marie Rogêt." But although the royal lady's affair might seem unintentional, the Minister's and Dupin's efforts to exploit those circumstances are cleverly calculated. After discerning the hidden story through a brilliant act of reading in which his "lynx eye immediately perceives the paper, recognises the handwriting of the address, observes the confusion of the personage addressed, and fathoms her secret," the Minister conceives the plan of pocketing the letter and then blackmailing the lady (*P&T*, 682). What is particularly intriguing here is not the scheming itself but the way the Minister's cunning parallels the behavior of the detective. A skillful reader like Dupin, the Minister also displays an ability to script the action. Just as Dupin directs the scenes in which he claims the letter, so the Minister fashions that earlier mini-drama in which he gains possession: "he produces a letter somewhat similar to the one in question, opens it, pretends to read it, . . . then places it in close juxtaposition to the other," and, at the end of the conversation, takes her letter, knowing that in the role the royal lady inhabits she cannot object (*P&T*, 682). Ultimately, of course, the Minister, who has incorporated the lady's story into his own plot of blackmail, proves less masterful than Dupin, who absorbs the machinations of the Minister into his more encompassing counterplot. Symbolic of Dupin's triumphant management of narrative is the artfully crafted moment when the detective trades the letter for a check of 50,000 francs. Here, as the twice-stolen letter is exchanged, we are reminded of the criminal's profiteering and, consequently, of the dubious motives of the detective who, in each of the three tales, exploits his control of the hidden story.

Not content with engineering the structure of detective fiction – the movement from mystery to solution – Poe proceeds to destabilize what he has wrought by challenging the apparent opposition between *good* detective and *bad* criminal. Like William Godwin's *Caleb Williams* (1794), one of detective fiction's most important forerunners, and like the work of Poe's successors in the nineteenth century, Charles Dickens, Wilkie Collins, and Arthur Conan Doyle, the Dupin stories critique the authority of the detective, subvert his solutions, and thus resist closure. In "The Purloined Letter" Dupin and the criminal Minister D— are similar in a variety of ways: for example, both are poets (*P&T*, 684), authorial figures who, we discover, can read circumstances and script the action; they share the initial D; and they both purloin the letter, an action which promises profit and allows us to see more clearly how detection becomes a kind of thievery as the investigator assumes possession of the hidden story and of the characters contained within it.[12] From the making of the facsimile and the act of re-stealing in "The Purloined Letter," to the imitative orangutan shaving before the mirror in "The Murders in the Rue Morgue," to the extended parallel between Mary Rogers and Marie Rogêt, the three Dupin stories seem preoccupied with reflection, repetition, and the blurring of boundaries. In "The Murders in the Rue Morgue" we witness how Dupin, like the sailor and the orangutan, trespasses upon private space, and in all three stories we glimpse how the imaginative Dupin – whom John Douglas and Mark Olshaker describe as possibly "history's first behavioral profiler"[13] – adopts the character and perspective of the ostensible criminal.

This entanglement of apparent opposites also emerges in the stories' portrayal of the interdependence of detective and criminal. Just as the detective's existence depends on criminals, so, in an odd way, criminality relies on detection and the threat of exposure. The proliferation of detectives (as police, amateur investigators, and the curious public itself) supposedly works to ensure the self-regulation of society as individuals, in fear of surveillance, monitor their own behavior.[14] But as the Dupin stories suggest, surveillance also helps to generate transgressive acts as individuals struggle to avoid exposure and to preserve their reputations. In "The Purloined Letter" the royal lady's desire to maintain her respectability in the public eye drives her to behave dishonorably: the story suggests that she has cooperated with the blackmailing Minister D—, whose power "has, for some months past, been wielded, for political purposes, to a very dangerous extent" (*P&T*, 683). In its allusions to an abortion, "The Mystery of Marie Rogêt" also draws a link between transgression and the fear of exposure. Perhaps seeking to elude detection and thus preserve the secrets of her own sexual conduct, Marie (who has disappeared once before) ventures to the other side of the river, where one might "escape from the restraints and conventionalities of society" and act "unchecked by any eye" (*P&T*, 542). In such a version of events, the death of Marie during the operation would necessitate one further act of evading the public eye: the depositing of her corpse in the river. Such a strategy echoes the behavior of the orangutan, which "[c]onscious of having deserved punishment . . . seemed desirous of concealing its bloody deeds," and thus proceeds to commit further indignities upon the bodies by thrusting the daughter up the chimney and hurling the mother through the window (*P&T*, 430). In each story we find this unsettling connection between the operation of surveillance (in which the detective is a major participant) and transgression; even "The Murders in the Rue Morgue," a story that purportedly has no crime, reveals the lengths an individual might go to escape detection. Here that individual is the detective whose crafting of a solution (like Poe's own revisions in "The Mystery of Marie Rogêt") reflects his need, in the face of scrutiny, to design a favorable self-image. As we have seen, Dupin overlooks the moral crimes of the sailor and the implicit connections between power and violence in order to conceal his own failings.

In addition to detailing Dupin's motives and his connections to criminality, Poe's stories also reveal how the detective actually seems fond of manufacturing the very anxiety he is supposed to soothe. Fashioning moments that astonish and shock others appeals to the detective's aesthetic sensibility and appetite for power; like detectives of the second half of the century such as Inspector Bucket of Dickens's *Bleak House* and Sherlock Holmes, Dupin enjoys enforcing his authority and others' submission. That shock can disempower is dramatically depicted at the conclusion of Poe's " 'Thou Art the Man,' " when the narrator, who suddenly emerges as the story's amateur detective, produces a scene of horror to unnerve and expose the criminal. Used in this way, shock becomes a legitimate and useful tool, a weapon that

Dupin wields in his confrontation with the sailor in "The Murders in the Rue Morgue." By luring the sailor to his home, making him comfortable, and then stunning him with his true intention of extracting information about the murders, Dupin disempowers his opponent, who then confesses "all I know about this affair." The "tall, stout, and muscular-looking person, with a certain dare-devil expression of countenance, not altogether unprepossessing" who enters the room is subdued by Dupin's sudden revelation: "The sailor's face flushed up as if he were struggling with suffocation. He started to his feet and grasped his cudgel; but the next moment he fell back into his seat, trembling violently, and with the countenance of death itself" (P&T, 426–428).[15]

Dupin, however, does not employ these tactics solely in the service of solving the case. For example, Dupin's companion, like Holmes's Watson, becomes the innocent victim of the competitive detective who feels the need to dominate, control, and witness his power as it is registered on others' nervous systems. In "The Murders in the Rue Morgue" Dupin manages his narrative disclosures so that his companion (his immediate audience) "stared at the speaker in mute astonishment"; "felt a creeping of the flesh"; was "completely unnerved" (P&T, 414, 423). Dupin's most sensational revelation occurs in "The Purloined Letter," where the detective brilliantly plots the narrative climax of his case, the moment when he suddenly produces the stolen object and stuns his two onlookers: his companion and the Prefect. If Dupin was primarily interested in quickly recovering the letter and thus quickly rescuing the royal lady from blackmail, he would have volunteered to accompany the Prefect on one of his searches of the Minister's hotel. But Dupin seeks to execute his case artfully. When G— first visits, Dupin advises him to "make a thorough re-search of the premises," a strategy guaranteed to heighten both the Prefect's frustration and the astonishment generated by his own eventual production of the letter. After obtaining "a minute account of the internal, and especially of the external appearance of the missing document," and secretly and successfully implementing his own plan of recovering the letter, Dupin patiently waits for the Prefect's next visit, which occurs "about a month" after the first. Thus, like the author who created him, Dupin carefully shapes the unfolding action so that his revelation springs most unexpectedly upon his audience. As Dupin's companion reports, "I was astounded. The Prefect appeared absolutely thunder-stricken. For some minutes he remained speechless and motionless, looking incredulously at my friend with open mouth, and eyes that seemed starting from their sockets" (P&T, 686–688). By constructing such a forceful surprise, Dupin emphasizes his superiority, creating a significant gap between his composure and control and the vulnerability of both his companion (whom the detective has coolly kept in the dark until now) and the Prefect (now a comic figure who, without the power to speak or adequately control his body, manages to follow Dupin's directions before "scrambling and struggling to the door").

In contriving shocks, Dupin generates, at least momentarily, the disorientation that he is supposed to assuage; and in manipulating others, Dupin reproduces that pattern of victimization evident in the crime itself. Thus the Dupin stories resist closure, for the criminal dynamic of authority and submission is not so much eradicated as reformulated in the relationships forged by the detective. In "The Purloined Letter," the cunning Dupin becomes a more than apt replacement for the Minister, and in "The Murders in the Rue Morgue" the domination exercised by the sailor over the orangutan and the orangutan over the L'Espanayes reappears in Dupin's treatment of the sailor, the Prefect, and the narrator. Of course, reappearance and repetition are inherent in the very structure of detective fiction, as the investigator rewrites and, in explaining his case, retells the hidden story of the crime; consequently, to some extent, the detective necessarily reproduces the original anxiety, which is re-experienced by his audience. Indeed, in each of the stories, the tension between power and subjection is eventually channelled into the relationships between storyteller and audience: between Dupin and the companion-narrator, and the companion-narrator and the reader. In the final relationship, however, the submissive party (now the reader) willingly chooses to acquiesce to the powerful party (the teller), trusting that the infliction of suffering (the nervousness engendered by the story) can paradoxically bring pleasure. Voluntarily, we embark on such stories, knowing (to quote Poe's review of Hawthorne's *Twice-Told Tales*) that "[d]uring the hour of perusal the soul of the reader is at the writer's control," and subject to the "*effect*" he has established (*E&R*, 572).

The inherent tension of the Dupin stories, as they simultaneously pull towards and away from solution, is particularly satisfying. As readers, we intellectually approve of irresolution, of the avoidance of the facile conclusion, and emotionally relish the narrative unrest that sustains the possibility of both order and disorder. For just as we identify with the detective in his effort to eradicate mystery, we also, paradoxically, identify with the fiction's victims. In our willingness to submit to the nervous trials of the text and masochistically enjoy shock and disorientation, we align ourselves not with the power of the knowing detective but with the disempowered. Thus we seek the "intense excitement" that the "agitated" public experience in "The Mystery of Marie Rogêt" (*P&T*, 509–510); and thus we return to the scene of the crime not only to investigate but also to relive vicariously the terror of the supposed original moment. As onlookers, we seek the emotions experienced by Mademoiselle L'Espanaye and the sailor in "The Murders in the Rue Morgue," who are overcome by what they see. She "lay prostrate and motionless; she had swooned," while "he nearly fell from his hold through excess of horror"; later, as Dupin's victim, the sailor "fell back into his seat, trembling violently" (*P&T*, 427–430). The vulnerability conveyed by these references to falling and to mental and physical collapse seems, however, at odds with the power implicit in the modern reader's *decision* to pursue such discomforts and to allow the author to assume the dominant position. For, as informed readers of detective fiction with its formalized structure and series characters, we choose our pleasure; we allow ourselves to play the game. We willingly suffer the narrative thrills that disorient (and enliven) us; and, like Dupin, who has fallen socially and figuratively seeks to reclaim his position through detection, we hunt for the security of solution (*P&T*, 400). Content with neither order nor disorder and seemingly satisfied only with the possibility of both, we keep reading fiction after fiction or, in the case of Poe's stories, the same fiction. For in their compelling mysteriousness, in the way that they sustain that condition of tension and unrest so desired by readers, these first detective fictions continue to give us pleasure.

NOTES

Some of the ideas in this essay appear, in different form, in my book *Detection and Its Designs: Narrative and Power in Nineteenth-Century Detective Fiction* (Ohio University Press, 1998).

1. Although I focus on Poe's major contribution to detective fiction, the Dupin stories, students of the genre also note the presence of detection in other stories, particularly "The Gold-Bug" (1843), "The Man of the Crowd" (1840), and " 'Thou Art the Man' " (1844).

2. A. E. Murch, *The Development of the Detective Novel* (London: Peter Owen, 1968), p. 11.

3. Critics have noted that detective fiction contains two stories: the concealed story of the crime and the visible story of the investigation, which unfolds as the uncovering (or figurative writing) of the criminal story. See, for example, Dennis Porter, *The Pursuit of Crime: Art and Ideology in Detective Fiction* (New Haven: Yale University Press, 1981), p. 29.

4. Liahna Klenman Babener, "The Shadow's Shadow: The Motif of the Double in Edgar Allan Poe's 'The Purloined Letter,' " in *The Purloined Poe: Lacan, Derrida, and Psychoanalytic Reading*, ed. John P. Muller and William J. Richardson (Baltimore: Johns Hopkins University Press, 1988), p. 328, makes a similar point in describing how Dupin, like the Minister, "employs deception to confound his opponent."

5. Walter Benjamin, "The Storyteller: Reflections on the Works of Nikolai Leskov," in *Illuminations*, ed. Hannah Arendt, trans. Harry Zohn (New York: Harcourt, Brace and World, 1968), p. 101.

6. See Walter Benjamin's remarks on how "the masses appear as the asylum that shields an asocial person from his persecutors" in *Charles Baudelaire: A Lyric Poet in the Era of High Capitalism*, trans. Harry Zohn (London: NLB, 1973), p. 40.

7. Shawn Rosenheim, "Detective Fiction, Psychoanalysis, and the Analytic Sublime," in *The American Face of Edgar Allan Poe*, ed. Shawn Rosenheim and Stephen Rachman (Baltimore: Johns Hopkins University Press, 1995), p. 161, points out that "the description of the orangutan virtually reverses Cuvier's actual claims." See also Burton R. Pollin, "Poe's 'Murders in the Rue Morgue': The Ingenious Web Unravelled," in *Studies in the American Renaissance: 1977*, ed. Joel Myerson (Boston: Twayne, 1978), p. 253.

8. Poe to George Roberts, 4 June 1842, *Letters*, 1: 200.

9. Qtd. in John Walsh, *Poe the Detective: The Curious Circumstances behind "The Mystery of Marie Roget"* (New Brunswick, NJ: Rutgers University Press, 1968), p. 55.

10. Walsh, *Poe the Detective*, pp. 61, 63, 69.

11. Poe to George Roberts, 4 June 1842, *Letters*, 1: 200.

12. Many readers have noted similarities between Dupin and the Minister. Joseph J. Moldenhauer, "Murder as a Fine Art: Basic Connections Between Poe's Aesthetics, Psychology, and Moral Vision," *PMLA* 83 (1968): 294, describes Dupin as "the double of the criminal" and remarks that "the investigator's motives are hardly more philanthropic than the Minister's." Babener, "The Shadow's Shadow," 329–331, explores the links between detective and criminal and notes, like my discussion, Dupin's "morally dubious" motives. See also Stephen Knight, *Form and Ideology in Crime Fiction* (London: Macmillan, 1980), p. 64, and Martin Priestman, *Detective Fiction and Literature: The Figure on the Carpet* (London: Macmillan, 1990), p. 54.

13. John Douglas and Mark Olshaker, *Mindhunter: Inside the FBI's Elite Serial Crime Unit* (New York: Scribner, 1995), p. 32.

14. Michel Foucault, *Discipline and Punish: The Birth of the Prison*, trans. Alan Sheridan (New York: Vintage Books, 1979), pp. 202–203, writes: "He who is subjected to a field of visibility, and who knows it, assumes responsibility for the constraints of power; he makes them play spontaneously upon himself; he inscribes in himself the power relation in which he simultaneously plays both roles; he becomes the principle of his own subjection."

15. J. Gerald Kennedy, *Poe, Death, and the Life of Writing* (New Haven: Yale University Press, 1987), pp. 120, 124–126, also discusses how Dupin stuns his opponents.

9

KAREN WEEKES

Poe's feminine ideal

Poe's vision of the feminine ideal appears throughout his work, in his poetry and short stories, and his critical essays, most notably "The Philosophy of Composition." Especially in his poetry, he idealizes the vulnerability of woman, a portrayal that extends into his fiction in stories such as "Eleonora" and "The Fall of the House of Usher." In these tales, and even moreso in "Morella" and "Ligeia," the heroines' unexpected capacities for life beyond the grave indicate that females may have more strength and initiative than the delicate models of his verse. The most significant trait of his ideal, however, is her role as emotional catalyst for her partner. The romanticized woman is much more significant in her impact on Poe's narrators than in her own right.

The concept of using females merely as a means to a (male) end appears explicitly in "The Philosophy of Composition," wherein Poe also supplies his philosophy of beauty: "When, indeed, men speak of Beauty, they mean, precisely, not a quality, as is supposed, but an effect – they refer, in short, just to that intense and pure elevation of *soul – not* of intellect, or of heart – upon which I have commented, and which is experienced in consequence of contemplating 'the beautiful'" (*E&R*, 16). Thus the value of what is viewed lies solely in the response induced in the observer, and the subject takes complete precedence over its object. Scenic images in Poe's work fall more into the realm of the sublime than the beautiful, so instead, the inspiration for the experience of Beauty in all its melancholy extremity is "the death . . . of a beautiful woman" and, appropriately, "equally it is beyond doubt that the lips best suited for such topic are those of a bereaved lover" (*E&R*, 19). The woman must die in order to enlarge the experience of the narrator, her viewer. Poe indulged his "most poetical topic in the world" by repeating this idea obsessively: poems on the subject include "Lenore," "To One in Paradise," "Sonnet – To Zante," "The Raven," "'Deep in Earth,'" "Ulalume," and "Annabel Lee"; tales include "Eleonora," "Ligeia," "The Oval Portrait," "Berenice," "Morella," "The Fall of the House of Usher," "The Murders in the Rue Morgue," "The Mystery of Marie Rogêt," "The Assignation," "The Oblong Box," and "The Premature Burial." Floyd Stovall comments that Poe's poetic theory "has been partly substantiated by the excellence of these productions, most of which are among the best things that he did. There is in them, however, much repetition . . . and in spite of the poet's excellent art the theme grows monotonous."[1]

Critics have used biographical and psychological arguments to explain this preoccupation of Poe's. Doubtless, Poe lost an unusual number of beautiful, relatively young, nurturing females in his lifetime: his mother, Eliza Poe; his foster mother, Fanny Allan; the mother of one of his friends, Jane Stanard; and his own wife, Virginia Clemm. Poe witnessed his mother's death before he turned three, and this traumatic event caused him not only to seek desperately for replacement caregivers but to re-enact this bereavement in his poetry and prose. Kenneth Silverman believes that in his tales Poe "nourished himself on a young woman's death, in the sense that art was for him a form of mourning, a revisitation of his past and of what he had lost, as if trying to make them right. Since nothing could, he returned to the subject of 'the one and only supremely beloved' again and again."[2] All three of these key biographical figures show signs of consumption, a disease that kills its victims without destroying their appearance.

In fact, often the consumptive woman ironically becomes increasingly beautiful as her skin pales to translucence and her cheeks and lips redden from fever. Washington Irving depicted the demise of a young girl whom he observed in the throes of consumption as exemplifying "a kind of death that seemed devoid of pain, deformity, filth, or horror." Examining Poe's depictions of death, Gerald Kennedy comments:

> Poe implies that through this insidious transformation, temporal loveliness approaches the perfection of eternal beauty, and theoretically at least the corpse of the dead woman briefly incarnates an ideality. But because death also entails physiological decay, the beauty of the just-departed contains an element of terror, since the passage of time implies a subsequent and inevitable mutation to loathsomeness. . . . The dying woman became a sign of her own fate, and her dissolution presented a spectacle at once irresistible and unbearable.[3]

One is immediately reminded of the scene from "Ligeia" in which the body of Rowena revivifies and then collapses back into death, each cycle falling farther into decay. The vacillation between flushed, warm cheeks and the shrunken-lipped, clammy corpse is horrific because of the stark contrast between these states. The repugnant aspects of death usually happen beyond the narrator's ken; his poetic ladies are already entombed, and he is informed of, rather than called to witness, the non-consumptive "deaths" of the wasting Madeline Usher and Berenice, whose emaciated body, "hollow temples," and "thin and shrunken lips" revolt the narrator almost as much as her teeth do (*P&T*, 230). In other cases where the female falls ill without lessening her beauty ("Morella," "Ligeia," "Eleonora"), he is at the bedside of his wife for her last breath.

Serving chiefly as inspiration for the narrator's melancholy experience of "Beauty" in the loss of this increasingly attractive figure, Poe's poetic and fictional females lack individual development. The dying woman passes silently from this life, rarely expressing her feelings on the matter. Madeline Usher is speechless in her only pre-entombed appearance; Berenice smiled her ghastly grin but "spoke no word" (*P&T*, 230), and the wife in "The Oval Portrait" disturbs her husband's labor not at all but instead quietly dies in her chair as he paints. In other cases, such as those of Ligeia, Morella, and Eleonora, their dying thoughts focus not on their own plight but on that of the narrator. In Poe's fictional and poetic world, the suffering and death of the beloved figure repeatedly pales into insignificance beside the self-absorption of her survivor.

Poe's female characters thus become a receptacle for their narrator's angst and guilt, a *tabula rasa* on which the lover inscribes his own needs. His fictional "ideal" is a woman who can be subsumed into another's ego and who has no need to tell her own tale; she is killed off so quickly that her silence is inscribed quite irrevocably. Instead her image functions merely as a mirror that reflects man at twice his size, as Virginia Woolf has described.[4] I join other critics in arguing that Poe never truly wrote about women at all, writing instead about a female object and ignoring dimensions of character that add depth or believability to these repeated stereotypes of the beautiful damsel. Nina Baym asserts that there "are neither portrayals of women, nor attitudes toward them, in Poe's fiction and biography," since he uses females to stand for ideas that can almost be construed as morals of his tales.[5] On the other hand, Joseph Moldenhauer points out that Poe's women, although admittedly representing ideals, are disturbingly "wishe[d] into death" in order for Poe to fulfill his art, thus making him "symbolically, a killer of beautiful women."[6] It is hard to determine which repeated treatment of women is more demeaning: to see them as creatures in their own right, but ones who must die in order to serve a larger, androcentric purpose, or to utilize them as lifeless pasteboard props for the purposes of the narrator's emotional excesses.

Poe's feminine ideal thus is merely a placeholder, the less obtrusive the better, for some need in the narrator himself. As Joan Dayan remarks Poe's tales about women "are about the men who narrate the unspeakable remembrance."[7] Just as Poe's female characters have similarities in demeanor, his narrators peculiarly resemble each other as well. These bereaved men wax eloquent on the subject of the beauty of their spouses, but even in the cataloguing of features, Poe uses "attributes repeated and recycled no matter for whom or when he wrote, [and] the writer himself seems to be most 'heartfelt' when most vague. Poe's narrators ... become as vain, abstract, and diseased as their objects of desire."[8] This vagueness is evident when they attempt to describe the nature of the disease that fells these women. When Berenice is stricken, the narrator reports that "a fatal disease – fell like the simoom upon her frame, and, even while I gazed upon her, the spirit of change swept over her, pervading her mind, her habits, and her character, and, in a manner the most subtle and terrible, disturbing even the identity of her person!" (P&T, 226). How she is changed is never delineated; we are only persuaded that the narrator believes it is for the worse.

These males also have surprising lapses about quite significant points; Ligeia's husband not only does not remember her last name, he asserts that he may never have known it, a quite surprising admission from someone whose vast wealth derives from inheriting her presumably paternal riches.[9] They marry for unknown reasons at questionable times: Berenice is betrothed only after she is fatally ill, and Morella and her husband are bound by "fate" despite the narrator's lack of love or passion for her. The narrators are obviously repelled by visible signs of their partner's illness ("Berenice," "Morella") and seem curiously removed from physical passion or any vestige of empathy for their wives. When they are overcome with emotion, they become corpselike: as the narrator reads the words of Ebn Zaiat in "Berenice," the blood congeals in his veins. Upon the revivification of Rowena, the narrator's heart ceases beating and his limbs grow rigid; the ultimate sight of Ligeia's face renders him cold as stone.[10] The vision of Madeline Usher sends that story's narrator into a stupor.

Mary Oliver conflates these figures into "a single sensibility, as one character," and sees this persona as "other than rational. He is a man of nervous temperament; he is capable of great love, loyalty, grief, of 'wild excitement' (a recurring phrase); he owns a strange and unfettered imagination.... The question of madness is always present. The actions of the narrator are often clearly, recognizably insane.... Illness, as well, is a presence, an excuse."[11] Opium use is another rationale for the narrator's incredible behavior. Oliver's designation of these characters as mad would certainly be a logical conclusion based on their actions as well as their "wild words." Their odd betrothals or marriages (to cousins, in two cases) are the least of their strange indulgences, as one later violates his fiancée's grave to extract her teeth and take them to his library, one builds a bedroom filled with sarcophagi and literally frightens his bride to death, one does not name his daughter until she is ten years old (and then gives her the name of the deceased mother whom he abhorred and of whom he has never spoken to the child), and one helps his emotionally deranged friend entomb a living woman.

These bizarre behaviors do not generally appear in poems, although the husband who nightly sleeps with Annabel Lee in her tomb and the mysterious visit to Ulalume's grave are consistent with the macabre activities of the prose narrators. But the melancholy narrator in "The Raven" is "ponder[ing], weak and weary" at the point of his visitation, and this passive state of bereaved grief is more typical of the poetry than the tales.

"Annabel Lee" exemplifies several traits of Poe's feminine ideal, especially that of being wholly subsumed by the male. Her unnaturally young age for marriage (she and the narrator are each described as "a child") is, of course, evocative of Poe's own child-bride, his thirteen-year-old cousin Virginia. The youth of several of the poetic figures, including "Annabel Lee," "Lenore," "Ulalume," and "Eulalie," is specifically remarked. A young "maiden" would be more easily dominated than the philosophical Morella or learned Ligeia, and the narrator appreciates the fact that Annabel Lee "lived with no other thought / Than to love and be loved by me" (P&T, 102). She is also victim of one of those swift illnesses that so beset Poe's women; he appears to be spared the decay of his beloved, as she is whisked away by her kinsmen and buried safely out of sight.

"Lenore" is one of the many poems that celebrate the fairness of the beloved, in hair, skin, or eyes. When the poetic women are described, they are often fair, with "hyacinth" or yellow hair ("Eulalie," "To Helen") and light eyes; they are never described as having the black hair and eyes of the "Dark Ladies" of Poe's tales. The bride "Eulalie" has violet eyes, and "To One in Paradise" is an elegaic for a grey-eyed beloved.

Poe's feminine ideal also appears in several of his biographically-based poems, such as "For Annie," "To Helen [#2]," and "To F—s S. O—d." The subjects of these poems have basis in Poe's own romantic quests, as "Annie" is actually Nancy Richmond; this "Helen" is his future fiancée Sarah Helen Whitman rather than the Jane Stanard of his youth, and "F—s S. O—d" is poet Frances Sargent Osgood. Although these mature females have lives and accomplishments of their own, they are lauded for the same doting, feminine qualities that imbue his imagined poetic females. Instead of praising Osgood's poetic skill or intelligence, for example, he casts her in the stereotypical female mold, extolling her "gentle ways," "grace," and "more than beauty" that, according to the poem, will be her means of ensuring the world's "love" (P&T, 73).

"For Annie" ennobles the same stereotypical traits; he lauds her "truth" equally with her "beauty," but it is her nurturing capacity that seems most impressive. "She tenderly kissed me, / She fondly caressed, / And then I fell gently / To sleep on her breast," is as much a maternal image as a romantic one and becomes even more motherly as Annie tucks him into bed and says a prayer "to the angels / to keep [him] from harm" (*P&T*, 100). This conflation of the maternal with the romantic appears more insidiously in tales such as "Morella" and "Ligeia," in which the husband's status is explicitly stated as child-like compared to the erudition of his spouse and in which both these learned women mysteriously die.

In both verse and fiction Poe emphasizes his heroines' eyes. Annabel Lee, Annie, Eulalie, the beloved in "To —," Isabel ("Fairy Land"); and the bride in "Song" are all described as having glowing or bright eyes, often likened to stars. But most extreme in Poe's paeans to lovers' eyes occurs in "To Helen [#2]," in which the lover disappears except for her eyes:

> Only thine eyes remained.
> They would not go – they never yet have gone,
> Lighting my lonely pathway home that night,
> They have not left me – they lead me through the years.

Helen's eyes fill the poet's soul with Beauty and Hope, and at last are recognized as not only brighter than stars but even outshining daylight: "I see them still – two sweetly scintillant / Venuses, unextinguished by the sun!" (*P&T*, 96–97).

The "light" that shines in these myriad eyes is synonymous with these capitalized traits, Beauty and Hope. Remember that Beauty, in Poe's cosmology, is the experience in the breast of the perceiver of the beautiful object, not the object itself. These usually passive, vulnerable, even dead, women are ripe for this objectification, the epitome of which is to fragment the female into parts and idealize or fetishize one aspect of her body, such as her eyes or teeth.

As for "Hope," I would argue that this trait is linked to the youth of his females; there is Hope not only for a long and fruitful life for the beloved as she is seen in her innocent young state, but for the narrator as he views his own prospects in this reflective surface. Kennedy draws on the work of Ernest Becker in his argument about "the idealizing of the Other," in which "the wife (for example) is expected to assure the happiness of the husband and by maintaining her own youthfulness and vitality to affirm his youth – that is, to save him from aging and death. The discovery of her vulnerability seems to deprive him of the illusion of his own immortality."[12] The poet can either depict the Hopefulness of healthy youth, in all its resonance of immortality, or the Beauty of the death of a beautiful woman. However, if a *young* woman dies, he can do both, her death ultimately foiling Hope and so becoming even more poignant for the narrator.

Thus a dying woman who remains beautiful is to be adored as a poetic inspiration, but one who has the poor grace to show the ravages of disease is to be eschewed, as she is merely a token of inevitable decay without the redeeming virtue of impregnable beauty. As Becker explains, "If a woman loses her beauty, or shows that she doesn't have the strength and dependability that we once thought she did . . . then all the investment we have made in her is undermined. The shadow of imperfection falls over our lives, and with it – death and the defeat of cosmic heroism."[13] The narrators' inability to accept their own mortality leads them to reject this tangible reminder of human frailty; however, someone who dies while still lovely provides an opportunity both for romantic idolizing of the beloved and romantic idealizing of Poe's "*most* melancholy" topic, death (*E&R*, 19). Emblematic of the abhorrence of decay is the narrator's characterization in "The Spectacles" of Madame Lalande as a "wretch" and a "villainous old hag" upon his discovering her true age on their wedding day (*P&T*, 638). The narrator's passionate outcry against her is clearly a farcical element, but his rage is not at his own pride and inanity but at the audacity of a woman. Mme. Lalande's chief wrongs against him are daring to have lost her youth and using artifice in order to enhance her beauty. Lalande is the opposite of Poe's feminine ideal: she is more than a match for the narrator in intelligence; she is active; she is not young nor delicately beautiful; and although she is his own great-great-grandmother she seems completely uninterested in nurturing him. She terrifies him not only with her subliminal reminder of his own mortality, but also with her violation of what Poe's narrators have come to expect in their brides. Once a woman steps out of the narrow boundaries of the stereotypical feminine role, she is reviled rather than revered. This argument is borne out by others of Poe's tales, including Eleonora, Berenice, and Morella.

Eleonora epitomizes Poe's ideal: young, unlearned, impressionable, and completely dedicated to her love for him. Only fifteen years old, compared with her lover's age of twenty, she is, significantly, also his cousin. A combination of the poetic ideal and the more complex prose females, she has eyes that are brighter than a flowing river, and, in the original publication, "the lilies of the valley were not more fair," but she also has the prerequisite "majestic forehead" and "large luminous eyes of her kindred." She is exceptionally frail and beautifully sickly, "slender even to fragility," with an "exceeding delicacy" of frame. Her complexion speaks "painfully of the feeble tenure by which she held existence."[14] After plumbing the depths of "the fervor of her love" for the narrator, her main concern at death is whether the narrator will remain true to her memory or will marry another. These scenes are reminiscent of Ligeia's "idolatrous love" and the narrator's subsequent remarriage in that tale. They are also prescient of Poe's own experience with

Virginia's youthful death and his subsequent years spent with her mother, "Muddy"; however, this narrator remains faithful to the memory of his departed longer than Ligeia's widower or Poe himself, as years pass before he leaves the Valley of Many-Colored Glass and courts again.

Eleonora's love is as all-consuming as the narrator could wish, but her jealous acceptance of the promise of fidelity introduces a question of power that does not arise in the poetry, in which Poe's females are romantically submissive. However, the power struggle is absolutely resolved in favor of the narrator, who not only loves Ermengarde with the passion he once felt for Eleonora, he even denigrates the previous relationship, thus proving faithless not only to his pledge but also to the memory of his earlier beloved. Conveniently, the "Spirit of Love" absolves the narrator for breaking his vow, removes whatever curse has been invoked by his marrying Ermengarde, and releases him from the claims of Eleonora. First published in 1841, this tale is perhaps wishful thinking on Poe's part as Virginia's illness intensifies. However, earlier tales of conflicted emotion emphasize the narrator's struggle with strong-willed, threatening women and offer complex conclusions rather than this pat *deus ex machina*.

The silent Berenice at first seems remarkably similar to Eleonora: she, also, is the cousin of her betrothed, has a high, pale forehead, is "unparalleled" in her beauty, and "had loved [the narrator] long" (*P&T*, 229). But instead of reciprocating this love, the narrator plainly states his objectification of Berenice: "I had seen her – not as the living and breathing Berenice, but as the Berenice of a dream...not as a thing to admire, but to analyze – not as an object of love, but as the theme of the most abstruse although desultory speculation" (*P&T*, 229). Jacqueline Doyle points out that as Berenice's disease progresses, this "distancing" of Egaeus from his fiancée becomes even more pronounced through his use of the definite article to describe "the" forehead, etc., rather than "her."[15] Egaeus proposes marriage despite his passions that were purely "of the mind" and despite his revulsion at the changes wrought in her "identity" – however that is to be interpreted – by this disease.

His horror becomes unbearable as her physical condition deteriorates. When he last sees Berenice, she is drastically emaciated, and her alteration is manifested in the change in hair color from black to a "vivid yellow" that is out of keeping with her fatal state. Her sickness manifests the poetic traits to an extreme, moving from the realm of the beautiful to that of the bizarre and repellent. Her hair is an incongruous yellow, she is emaciated rather than merely slender, and her delicate pallor becomes a deathlike pall. Instead of the bright eyes of Poe's poetic heroines, hers are "lifeless, and lustreless, and seemingly pupil-less," with a "glassy stare" (*P&T*, 230). Her lips are "thin and shrunken," offering a smile of "peculiar meaning" that so horrifies the narrator that he apparently swoons or looks down, or it would seem so, since when the text resumes after the major ellipsis the narrator must look up to see the door close behind Berenice.

Drawing on the earlier comments of Becker and Kennedy, I would interpret the meaning of Berenice's smile as a suggestion of the inevitability of the narrator's similar fate.[16] Upon seeing Berenice, her fiancé has already become corpse-like: he suffers an "icy chill" throughout his frame, he falls "for some time breathless and motionless." Upon seeing her teeth and ghastly smile, he wishes for death and then fades from the reader's sight into the void of the major ellipsis. The teeth are horrific because, as Liliane Weissberg points out, the "symmetry and lifeless lustre of her teeth – indicators of health and beauty – become noticeable only in their difference from the decaying body."[17] Her emaciated, bleached features are already skeleton-like, and these teeth are a source of horror in the skull-like face.

The narrator's terror is evoked by the specter of his own decay and demise, but an erotic specter rises before him as well. Showing one's teeth in a smile can indicate sexual interest, and if the "peculiar meaning" of Berenice's grin is of carnal desire, the cerebral narrator would be doubly overcome. The nature of Berenice's ailment has not been revealed, nor has its complete manifestation. But it has somehow altered her identity, both in her "*moral and physical being*" (*P&T*, 227, my italics); Egaeus notes the "alteration produced by her unhappy malady in the *moral* condition of Berenice" (*P&T*, 229, original italics). If her most disturbing change is in the moral realm, one could assume that she is exchanging her innocence for sexuality, a prospect that would terrify her reclusive, passionless fiancé.[18] Another moral shift might be her foregoing her contented, naive feminine role for that of the male sphere of knowledge, signaled by her appearing to Egaeus in his hallowed library – the site of male birth and female death. Either interpretation involves a threat to his power in his bookish realm or in their relationship.

Whichever of these readings – Berenice as sign of mortality, as sexualized creature, or emerging New Woman – is most convincing, they are all fulfilled in Egaeus's pulling her teeth in order to gain mastery over the ideas they represent. He destroys the vision of the ghastly grinning skull and also desexualizes the corpse by removing this token of devouring carnality. The threat of the first of Poe's "Dark Ladies" has been contained, but Morella and Ligeia prove more difficult to control.

"Morella" presents another passionless, apparently motiveless, marriage, this time to the narrator's "friend" rather than his cousin. His admiration for her is mental rather than emotional, as he is impressed with his wife's vast knowledge. He abandons himself to her educational guidance, silently listening for hours to her disquisitions. However, despite her typically attractive appearance (melancholy eyes, high forehead, wan complexion, and "ringlets of silken hair" that both she and their daughter share), the narrator comes to revile Morella without being able to say why.

One theory for the rejection of his wife is her intellectual threat. His wife is "a woman of emotional intensity and determined will who threatens the narrator with complexities which he cannot understand, let alone reciprocate." Her dominant role as mentor eventually "becomes insupportable, and he rejects her as a threat to his masculine superiority and leadership. . . . His ensuing revulsion diminishes her life."[19] She is wise enough to know the cause of his disregard and calls it "Fate"; ironically, her explanation for their intellectual incompatibility also is her husband's weak rationale for their having been originally "bound" at the altar.

Another reason for his repugnance could be her representation of death. As her skin pales and her veins become apparent, she develops an expression in her "meaning eyes" that affects the narrator with "the giddiness of one who gazes downward into some dreary and unfathomable abyss" (P&T, 236). The narrator sees his own demise prefigured in this grave-like image. From then on, he longs for Morella's death, and considers the time "irksome" before she is in the grave.[20] The husband is "furious" and "cursed the days, and the hours, and the bitter moments" until her decease" (P&T, 236), much as Morella curses him by reappearing in the person of their daughter.

This daughter, who is born as the mother dies, raises the specter of sex in the story. Although their conjugal union is supposedly passionless, a child results, and his revulsion could be directed both at Morella's pregnant body and the incipient child. His "gradual alienation" could be the result of sexual terror, though; when he "felt a forbidden spirit enkindling within," she takes his hand and speaks "some low singular words." Eventually, he says, "joy suddenly faded into horror, and the most beautiful became the most hideous" (P&T, 234–235). The husband is terrified of Eros, and he rejects Morella because she reminds him of both carnality and maternity. As Debra Johanyak remarks, "It is the narrator's failure to live up to his marital and paternal duties, and his reactionary horror to his wife's and daughter's achievements, that constitute the evil in this tale."[21]

Although Morella appears to accept passively her husband's disregard, her deathbed curse and reincarnation in the person of their daughter proves otherwise. Although the narrator does what he can to forget that Morella ever existed, never even speaking her name to their daughter, Morella is clearly manifested in the unearthly knowledge of their precocious offspring. Johanyak points out that the daughter "represents even more strongly the independent strengths and talents for which her mother died."[22] And the child's death is as inevitable as that of her threatening mother. By invoking the name of the mother, the narrator imparts her fate to the daughter as well, and both "Dark Ladies" are struck down. The closing scene is of the narrator giving a "long and bitter laugh" at both Morellas' tomb – an ambiguous response, at best, as it is unclear whether he is commemorating Morella's revivification or her final laying to rest in the person of the daughter. The former response would emphasize Morella's power, the latter the narrator's.

The power struggle between Ligeia and her husband is much more clearly resolved, as at the end of her tale she shrinks from his touch and stands, regally, while he is at her feet. Ligeia's mighty will proves more than an equal for the protagonist; she is the only female in Poe's tales or poems to triumph both over death and, more significantly, over her narrator. Stovall argues that Ligeia is Poe's "incarnation of feminine perfection" but also points out that "she was no more than a feminine portrait of [Poe] as he wished to be. Her personal beauty, analytic mind, immense learning, powerful will, and supreme love were qualities which he himself possessed in varying degrees."[23] Thus, through Ligeia's triumph, Poe disproves death's finality for the women in his life and denies his own mortality.

Ligeia is the quintessential "Dark Lady," except that her black hair and eyes, low voice, and quiet step are all described in surreal or ethereal terms that differentiate her from the rest of Poe's heroines. This physical description already sets her apart as "Other" from the narrator and all humanity; thus her immense learning and active will are both acceptable traits in this extraordinary being.[24] Also defying the norm is her "idolatr[ous]" love for the narrator, as her devotion to her husband, entangled as it is with her indomitable will to live, is possibly surpassed only by that of Annabel Lee.

Like the loving and learned Morella, Ligeia is the nurturing mentor figure for her husband. Cynthia Jordan notes that "Ligeia's authority over him was like a mother's over her child; his language speaks of emasculation." She dominates him even on her deathbed, as she "peremptorily" commands him to recite the poem she wrote, and he immediately obeys. Jordan also speculates that Ligeia's sexuality was a source of anxiety for the narrator; Ligeia bends over him in his studies and fills his mind with "vivid delight" at a prospect of "that delicious vista by slow degrees expanding before me, down whose long, gorgeous, and all untrodden path, I might at length pass onward to the goal of a wisdom too divinely precious not to be forbidden!" (*P&T*, 266). Jordan emphasizes this passage as proof of Ligeia's "usurp[ing] the male prerogative" as sexual aggressor,[25] but it also conflates knowledge and carnality and shows Ligeia's domination in both these areas.

Although Ligeia differs in significant ways from other Poe females, the narrator is as repetitive as ever, a weak-willed, fearful narcissist who escapes from memories of his wife by spending her bequest on travel, opium, and a macabre bedroom for his new bride. The brevity of his solitary state is in keeping with his self-absorption at Ligeia's deathbed: rather than expressing grief at his wife's loss of life, or at humanity's loss of her potential intellectual contributions, the narrator bemoans *only* his own fate, asking how he had "deserved to be so blessed by such confessions? – how had [he] deserved to be so cursed with the removal of [his] beloved in the hour of her making them?" (*P&T*, 267). Terrence Matheson adds that the narrator is "[p]reoccupied only with his loss of Ligeia in her role as his worshiper, [and] her capacity to feed his craving for self-esteem and the deprivation of this source of adoration are all that concern him."[26] Matheson argues that the narrator's resentment and greed cause him to murder both Ligeia and Rowena, who although a "fair" heroine, with the delicacy, youth, and vulnerability of Poe's poetic idols, meets an even worse fate than Ligeia.

If not murdered, Rowena is at least emotionally abused by her husband, and her body is possessed by the dominating Ligeia. The scene of revivification enacts the struggle between the "Dark" and "Fair" Ladies of Poe and crystallizes the symbolism of his two female types. The Feminine Ideal, the beautiful, naive maiden who dies an untimely death, is opposed to the willful, dark-haired woman who fascinates but also threatens the narrator with reminders of his own vulnerability and decay. (Berenice is Poe's prototypical "Dark Lady," and it is her sudden hair-color change combined with her otherwise decaying features that initially unsettles the narrator.) Upon conquering her foe, Ligeia scorns the touch of the narrator, offering no solace: although her will has triumphed over death, she is still a manifestation of the decay that rives Rowena's body as the two spirits fight for its possession.

Ligeia and Morella both challenge the narrator in ways that Poe's stereotypical feminine heroines do not. For the narrator, the true horror in these particular "tales of terror" is that a beautiful woman can wield her own power. Craig Howes argues that Poe's

> whole aesthetic rests on the *a priori* assumption that beautiful women are passive, weak, and therefore especially vulnerable to the terrifying powers of death. Women cannot consciously direct or cause death; they can only embody or fall victim to it. Poetic melancholy is male – a sorrow for the loss of a beautiful, and therefore pitiful, object.... the narrator sees, if only for a moment, the incipient, hidden power residing within the beautiful – a power that can triumph over even that most sublime of subjects, death itself."[27]

The narrator is terrified by Ligeia's reappearance not so much because it means she has conquered death but because she does it through an act of vehement will, a powerful volition that renders him prostrate.

Stovall terms Ligeia as Poe's feminine ideal,[28] but I would disagree. Poe's idealized woman, whose figure reappears throughout his work, is not the sexualized, intellectually overpowering Ligeia, but rather a passive, blonde version of the women who nurtured him and then died. Oliver has pointed out the similarities between the appearance of Poe's heroines and the portraits or descriptions of Eliza Poe, Frances Allan, and Virginia Clemm. Eliza and Virginia both feature a high forehead, and they all had long, black hair and dramatically dark eyes; these are features that figure prominently in Poe's descriptions.[29] The wide or high brow and "bright" or "luminous" eyes are included in nearly every depiction of females.

Ligeia has her own voice; she writes poetry, and by having her husband recite it even places her words in his mouth. Much more often, the narrator chooses women who are nearly speechless, as even this husband does in the person of Rowena. The poetic women are already in the grave, and the fictional ones are not far from this permanently silenced state. Stereotypical "feminine" quiescence most typifies the still-living heroine, whether she is light- or dark-featured. Even Morella and Ligeia have low, musical voices, and many have unnaturally light footsteps (Eleonora, Ligeia, Berenice).

Rather than his ideal as a partner, Ligeia is Poe's ideal of himself. She is Poe's own version of Madeline Usher: his haunting, beautiful twin. Berenice, Morella, and Madeline Usher, the other "Dark Ladies," are not eulogized to nearly the same extent as the fair, ethereal beings in the poetry. Even Ligeia's husband travels only a few months before buying a home and preparing it for his new bride, while Eleonora's husband languishes for years before courting Ermengarde. Gentle, vulnerable, delicate females, such as Eleonora and Annabel Lee, pose no sexual or intellectual threat, and their sudden, poignant deaths serve several purposes: they end the relationship while it is still in its early stages of absolute devotion, and they prevent the narrator from having to face the grisly terms of his own mortality. But most importantly for Poe, their dying serves the poetic purpose of enhancing the male's experience of melancholy Beauty, "that pleasure . . . at once the most intense, the most elevating, and the most pure" (*E&R*, 16).

NOTES

1. Floyd Stovall, "The Women of Poe's Poems and Tales," *Texas Studies in English* 5 (1925): 197, 200.
2. Kenneth Silverman, "Introduction," in *New Essays on Poe's Major Tales*, ed. Kenneth Silverman (Cambridge University Press, 1993), p. 21.
3. J. Gerald Kennedy, *Poe, Death, and the Life of Writing* (New Haven: Yale University Press, 1987), pp. 65–68, 87–88, discusses Irving's response as well

as other literary representations of young women's deaths that would have been contemporaneous or slightly previous to Poe's own accounts.

4. Virginia Woolf, *A Room of One's Own* (1929; reprinted, London: Hogarth Press, 1967), p. 77. Laura Saltz, "'(Horrible to Relate!)': Recovering the Body of Marie Rogêt," in *The American Face of Edgar Allan Poe*, ed. Shawn Rosenheim and Stephen Rachman (Baltimore: Johns Hopkins University Press, 1995), p. 237, draws on the same metaphor in her remark that "[t]he story's eponymous victim becomes a kind of reflecting surface on which certain masculine identities are super-imposed: the criminal, the narrator, Dupin, even Poe himself."

5. Nina Baym, "Portrayal of Women in American Literature, 1790–1870," in *What Manner of Woman: Essays on English and American Life and Literature*, ed. Marlene Springer (New York University Press, 1977), p. 222.

6. Joseph Moldenhauer, "Murder as Fine Art: Basic Connections between Poe's Aesthetics, Psychology, and Moral Vision," *PMLA* 83 (1968): 294.

7. Joan Dayan, "Amorous Bondage: Poe, Ladies, and Slaves," *American Literature* 66 (1994): 244.

8. Joan Dayan, "Poe's Women: A Feminist Poe?" *Poe Studies/Dark Romanticism* 26 (June-December 1993): 9.

9. Cynthia S. Jordan, *Second Stories: The Politics of Language, Form, and Gender in Early American Fictions* (Chapel Hill: University of North Carolina Press, 1989), p. 136.

10. See Joan Dayan, *Fables of Mind: An Inquiry Into Poe's Fiction* (New York: Oxford University Press, 1987), p. 188.

11. Mary Oliver, "The Bright Eyes of Eleonora – Poe's Dream of Recapturing the Impossible," *Ohio Review* 58 (1998): 125.

12. Kennedy, *Poe, Death, and the Life of Writing*, p. 81. See also Ernest Becker, *The Denial of Death* (New York: The Free Press, 1973).

13. Becker, *The Denial of Death*, p. 167; Kennedy, *Poe, Death, and the Life of Writing*, p. 81.

14. *Collected Works* (Mabbott), 2: 641.

15. Jacqueline Doyle, "(Dis)Figuring Woman: Edgar Allan Poe's 'Berenice,'" *Poe Studies/Dark Romanticism* 26 (June-December 1993): 14.

16. Kennedy, *Poe, Death, and the Life of Writing*, p. 80, observes: "Egaeus can do nothing about the disease of Berenice, and her hideous transformation confronts him with a reminder of his own impotence and vulnerability. In particular the woman's teeth signify the problem of death; the narrator wants to possess them to control the reality which they represent."

17. Liliane Weissberg, "In Search of Truth and Beauty: Allegory in 'Berenice' and 'The Domain of Arnheim,'" in *Poe and His Times: The Artist and His Milieu*, ed. Benjamin Franklin Fisher IV (Baltimore: The Edgar Allan Poe Society, 1990), p. 69.

18. Several critics have noted the vampire theme in "Berenice," casting either Egaeus or Berenice as this Gothic figure. This reading supports the idea of a sexualized Berenice who threatens Egaeus with both literal and figurative consumption and thus suffers the resulting mutilation. See Hal Blythe and Charlie Sweet, "Poe's Satiric Use of Vampirism in 'Berenice,'" *Poe Studies/Dark Romanticism* 14 (December 1981): 23–24.

19. Debra Johanyak, "Poesian Feminism: Triumph or Tragedy," *College Language Association Journal* 39 (September 1995): 64–65.

20. Kennedy, *Poe, Death, and the Life of Writing*, p. 82, remarks that "By avoiding Morella, the narrator endeavors to protect himself from the contagion of dying. But he cannot escape . . . the child whom he imagined to embody the principle of life and the proof of his own immortality becomes herself the emblem of inescapable death."

21. Johanyak, "Poesian Feminism," p. 66.

22. Johanyak, "Poesian Feminism," p. 66.

23. Stovall, "The Women of Poe's Poems and Tales," pp. 202, 208.

24. Jordan, *Second Stories*, p. 136; Johanyak, "Poesian Feminism," p. 67. Other explanations for Ligeia's unusual traits are that she is either a vampire or a Siren. See Daryl E. Jones, "Poe's Siren: Character and Meaning in 'Ligeia,'" *Studies in Short Fiction* 20 (Winter 1983): 33.

25. Jordan, *Second Stories*, pp. 137–138.

26. Terrence J. Matheson, "The Multiple Murders in 'Ligeia': A New Look at Poe's Narrator," *Canadian Review of American Studies* 13 (Winter 1982): 285.

27. Craig Howes, "Burke, Poe, and 'Usher': The Sublime and Rising Woman," *ESQ* 31 (1985): 184–185.

28. Stovall, "The Women of Poe's Poems and Tales," p. 206.

29. Oliver, "The Bright Eyes," pp. 121–122. Stovall "The Women of Poe's Poems and Tales," pp. 197–198, 207, has also remarked on these physical similarities; he goes on to argue that Annabel Lee and Eleonora are "idealized portraits" of Virginia and that Berenice, the bride in "The Oval Portrait," and the heroine of "Three Sundays in a Week" are also derivative of her.

IO

GEOFFREY SANBORN

A confused beginning: *The Narrative of Arthur Gordon Pym, of Nantucket*

Why must Arthur Gordon Pym, the protagonist of Poe's only book-length fiction, be identified on the title page as someone who is *of Nantucket?* Nantucket is of no apparent interest to Pym and plays no memorable part in his narrative. Psyche-wise and plot-wise, it seems to be nothing more than what westering Americans in the mid-nineteenth century called a "jumping-off place," a town where travelers assemble to make preparations for an upcoming journey. Why must Pym be identified as belonging to, or hailing from, this place? Other questions are implicated in that one. Why must a person be identified as the product of his or her influences? Why must an idea be identified as the precipitate of prior ideas? Why must an action be identified as the effect of prior actions? Why, more generally, must it be taken for granted that every element of one's existence is subject to genealogical criticism?

I raise these questions here because they are the kinds of questions that are obsessively raised in Poe's fictions, very often in their opening pages. "Of my country and of my family I have little to say," writes the narrator of "MS. Found in a Bottle" (*P&T*, 189). "It is impossible to say how first the idea entered my brain," declares the narrator of "The Tell-Tale Heart" (*P&T*, 555). Most tellingly, in "The Fall of the House of Usher," the narrator reports having detected around the Usher mansion "an atmosphere peculiar to themselves and their immediate vicinity – an atmosphere which had no affinity with the air of heaven" (*P&T*, 319). This is precisely what so many of Poe's narrators and protagonists desire: the air of self-generation, "the gigantic force of *the new*" (*E&R*, 1359). That they often do not achieve the new, and that they often make the prospect of achieving the new seem distasteful, does not cancel out the force of the desire that sets their tales in motion.

In the opening chapters of *The Narrative of Arthur Gordon Pym, of Nantucket*, that desire drives Pym with a vengeance. But after an extended howl of protest against the conventions of belonging that are concentrated in the word "of," the narrative undergoes a strange shift. For a brief time, Pym enters into an identification with the universal human subject of the Enlightenment, that extrapolated intellect whose "aggregate of useful knowledge . . . is the common property of all" (*E&R*, 1231). The justly famous conclusion of the narrative, in which Pym, a listless man, and a dead man hurtle toward the South Pole in a canoe and are confronted by a huge human figure in a cataract of vapor, does not resolve this tension. It does, however, hold out a third possibility: another future for the word "of." For "the hue of the skin of the figure was of the perfect whiteness of the snow" (*P&T*, 1179).

These are the first sentences of the narrative: "My name is Arthur Gordon Pym. My father was a respectable trader in sea-stores at Nantucket, where I was born. My maternal grandfather was an attorney in good practice" (*P&T*, 1009). Pym goes on to say a little more about his grandfather in the remainder of the paragraph, and in the second chapter, after he has decided to set out on a whaling voyage, he tells us, in a sentence, that his father, mother, and grandfather opposed the decision. The last glimpse of his family comes later in that chapter, when he unexpectedly encounters his grandfather while en route to the *Grampus*. His grandfather asks him why he is wearing such a dirty cloak; Pym pretends he is an Irishman who *likes* his dirty cloak. "For my life," he writes, "I could hardly refrain from screaming with laughter at the odd manner in which the old gentleman received this handsome rebuke" (*P&T*, 1020–1021). His grandfather retreats, turns pale, turns red, lifts his glasses, lowers them, runs at him with his umbrella raised, stops, turns, and hobbles away.

A comprehensive refusal is embedded in these passages. As David Halliburton points out, Pym does not provide any semantic connections between the first three sentences; all that links him to his father and his grandfather is "bare seriality."[1] Neither does he evince any emotional connection to these two men. The father is mentioned only to be passed over in favor of the grandfather and the grandfather's more extensive presence in the narrative only exposes him to more extensive abuse. (In a quietly vicious sentence, Pym writes, "He was more attached to myself, I believe, than to any other person in the world, and I expected to inherit the most of his property at his death" [*P&T*, 1009]). The mother, like the father, shows up only long enough to be kissed off. The only physical response that we see provoked in Pym by any of these three figures is an apt one: a laugh-like scream, or a scream-like laugh, choked down.

I say "physical" because we do witness, just before that scene, a crucial psychic response to his family's opposition to his seafaring plan. "[F]ar from abating my desire," he says, their resistance "only added fuel to the flame" (*P&T*, 1019). This desire, which is most ardently opposed by his grandfather, a man who has been "fortunate in everything," is a desire to be unfortunate. "For the bright side of the painting I had a limited sympathy," Pym says. The visions that animate him are "of shipwreck and famine; of death or captivity among barbarian hordes; of a lifetime dragged out in sorrow and tears, upon some gray and desolate rock, in an ocean unapproachable and unknown" (*P&T*, 1018). He is, accordingly, *excited* by his grandfather's vow "to cut me off without a shilling if I should ever broach the subject to him again." To be "cut off," to be without lineage or social opportunity, to be "of" no one and nowhere, is what he most wants.

This is where his seemingly normative adolescent rebelliousness begins to get interesting. Rather than desiring to supplant socioeconomic dependence with socioeconomic control, interpersonal submission with interpersonal mastery, he longs, as I have suggested, to decompose his identity – not as a prelude to maturity, but as a finale. If the "bright side of the painting" presents no attractions to him, then he cannot be reasoned or bullied into the kinds of behaviors that would eventually install him as a figure on that canvas. His willingness to extend his flight to the end of the line – the wreck, the barbarians, the unapproachable, unknown rock – makes him an icon of cultural dissolution: the white boy who will not accept his patrimony, who represents the end of the familial and national line.

That icon was everywhere in the 1830s. As Karen Halttunen has shown, anxiety about white youth, particularly boys, greatly increased during that decade, evidently in response to "the major social forces transforming American society: a high rate of geographical mobility . . . the decline of social deference and a loosening of ties between family generations . . . and in general a replacement of traditional hierarchical social relationships with modern peer relations."[2] To many older Americans, these transformations were portents of disaster. How could a white boy cut off from his town and family of origin be expected to carry on the traditions of town and family? More broadly, how could he be expected to have any kind of identity at all, if his location was, to use a word favored by Emily Dickinson, illocality?[3]

In an effort to dampen the desire to be cut off, the guardians of culture flooded the print market with warnings about the illness that attended the condition of illocality. Popular advice books were packed with vivid accounts of the fate of white boys who allowed themselves to be sucked into what Lyn Lofland has called the "world of strangers."[4] That world was, or was next to, the urban underworld of confidence men, prostitutes, drunkards, and gamblers, a place where the wandering white boy might experience disaster, famine, death, captivity, and the sorrow common to those who are unapproachable and unknown. It was a world very much like the one that a white boy could expect to find on an unfortunate whaling voyage, or, as

Henry Ward Beecher suggested, the one that he could expect to find if he were an African on the middle passage. In the world of strangers, Beecher warned his young listeners, there were men who would

> coolly wait for character to rot, and health to sink, and means to melt, that they may suck up the last drop of the victim's blood.... The agony of midnight massacre, the phrenzy of the ship's dungeon, the living death of the middle passage, the wails of separation, and the dismal torpor of hopeless servitude – are these found only in the piracy of the slave-trade? They are all among US! worse assassinations! worse dragging to a prisonship! worse groans ringing from the fetid hold! worse bondage of intemperate men, enslaved by that most inexorable of all taskmasters – sensual habit![5]

To avoid such a fate, the white boy had to construct, or have constructed for him, a character that would not rot. The problem was that the feature of youth that made it possible to imagine such a construction – malleability – simultaneously portended the impossibility of the project. "You will have *associates*," one advice-book writer told his young readers, "and you will feel their influence."[6] If the terrorism of the depictions of suffering did not succeed in making the white boy shy away from the influence of associates, nothing could be done to prevent him from slipping out of the normative sphere of influence. Intimacy with an associate would lead, as in the case of Pym and Augustus, to "a partial interchange of character," and henceforward the boy would belong as much to the world of strangers as to the world of the familial and familiar.

Some speakers and writers held out hope that the boy would never entirely lose his sanctified impressions of home. "Whithersoever the sons of the thirteen states shall wander," Edward Everett declared, "they will send back their hearts to the rocky shores, the battlefields, the infant settlements of the Atlantic coast. These are places beyond the reach of vicissitude."[7] But the more common belief was that the phantasmatic tutelage of the Atlantic coast settlements would persist only if the wandering white boy actively maintained it in memory. Young travelers like Richard Henry Dana reported that they made a point of performing rites of memory while away from home in order to fend off the otherwise inexorable process of becoming insensible to the value of what they were leaving.[8] In the absence of such rites, early impressions would tend to become isolated from subsequent experiences, the cathexis that caused them to "live" in memory would gradually be withdrawn, and the travelers would no longer perceive them as, in Pym's words, "events which had taken place in sober and naked reality" (*P&T*, 1114). Personal and cultural continuity would be sacrificed to the genius, or demon, of illocality.

In this context, the image of a white boy who has no interest in "the bright side of the painting," who opens himself to the influence of associates, and who bears with him in his vagrancy no memory of home, is more than a little troubling. One might go so far as to say that Nat Turner, the black man whose leadership of a rebellion in 1831 exposed the fragility of the authority of whites, and of white men in particular, represents only half of a complex antebellum nightmare. Pym – isn't it strange that we conventionally refer to him by his patronymic? – represents the other half. As a white boy who dreams of pain without gain, who identifies promiscuously, who does not seem to remember the previous phases of his existence once a new phase begins, he is the logical complement of the figure of Nat Turner. Together, they compose a tableau that represented, to many white Americans in the 1830s and beyond, the end of history.

But Pym does not sustain the process of developing a version of white masculinity that "radiates a negativity inimical to the social order."[9] The bounce-back begins about halfway through the book, near the end of the chapter in which Pym, Augustus, Peters, and Parker, stranded on the floating wreck of the *Grampus*, see a sail. As the ship comes closer, they see that it is a "large hermaphrodite brig" that has "suffered much" (*P&T*, 1084). It is steered so awkwardly that they conclude the helmsman must be drunk. A man leaning on the bulwark seems to be nodding and smiling at them. But when the brig finally passes within fifty feet of them, they smell something "insufferable, inconceivable"; then they see bodies littering the deck; then they hear the cry of a sea gull that is feeding on the back of the nodding man. The bird rises, flaps over to them, and drops "a portion of clotted and liver-like substance" at the feet of Parker. "May God forgive me," Pym writes,

> but now, for the first time, there flashed through my mind a thought, a thought which I will not mention, and I felt myself making a step towards the ensan-guined spot. I looked upward, and the eyes of Augustus met my own with a degree of intense and eager meaning which immediately brought me to my senses. I sprang forward quickly, and, with a deep shudder, threw the frightful thing into the sea. (*P&T*, 1085–1087)

This is the limit of Pym's masochistic descent. He has been brought to his senses on several earlier occasions (*P&T*, 1024, 1027, 1030), but never before has the renewed ability to think entailed the awakening of a principle of righteous action. What he sees shining in Augustus's eyes is something beyond all the visions of suffering he had earlier entertained; if his own eyes are anything like Augustus's, he has forgotten, or almost forgotten, his humanity and his race. There is perversity and then there is perversity, it now appears. Though the "paradoxical something" that Poe calls *"perverseness"* is "an innate and primitive principle of human action," it cannot be safely surrendered to: "Man's chief idiosyncrasy being reason, it follows that his savage condition – his condition of action *without* reason – is his *un*natural state" (*E&R*, 1313). To act without reason, to move impetuously toward the ensanguined spot, is to approach the precincts of the racially defiled.

As I have demonstrated elsewhere, whites who ate human flesh under the pressure of famine were understood, in Poe's day, to have a conditional racial identity.[10] If they exhibited a positive desire to eat human flesh, they could be branded with the racial epithet "cannibal." The two survivors of the wreck of the *Magpie* are described as gazing upon each other with "silent pity, not unmixed with fear," for "the cannibal was, already, in their looks."[11] Likewise, in *Don Juan*, Byron describes the reactions of survivors when they had run out of provisions after a week in an open boat:

> They glared upon each other – all was done,
> Water, and wine, and food, – and you might see
> The longings of the cannibal arise
> (Although they spoke not) in their wolfish eyes.[12]

But if this inner cannibal did not appear in their eyes, if the survivors exhibited nothing more than a piteous physical need, then their acts could be reconciled with a putatively natural, rational white identity. As long as they held off until "the last extremity," wrestled with the morality of the act, drew lots when someone had to be killed, and divided the body equally, their cannibalism was merely situational, and therefore not really cannibalism at all. In the wake of this scene, Pym is not just more rational, but more committed to what Poe calls, in "The Imp of the Perverse," the "desire to be well" (*P&T*, 827). After the others have failed to find anything to eat or drink in the flooded hold, he succeeds in discovering a bottle of port wine; when the others are crazed by the wine, he remains sane, and revives their reason by means of the technique of "sudden immersion," which he remembers having read about "in some medical work" (*P&T*, 1091). Even more strikingly, he is conscious of, and proud of, his reason and wellness: he remarks that "although at the commencement of the voyage I had been in bad health, and was at all times of a delicate constitution, I suffered less than any of us, being much less reduced in frame, and retaining my powers of mind to a surprising degree, which the rest were completely prostrated in intellect" (*P&T*, 1092). It is as though the meandering death ship has drawn out and drawn away Pym's waywardness and masochism, enabling him to be reborn as a rational, temperate leader of men.

Throughout their ensuing sufferings, which culminate in the killing and eating of Parker, Pym never again exhibits any desire for human flesh. Though he dwells in secret "upon the prospect of our being reduced to this last horrible extremity," Parker is the one who proposes "that one of us should die to preserve the existence of the others," and Pym instantly and energetically resists his "bloody and cannibal designs" (*P&T*, 1094, 1096). Only after all of his appeals to the consciences of his shipmates have failed does he finally submit to the necessity of drawing lots, and then to the necessity of "the fearful repast" (*P&T*, 1099). This is how one eats human flesh without surrendering one's racial identity; this is how Pym can get away with assigning the word "cannibal" to Parker's designs, but not to his own actions.

If Parker represents "action *without* reason," the "unnatural state" of man, Pym represents "man" rising toward his natural state, propelled by reason. "The more [man] reasons," Poe writes, "the nearer he approaches the position to which this chief idiosyncrasy irresistibly impels him; and not until he attains this position with exactitude – not until his reason has exhausted itself for his improvement – not until he has stepped upon the highest pinnacle of civilisation – will his *natural* state be ultimately reached, or thoroughly determined" (*E&R*, 1313). Hence Pym's commitment, after he and Peters have been rescued by the *Jane Guy*, to "the progress of discovery" (*P&T*, 1125), the advancement of a knowledge that belongs not to any one individual, but to the universal human subject conjured up by the philosophers of the Enlightenment. Augustus, with whom Pym had once identified, putrefies, dies, and goes to pieces; the universal human subject, with whom Pym now identifies, is eternally clean and whole. By identifying with this subject, by developing, all of a sudden, a narratorial eye that gazes on behalf of "the eye of science" (*P&T*, 1134), Pym attempts to stay clear of all the unnaturalness that he had once perversely pursued.

Now that he is "of" a consciousness that is remote from his own private self, the details of his bodily and psychic life no longer occupy center stage. In their place, he presents accounts of the nesting behavior of penguins and albatrosses, whose "spirit of reflection" is "calculated to elicit reflection in every well-regulated human intellect"; accounts of Captain Guy's "search for a group of islands called the Auroras, respecting whose existence a great diversity of opinion has existed"; and accounts of "the very few attempts at reaching the southern pole which have hitherto been made." In every instance, the motive force behind his narration is a desire to "settle the question," to solve "the great problem." He burns to reach a place of total revelation, a place something like Aidenn, the supramundane realm in "The Conversation of Eiros and Charmion," where he might finally experience "the majesty of all things – of the unknown now known – of the speculative Future merged in the august and certain Present" (*P&T*, 1119, 1123–1125, 1134, 359).

This place, "the high Heaven of pure knowledge," is the polar opposite of the place he had been journeying toward before. It is approached not through divestiture but accumulation, not through degradation but rarefaction. Now that he identifies with what is, quite literally, a body of knowledge, Pym can disidentify with the perverse fleshly body that had moved of its own accord toward the ensanguined spot. Now that he views the world from the perspective of that ideal body, he can abjure the dream of outsideness, for everything that appears to exist outside the region controlled by the gaze of that body will eventually come into sight. No area exists that will not be mapped; no code exists that will not be cracked; nothing, in theory, is capable of deferring the "apocalypse of signification."[13]

But then the *Jane Guy* stops at Tsalal, a previously unknown island whose occupants are profoundly black and profoundly savage. Everything about the Tsalalians appears to transcend the usual standards of measurement. Upon boarding the *Jane Guy*, they exhibit "a degree of ignorance for which we were not prepared" and an amazement that "exceeded all bounds" (*P&T*, 1137–1138). Their dwellings are "unlike those of even the lowest of the savage races with which mankind are acquainted," and their boats differ "vastly in shape from those of any other inhabitants of the Southern Ocean with whom civilized nations are acquainted" (*P&T*, 1142, 1175). During their assault on the *Jane Guy*, which Pym views from a hiding place in the mountains, over two thousand of them surround it "as if by magic" and demolish everything on board, again "as if by magic" (*P&T*, 1157–1159). When they see a chance to prevent Pym and Peters from escaping, they race toward them "with inconceivable rapidity"; when their efforts fail, they "set up the most tremendous yell of rage and disappointment conceivable." Overwhelmed by this barrage of seeming anomalies, Pym sinks, increasingly, into "a species of stupid contemplation" (*P&T*, 1172).

In the "Note" that follows Pym's narrative, an anonymous writer points out that the shape of the Tsalalian chasms, together with the pattern of the indentures on the wall of one of the chasms, may be read as a set of Ethiopian, Arabic, and Egyptian words signifying the structural oppositions of black and white, north and south. The writer thereby suggests that Tsalal is not as prodigious as it appears to be, that it lies within what Poe calls, in his 1837 review of John L. Stephens's *Incidents of Travel in Egypt, Arabia Petraea, and the Holy Land*, "the regions of biblical history" (*E&R*, 928). That is to say that the "outsideness" of the Tsalalians is no more than an element of a structural opposition between those who are inside and those who are outside the space of God's pleasure, but who are each equally ensconced within the space of God's word. If the Tsalalians are, in a phrase that Poe applies to modern-day Egyptians, the "basest of the base," they are, as such, "but a portion of the providential plan of the Deity for bringing more visibly to light, in after-ages, the *evidence* of the fulfillment of his word" (*E&R*, 926, 929). For the writer of the "Note," no place exists outside the space of God's word. Even within the hills, at the ends of the earth, God has caused his word to be engraved, and everything outside that word – even the dust that crumbles out of the rock during the process of engraving – is the object of his implacable vengeance.

But this line of thinking is noticeably absent from Pym's account of his experiences on Tsalal. If the philological analysis of the "Note" may be described as a form of scientific racism, a hierarchical ordering of human types, Pym's refusal of analysis may be described as a form of teratological racism, an agapeness before the phenomenon of monstrosity. Confronted by what he takes to be the incarnations of absolute savagery and blackness, he cannot set the wheels of analysis in motion. As a result, he foregrounds the "apparitional" as opposed to the "representational" quality of the Tsalalians, and thereby obstructs the process of cataloging and shelving them in the storehouse of reason.[14] It seems to be a general law, Legrand observes in "The Gold Bug," that whenever the "mind struggles to establish a connexion – a sequence of cause and effect – and [is] unable to do so," it "suffers a species of temporary paralysis" (*P&T*, 581). In the final chapters of *Pym*, this paralysis steadily deepens, until our hero is, in W. H. Auden's words, "as purely passive as the I in dreams" (*Recognition*, 222).

Where, then, do we find ourselves? Back in the downward arc of masochism? The famous scene in which Pym swoons on a cliffside might seem to indicate as much. Despite his efforts *"not to think,"* he pictures to himself "the sickness, and dizziness, and the last struggle, and the half swoon, and the final bitterness of the rushing and headlong descent," and is soon "pervaded with *a longing to fall*; a desire, a yearning, a passion utterly uncontrollable" (*P&T*, 1170). But the scene is something of a set piece; it is confined to two incidental paragraphs, and its mood does not carry over to the rest of the descriptions of the events on Tsalal. It is more a reminder of the ongoingness of perversity than a restoration of the once-fierce desire to be other than upright.

Do we find ourselves still within the upward arc of Enlightenment, via the writer of the "Note"? Many critics have thought so. Beginning in the 1950s, when *Pym* was first judged fit for serious analysis by critics outside France, the standard practice has been to assume that we are meant to identify not with Pym but with Poe, or with the hallucinatory figure of the masterful author that is generated by the "Preface" and the "Note."[15] But if *Pym* is, in Garrett Stewart's words, "a novel about the production of textuality," it is, by the same token, "a metanarrative of reading concerned with reading's own nervous perversity, its surrogate pleasure and pain, its psychosomatic risks."[16] That is to say that Poe's occasionally ironic treatment of Pym does not foreclose the possibility of the reader's identification with Pym. Quite the contrary: by calling our attention to the existence of the text, and thereby intimating the textuality of existence, Poe calls our attention to the dream he thereby interrupts, the surrogate pleasure and pain that we have been sharing with his narrator and with him. Like the knocking at the gate in *Macbeth*, the metanarrative elements in *Pym* awaken us to our irrational, unpredictable, even perverse investments in the story. If these elements do not, if they merely confirm what the reader always already knows about textuality and thereby offer a brief respite from the wearisome business of scanning, at a distance, a series of insufferably naive fantasies, then he or she is a heroically resistant reader – so resistant that one wonders why he or she bothers to read at all.[17]

We are left, then, in an in-between space created by the weakening of the masochistic and rationalistic vectors. In that space, a third undercurrent, a third motive force, stirs. That force manifests itself first in the kind of racism I have already described. It manifests itself next in Pym's reactions to natural objects. "At every step we took inland," Pym writes, "the conviction forced itself upon us that we were in a country differing essentially from any hitherto visited by civilized men.... The very rocks were novel in their mass, their color, and their stratification." The "magical-looking" water, striated by veins, "excited as profound [an] astonishment in the minds of our party as the mirror had done in the case of Too-wit." The water, in fact, "formed the first definite link in that vast chain of apparent miracles with which I was destined to be at length encircled" (*P&T*, 1140–1142). Rather than rising toward knowledge or falling toward obliteration, Pym is now spinning in place, finding "apparent miracles" everywhere he turns.

The circle of miracles closes swiftly over the course of the final chapter. Barreling south in a canoe, Pym notes "Many unusual phenomena now indicated that we were entering upon a region of novelty and wonder." The ocean is hot, and "of a milky consistency and hue"; a "high range of light gray vapor appeared constantly in the southern horizon." But he feels none of the alarm that one might expect him to feel, only "a *numbness* of mind and body – a dreaminess of sensation." Here as elsewhere in the chapter, the features of things are strangely dissociated from the things themselves, though they remain tied to those things grammatically, by means of the word "of." He goes on to report changes in the "heat of the water," the "agitation of the water," and the "glare of the water." He observes the "flaring up of the vapor," its decreasing "grayness of tint," and its increasing "distinctness of form." And when the figure in the vapor finally appears, he tells us first that it is "very far larger in its proportions than any dweller among men," and then that "the hue of the skin of the figure was of the perfect whiteness of the snow" (*P&T*, 1176–1179).

The peculiar structure of that climactic sentence causes the hue of the figure's skin to lift away from its skin, to become an instance of a formal quality – perfect whiteness – rather than an element in the description of the figure in the vapor.[18] It exemplifies what Gérard Genette calls "aspectual attention," a type of attention that concerns itself "not with the identity of the object ('what is it?') – and even less with its function ('what purpose does it serve?') – but rather with its outward appearance, its *aspect* – its contours and colors: 'what does it look like?' "[19] This is the kind of attention that Pym gives to the Tsalalians and to the natural objects on and beyond Tsalal. Because the Tsalalians transcend ordinary standards of ethnological measurement, they increasingly appear to him to be instances of a formal quality – perfect blackness – rather than beings with historical identities (as the writer of the "Note" would have it) or commercial functions (as the captain of the *Jane Guy* would have it). The natural objects on and beyond Tsalal are even more obviously without identities or functions: Pym's descriptions of these objects are no more than accounts of their color, shape, volume, heat, viscosity, and luminousness. In this context, the final sentence of Pym's narrative may be seen as the culmination of a brief but still distinctive movement toward a mode of existence that is predicated neither on a fantasy of going to pieces nor on a fantasy of wholeness. It is predicated, instead, on *not going beyond* the aspectual attention that characterizes the first moments of all perceptual encounters.

According to Henry James, it is this refusal to go behind appearances that causes the climax of the narrative to fail. In a famous reading, James declares that Pym "stops short, and stops short for want of connexions." The connections James refers to are those that are produced by the reader's identification with the "thickness" of "the human consciousness that entertains and records, that amplifies and interprets" the elements of its experience. If that consciousness is "thin," if it does nothing but detail the aspects of the elements of its experience, then there is no "further relation to the elements, which hang in the void; whereby we see the effect lost, the imaginative effort wasted."[20]

But identification with and through a thick consciousness is not the only possible mode of readerly identification. As Poe repeatedly insists, it is possible to imbibe delight from an aspectual attention to elements of experience that hang, successively, in a void. "In the quivering of a leaf – in the hue of a blade of grass – in the shape of a trefoil – in the humming of a bee – in the gleaming of a dew-drop – in the breathing of the wind – in the faint odors that came from the forest, there came a whole universe of suggestion – a gay and motley train of rhapsodical and immethodical thought," says the morphine-addicted Augustus Bedloe in "A Tale of the Ragged Mountains" (*P&T*, 658). In "The Poetic Principle," Poe writes that the poetic sentiment finds its origin and continuance "in the waving of grain fields – in the slanting of tall Eastern trees – in the blue distance of mountains – in the gleaming of silver rivers – in the repose of sequestered lakes – in the star-mirroring depth of lovely wells" (*E&R*, 93). One of the essential functions of poetry, for Poe, is to awaken in readers a sense of identity with a consciousness so "thin" that it perceives, everywhere, aspect alone – not a blade of grass, but "the hue of a blade of grass"; not grain fields, but "the waving of grain fields."

If it is a fantasy to imagine that one might permanently arrest one's consciousness in the perception of aspect alone, it is not at all fantastical to propose that the perception of aspect is the precondition of all conscious perception. One of Freud's most important postulates is that there is a delay between perception and consciousness, that we sense things before we know ourselves to be sensing things. Between these two activities, between perception and conscious perception, we classify according to aspect. "When I look at a red chair," Kaja Silverman writes, "it is classified at the level of my preconscious, at the very least, under the categories 'chair' and 'red object.'" The object is additionally classified "in more overtly evaluative ways," as, for instance, "cheap," or "only appropriate for children," or "art."[21] Only then does it enter the domain of conscious perception. According to this theory, which remains a crucial element of contemporary psychoanalysis, we receive each object that we consciously perceive in a doubly worked-over condition. By the time the representation of the object arrives in the domain of the ego, it has already been classified by aspect and evaluated, associatively, on that basis.

Why would Poe want to halt our awareness of what surrounds us and hold it, as long as possible, in an attention to aspect? Perhaps because he wishes to naturalize a cultural system in which differences of physical features – particularly those features associated with sex and race – are tacitly equated with differences of capacity and status. If Poe looks at an object and sees "white" and "woman," and associates these features with "purity," "docility," and "comfort," then the subsequent efforts of a Margaret Fuller to classify white woman as "nervous, forcible, thoughtful, suggestive, brilliant, and to a certain extent scholar-like" may appear to be little more than curious exceptions to an untroubled rule (*E&R*, 1172). Given that our unconscious associative linkages are culturally conditioned, it could be argued that Pym's rapt attention to aspect is a form of quietism, a luxurious immersion in the warm milk bath of the representational status quo.

But racist and patriarchal associations are not the only ones that wait alongside the road traversed by sense-images on their way toward consciousness. To quote Kaja Silverman again, "The attribution of psychic value to the red chair may work in ways that consolidate the dominant fiction, but...the reverse is also possible."[22] Toni Morrison's reading of the end of *Pym* is a case in point. "Whiteness" conventionally signifies privilege, competence, innocence, enterprise, refinement, and a whole host of other positive attributes.[23] But the whiteness of the figure in the vapor is, in Morrison's reading, "mute, meaningless, unfathomable, pointless, frozen, veiled, curtained, dreaded, senseless, implacable."[24] Though an attention to aspect may make it temporarily impossible to apply conscious scrutiny to unconscious aversions and affinities, it also provides more time for associations and feelings to cluster around the image. Stare too long at the wonder of whiteness, as Ishmael does in *Moby-Dick*, and it may begin to accrue a degree of horror. Stare too long at the horror of blackness, as Pym does on Tsalal, and it may begin to accrue a degree of wonder.

More than that: stare too long at the formal aspects of anything, and strange correspondences between oneself and that other thing may begin to emerge, throwing into question our most basic assumptions about the supposedly individual and inviolate ego. As Kaja Silverman observes, "what we are at the level of the ego may be a much more complex issue than we are accustomed to imagining, having to do not only with mothers, fathers, lovers, etc., but also with line, shape, composition, color."[25] During the stage of what Leo Bersani and Ulysse Dutoit call "prenarrative perception," we are all in communication with the formal aspects of the human and non-human worlds. One of the most important functions of art is to help us remember what it was like to have been born as a subject into a world of lines, shapes, colors, densities, and positions – to return us to the simultaneously painful and pleasurable "confusion of the 'I' and the 'non-I.'" "At its very highest," Bersani and Dutoit write, "art perhaps knows nothing but such confused beginnings, and in pushing us back to them it beneficently mocks the accumulated wisdom of culture."[26]

The conclusion of *Pym* may be read as just such a confused beginning, as an invitation to stop short, and so to start over. It may be read as an alternative to Pym's first effort to start over, in which he attempted to become the antithesis of the good white son, embracing all the pain that is promised to such apostates. That effort failed because it never took him outside the domain of the social; his identity as an apostate only existed by virtue of its contrast to the image of the disciple, and as he discovered on the wreck of the *Grampus*, he was not entirely willing to give up on the privileges associated with that idealized cultural image. But in the monstrous domain of "blackness" that is shadowed forth by the specter of cannibalism, he discovers another exit. It is as though the masochistic voyage of negation brings him to the edge of the social, where he discovers a strange pool, oscillating in appearance between dark opacity and silvered reflectiveness. The pursuit of transhuman knowledge is shadowed by the memory of this pool, and finally gives way, on Tsalal, to a simple contemplation of its occult transformations and relations. Seeing otherwise, Pym vanishes; the "Note" shows up to mark his absence, and to warn us away from any interest in Pym's subsequent life and death. The sequel to *Pym* begins at the vanishing point, and it belongs to us.

NOTES

1. David Halliburton, *Edgar Allan Poe: A Phenomenological View* (Princeton University Press, 1973), p. 257.
2. Karen Halttunen, *Confidence Men and Painted Women: A Study of Middle-class Culture in America, 1830–1870* (New Haven: Yale University Press, 1982), p. 20.
3. Emily Dickinson, *The Poems of Emily Dickinson*, ed. Thomas H. Johnson, 3 vols. (Cambridge, MA: The Belknap Press of Harvard University Press, 1955), poem 963.
4. Lyn Lofland, *A World of Strangers: Order and Action in Urban Public Space* (New York: Basic Books, 1973), p. 3.
5. Qtd. in Halttunen, *Confidence Men*, p. 6.
6. Qtd. in Halttunen, *Confidence Men*, p. 4.
7. Edward Everett, *Orations and Speeches on Various Occasions*, 2 vols. (Boston: C. C. Little and J. Brown, 1850), 1: 38.
8. Donald E. Pease, *Visionary Compacts: American Renaissance Writings in Cultural Context* (Madison: University of Wisconsin Press, 1987), p. 174.
9. Kaja Silverman, *Male Subjectivity at the Margins* (New York: Routledge, 1992), p. 206.
10. Geoffrey Sanborn, *The Sign of the Cannibal: Melville and the Making of a Postcolonial Reader* (Durham: Duke University Press, 1998), pp. 38–46.
11. R. Thomas, ed., *Interesting and Authentic Narratives of the Most Remarkable Shipwrecks, Fires, Famines, Calamities, Providential Deliverances, and Lamentable Disasters on the Seas* (Hartford: E. Strong, 1837), p. 183.
12. George Gordon, Lord Byron, *Byron's Don Juan: A Variorum Edition*, ed. Truman Guy Steffan and Willis W. Pratt, 4 vols. (Austin: University of Texas Press, 1971), canto 2, stanza 72.
13. Shawn James Rosenheim, *The Cryptographic Imagination: Secret Writing from Edgar Poe to the Internet* (Baltimore: Johns Hopkins University Press, 1997), p. 89.
14. Pease, *Visionary Compacts*, p. 167.
15. To get a sense of how pervasive this reading has been, see the excellent analytical surveys of criticism on Pym in Douglas Robinson, "Reading Poe's Novel: A Speculative Review of Pym Criticism, 1950–1980" *Poe Studies* 15 (1982): 47–54;

David Ketterer, "Tracing Shadows: Pym Criticism, 1980–1990," in Richard Kopley, ed., *Poe's Pym: Critical Explorations* (Durham: Duke University Press, 1992), pp. 233–274; J. Gerald Kennedy, *The Narrative of Arthur Gordon Pym and the Abyss of Interpretation* (New York: Twayne, 1995), pp. 14–28; and Ronald C. Harvey, *The Critical History of Edgar Allan Poe's The Narrative of Arthur Gordon Pym: "A Dialogue with Unreason,"* New York: Garland, 1998).

16. Garrett Stewart, *Dear Reader: The Conscripted Audience in Nineteenth-Century British Fiction* (Baltimore: Johns Hopkins University Press, 1996), p. 347.

17. It is worth noting in this context that Poe consistently praises the "power of *identification* with humanity at large" (*E&R*, 273). He ascribes this "power of simulation" (*E&R*, 873) on various occasions to Defoe, Boccaccio, Scott, Shakespeare, Lambert A. Wilmer, and himself. He asserts, moreover, that the author can only achieve this effect when he, too, "utterly loses sight of himself in his theme, and, for the time, identifies his own thoughts and feelings with the thoughts and feelings of fictitious existences" (*Complete Works* [Harrison], 8: 234). During the writing and reading of literature, we ideally "become perfect abstractions in the intensity of our interest" (*E&R*, 202).

18. My analysis here is indebted to Stephen Rachman's reading of "-ness" words in "Melville's *Pierre* and Nervous Exhaustion: Or "The Vacant Whirlingness of the Bewilderingness," *Literature and Medicine* 16 (1997): 226–249.

19. Gérard Genette, *The Aesthetic Relation*, trans. G. M. Goshgarian (Ithaca: Cornell University Press, 1999), p. 6.

20. Henry James, *Literary Criticism: French Writers, Other European Writers, The Prefaces to the New York Edition*, ed. Leon Edel and Mark Wilson (New York: Library of America, 1984), p. 1259.

21. Kaja Silverman, *The Threshold of the Visible World* (New York: Routledge, 1996), p. 180.

22. Silverman, *The Threshold of the Visible World,* p. 180.

23. Richard Dyer, *White* (New York: Routledge, 1997), pp. 21–24.

24. Toni Morrison, *Playing in the Dark: Whiteness and the Literary Imagination* (Cambridge: Harvard University Press, 1992), p. 59.

25. Tim Dean, Hal Foster, and Kaja Silverman, "A Conversation with Leo Bersani," *October* 82 (1997): 9.

26. Leo Bersani and Ulysse Dutoit, *Arts of Impoverishment: Beckett, Rothko, Resnais* (Cambridge, MA: Harvard University Press, 1993), pp. 89, 91.

11

SCOTT PEEPLES

Poe's "constructiveness" and "The Fall of the House of Usher"

Speaking at the University of Virginia's 1909 commemoration of the centenary of Poe's birth, University of North Carolina Professor C. Alphonso Smith described Poe's work habits in terms that might seem out of place with Poe's current popular reputation: "a patience and persistence worthy of Washington...a husbandry of details that suggest the thriftiness of Franklin...a native insight and inventiveness that proclaim him of the line of Edison." Like these other notable Americans, the practical-minded Poe excelled at putting things together. Indeed, according to Smith, Poe's contribution to world literature was his "constructiveness," his "structural art."[1] Although Smith put an unusually patriotic spin on his description, critics through the nineteenth and into the twentieth century had characterized Poe in similar, if less flattering, terms. Evert Duyckinck, in an 1850 review of Poe's collected works, compared him to a mechanical Swiss bell ringer, an "excellent machine," a writer who "lived apart from the solidities and realities of life: was an abstraction; thought, wrote, and dealt solely in abstractions"; and was "indifferent to flesh and blood subjects" (*CH*, 337). Alongside the more prevalent popular image of Poe the impoverished, drunken, misunderstood Romantic visionary, the image of Poe-the-engineer has persisted, mostly among scholars who explore Poe's interest in intellectual games and detection.[2] When these two Poes meet, it is usually in discussions of his theories of fiction and poetry, in which he applies something that sounds like a mathematical principle to the creation of art. In "The Philosophy of Composition," particularly, Poe fostered the image of himself as a mechanic who, with words, could inspire emotion without actually feeling it. Similarly, in his theory of the short story, he emphasizes the high ratio of calculation to inspiration required to create lasting art.

Teachers and critics like to use "The Fall of the House of Usher" to demonstrate Poe's adherence to his own principles of good construction – it has long been recognized as one of his best stories – but "Usher" is a particularly apt story for examining Poe's "constructiveness" for other reasons as

178

well. First and foremost, it is about a house, and in no other Poe tale is the house itself so central to both a story's plot and its network of symbolism. If, as he claimed, Poe saw himself as a builder, he might well inscribe his personal philosophy of architecture into this fictional house. Indeed, the stories Poe wrote immediately before and after "Usher" in 1838 and 1839 show a preoccupation with building and arranging. "Ligeia" (September 1838), a story closely related to "Usher" in its themes and Gothic atmosphere, hinges upon a description of the design and decoration of a single room, the pentagonal chamber in which the narrator psychologically tortures his second wife Rowena and witnesses the return of his deceased first wife Ligeia. In "William Wilson" (October 1839), the story Poe published immediately after "Usher," he raises the symbolic stakes by having Wilson describe the structure of his old schoolhouse in a manner that clearly suggests the "subdivisions" of the human mind. The three comic tales Poe wrote between "Ligeia" and "Usher" satirize other forms of architecture, the formulaic construction of magazine stories in "How to Write a Blackwood Article" (November 1838, originally titled "The Psyche Zenobia") and the (literal) making of a hero in "The Man That Was Used Up" (August 1839). Even "The Devil in the Belfry" (May 1839) takes a kind of construction – clock time and the "structured" life – as its target. Moreover, Poe's fondness for metafictional self-reference seems to have peaked around this same time. "How to Write a Blackwood Article" lampoons the style of the magazine Poe studied and imitated; "William Wilson" contains more autobiographical references than any other tale by Poe, including the birthday shared by Poe and Wilson and the setting at the English school Poe attended in 1818; and *The Narrative of Arthur Gordon Pym*, published the year before "Usher," contains numerous winking references to Poe, the ostensible "editor" of Pym's narrative. In short, other works from the late 1830s show Poe to be preoccupied with construction as a theme or trope and unusually prone to self-reference in his fiction, supporting the idea that "Usher" might be read in terms of Poe's own concerns as a builder of literature.

As critics have long noted, "The Fall of the House of Usher" is carefully structured, with the interpolated (and previously published) poem, "The Haunted Palace," positioned appropriately in the middle to function as a *mise en abyme*, a miniature of the story that contains it. One can see the tale, as Thomas Woodson does, as divided into three parts: the first introducing the house and the Ushers, the second developing Roderick Usher's aesthetics and his relationship with his sister, and the third beginning after Madeline's burial with the build-up toward her reappearance and ending with the house's collapse.[3] Alternatively, one can simply see "The Haunted Palace" dividing the story in two, in keeping with its dominant motif of doubling and reflection. The list of paired characters, events, places, and objects that can be regarded as doubles for their more-than-coincidental resemblance testifies to the density of Poe's construction, and perhaps to the ingenuity of literary critics: the twins Roderick and Madeline; Roderick and the narrator, who eventually becomes "infected" by his friend's condition; Roderick's abstract but vault-like painting and the vault where Madeline is buried; "The Haunted Palace" and "The Fall of the House of Usher"; "The Mad Trist" – the Gothic romance the narrator reads to Usher – and the events that echo its sounds in the house; the thunderstorm and the tumultuous climax of the story. Then there is the house, which is "doubled" or reflected in the tarn, but also reflected in the double-meaning of "house," referring to the family as well as their dwelling, and more specifically reflected in Roderick, whose poem likens the "palace" to its master; or, if the story is a kind of dream or psychological journey of the narrator, as several critics have suggested, the house may express the psyche of the narrator.[4] In addition to these (and other) instances of doubling, the House of Usher reflects "The Fall of the House of Usher" in the sense that I have already suggested, that Poe uses the house to reflect upon literary structures.

The doubling motif is itself doubled by Poe's tendency to repeat words and verbal structures throughout "The Fall of the House of Usher," which begins with the following sentence:

> During the whole of a dull, dark, and soundless day in the autumn of the year, when the clouds hung oppressively low in the heavens, I had been passing alone, on horseback, through a singularly dreary tract of country; and at length found myself, as the shades of the evening drew on, within view of the melancholy House of Usher. (*P&T*, 317)

The motionlessness of this opening sentence, reflecting the morbid scene it describes, can be best illustrated by a sentence diagram (see Figure 11.1). The main subject-verb constructions – "I had been passing," "I found (myself)" – are so weak and buried as to be unnoticeable amidst the evocative but hardly vivid descriptions conveyed by the sentence's thirteen prepositional phrases, which, when read aloud, seem to echo one another without moving the sentence forward. The verbs of the subordinate clauses similarly evoke atmosphere without activity: "clouds hung," "shades...drew." By diagramming and counting prepositional phrases, I am in a sense replicating the narrator's attempt to analyze the house before him; but as the narrator observes later in the first paragraph, you can rearrange "the particulars of the scene...the details of the picture," and still find yourself under its spell. His comments on the scene before him – the house reflected in the tarn – might well apply to our reading of that first sentence, or the entire

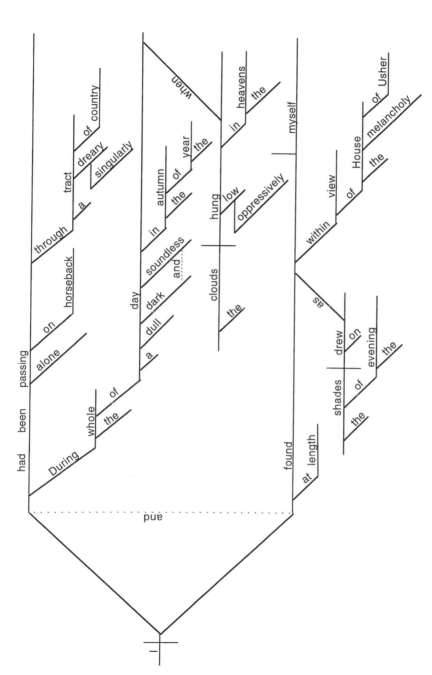

Figure 11.1 A diagram of opening sentence of "The Fall of the House of Usher." Prepared by Scott Peeples and Myung-Sook Hayes.

story: "What was it – I paused to think – what was it that so unnerved me in the contemplation of the House of Usher? It was a mystery all insoluble" (*P&T*, 317).

Repetitions such as "What was it" in the sentence just quoted abound in the story, increasing the sense of inertia and textual opacity. Examples are concentrated in the opening paragraph: one sentence contains six phrases beginning with "upon"; another contains four consecutive three-word phrases beginning with "of" – "of the particulars of the scene, of the details of the picture"; the second half of that same sentence contains seven "and"s. Another sentence slithers through the alliterative compound adjectives: "an iciness, a sinking, a sickening of the heart." More subtle examples of verbal repetitions occur throughout the story: "very trifling and very temporary variation"; "there grew in my mind a strange fancy – a fancy so ridiculous"; "Our books – the books which, for years" (*P&T*, 317–319, 328). While supporting the structural principal of doubling, these repetitions call attention to the words *as words*. Perhaps not surprisingly, two of the most recent articles on "Usher" have referred to the story as a hall or house of mirrors, suggesting the way that words in this story give the illusion of depth while actually keeping readers focused on the mirror-like surface of words.[5]

Poe's wordplay reinforces the parallel between house and text. Dennis Pahl, understanding the word "text" as Quintilian did, that is, to mean the woven tissue of a literary work, enumerates the references to woven material in descriptions of the house and its owner: "The house is composed of a 'fabric [that at the narrator's first glance] gave little token of its instability,'"[6] to which I would add that the house is specifically referred to as "fabric" in "The Haunted Palace," through the metaphor that closes the first stanza: "Never seraph spread a pinion / Over fabric half so fair" (*P&T*, 326). Pahl then points out the "wild gossamer texture" of Roderick's hair, the fact that "he could wear only garments of a certain texture," the walls covered with tapestries and the fretted or interlaced ceiling.[7] Even the "ebon blackness of the floors" of the house can reasonably be read as an allusion to Poe's literary architecture: Stuart and Susan Levine argue that this ebony wood is a code name for *Blackwood's Edinburgh Magazine*, a major influence on Poe, who had lampooned its tales of sensation in print less than a year before "Usher."[8]

The narrator's paradoxical description of the house's construction has suggested to various readers an Enlightenment tradition still standing but about to collapse, the similarly precarious conventions of Gothic fiction employed and parodied in "Usher," and Usher's (or the narrator's, or anyone's) fragile psyche,[9] but it also evokes the construction of "The Fall of the House of Usher," and by extension every Poe text and, one might argue, every text: the house is greatly discolored and covered with fungi, "[y]et all this was apart from any extraordinary dilapidation. No portion of the masonry had fallen; and there appeared to be a wild inconsistency between its still perfect adaptation of parts, and the crumbling condition of the individual stones" (*P&T*, 318–19). Pahl and, more recently, Harriet Hustis have equated the house's stones to individual words, and their "perfect adaptation of parts" to "the syntax of sentences, the careful arrangement of words."[10] Roderick believes that the dead stones that make up his house are sentient, and given the fact that they collapse in sympathy with his fall, the story suggests that the house *is* in some way alive. Likewise, the words themselves, like the Gothic conventions that Poe pieces together, are "dead," but Poe's construction brings the house to life.[11] Poe's description in the *Twice-Told Tales* review of the work of "a skillful literary artist" who had "constructed" a tale suggests a further correspondence, with its emphasis on careful arrangement of sentences and incidents to serve a preconceived effect:

> In the whole composition there should be no word written, of which the tendency, direct or indirect, is not to the one pre-established design. And by such means, with such care and skill, a picture is at length painted which leaves in the mind of him who contemplates it with a kindred art, a sense of the fullest satisfaction. The idea of the tale has been presented unblemished, because undisturbed. (*E&R*, 572)[12]

This brief passage not only reinforces Poe's emphasis on arrangement of parts, but also suggests the scene of the narrator's confrontation of the house in two other respects. Like the "undisturbed" tale, the house reminds the narrator of "the specious totality of old wood-work which has rotted for long years in some neglected vault, with no disturbance from the breath of the external air" (*P&T*, 320). And because the narrator, in crossing the causeway, is about to enter this closed universe of Usher, he resembles the ideal reader who "contemplates it with a kindred art."

As Pahl argues, the notion of being "inside" a container is a key structural element in the story. Indeed, in most instances of doubling in the story, one of the doubles is in fact contained by the other: the two interpolated texts, "The Haunted Palace" and "The Mad Trist," are performed inside a haunted palace where a really mad tryst takes place; the painting of the vault is displayed inside a house that is itself sealed up in its own atmosphere; Roderick is inside (and never leaves) the house that reflects his psyche; at the story's end the storm outside reflects the tumult within the house; the house, in turn, is ultimately swallowed by the tarn that reflects it.[13] The emphasis Poe places on containment through his network of images and symbols underscores a reading of the story as a tragedy brought about by the Usher family's attempt to control or seal in their private world, in the manner of Prospero in "The Masque of the Red Death." The Usher line, whether literally incestuous or not, has, paradoxically, contaminated itself by trying to remain pure – that is, by trying to contain and control the family lineage just as they have secluded themselves in a house so isolated that it has its own weather system. Both "houses," for all their careful arrangement, are doomed to collapse.[14]

What does that collapse suggest about Poe's carefully constructed fiction? For Charles May, the house's implosion demonstrates Poe's proto-deconstructionist vision, for the "story deconstructs just as the house does, just as everything collapses back into formulated precreation nothingness and the tale ends on the italicized words of its own title."[15] Similarly, Pahl argues that "the structure of the story, like the structure of the house, is always already in a state of collapse."[16] Yet the fall of "The Fall of the House of Usher" is not an admission of failure on Poe's part but a further assertion of the writer's control; what matters is that the writer or artist controls the structure, even when that means bringing down the house through what might be described as "controlled demolition."

Poe emphasizes the writer or artist's uncanny power over his audience throughout the story – Usher's letter imploring the narrator to visit "allowed [him] no room for hesitation" (*P&T*, 318), and Usher's vault-like painting and musical performances seem to cast a spell over him. Introducing Usher's "The Haunted Palace," the narrator remarks, "I was, perhaps, the more forcibly impressed with it, as he gave it, because, in the under or mystic current of its meaning, I fancied that I perceived, and for the first time, a full consciousness on the part of Usher, of the tottering of his lofty reason upon her throne" (*P&T*, 325). In other words, the narrator now understands that Usher understands his own loss of reason, but the sentence emphasizes the *narrator's* reception of Usher's song: "I" was impressed, "I fancied," "I perceived." By the night of Madeline's return, the narrator's movements imitate Usher's: while Usher "roamed from chamber to chamber with hurried, unequal, and objectless step," the narrator "endeavored to arouse myself from the pitiable condition into which I had fallen, by pacing rapidly to and fro through the apartment." At the same time, he reports that Usher's condition not only "terrified" but "infected" him: "I felt it creeping upon me, by slow yet certain degrees, the wild influences of his own fantastic yet impressive superstitions" (*P&T*, 330–331).

For all his power over the narrator, Usher is himself susceptible to the influence of other writers' texts; as if answering the call of his own imp of the perverse, Usher, who, claims he has nothing to fear but fear itself, surrounds himself with occult literature.[17] But the most forceful insistence upon the power of writing or art to "move" its audience comes at the story's climax, as the narrator reads to Usher from "The Mad Trist" of Sir Launcelot Canning. The narrator's reference to the "well-known portion of the story" is a tease, of course, since both the "antique volume" and its author are Poe's inventions, and as a number of critics have pointed out, "The Mad Trist" is parodic, "purposefully ludicrous," according to G. R. Thompson.[18] This story, which the narrator calls "uncouth and unimaginative," full of extreme "folly," breaks Poe's spell, for how can we take this dungeons-and-dragons tale seriously? But then, how can we take *any* of this outdated haunted-palace Gothicism seriously? That is precisely the mirror Poe turns back on us in planting "The Mad Trist" into the story's climax: Usher does take it seriously; Madeline seems to be summoned by it; the house itself is awakened to life by it. Although I don't want to overstate the comic effect of "The Mad Trist" (much less "Usher"), the inner narrative functions much like the Mickey Mouse cartoon at the climax of Preston Sturges' film *Sullivan's Travels*: the inner text or film is not a *mise en abyme* reflecting the plot of the story that contains it, but it represents a crude form of the larger story's genre – film comedy, Gothic tale – and, through its very crudeness, releases the energies that give the genre much of its appeal. The cartoon appears in *Sullivan's Travels* after the film has taken a decidedly serious turn; but when Sullivan and the rest of the audience of prisoners watching the cartoon laugh uncontrollably, *Sullivan's Travels* not only becomes a comedy again but in so doing asserts the power and purpose of comedy. Similarly, "The Mad Trist" calls out the supernatural in Poe's house: Madeline (who up until now has merely been making some barely perceptible noise down in the cellar) suddenly has the impossible strength to break through a screwed-down coffin lid and open a heavy iron door, and the house, whose sentience was previously described as a delusion of Usher's, now actually seems animate, if only for the time it takes to fall. Oddly, the very moment at which Poe reminds us, via "The Mad Trist," that this is only a story, only another example of Gothic clap-trap, he shows how powerful such stories can be, and, according to many readers I have talked to over the years, achieves the spine-tingling effect that can come only when one is not thinking "this is only a story" but is instead under the spell of, or "inside," the text.[19]

That paradox of the author telling us not to fall for what the author actually does intend us to fall for recurs throughout Poe's work. Montresor cannot murder Fortunato without repeatedly tipping him off as to his intentions, knowing his enemy will fall into his trap anyway; the Minister D— hides the purloined letter in plain sight, as if to say, "Here it is, but you won't see it." Virtually all of Poe's hoaxes or near-hoaxes – "Hans Pfaall," "The Facts in the Case of M. Valdemar," "Von Kempelen and His Discovery" – contain overt warnings not to be duped. Poe even "exposes" his own mechanical approach to writing in "The Philosophy of Composition," however much he fabricated the explanation, in order to demonstrate his ingenuity, as if his poetic masterpiece had really been a kind of trick; he knew that to reveal the "wheels and pinions . . . the step-ladders and demon-traps" (*E&R*, 14) would not lessen the emotional effect the poem had on readers. While readers too often assume that Poe closely resembles his own perverse characters, one respect in which he really does resemble them is that he insists on showing his work, hiding his "signature" in plain sight. Louis Renza describes this tendency as Poe's "verbal static," directed "toward revealing to its imagined reader the word-mediated traces of its author, the man in the text-as-machine [a reference to Poe's essay on Maelzel's automaton chess player], for no apparent reason other than to confront his reader with an autobiographical terminus."[20] Even as we're getting "lost" in the House of *Usher*, the self-referential devices – elaborate sentence structures, texts within the text, relentless use of doubling and reflection – keep pushing us back outside the story, reminding us that *Poe* is the real master of the house. Commentators have long noted that the narrator's description of Usher bears a striking resemblance to Poe:

> A cadaverousness of complexion; an eye large, liquid, and luminous beyond comparison; lips somewhat thin and very pallid, but of a surpassingly beautiful curve; a nose of delicate Hebrew model, but with a breath of nostril unusual in similar formations; a finely moulded chin, speaking, in its want of prominence, of a want of moral energy; hair of a more than web-like softness and tenuity; these features, with an inordinate expansion above the regions of the temple, made up altogether a countenance not easily forgotten. (*P&T*, 321)

Perhaps the most suggestive details – the pale complexion, large eyes, alleged want of moral energy, and large forehead – are coincidental, or perhaps they are another example from the period of *Pym* and "William Wilson" of Poe playfully embedding his signature into the text. If this is the case, we might regard it as another signal to read the house of Usher as Poe's house of fiction.

While Poe theorized the tale as a closed system, with every word contributing to a single pre-conceived effect, his own tales often present situations where a closed space ("Loss of Breath," ' "The Murders in the Rue Morgue," "The Masque of the Red Death," "The Premature Burial," ' "Thou Art the Man!' " "The Purloined Letter") or a perfect plot ("The Tell-Tale Heart," "The Black Cat," "The Imp of the Perverse") is disrupted: the closed space wasn't really closed, the perfect crime was foiled by conscience or perversity, or, as in "Usher," the "corpse" wasn't really dead. Again and again Poe tells us that control is an illusion, and yet he insists that the work of fiction itself remain under control. Accordingly, when all hell breaks loose in "Usher," the house, which in so many ways seems to represent Poe's storymaking, consumes itself, collapsing violently but completely, into the tarn: the story is over, the text vanishes as the narrator escapes the collapsing building just as the reader closes the book.

But of course, the book will be opened again, the narrator will go back over the causeway and the reader will follow him through that maze of prepositional phrases; Poe suggests as much by ending the story with an echo of the title, "the fragments of the *House of Usher*.'" Almost a decade after the publication of "Usher," Poe would write at length about that process of repeated collapse and rebirth, and apply it to the workings of the universe, in his cosmological prose poem *Eureka*. According to Poe, the universe is contracting, as gravity pulls all matter together:

> In sinking into Unity, it will sink at once into that Nothingness which, to all infinite perception, Unity must be – into that Material Nihility from which alone we can conceive it to have been evoked – to have been *created* by the Volition of God.... But are we here to pause? Not so. On the Universal agglomeration and dissolution, we can readily conceive that a new and perhaps totally different series of conditions may ensue – another action and reaction of the Divine Will.... [A]re we not, indeed, more than justified in entertaining a belief – let us say, rather, in indulging a hope – that the process we have here ventured to contemplate will be renewed forever, and forever, and forever; a novel Universe swelling into existence, and then subsiding into nothingness, at every throb of the Heart Divine? (*P&T*, 1355–1356)

As Maurice Beebe points out, "The house of Usher is like the universe not only in that everything is related but also in that it is limited."[21] That is, this universe that repeatedly contracts into nothingness and then is reborn with a big bang can be entered and left, just as the closed system of the Usher house is entered and left by the narrator, and just as the closed system of a work of fiction can be entered and left by a reader; in Beebe's words, "Poe permits us to crack the shell with the narrator."[22]

Poe explicitly parallels this vision of the universe with his theory of the short story as a closed system. He argues that if humans were confronted with evidence of the universe ceasing to exist, we

> should have been forced to regard the Universe with some such sense of dissatisfaction as we experience in contemplating an unnecessarily complex work of human art. Creation would have affected us as an imperfect *plot* in a romance, where the denouement is awkwardly brought along by interposed incidents external and foreign to the main subject; instead of springing from the bosom of our thesis ... as inseparable and inevitable part and parcel of the fundamental conception of the book. (*P&T*, 1352)

Elsewhere in *Eureka* he proclaims that we appreciate "fictitious literature" to the degree that it accords with the perfection of the universe: "In this sense, of course, perfection of plot is really, or practically, unattainable – but only because it is a finite intelligence that constructs. The plots of God are perfect. The Universe is a plot of God" (*P&T*, 1342). This human longing to achieve a perfection reserved for the heavens recalls Poe's early poem "Israfel," in which the poet compares himself to the angel "whose heartstrings are a lute," a model of artistic perfection Poe invokes in the epigraph to "Usher":

> Son coeur est un luth suspendu;
> Sitôt qu'on le touche il résonne.
>
> [His heart is a lute;
> touch it, and at once it sounds.]
> (*P&T* 317, 1392)

The ethereal artist whose heartstrings are a lute would seem to be Usher, who looks a lot like Poe, the cosmologist who understands the universe as a work of art. Reading *Eureka*, in fact, one comes to see the work not so much as a theory of the known universe but as a parallel universe created by Poe; the text and its subject merge in his preface when he claims, "*What I propound here is* true: – therefore it cannot die: – or if by any means it be now trodden down so that it die, it will 'rise again to Life Everlasting'" (*P&T*, 1259). In other words, the plots of Poe are perfect.

The similarities to *Eureka* testify to the centrality of "The Fall of the House of Usher" in the Poe canon; moreover, these similarities suggest that "Usher" is not just an example of Poe's "constructiveness" but a story about its own construction. It is also a story about control: just as *Eureka* is a kind of control fantasy in which Poe identifies himself with the creator of the universe, in "Usher" he identifies himself with an artist who has made his house a universe, and then he enacts the artist's fantasy of bringing that dead house to life: the "blood-red moon" through the fissure gives the appearance of blood gushing from the house, and the last sound the narrator hears is "a long tumultuous shouting sound like the voice of a thousand waters" (*P&T*, 335–336). Paradoxically, the house comes to life only to collapse and die, but for Poe, the paradox works both ways: the fall of the house gives rise to the story, which "lives" off paradox and other uncanny verbal structures.

NOTES

1. C. Alphonso Smith, "The Americanism of Poe," in *The Book of the Poe Centenary: A Record of the Exercises at the University of Virginia January 16–19, 1909, in Commemoration of the One Hundredth Birthday of Edgar Allan Poe*,

eds. Charles W. Kent and John S. Patton (Charlottesville: University of Virginia, 1909), pp. 163–164.

2. See, for instance, John T. Irwin, *The Mystery to a Solution: Poe, Borges, and the Analytic Detective Story* (Baltimore: Johns Hopkins University Press, 1994), and Shawn James Rosenheim, *The Cryptographic Imagination: Secret Writing from Edgar Poe to the Internet* (Baltimore: Johns Hopkins University Press, 1997).

3. Thomas Woodson, "Introduction," *Twentieth-Century Interpretations of "The Fall of the House of Usher": A Collection of Critical Essays*, ed. Thomas Woodson (Englewood Cliffs, NJ: Prentice-Hall, 1969), p. 15.

4. Richard Wilbur, "The House of Poe," in *Recognition*, pp. 265–267; Daniel Hoffman, *Poe Poe Poe Poe Poe Poe Poe* (1972; reprinted, Baton Rouge: Louisiana State University Press, 1998), pp. 299–300; and G. R. Thompson, *Poe's Fiction: Romantic Irony in the Gothic Tales* (Madison: University of Wisconsin Press, 1973), pp. 96–97.

5. David Ketterer, " 'Shudder': A Signature Cryptogram in 'The Fall of the House of Usher,' " *Resources for American Literary Study* 25 (1999): 197; Harriet Hustis, " 'Reading Encrypted But Persistent': the Gothic of Reading and Poe's 'The Fall of the House of Usher,' " *Studies in American Fiction* 27 (Spring 1999): 19.

6. Dennis Pahl, *Architects of the Abyss: The Indeterminate Fictions of Poe, Hawthorne, and Melville* (Columbia: University of Missouri Press, 1989), p. 9. For other readings that regard the house as analogous to the story, see Ib Johansen, "The Madness of the Text: Deconstruction of Narrative Logic in 'Usher,' 'Berenice,' and 'Doctor Tarr and Professor Fether,' " *Poe Studies* 22 (June 1989): 1–9; and Hustis, "Reading Encrypted but Persistent."

7. Pahl, *Architects of the Abyss*, p. 9.

8. Stuart Levine and Susan Levine, eds., *Edgar Allan Poe: Thirty-Two Stories* (Indianapolis: Hackett, 2000), p. 90n.

9. See Michael J. Hoffman, "The House of Usher and Negative Romanticism," *Studies in Romanticism* 4 (Spring 1965): 159–168; Benjamin Franklin Fisher IV, "Playful 'Germanism' in 'The Fall of the House of Usher,' " in *Ruined Eden of the Present: Hawthorne, Melville, and Poe: Critical Essays in Honor of Darrel Abel*, eds. G. R. Thompson and Virgil L. Lokke (West Lafayette: Purdue University Press, 1981), 355–374; and Edward H. Davidson, *Poe: A Critical Study* (Cambridge, MA: Harvard University Press, 1957), pp. 196–198.

10. Pahl, *Architects of the Abyss*, p. 18.

11. Pahl, *Architects of the Abyss*, p. 19.

12. See E. Arthur Robinson, "Order and Sentience in 'The Fall of the House of Usher,' " *PMLA* 76 (March 1961): 68–81, esp. 69, where he makes a similar connection to Poe's review of *Twice-Told Tales*. Robinson also draws useful parallels among "Usher," *Eureka*, and "The Colloquy of Monos and Una."

13. See Maurice Beebe, *Ivory Towers and Sacred Founts: The Artist as Hero from Goethe to Joyce* (New York University Press, 1964), pp. 120–121; Pahl, *Architects of the Abyss*, pp. 19–21.

14. In *Edgar Allan Poe Revisited* (New York: Twayne), pp. 84–88, I assert that Roderick and Madeline are "children of incest," a claim that should be qualified, since there is no "proof" of it in the story.

15. Charles E. May, *Edgar Allan Poe: A Study of the Short Fiction* (Boston: Twayne, 1991), p. 107.

16. Pahl, *Architects of the Abyss*, p. 21.
17. Levine and Levine, eds., *Edgar Allan Poe: Thirty-Two Stories*, p. 97n.
18. Thompson, *Poe's Fiction*, p. 95. See also Fisher, "Playful 'Germanism,'" p. 363; Darrel Abel, "A Key to the House of Usher," in *Twentieth-Century Interpretations*, p. 53; and James M. Cox, "Edgar Poe: Style as Pose," in *Twentieth-Century Interpretations*, p. 115.
19. See Michael T. Gilmore, "Words and Things in Antebellum American Literature: Notes Toward an Interpretation," in *Brandeis Essays in Literature*, ed. John Hazel Smith (Waltham, MA: Brandeis University, 1983), pp. 90–91.
20. Louis Renza, "Poe's Secret Autobiography," in *The American Renaissance Reconsidered*, ed. Walter Benn Michaels and Donald E. Pease (Baltimore: Johns Hopkins University Press, 1985), p. 62. See also Ketterer, "'Shudder.'"
21. Beebe, *Ivory Towers and Sacred Founts*, p. 120.
22. Beebe, *Ivory Towers and Sacred Founts*, p. 120.

12

RICHARD KOPLEY AND KEVIN J. HAYES

Two verse masterworks: "The Raven" and "Ulalume"

Many poets who have commented on Poe's verse have expressed amazement regarding the relative paucity of his poetic output in relation to his status as a great poet. William Carlos Williams observed that though Poe is known as a poet, "there are but five poems, possibly three." In his essay, "From Poe to Valéry," T. S. Eliot noted, "He wrote very few poems, and of those few only half a dozen have had a great success: but those few are as well known to as large a number of people, are as well remembered by everybody, as any poems ever written." Daniel Hoffman has called Poe's poetic oeuvre "one of the teeniest bodies of verse of any poet the world has applauded for over a century." In his sonnet, "For a Copy of Poe's Poems," Edward Arlington Robinson eloquently characterized Poe's poetic output as "wonder-songs, fantastically few."[1] Some have their special favorites – H.D., who named Poe her "favorite among American writers," preferred "To Helen"; William Carlos Williams, "To One in Paradise"; Robert Pinsky, "Fairy-Land"[2] – yet many agree that Poe's two finest poems are "The Raven" and "Ulalume."

"The Raven": composition, thematics, influence

More than one hundred and fifty years after Poe's death, "The Raven" is alive and well. The poem about the bird of ill omen visiting the melancholy student is a shared cultural property, its first line adapted for the first line of Blues Traveler's "Runaround," its immortal visitor comically re-immortalized on television as Bart Simpson and on the playing field as the Baltimore Ravens. Regularly anthologized, "The Raven" is read, analyzed, and discussed in middle schools, high schools, colleges and universities, and elderhostels. In myriad translations, it is studied around the world. If it does not have the cachet of modernist or postmodernist poetry, it does have an alluring mix of accessibility and mystery that earns it enduring affection. It is a remarkable poem about remembering – and a work that readers never forget. It invites our continued attention.

Of some details we cannot be certain. Poe stated in his revealing but not-always-reliable essay on his writing "The Raven," "The Philosophy of Composition," that the raven had originally been a parrot (*E&R*, 18). Susan Archer Weiss tells us in her informative but not-always-dependable book on Poe that he said that it had once been an owl.[3] According to Poe, he had preferred the raven for its tone; according to Weiss, he had preferred it for the sake of the refrain, "Nevermore." Probably both parrot and owl have a legitimate claim. And probably the raven had been encouraged by Poe's encounter with the raven in Charles Dickens's novel *Barnaby Rudge*. Poe had reviewed the book in 1841 and 1842: he first stated that the raven's "croakings are to be frequently, appropriately, and prophetically heard in the course of the narrative," but he later shifted his view, wishing that its "croakings might have been *prophetically* heard in the course of the drama" (*E&R*, 222, 243). Perhaps he was coming to consider how Dickens's raven might be improved upon effectively.

We cannot know for sure if, as Weiss maintained, "The Raven" had been written intermittently over a period of ten years – or, as F. W. Thomas asserted so improbably, in a day.[4] We cannot know for sure what form the poem took when Poe apparently recited it near Saratoga, New York (now the Yaddo Artists' Colony), in 1843, or when he apparently submitted it to *Graham's Magazine* in Philadelphia, also in 1843. However, we can be reasonably sure that, as Poe says in "The Philosophy of Composition," he wanted to write a popular and critically successful poem, he wished the poem to be readable at a single sitting, and he intended the work to elevate the soul of the reader. Probably, in its earlier versions, the poem already concerned "the most poetical topic in the world": "the death . . . of a beautiful woman" (*E&R*, 19).

We can be confident that in 1844 Poe was working on a version of "The Raven" close to that finally published since it was in that year Elizabeth Barrett Barrett's poem "Lady Geraldine's Courtship" appeared. This work, reviewed by Poe in early January 1845, offered the metrical model for "The Raven." Indeed, Poe candidly acknowledged in "The Philosophy of Composition" that he had offered "no originality" with regard to the poem's rhythm or meter (*E&R*, 21). Suggestively, Poe's 1845 collection *The Raven, and Other Poems* was dedicated to Barrett.

The meter of both Barrett's poem and Poe's is generally trochaic octameter. That is, the lines of each work are built of a series of paired syllables (feet), the first syllable of which is stressed and the second unstressed; there are eight feet to each line. We may compare the meter of the first line of "Lady Geraldine's Courtship" with that of the first line of "The Raven."

"Lady Geraldine's Courtship":
> Dear my friend and fellow-student, I would lean my
>   spirit o'er you![5]

"The Raven":
> Once upon a midnight dreary, while I pondered, weak and
>   weary   (*P&T*, 81)

It should be added that Poe is reported to have said that his poem had been prompted by a particular line of Barrett's poem.[6] A comparison of that line and the relevant one of Poe's will indicate that he was at least indebted to her line, which he ably transformed.

"Lady Geraldine's Courtship":
> With a rushing stir, uncertain, in the air, the purple
>   curtain[7]

"The Raven":
> And the silken, sad, uncertain rustling of each purple
>   curtain   (*P&T*, 82)

And scholarship has noted that the refrain "Nevermore" had many possible origins, from Byron to Longfellow.[8] Doubtless Poe's reading contributed in significant ways, known and unknown, to his writing "The Raven." But his probable indebtedness in no way lessens his achievement. As he wrote himself in 1840, a work of imagination is akin to a griffin – a creature half lion, half eagle – that is, an unusual combination of already-existing elements (*E&R*, 334). What matters, then, is the author's power of combination, his or her ability to bring together and transform. In the case of "The Raven," Poe created a work truly as fantastic as any griffin.

We may note literary techniques that Poe employed beyond a sophisticated meter and a haunting refrain. His rhyme scheme is consistently ABCBBB, and, like Barrett, he occasionally offered a rippling internal rhyme – "dreary," "weary"; "napping," "tapping"; "uttered," "fluttered." His use of alliteration is compelling, effectively contributing to the lulling, incantatory quality of the language. Alliteration is evident in the two lines already quoted from "The Raven" (as is internal rhyme in the first of these lines); both of these literary techniques are employed repeatedly throughout the poem, as in the following couplet:

> Deep into that darkness peering, long I stood there
>   wondering, fearing,
> Doubting, dreaming dreams no mortal ever dared to dream
>   before   (*P&T*, 82)

Occasionally, too, Poe offered suggestive allusion – to mythology ("Pallas" – Pallas Athena, the goddess of wisdom; "Plutonian" – related to Pluto, god of the underworld) and to the Bible ("is there balm in Gilead?" drawn from the biblical "Is there no balm in Gilead; is there no physician there? why then is not the health of the daughter of my people recovered?" [Jeremiah 8:22]).

Clearly Poe was a consummate craftsman. And he asserts in "The Philosophy of Composition" the primacy of reason in his constructing the poem – including his developing the ending first, his concentrating on a single unity of effect, and his intensifying the effect with a limited physical space and the progression of the student's questions. Yet the highly-reasoned process that Poe argues for also honors emotion: the student mourns his lost beloved and seems to enjoy perversely the pain of his loss. (See, in this connection, Poe's tale "The Imp of the Perverse.") Furthermore, there was in Poe's life a personal connection with "the death...of a beautiful woman," one not explicitly acknowledged in "The Philosophy of Composition." The impetus for the poem doubtless arose, at least in part, from Poe's loss of his mother – and of others whom he had loved. Although Poe contends that the process of composition of the poem was ultra-rational, the motive for the poem seems to have been unreasoning sorrow.

Edgar Poe was not yet three years old when his mother, Eliza Arnold Poe, died in Richmond, Virginia – probably of "consumption" – tuberculosis. She had been a gifted comic actress and a great beauty – her presence on stage had regularly elicited "involuntary bursts of rapture" (*Log*, 11). Poe grew up to know well of his mother's renown and radiance, and he wrote in 1845 that "no earl was ever prouder of his earldom than he of his descent from a woman who, although well-born, hesitated not to consecrate to the drama her brief career of genius and of beauty."[9] The death of his mother very probably contributed to his writing "The Raven."

And there were losses of other women whom Poe had loved, as well: the death of surrogate mother Jane Stith Stanard in 1824, the termination of his romance with young Elmira Royster in 1826, the death of foster mother Frances Allan in 1829. Moreover, as he worked on "The Raven," he may well have anticipated the death of his "young, gentle, and idolized wife" Virginia[10]: the onset of her tuberculosis occurred three years before the poem was published (and she died two years after it appeared).

Finally, there was another critical loss for Poe – the death of his brother Henry, which recalled the death of his mother. In 1829, Poe wrote of the connection, asserting that "there can be no tie more strong than that of brother for brother – it is not so much that they love one another as that they both love the same parent."[11] Clearly, they both loved their mother Eliza (certainly not their father David, who had abandoned them). Notably,

Henry was said to have "often deplored the early death of his mother."[12] Brother Henry died in the bedroom that he shared with Edgar – perhaps even in the same bed – in their aunt Maria Clemm's apartment in Baltimore on 1 August 1831. Poe's loss of Henry resonated with his loss of his mother Eliza – and the resonance is clear in *The Narrative of Arthur Gordon Pym* (1838), where the central image of the death of the Henry-like Augustus Barnard on 1 August is linked with the final apocalyptic image of the novel, suggestive of Eliza's performing as a bride in the play *Tekeli*.[13]

Poe does hint at the autobiographical significance of "The Raven" towards the close of "The Philosophy of Composition": he states there that the raven is "emblematical of *Mournful and Never-ending Remembrance* (*E&R*, 25). Here we have what may well be the key to the poem: the black bird represents the student's infinite memory of his lost Lenore – Poe's ceaseless memory of those he loved and lost – and, indeed, our own unending memory of our own lost loved ones. Although there may be no "surcease of sorrow," this poem does help to create, over time and around the world, a community of shared sorrow.

"The Raven" was first published on 29 January 1845, in N. P. Willis's New York *Evening Mirror*; it was introduced as "the most effective single example of 'fugitive poetry' ever published in this country." It then appeared, attributed to the pseudonymous "Quarles," in the February 1845 issue of George H. Colton's *American Review*, where the poem was described as "one of the most felicitous specimens of unique rhyming which has for some time met our eye" (*Log*, 496). (We are told, however, that the *American Review* paid Poe for "The Raven" only nine dollars.[14]) Benjamin Blake Minor, editor of Poe's former monthly the *Southern Literary Messenger*, quoted newspaper editor James Brooks as stating, "In power and originality of versification the whole is no less remarkable than it is, psychologically, a *wonder*" (*CH*, 143). And the critically acclaimed work was a great hit: Poe wrote in May 1845, comparing the popularity of "The Raven" with that of his 1843 short story "The Gold-Bug," "The bird beat the bug...all hollow."[15]

People quoted the refrain aptly – Poe had the pleasure of hearing the allusion at a play in New York City – and Poe himself was referred to as "the Raven" (*Log*, 497–498). The poem was readily parodied in such works as "The Owl," "The Craven," "The Gazelle," "The Whippoorwill," and "The Pole-Cat" (the last admired by Abraham Lincoln). And in his final years, Poe was repeatedly asked to recite "The Raven," which he did on a variety of occasions, including at a high school graduation ceremony (*Log*, 703).

The Raven and Other Poems was published by Wiley and Putnam in November 1845 at the peak of Poe's fame. But Poe's situation was quickly worsening – in part because of his drinking (which caused his loss of the *Broadway Journal*, a magazine that he had edited and briefly owned). Still, interest in "The Raven" continued. In April 1846, Elizabeth Barrett, now Mrs. Browning, wrote to Poe, who had sent her an inscribed copy of *The Raven and Other Poems* bound with the *Tales*, "I thank you as another reader would thank you for this vivid writing, this power which is felt! Your 'Raven' has produced a sensation, a 'fit horror,' here in England" (*CH*, 144). And in the same month, *Graham's Magazine* published Poe's explanation of his writing "The Raven," the aforementioned essay, "The Philosophy of Composition."

The process that this essay describes was taken as a guide by subsequent poets – unsuccessfully by the anonymous author of the 1855 poem "Elenor,"[16] but successfully by symbolist Stephane Mallarmé, who wrote, "The more I work, the more I will be faithful to the strict ideas that my great master Edgar Poe bequeathed to me. The remarkable poem 'The Raven' was created according to his ideas. And the soul of the reader responds absolutely as the poet intended."[17] Furthermore, "The Philosophy of Composition" endures as a provocative complement to Poe's most famous poem; indeed, the essay is frequently included in anthologies and regularly taught with "The Raven" today.

The reputation of "The Raven" is evident in its frequent translations – including the French (by Baudelaire and Mallarmé, among others) and the Czech, the Hungarian and the Romanian, the Polish and the Croatian, the Portugese and the Chinese. Also, the poem has been widely illustrated – most famously by Gustave Doré, Edouard Manet, and James Carling. And it has been the basis for a variety of films, including D. W. Griffith's *Edgar Allen Poe* (1909); Louis Friedlander's *The Raven* (1935), with Boris Karloff and Bela Lugosi; and Roger Corman's *The Raven* (1963), with Vincent Price, Peter Lorre, and Jack Nicholson. Its influence may be seen in a variety of literary works, including Walt Whitman's "Out of the Cradle Endlessly Rocking," Vladimir Nabokov's *Lolita*, Bernard Malamud's "The Jewbird," and Ray Bradbury's "The Parrot Who Knew Papa."

And Poe's poem is honored in a variety of other ways. On the 150th anniversary of the publication of the poem, 1995, a scholarly conference on "The Raven" was held at the University of Baltimore. *Quoth the Raven* is the name of a popular 1991 novel by Jane Haddam; it is also the title of two of the greatest Poe exhibits ever mounted – the Yale University Library's 1959 exhibit of the Poe collections of H. Bradley Martin and Colonel Richard Gimbel and the Poe Museum's 1997 exhibit of the Poe collection of Susan Jaffe Tane. *Nevermore* is the title of a 1994 novel by William Hjortsberg and a 1999 novel by Harold Schechter; *Evermore* is the title of the newsletter of the Poe Museum (located in the city of Poe's childhood, Richmond, Virginia). And "Edgar's Cafe" is the name of the restaurant on Edgar Allan Poe Street (West 84th Street between Broadway and West End Avenue) in New York City, the site of the Brennan Mansion, where, in 1844, Poe worked on "The Raven."

Poe's final recitation of "The Raven" occurred, fittingly, in the city where he had grown up, Richmond, Virginia. On 24 September 1849, in the Exchange Hotel, Poe concluded his lecture on "The Poetic Principle" with a presentation of his most famous poem. The editor of the *Semi-Weekly Examiner*, John M. Daniel, asserted on the following day, in his piece on "The Raven," "It is stamped with the image of true genius – and genius in its happiest hour. It is one of those things an author never does but once."[18]

Putting "Ulalume" in its place

While visiting Maryland, Amory Blaine, the self-centered protagonist of F. Scott Fitzgerald's *This Side of Paradise*, gets into the habit of wandering through the countryside "reciting 'Ulalume' to the corn-fields." On one such walk, he encounters Eleanor Savage, who, having heard his recitations earlier, calls him the "auburn-haired boy that likes 'Ulalume'" and, caught with him in a thunderstorm, offers to play Psyche, his soul, as he recites.[19] Besides capturing Fitzgerald's personal enjoyment of Poe, an author his father had read to him in his boyhood,[20] *This Side of Paradise* captures a prominent theme of "Ulalume," the clash between the physical landscape and the landscape of the mind. By no means has Fitzgerald been the only prominent literary figure to appreciate and be influenced by the poem, for it has helped to shape the work of numerous others. The Spanish verse of Francisco Villaespesa, Antonio Machado, and Rubén Dario embody their enthusiasm for "Ulalume," and in Russia the verse of Konstantin Balmont and Valery Bryusov reflects their appreciation.[21] For many readers, however, "Ulalume" is a difficult poem, and the richness of its language and the density of its imagery make it seem, at times, impenetrable. Disparaging the poem in his essay, "Vulgarity in Literature," Aldous Huxley called "Ulalume" "a carapace of jewelled sound," and Daniel Hoffman, somewhat more appreciative, equated reading the poem with "making a meal of marzipan."[22]

The critical history of "Ulalume" is not dissimilar to that of much other Anglo-American literature. Scholars identified the poem's topical references in the 1930s and 1940s, yet critics in subsequent decades denied the relevance of identifying topical references in favor of analyzing the poem's formal elements. For instance, T. O. Mabbott and Lewis Leary identified the references for the poem's imaginary geography in the 1940s, yet James E. Miller, writing a decade later, asserted that the placenames in the poem had value solely for the associations their sounds could evoke.²³ It is possible, however, to reconcile the topical references with the formal qualities of "Ulalume," for Poe used references to contemporary culture in the poem as a structural device, a way of establishing bonds between the real world and the poem's imaginative world.

According to tradition, "Ulalume" began as an answer to a challenge. The Reverend Cotesworth P. Bronson, a well-known teacher of elocution, challenged Poe to write "something suitable for recitation embodying thoughts that would admit of vocal variety and expression."²⁴ Another contemporary elocutionist, George Vandenhoff, had already anthologized "The Raven" in the second edition of his handbook, *A Plain System of Elocution* (1845), so Poe recognized that an additional poem suitable for recitation could help to enhance his renown. While the mellifluous sounds of "Ulalume" answer Bronson's challenge, the poem's setting may answer a personal challenge Poe set for himself. Relating how he chose the locale for "The Raven," Poe explained that he first thought to set "The Raven" outdoors – in "a forest, or the fields" – yet concluded that "a close *circumscription of space* is absolutely necessary to the effect of insulated incident: – it has the force of a frame to a picture" (*E&R*, 21). With "Ulalume," Poe challenged himself to write a poem set in forest and field, which nevertheless achieved a circumscription of space similar to that of "The Raven."

"Ulalume" begins: "The skies they were ashen and sober; / The Leaves they were crispèd and sere" (*P&T*, 89). Autumn settings were fairly common in contemporary verse, and the opening imagery establishes the poem's temporal setting – a gloomy autumn evening – and emphasizes its visual qualities. Furthermore, shifting from ashen sky to withering leaves, the first two lines of the initial nine-line stanza quickly direct the reader's eyes from the sky to the ground and therefore circumscribe the setting vertically. The following stanza, which encloses the speaker of the poem within an alley of cypress, circumscribes the setting horizontally. The explicit reference to the month of October in the first stanza confirms the temporal setting the opening imagery suggests while its last four lines establish the geographical setting:

> It was hard by the dim lake of Auber,
>   In the misty mid region of Weir:
> It was down by the dank tarn of Auber,
>   In the ghoul-haunted woodland of Weir.
>   (*P&T*, 89)

Such repetition with variation typifies a pattern that occurs throughout "Ulalume." William Carlos Williams may have had these lines in mind when he noticed that Poe's "passion for the refrain is like an echo from a hollow."[25] Williams made this comment in an essay refuting the commonplace notion that Poe's works were "out of space – out of time" and advocating the importance of place to Poe's work.

Using proper nouns to name the lake and its surrounding environs, Poe did give "Ulalume" a sense of place, yet these two names, instead of referring to actual geographical locations, recall the names of two contemporary figures prominent in the arts: Daniel-François-Esprit Auber and Robert Walter Weir. Auber, a prominent composer during Poe's lifetime, wrote many popular operas including *Le Lac des Fées* (*The Lake of the Fairies*), an unmistakable precedent for Poe's "dim lake of Auber." Weir, a contemporary American artist and art teacher, was on his way to establishing a significant reputation as one of America's most important history painters. Though Weir, a professor at the US Military Academy, did not come to West Point until a few years after Poe had been discharged, the two likely made acquaintance during the 1840s, for they travelled in the same literary circles, and both were friends with such men as N. P. Willis and "General" George Pope Morris.[26] Using names of artists as placenames, Poe clearly situated the poem in the realm of the imagination. The references specifically compare "Ulalume" to painting and opera and thus provide additional ways for Poe to circumscribe the space of the poem – within a frame and within a proscenium arch.

Like "The Raven," "Ulalume" offers an unusual combination of already-existing elements, for Poe combined the visual qualities of painting with the dramatic qualities of the stage to create his unique poem. Referring to both opera and painting, Poe placed "Ulalume" at the conjunction of performance and image. Opera, generally speaking, represents the collocation of story, music, and verse, and much the same might be said about "Ulalume." Placing his reference to the theater prior to the painting reference, Poe figuratively set the stage and then opened the curtain onto the picture. He therefore juxtaposed the physical location of the theater with the imaginative location of the events that occur on stage. He also made use of popular superstition. Traditionally, pictures were covered after a death to prevent spirits from haunting a home. Figuratively uncovering a picture, Poe woke the spirits of the dead. Read in relation to the remainder of "Ulalume," Poe's allusions to Auber and Weir take on additional significance, for they are virtually the poem's only contemporary references. Making reference to real persons in the opening stanza and not in the later ones, Poe established a connection between the poem and the world external to it only to sever that connection, allowing contemporary reality to give way to the world of imagination.

Poe used a variety of poetic devices to develop the action of the poem. "Ulalume," too, is about a man attempting to cope with the grief arising from the death of his lover. Though the title character has no physical presence in the poem, the absent female image, according to Tiziana Rossi, forms the center of "Ulalume."[27] The name of the lost love, like so many of Poe's female characters – Annabel Lee, Eulalie, Helen, Lenore, Ligeia, Morella – favors the letter "L," an aspect of Poe's use of sound that poets from Konstantin Balmont to Thomas Hardy have appreciated. As Rachel Polonsky observed, Balmont so enjoyed Poe's alliteration that he multiplied the number of l-sounds in his translations of Poe's verse.[28] Furthermore, "Ulalume" abounds with figurative language. Most importantly, the speaker of the poem figures his soul as something external to himself, Psyche, his winged companion. Externalizing his soul, he indicates how grief has fractured his mental and physical state. To indicate his fractured state further, he contrasts the feelings of his heart and body using what can be considered an epic simile. His heart is as volcanic

> As the scoriac rivers that roll,
>   As the lavas that restlessly roll
> Their sulphurous currents down Yaanek
>   In the ultimate climes of the pole,
> That groan as they roll down Mount Yaanek
>   In the realms of the Boreal Pole.
>
> (*P&T*, 89)

Recognizing Poe's reference to the polar regions, J. O. Bailey suggested that "Ulalume" was set in a mythical land inside the earth that could be entered through an opening in the poles, theories about which were current in the popular culture of Poe's day.[29] While Bailey's argument is unconvincing, it does provide one way to reconcile the poem's conflation of the external and the internal. The work of Victoria Nelson, drawing upon some of the same source material as Bailey and specifically discussing *The Narrative of Arthur Gordon Pym*, offers a more balanced approach for interpreting "Ulalume," for these lines reflect what Nelson identified as the human tendency to project inner psychological states onto the contours of the earth.[30]

Poe derived his unusual adjective – the first recorded use of "scoriac" in the English language – from scoriae, the jagged blocks of loose igneous rock he associated with the regions of the South Pole in *Pym*.[31] Decades later, Theodore Roosevelt, borrowing diction from Poe, reused the adjective "scoriac" and, in so doing, described some particularly jagged rock formations in *Hunting Trips of a Ranchman* (1885), a work in which Roosevelt recommends a copy of Poe for the Dakota ranchman's bookshelf because the Badlands "somehow *look* just exactly as Poe's tales and poems *sound*."[32]

Roosevelt's comments reveal his impulse to use Poe's imagery as a way to interpret the physical environment. Whereas "Ulalume" shifts from external reality to the world of imagination, Roosevelt used his reading of Poe's imaginative verse as a way to interpret the natural environment. Valery Bryosov, alternatively, reinforced the interiority of Poe's geographic description with an explicit reference to "Ulalume" in his poem, "Domovoj":

> In a dark crowd – I am the dark house,
> where there are volumes, shadows, dreams and portraits;
> The Yaanek of Edgar – that is I; under the ice
> of lava, burning with memory.[33]

In the third and fourth stanzas of "Ulalume," the speaker of the poem characterizes his conversation with Psyche ("Our talk had been serious and sober"), describes his distracted state of mind ("we knew not the month was October, / And we marked not the night of the year"), and explains how they paused on their walk at the sight of a heavenly body ("At the end of our path a liquescent / And nebulous lustre was born") (*P&T*, 89). His words, especially the pronouns, further blur the distinctions between internal and external, self and other. The speaker's use of "we" and "our" in "Ulalume," which recall Poe's use of the editorial plural in his critical writings, conveys his feeling that he is incomplete, that a part of himself exists separately from him. His inability to recognize where he is or what day of the year it is reinforces the difficulty he has distinguishing between external reality and his interior mental state. The fact that the action of the poem takes place on Halloween, a time when spirits of the dead were free to roam the earth, reinforces the body / soul dichotomy. Only with the appearance of a rising crescent, which has been alternately interpreted as either the moon or Venus, does he become cognizant of something external to him. His interpretation of this heavenly body as Astarte, the Phoenician goddess of fertility, indicates that his understanding of the environment is still highly subjective.

Over the next three stanzas, he argues with Psyche, his soul, over whether or not they should approach Astarte, he taking the affirmative and she the negative. A cross between a political debate and a lover's quarrel, the argument continues the external/internal dichotomy as it juxtaposes public and private modes of discourse. It ends with the speaker of the poem winning out over Psyche and the two proceeding forward. They reach a tomb, and the legend inscribed on its door lets them know that Ulalume lies within. Introducing the written word as a motif, Poe juxtaposed a written message with the preceding speeches and thus established an opposition between writing and speech. Speech is associated with actions of the moment whereas writing, while linked to the stillness of death, is also associated with permanence.

Explaining his feelings at the sight of the "legended tomb," the speaker of the poem observes, "Then my heart it grew ashen and sober / As the leaves that were crispèd and sere" (P&T, 91). This, his first use of the first person possessive since the second stanza, indicates his re-emerging sense of self. Describing himself by recalling his description of the surrounding environment in the opening lines, the speaker of the poem suggests that he is finally becoming in tune with his environment. In addition, he now realizes what night it is, Halloween, the same night he had buried Ulalume the year before. He also recognizes where he is: "Well I know, now, this dank tarn of Auber, / This ghoul-haunted woodland of Weir" (P&T, 91).

In the final stanza, the speaker's voice harmonizes with Psyche's. Speaking in unison, they express their recognition that the ghouls were responsible for having "drawn up the spectre of a planet / From the limbo of lunary souls" (P&T, 91). Poe's diction cleverly recalls the topical references in the poem's opening stanza and thus gives the poem a fine sense of closure. His use of the word "drawn" is a double entendre. At the literal level he meant the ghouls had drawn up the spectre in the sense of bringing it forth, yet the verb also suggests the act of drawing in an artistic sense and thus subtly recalls the reference to Weir in the opening stanza. Similarly, the word "spectre" recalls the reference to Auber, for it, too, can be interpreted as a reference to another popular form of entertainment in Poe's day. Contemporary producers of phantasmagoria often advertised their ability to call forth spectres.

In *The Histrionic Mr. Poe*, Bryllion Fagin argued that Poe's dramatic sense offered the key to his writings. While Fagin may have overstated his case, his understanding of dramatic elements in Poe's work does apply to "Ulalume."[34] Though Fagin did not discuss "Ulalume" in terms of its theatrical elements, the poem, more than many of Poe's other works, possesses a fine dramatic sense. The first stanza opens the curtains. The action of the poem occurs largely in dialogue, and, with a subtle invocation of phantasmagoria, the last stanza closes the curtain. With the first stanza, Poe makes deliberate reference to external reality but then opens the curtain to allow readers to enter his imaginative world. In the final stanza, Poe closes the curtain, allowing readers to return to reality and letting them know, as the producers of phantasmagoria let their audiences know, that the spectres they had witnessed were not real but the creation of showmen. While they may have been frightened during a phantasmagoria performance, contemporary audiences left the theater comfortable that all they had seen was artifice. Poe does not let his audience go so easily, for he leaves one ligature between the worlds of imagination and reality unsevered. Though he lets them know that the poem's visions had been artifice, he reveals that its showmen are not men. They are ghouls.

NOTES

1. William Carlos Williams, *In the American Grain* (1925; reprinted, New York: New Directions, 1956), p. 232; *Recognition*, pp. 205–206; Daniel Hoffman, *Poe Poe Poe Poe Poe Poe Poe* (1972; reprinted, Baton Rouge: Louisiana State University Press, 1998), p. 36; *Recognition*, p. 81.

2. Diana Chisolm, *H.D.'s Freudian Poetics: Psychoanalysis in Transition* (Ithaca: Cornell University Press, 1992), pp. 43, 107; Williams, *In the American Grain*, p. 233; Robert Pinksy, ["Sesquicentennial Tribute to Poe,"] *NewsHour with Jim Lehrer*, 7 October 1999, transcript no. 6571.

3. Susan Archer Weiss, *The Home Life of Poe* (New York: Broadway Publishing Company, 1907), p. 185.

4. Edgar Allan Poe, *The Complete Poems of Edgar Allan Poe*, ed. J. H. Whitty (Boston: Houghton Mifflin, 1901), p. 195.

5. Elizabeth Barrett Barrett, *A Drama of Exile and Other Poems*, 2 vols. (New York: Henry G. Langley, 1845), 1: 223.

6. John H. Ingram, ed., *"The Raven" by Edgar Allan Poe, with Literary and Historical Commentary* (London: George Redway, 1885), pp. 12–13. See also *Collected Works* (Mabbott), 1: 357n.

7. Barrett, *A Drama of Exile and Other Poems*, 1: 261.

8. Robert S. Forsythe, "Poe's 'Nevermore': A Note," *American Literature* 7 (January 1936): 439–452.

9. Edgar Allan Poe, "The Drama," in *Writings in The Broadway Journal: Nonfictional Prose: Part 1, The Text*, ed. Burton R. Pollin (New York: Gordian, 1986), p. 176.

10. Arthur Hobson Quinn, *Edgar Allan Poe: A Critical Biography* (1941; reprinted, New York: Cooper Square, 1969), p. 480.

11. Poe to John Neal, October-November, 1829, *Letters*, 1: 32.

12. J. H. Whitty, "Memoir," *The Complete Poems of Edgar Allan Poe* (Boston: Houghton Mifflin, 1911), p. xxi.

13. Richard Kopley, "The Hidden Journey of *Arthur Gordon Pym*," *Studies in the American Renaissance: 1982*, ed. Joel Myerson (Boston: Twayne, 1982), pp. 29–52.

14. John Ward Ostrom, "Edgar A. Poe: His Income as Literary Entrepreneur," *Poe Studies* 15 (June 1982): 5.

15. Poe to F. W. Thomas, 4 May 1845, in *Letters*, 1: 287.

16. "Elenor," *The Rambles and Reveries of an Art-Student in Europe* (Philadelphia: Thomas T. Watts, 1855), pp. 61–68.

17. Lois Davis Vines, "Stephane Mallarmé and Paul Valéry," in *Poe Abroad: Influence, Reputation, Affinities*, ed. Lois Davis Vines (Iowa City: University of Iowa Press, 1999), p. 172.

18. Poe, *Complete Poems*, ed. Whitty, p. 199.

19. F. Scott Fitzgerald, *This Side of Paradise*, ed. James L. W. West III (New York: Cambridge University Press, 1995), pp. 206–209.

20. Andrew Turnbull, *Scott Fitzgerald* (New York: Scribner's, 1962), p. 15.
21. José Antonio Gurpegui, "Poe in Spain," in *Poe Abroad*, p. 111; Gustavo Pérez Firmat, "Antonio Machado and the Poetry of Ruins," *Hispanic Review* 56 (Winter 1988): 7; Susan F. Levine, and Stuart Levine, "Rubén Dario," in *Poe Abroad*, pp. 216, 218; Eloise M. Boyle, "Valery Brjusov and Konstantin Bal'mont" in *Poe Abroad*, p. 178; Rachel Polonsky, *English Literature and the Russian Aesthetic Renaissance* (New York: Cambridge University Press, 1998), pp. 101–102.
22. Huxley is quoted in Cleanth Brooks, Jr., and Robert Penn Warren, *Understanding Poetry: An Anthology for College Students* (New York: Henry Holt, 1938), p. 651. Hoffman, *Poe*, p. 69.
23. T. O. Mabbott, "Poe's 'Ulalume,'" *Explicator* 1 (February 1943), item 60; Lewis Leary, "Poe's 'Ulalume,'" *Explicator* 6 (February 1948), item 25; James E. Miller, Jr., "'Ulalume' Resurrected," *Philological Quarterly* 34 (April 1955): 203.
24. *Collected Works* (Mabbott), 1: 410.
25. Williams, *In the American Grain*, p. 233.
26. Betsy Fahlman, "Weir, Robert Walter," in *American National Biography*, ed. John A. Garraty and Mark C. Carnes, 24 vols. (New York: Oxford University Press, 1999), 22: 907–908.
27. Tiziana Rossi, "La Figura Femenina en las Poesias de E. A. Poe," *Nueva Estafeta* 40 (1982): 54.
28. Polonsky, *English Literature and the Russian Aesthetic Renaissance*, p. 103.
29. J. O. Bailey, "The Geography of Poe's 'Dream-Land' and 'Ulalume,'" *Studies in Philology* 48 (July 1948): 518–520.
30. Victoria Nelson, "Symmes Hole, or the South Polar Romance," *Raritan* 17 (Fall 1997): 136.
31. *Collected Works* (Mabbott), 1: 421.
32. Theodore Roosevelt, *Hunting Trips of a Ranchman* (New York: G. P. Putnam's Sons, 1885), p. 12.
33. Qtd. in Boyle, "Valery Brjusov and Konstantin Bal'mont," p. 178.
34. N. Bryllion Fagin, *The Histrionic Mr. Poe* (Baltimore: Johns Hopkins Press, 1949), pp. 155–156.

13

MARK NEIMEYER

Poe and popular culture

When the newly reformed Baltimore professional football team chose to call itself the Ravens in 1996, Poe received a fin-de-siècle apotheosis as one of popular culture's favorite sons. The fact that football and Poe have nothing to do with each other only highlights the extent to which this nineteenth-century American author has remained not only present, but much appreciated in the minds of the general public throughout the world. Poe pops up almost everywhere: from a commemorative stamp issued by the US Post Office to a somewhat confused John Wayne listening to Robert Mitchum recite lines from Poe's poem "Eldorado" in the Hollywood western of the same name. Poe's face appears amidst the crowd on the cover of the Beatles' *Sgt. Pepper's Lonely Hearts Club Band*; the enigmatic "I am the Walrus" on *Magical Mystery Tour* includes the line "Man, you should have seen them kicking Edgar Allan Poe." *The Simpsons* has made several allusions to Poe, including an admirable cartoon dramatization of "The Raven." *The Crow* (1994) offers a triple-level tribute as Eric Draven (Brandon Lee) quotes "The Raven" after returning from the dead and entering a pawn shop in search of his murdered fiancée's ring. In the world of consumer goods, Raven Beer uses a publicity poster incorporating an irresistible pun: "I Know You're in the Pits. How about a Raven?" The poster also features a photograph of a dark-haired woman holding a rose in front of the stone marking Poe's original burial place in Baltimore and, beneath that:

Raven Beer
The Taste is Poetic

Mont Blanc's special-edition Edgar Allan Poe fountain pen, Poe alarm clocks, refrigerator magnets, T-shirts, coffee mugs, bookmarks, postcards, and mouse pads can be added to the list of recent appropriations of Poe in contexts with little direct relation to the author's life or works. Various company names such as Poe's Pub in Richmond, the Raven Gallery in Charlottesville, and Edgar's Billiards Club in Baltimore also fall into this category (though all are in cities where Poe spent part of his life). Perhaps the strangest recent tribute is the naming of the *U. S. S. Raven*, a state-of-the-art minesweeper, at whose commissioning ceremonies in Baltimore harbor in 1998 the Navy served Raven Beer.

In addition yet in partial contrast to this cacophony of Poe references, the Edgar Allan Poe Awards ("Edgars") given annually by the Mystery Writers of America can be seen as a more justified use of the writer's name since they do pertain to literature. Still, the connection with Poe remains tenuous, and these awards reveal one of the roles into which "intellectual popular culture" (if that expression is not an oxymoron) has cast Poe: that of a symbol, or sort of shorthand, for "literature." Other examples of this tendency include *The Complete Idiot's Guide to American Literature*, whose cover features a photograph of Poe as its only illustration, the *New York Times Book Review*, which has recently made frequent use of a caricature of Poe with a raven sitting on his head in a space-filling advertisement for itself with the punning declaration that its pages discuss "Writers worth raving about," and *Word Up Baltimore* (1997), a CD anthology of poetry readings whose cover art features a close-up of Poe's face. None of these three images is identified, and, indeed, it is precisely because Poe has been absorbed into the popular consciousness as an icon of "literature" (among other things) that such a labeling is not only not necessary, but would intrinsically put the status of the icon into question since, almost by definition, figures of popular culture do not need to be identified. This relating of Poe and "literature" goes beyond the somewhat limited context suggested by these examples and can be seen as part of the appeal in the appropriations of Poe already mentioned. The person who buys a Poe coffee mug is also, to a certain extent, procuring a symbolic link or identification with "literature" and even with "culture" more generally. From one point of view, these references boast that, even if they are embedded in products of popular culture, neither their creators nor their audience is ignorant of highbrow culture.

I began this discussion of Poe and popular culture with the preceding list in part to give an idea of the incredible variety and contexts in which references to him occur, but also because these appropriations are mere allusions to Poe. His position as an icon of popular culture has become so powerful that these examples can be seen as representatives of a sort of "meta-popular culture" that tacitly recall not only Poe and his works, but simultaneously other more developed adaptations in popular culture. The purchase of Poe mouse pads and the naming of a minesweeper are due as much to Poe's already-established image in popular culture as to Poe himself. The presence of Poe in popular culture is so strong that it seems to have spawned a popular culture of its own. It could be argued that to a certain extent all popular culture is (or has the potential of becoming) at one and the same time what I am calling meta-popular culture because at some point or another products of popular culture break away from their original inspiration, gaining an often increasing independence and circularity in which they tend to make reference to themselves more than to their first referent. Nonetheless, a distinction between popular culture and meta-popular culture can be made, at least in cases of very well-known and widely exploited subjects like Poe. Possibly, meta-popular culture is only possible in cases where productions of popular culture have already made a person, writing or other subject known to a large and diverse public. A partial clarification of this conjecture might be found in the answer to the following question: would it be as easy to sell a Poe T-shirt if there was not already a ton of Poe movies? Or, to put it another way (and still insisting on the overlap, to a greater or lesser extent, in the referents of popular culture and meta-popular culture), in the extreme case, popular culture results in some people knowing the movie and not the short story, while meta-popular culture results in some people registering a certain level of recognition in the name of the football team but not necessarily even having seen the movie.

Generations have been fascinated with popular presentations of Poe's life and works. His writings have appeared in a multitude of editions, frequently illustrated, and in almost every major language. There have been collections designed specifically for children and comic book versions aimed at young and older readers alike. Film studios around the world have perhaps done the most to bring various renditions of Poe to the public, but the list does not end there. The author and his works have been the inspiration for musical compositions, dramatic readings and theatrical productions. Indeed, if Poe is alive and well in the ether of postmodern meta-popular culture, it is because his image, his life, and his words are so firmly anchored in the many dimensions of popular culture.

Poe's desire for popularity and popular culture in Poe

Poe might well have been happy to learn of his prominent, though posthumous, place in popular culture since he clearly, though largely unsuccessfully, sought popular success during his lifetime. Poe once wrote Washington Irving, one of the day's most famous and well-paid American authors, begging him for a favorable comment to use in the promotion of his forthcoming *Tales of the Grotesque and Arabesque* (1839). "If," Poe wrote, "I could be permitted to add *even a word or two* from yourself, in relation to the tale of 'William Wilson' (which I consider my best effort) *my fortune would be made*."[1] He did not consider such an aspiration a concession, however.

As Kenneth Silverman notes, Poe saw Charles Dickens "as having achieved what he aimed at himself, securing a large popular audience without compromising his aesthetic standards."[2] In "The Philosophy of Composition" Poe states that his goal in writing "The Raven" was "a poem that should suit at once the popular and the critical taste" (*E&R*, 15). If there are those who disparage the literary quality of Poe's most famous poem, it can nonetheless be said that he came fairly close to this stated objective. Through the publication of "The Raven" he gained popular acclaim a few years before his death but not the financial success and security he had dreamed would accompany it. If Poe's fame has endured into the twenty-first century, to a large extent it is due to his prominent place in popular culture.

It is not only Poe's concern to make his work pleasing to a large audience, however, that may help explain his widespread adoption by popular culture. Such an appropriation has its own logic since Poe himself integrated the popular culture of his own day into his tales and poems. Silverman notes, "In creating 'Berenice,' 'Morella,' and stories like them, Poe drew on a widely popular tradition of Gothic fiction. By the time he began treating the Gothic world in 'Metzengerstein,' it had been a staple of British, American, and Continental writing for nearly half a century."[3] Poe's use of popular contemporary subjects went well beyond the Gothic, however. Killis Campbell explains, "With an eye to his market, Poe turned for his themes largely to subjects of local and contemporary interest": ballooning, the cholera, astronomical speculation, German mysticism, the telegraph, the steamboat, the galvanic battery, the political evils of the day, industrial conditions, and fashions in dress.[4] Poe's work was of his time perhaps more than that of any other American author of the nineteenth century. His close ties to the periodical press go a long way in accounting for this extensive use of popular culture, but Poe had a natural fascination (though sometimes in the form of a revulsion) for the vogues of his day. Jonathan Elmer calls Poe "a mass-cultural writer."[5] Not meant to disparage Poe's "literary" status, Elmer's statement emphasizes Poe's ambiguous position between highbrow and lowbrow culture, which made him especially appealing to the general public. Furthermore, Elmer sees the element of the uncanny – of the combining of the alien and the familiar – in Poe's work as an important dimension of its equivocalness which, again, made him naturally and fundamentally a part of popular culture.[6] As Freud notes in his consideration of the uncanny in literature, such a sentiment can be evoked effectively only "so long as the setting is one of material reality," that is, only provided that the irrational or unexplainable appear on a contrasting backdrop of seeming normality.[7] At first such a characterization of Poe's work may seem inappropriate, but upon further consideration it becomes clear that there is almost always a dimension of reality, if not the banal, in Poe's works that contrasts with an element of the unusual or the extreme or the distorted. "The Black Cat," to take one example, is set in a household of simple and apparently harmonious domesticity, only to end in a horrible and unjustified murder. These ambiguities no doubt work towards meeting the simultaneous desires of the popular audience for escape through transcendence or the unusual, on the one hand, and for relaxation and reassurance through the familiar, on the other,[8] and if they helped make Poe a "mass-cultural writer" of the nineteenth century, I would suggest that they have also facilitated his posthumous appropriation by popular culture.

The allure of Poe's life: the man and the myth

A more specific accounting for Poe's strong presence in popular culture should begin, perhaps, with a mention of the widespread attraction of the Poe legend. Clearly, it is not only Poe's works in isolation that have fascinated generations. Poe has largely been taken up by popular culture because of its ability to exploit his personal suffering and the sad, and sometimes strange, realities of his life as well as the even more fantastic myths that have grown up around him. Poe has become the archetype of the mad genius or the tortured Romantic artist, the *poèt maudit* crushed by a crass and insensitive world. His problems with alcohol have frequently been exaggerated, and his one documented use of laudanum has, on occasion, been transformed into a lifelong opium habit. Poe's marriage, at twenty-six, to his thirteen-year-old first cousin, Virginia, is rarely mentioned without suggesting some sort of deviant or defective sexuality, and the mysterious circumstances surrounding his death have been the source of endless and apparently irresistible speculation.[9] If that's not enough material for popular exploitation, one wonders what it would take.

One of the ironies of the Poe legend, which says much about how popular culture (and popular psychology) operates, is that its single most important source, Poe's literary executor, Rufus Griswold, was not trying to create a myth. Despite his admiration for some of the writings, he attempted to expose, or rather malign, Poe as an irresponsible and drunken madman, deserving perhaps pity, but not admiration or enthusiasm. Griswold's "Memoir" can be considered as the first and perhaps the most important treatment of Poe's biography in popular culture since it was reprinted in the only available American edition of the author's works for decades after his death. Furthermore, in its willful lack of accuracy, one can see it as an "adaptation," rather than an objective account, of Poe's life, even if Griswold was convinced that the overall impression he was giving reflected a certain reality. He asserts, for example, that at the University of Virginia, Poe "led a very dissipated life," and that while working for the *Southern Literary Messenger*, he fell into "a condition of brutish drunkenness."[10] Parts of Griswold's account make Poe sound like a raving lunatic: "He walked the streets, in madness or melancholy, with lips moving in indistinct curses... or, with glances introverted to a heart gnawed with anguish, and with face shrouded in gloom, he would brave the wildest storms; and all night, with drenched garments and arms beating the winds and rain, would speak as if to spirits."[11] If Poe had his posthumous defenders, it was Griswold's portrayal and other exaggerations – either derived from it or following its tone – that gained the most widespread circulation. The Poe legend has proved so strong that popular presentations of the author's life cannot seem to resist perpetuating it, even when ostensibly striving for historical accuracy. For example, the biographical section of *Cliffs Notes on Poe's Short Stories*, a frequent first source of information about Poe for high school and college students, attempts to debunk the apocryphal stories surrounding the writer's life only to assert that "because the facts are scarce, Poe's claim to being America's first authentic neurotic genius will probably remain."[12] *The Complete Idiot's Guide to American Literature*, aimed at a more general audience, is meant to be humorous and informative at the same time, and the chapter on Poe is no exception. Not surprisingly, the amusement here comes primarily through an exaggeration of the Poe myth that the non-idiotic reader is supposed to recognize as such (I think). Tales of Poe's gambling and drinking during his days at the University of Virginia, for example, are presented thus: "Within a day of his arrival, Poe managed to gamble away his entire term's allowance. Just a few months later, he owed $2,500 in gambling debts. The skill Poe lacked in cards he more than made up with in drinking, and he managed to stay drunk for the entire semester."[13] It's rather funny, but it's also essentially false, with the possible exception of the dollar figure whose exact amount remains uncertain. A last example, which can be seen as a sort of summary of this conveniently ambiguous position so often exploited in popular treatments of Poe (when they do not abandon any pretense of accuracy altogether), can be found in a mini-poster on sale at the Poe Museum in Richmond. It demands, in bold type, "Sadomasochist, drug addict, manic depressive, pervert, egomaniac, alcoholic? When did Poe find time to write?" Beneath these lines, the smaller print, which frames an image of an overturned chalice of wine (or some other no doubt alcoholic beverage), repeats a few more of the Poe myths only, finally, to get around to the message that at the Poe Museum, "you'll find out something really startling about Poe's life. The truth." Significantly, "truth" is the last word on the poster, and, indeed, it's the last thing that seems of interest to people in popular depictions of Poe.

It should also be noted that the public has not been fascinated by Poe's biography (and the distortions of it) in isolation from his writings. The persistent identification of the two has accounted for much of Poe's popular attraction. This blurring can also be traced back at least as far as Griswold's defamatory "Memoir" in which, for example, he notes that "The remarkable poem of 'The Raven' was probably more nearly than has been supposed, even by those who were very intimate with him, a reflection and an echo of his own history."[14] This interpretation was not only picked up by many early popularizers of Poe, including Charles Baudelaire in France, but has been incorporated into many productions of popular culture. Indeed, the frequent fusion and confusion of author and works is one of the most pervasive aspects of the whole phenomenon.

Edgar Allan Poe slept here

One of the indications that Poe continues to interest a wide audience is the number of actual places related to his life that the public is able, and often willing to pay, to visit. Here again, there is a sort of sliding scale of sloppiness or mythologizing as far as respect for historical accuracy goes. The Edgar Allan Poe House and Museum in Baltimore, the Edgar Allan Poe National Historic Site in Philadelphia, and the Edgar Allan Poe Cottage in the Bronx are all former residences of the writer open to the public. It is also possible to see Poe's gravesite in Baltimore, including the stone indicating his original burial place and the larger monument, dedicated in 1875 and marking the present location of his remains. Additionally, the University of Virginia in Charlottesville preserves Poe's student room on the West Range of the historic "Lawn" laid out by Thomas Jefferson. At the time of the writing of this article, a controversy has erupted over the planned demolition of a Poe house in New York City. While defenders of the structure on West Third Street (named Amity Street when Poe lived there) seem engaged in a hopeless battle, the very existence of the movement attests to continued popular interest in Poe.

If these historical sites provide a relatively serious view of Poe, even here there is an occasional slippage. The University of Virginia, for example, simply cannot resist placing a stuffed raven just inside Poe's window. "Why not?" seems a reasonable enough reaction, but such a practice nonetheless reflects the tendency in popular culture to mix Poe's life and work. In a somewhat similar vein, the National Park Service, which administers the Philadelphia house, has, at no small cost, done up a room based on Poe's suggestions for interior decorating in his essay "The Philosophy of Furniture." It's not a bad idea, and the Park Service could be seen as being a bit more honest than the University of Virginia since the particular room it used is not part of the house in which Poe actually lived. However, since the room adjoins the original residence, the casual visitor could be excused for mistaking it for part of Poe's home and thus assuming that he had a salon far more elegant and sumptuous than was the case. More significantly, the activities sponsored by some of these historic sites often play on Poe's standing in popular culture. The Edgar Allan Poe House and Museum in Baltimore (the cover of whose official brochure includes the quotation from film actor Vincent Price, "This place gives me the creeps!") celebrates Halloween with theatrical presentations, and the Philadelphia site holds candlelit tours in October and organizes readings from time to time by authors working in the various popular genres associated with Poe such as detective fiction.

The Poe Museum in Richmond, though not one of the writer's residences, also attracts many visitors, who learn once inside that they are not seeing a place in which Poe lived. The museum houses an impressive collection of artifacts, but, somewhat in the spirit of the Philadelphia "Philosophy of Furniture" room, it has also created a garden inspired by Poe's poems "To One in Paradise" and "To Helen" (and which is available for weddings). All of these sites, of course, have giftshops offering a selection of popular cultural products for one's better and more blissful consumption of Poe. Indeed, if "many Americans," as Kurt Vonnegut has blithely suggested, are like Billy Pilgrim's mother in *Slaughter-House Five* who "was trying to construct a life that made sense from things she found in gift shops,"[15] inside the Poe Museum and the various Poe houses, one might get the idea that many tourists are constructing an image of Poe from the items they buy there.

Moving on to more purely commercial ventures, one could mention the Deer Park Tavern in Newark, Delaware, which uses the image of a raven in its logo (and on its souvenir beer mugs) on the claim that Poe stopped there in December 1843 when he gave his lecture on "American Poetry" at the Newark Academy. The fact that the original inn had a different name and was knocked down about a hundred and fifty years ago in no way diminishes the Deer Park's pride in its association with Poe and its willingness to capitalize on that past. Edgar's Billiards Club in Baltimore can serve as a logical conclusion to this section since while it exploits the city's association with Poe, it makes no pretense to having any historical link whatsoever with the author. The decision is just as well since one would have to have downed more than one or two Raven Beers to believe that this bar in the middle of a large modern building complex was frequented by Poe. Deception, however, is not the point, and Edgar's is content to advertise itself as "Baltimore's only upscale day and night club combining billiards with a full service restaurant and bar along with a varied selection of other activities in a setting fashioned after the classic era of Edgar Allan Poe."

Illustrated, children's, and comic book editions

If up until now I have been concentrating on aspects of Poe somewhat outside and beyond his works, it is of course through his writings that Poe is still known by most people. One of the most frequent ways in which Poe's texts have been adapted for the general public is through illustrated editions that not only render the works more appealing, but often provide popular interpretations of the writings. Burton Pollin, in *Images of Poe's Works*, provides over 1,600 entries, most of them illustrated editions, by more than 700 different artists in thirty-three countries, accounting for somewhere between 8,000 and 10,000 individual images. The numbers themselves go a long way in arguing Poe's widespread appeal, and, as Pollin suggests, his catalogue "might serve to establish Poe as the most popular modern author for visual illustration."[16] Images occasionally accompanied Poe's work during his lifetime, but, of course, the vast majority of illustrated editions appeared after his death. As early as 1858 Sampson Low set high standards in Great Britain with its *Poetical Works of Edgar Allan Poe* illustrated by some of the best artists of the day. Most famous among these is probably Sir John Tenniel, who would later gain added fame for his illustrations of *Alice's Adventures in Wonderland* and *Through the Looking-Glass*. His images for "The Raven" helped establish some of the classic Victorian features of Poe illustrations, which have been drawn on repeatedly over the years, such as the cluttered, book-strewn parlor, the disheveled, slightly-crazed looking character and the voluminous, wind-blown curtains. This style reached its apotheosis in Gustave Doré's edition of *The Raven*, first published in London in 1883. While employing, and indeed exaggerating, some of the theatrical elements present in Tenniel's version, several of Doré's scenes also include images of "the lost Lenore," thus rendering the speaker's memories concrete for the reader. Indeed, perhaps Doré's greatest innovation, which would be taken up by later popular adaptations, was to move well beyond a literal representation of Poe's text. As one contemporary reviewer of the edition noted, the artist "solved the difficulty of translating the stanzas into pictures by treating 'The Raven' as an inconsolable mourner's revery upon the vast and eternal Enigma of Death."[17]

There is a long history of illustrated editions of Poe, but those intended primarily for adults make up only one facet of the story. In part because Poe is frequently encountered for the first time in childhood or adolescence, he serves the ends of popular culture well. Furthermore, the way in which many people are first introduced to Poe is through editions aimed specifically at children and youthful readers. *Edgar Allan Poe* in the "Poetry for Young People" series offers a good example of the way Poe's work is sometimes toned down and adapted for children. The book's richly colored illustrations avoid the more grim subjects (no mean feat in illustrating Poe), and several of the images show embracing couples or, at worst, isolated figures, men or women, in romantically desolate or austere surroundings. The most macabre image, which accompanies "The Bells," depicts a skeleton swinging from a bell rope. The rather fleshy figure, however, has a huge smile, and the whole decor is reminiscent of a Hallmark Halloween card and about as disquieting. Indeed, most of the illustrations evoke this same mood, and, clearly, this is one of the ways Poe has been successfully transformed into a writer for children, on the one hand, and into a product of mass culture more generally, on the other. The frequent tendency of allowing Poe's biography to creep into his work is demonstrated in this book's presentation of "For Annie." The headnote informs the young reader that "In this poem you can find the real Edgar Allan Poe," and the accompanying illustration depicts a bedridden Poe being nursed by "Annie." Furthermore, in the introduction, Poe's life is held out, at least indirectly, as an exemplary tale of the dangers of alcohol, thus echoing some of the earliest commentaries. Near the end, it concludes, "Like his father, Poe was destroyed by alcoholism."[18]

An example of an edition designed for slightly older readers is the Puffin Classics *Tales of Mystery and Terror*. Here, there are no illustrations, but the brief introduction – surprisingly silly for such a prestigious publishing company – informs readers that at the University of Virginia Poe "spent his first term on wine, women and song."[19] The characterization is comparable to that of *The Idiot's Guide*, which, in its defense, makes no pretence to exactitude. The newcomer to Poe also learns that after his wife's death, he was "more or less mad" and "still drinking." In the last paragraph the anonymous author of the introduction states, "Almost his last words were: 'I wish to God someone would blow my damned brains out.'" Aside from the awkward wording, which betrays the fact that these were not Poe's last words, the addition of the word "damned" is pure invention. Dr. John J. Moran, the source for Poe's delirious declaration of wanting to have his brains blown out, recorded the author's dying words as "Lord help my poor soul."[20] Those last words were, of course, of no interest to the writer of the Puffin Classics introduction since they do not accord with the popular stereotype of the tormented writer.

Since the 1940s Poe stories have also been a favorite subject of comic books, a genre between or outside the realms of classic adult and children's editions. Thomas Inge, in an on-going project, has already identified over seventy adaptations of Poe stories,[21] and as more are discovered and production continues, the list will continue growing. A somewhat hybrid version can be seen in the Classics Illustrated publications,[22] which, through comic book presentations, are meant to make literature fun, or at least accessible, for young readers. Like the "Poetry for Young People" edition, they tend to tame down Poe for what they seem to regard as the more delicate sensibilities of their audience. They also frequently suggest morals either not present in Poe or, worse, in flagrant violation of the whole spirit of his originals. In the first panel of "The Cask of Amontillado," for example, the narrator tries to justify his actions: "There's an old saying that 'man can stand so much and no more.' So it was with me. And one day, I could stand no more. What I did was surely wrong and sinful. But is there a man to say I was not at least partially justified? Hear my story and then judge for yourself." In the original story, of course, there is no open admission of wrong, and even less so of sin, nor is there any overt attempt at arguing or proving that the murder was justified. Not only do these changes moralize and rationalize the tale, they also seriously reduce its psychological interest. Interpretations of other works are also clarified for, or forced upon, the young reader. The last panel of "The Tell-Tale Heart," for example, shows the narrator wearing a straitjacket and sitting in a padded cell, enough of a gloss on his final words ("That's all to the story. Do you still think me mad? I think I was very clever.") for even an eight-year old to be able to figure out that we're talking about someone who's crazy here. The tendency to mix Poe's life and works is also demonstrated in the Classics Illustrated versions. In the first panel of the adaptation of "The Murders in the Rue Morgue," for instance, the reader is introduced to "the great amateur detective, Dupin, and his friend, Poe," and in the illustrations accompanying "The Raven," the speaker is clearly a caricature of Poe. In general, most of the alterations give the Classics Illustrated adaptations a watered-down quality. Despite their weaknesses, however, these editions could be considered as good an introduction to Poe as any other for young readers, some of whom perhaps are not yet ready for the nastier aspects of the stories and even more of whom, I suppose, do benefit from the coherence gained through an imposed moral or unambiguously suggested interpretation.

The more traditional type of comic books exhibit many of the same traits as the Classics Illustrated. For example, the adaptation of "William Wilson" published by Eternity Comics turns the tale into a moral lesson.[23] In the last panel, the dying Wilson exclaims, "Not real? Perhaps you suggest Wilson-the-Other was . . . not . . . real? Oh yes! Wilson the Other was real – real as my wretched dead conscience." In contrast to Classics Illustrated, however, the Eternity Comics versions tend to play up some of the gruesome aspects of the stories and occasionally add sexual innuendoes that are not in the original. In "The Tell-Tale Heart," for example, the narrator does not just dismember the body of the old man, but somehow ends up with a head and a pile of bones, and, to return to "William Wilson," at one point the apparently sex-crazed character is shown at a high-society soirée tying the hands of a woman behind her back and shouting, "Let's . . . have some fun." This sort of reveling in the gruesome and, to a lesser extent, the addition of sexual overtones, along with the frequent confusion of Poe's life and works, are distinguishing aspects of comic book versions of Poe and are no doubt keys to understanding Poe's success in this form of adaptation.

Poe at the movies

Many of the aspects relating to comic book versions are also present in what is probably the single most significant medium to have exploited Poe: the cinema. Since almost the first decade of the twentieth century, directors have been turning to Poe for inspiration, adapting his works with greater or lesser faithfulness, and incorporating aspects of his life or biographical legend into his stories. Fascinated by the myth, some directors have focused solely on Poe the man, and many have exploited his name and legend in movies with only the most tangential relationship with either the real Poe or the real works of Poe. If one includes made-for television versions, there are over a hundred films, but, due to the various and sometimes partial or unacknowledged ways in which the cinema has made use of him, no list of Poe films can really claim to be definitive. D. W. Griffith directed two silent movies, *Edgar Allen Poe* (1909) and *The Avenging Conscience* (1914). The first, a nickelodeon release lasting less than ten minutes, is ostensibly biographical, illustrating Poe's devotion to Virginia and the tragedy of her illness and death, but totally fanciful in its chronology and in its dramatization of how Poe came to write "The Raven." The story line of Griffith's second Poe film, subtitled *Thou Shalt Not Kill*, is loosely based on "The Tell-Tale Heart." Some aspects of the plot, in which the central character is an orphan as well as an aspiring author, are also reminiscent of Poe's life. The story includes echoes of other writings including "Three Sundays in a Week," "The Pit and the Pendulum," "The Black Cat" and "Annabel Lee" (lines from the poem are displayed from time to time, and the main character's love interest in the film is called Annabel). All of these threads are spun together in a story of love, murder, and vengeance, which nonetheless ends happily. Indeed, somewhat in the spirit of the comic book versions, Griffith simplifies and clarifies Poe's work.

The advent of the talkies combined with the vogue for horror pictures kicked off in 1931 by *Dracula* and *Frankenstein* resulted in several Poe adaptations in the 1930s. The two most famous actors of this genre, Bela Lugosi and Boris Karloff, teamed up to make *The Black Cat* (1934) and *The Raven* (1935). These two productions are good examples of how free and indiscriminate Hollywood can be in exploiting Poe's popularity for its own ends by borrowing titles from his works for movies with only the slightest relationship with the originals. Capitalizing partly on public interest in the still relatively new field of psychiatry, the first boasts the presence of a black cat as its only clear tie with Poe's story. Set in post-World War I Europe, the film focuses on the rivalry between Dr. Vitus Werdegast (Lugosi), a psychiatrist with an extreme cat phobia, and Hjalmar Poelzig (Karloff), a Satan-worshipping war criminal. Despite, or perhaps due to, its setting in a house featuring modern minimalist architecture, the film evokes a Poe-like atmosphere, and the cat's strange effect on Werdegast as well as the reappearance of another (or the same) black cat after he kills it vaguely recall Poe's story. Essentially, however, the plot has nothing to do with "The Black Cat" as Poe wrote it, and, to give the film credit for a certain amount of honesty, like *The Raven*, it claims only to have been "suggested by the immortal Edgar Allan Poe's classic." *The Raven* concerns Poe and his work more directly, but it is certainly not a simple reworking of Poe's poem of the same name. Here Lugosi plays Dr. Richard Vollin, a rather bizarre Poe enthusiast, who, early in the movie, is heard reciting "The Raven." Later it is revealed that he has constructed some of Poe's torture devices in his cellar (including a scimitar-shaped pendulum and a room with moving walls, both inspired by "The Pit and the Pendulum"), which become part of a revenge scheme plotted by the good doctor. While *The Raven* can be seen as a movie about the kind of madness often depicted by Poe, it can also be interpreted as being just as much about a latter-day popular obsession with Poe, a sort of metafictional comment on Hollywood's and, more generally, popular culture's focus on and exploitation of frequently distorted views of the writer and his works.

In the world of cinema, Poe is probably best known through the works of American actor Vincent Price. Indeed, as Ron Haydock has noted, "It's difficult anymore *not* to think of Vincent Price whenever anybody, for whatever reason, even mentions the name of Edgar Allan Poe."[24] While such a comment may be less true today than it was in the 1970s, Price still seems intimately linked to Poe and the movies, and indeed to Poe and popular culture, perhaps more than any other person. From 1960 to 1970 Price starred in eleven Poe films, which were produced by American International Pictures and directed, for the most part, by Roger Corman.[25] Haydock finds the Corman films particularly notable for the dream sequences: "usually bizarre, camera-distorted scenes that actually came the closest in any of the films to capturing the authentic nightmare quality so prevalent in Poe's tales of horror."[26] While that may well be, these productions are sometimes no more faithful to Poe's stories than the works of Lugosi and Karloff. The first collaboration between Price and Corman, *The Fall of the House of Usher*, basically follows Poe's storyline, but there are major departures. Philip Winthrop, the film's character corresponding to Poe's unnamed narrator, is engaged to Madeline Usher, which is the reason given for his visit to the sinister house. This allows the introduction of a love theme and sets up Philip as an adversary to Roderick, who does everything in his power to keep his sister entombed despite his knowledge that she is not dead. Poe's ending, of course, was irresistible, but not quite dramatic enough, for Corman, and as a grand finale the house collapses *and* is engulfed in flames just after Philip escapes outside to witness its final sinking into the tarn. *The Haunted Palace* (1963) is an example of a much more liberal use of Poe, and its main source is H. P. Lovecraft's *The Case of Charles Dexter Ward* and not Poe's poem, which the film uses for its title. As if to apologize for, or perhaps rather to cover up, that fact, the first four lines of the last stanza are quoted near the beginning of the story and the last four lines of the poem appear on the screen at the end. It's just what's in between that has little, if any, relation to "The Haunted Palace." Though Price would go on to make four more Poe films, *The Tomb of Ligeia* (1965) was the last one in which he was directed by Corman, and Price considered it the best of their collaborations. Filmed in England, it broke the rules of Corman's previous works by including sunny outdoor scenes and a more realistic, less claustrophobic, setting. The story is based on Poe's "Ligeia," but is rather free with the original. Hypnotism plays an important role in the revised plot, introducing a possible rational explanation for some of the strange goings-on, and Ligeia seems eternally present in the form of a black cat that spends much of its time trying to do in Lady Rowena. If Price and Corman were not terribly faithful to Poe's texts, they are perhaps the two men who have done the most to ensure the author's continuing presence in popular culture. Their work is one of the highpoints in the commodification of Poe, imposing a theatrically Gothic aspect on the writings, much in the tradition of Victorian illustrations, and making him a favorite to a wide range of audiences. If the power of these films seems diminished today, they have taken on new life through a semi-cult status that allows viewers to appreciate, and indeed revel in, the cheap special effects, campy dialogue, and kitsch atmosphere. This latter type of admiration, in fact, can be seen as a hallmark of a postmodern view of popular culture since, at least partly, it celebrates the distance between the original source and the indulgently unfaithful adaptation and embraces the fact that the product is unabashedly low brow.

Poe films did not stop, of course, when Price and Corman moved on to other things, though production did slow a bit. One notable work is the made-for-television version of *The Murders in the Rue Morgue* (1986) starring George C. Scott (who plays Dupin), Val Kilmer, and Rebecca De Mornay. In contrast to many other Poe films, it follows the text fairly closely (despite added details necessary to make it into a full-length picture) and avoids exaggerated Gothic trappings (though not a certain amount of stilted acting). Such seriousness, of course, cannot be tolerated for too long in the world of popular culture, and, at the time of the writing of this article, plans are already underway for a new Poe movie starring Michael Jackson. The script, apparently, includes characters from the writer's works coming back to haunt him during the last week of his life. Once again, biography and writings seem on a popular cultural collision course, and if Poe were alive today he might interpret the movie's announced title differently than the people who have chosen to call it *The Nightmare of Edgar Allan Poe.*

In addition to the films produced by American studios, many foreign countries have made their own adaptations of Poe, and this activity also goes back to the earliest days of cinema. Italian adaptations include *The Pit and the Pendulum* (1910), *Hop Frog the Jester* (1910), and *The Masque of the Red Death* (1911), three period pieces characteristic of their producer Ambrosio, who had established his reputation with *The Last Days of Pompeii* (1908).[27] The French, too, adapted Poe for the silent screen, though, contrary to general opinion, *Le Scarabée d'Or* (Kleine-General, 1911) or *The Golden Beetle*, a four-reel French film directed by Henri Desfontaines, has nothing to do with "The Gold Bug."[28] *Le Système du Docteur Goudron et du Professeur Plume* (Eclair, 1912) or, as the American release was titled, *The Lunatics*,[29] Maurice Tourneur adapted from a stage-play based on the Poe story. (Decades later Jean Renoir considered re-adapting Tourneur's version of Poe and went so far as to write a detailed treatment.[30]) Poe films have also been produced in many other countries including Argentina, Australia, Austria, Czechoslovakia, Germany, Great Britain, Mexico, Russia, South Africa, and Spain. *Histoires Extraordinaires* (a joint French-Italian production composed of three separate stories and also released under the title *Spirits of the Dead*) attracted directors Roger Vadim for the adaptation of "Metzengerstein," Louis Malle for that of "William Wilson," and Federico Fellini for that of "Never Bet the Devil Your Head." A relatively recent example of foreign interest in Poe can be seen in a series of French made-for-television films released in 1980 which includes *La Chute de la Maison Usher*, *Ligeia*, and *Le Système du Docteur Goudron et du Professeur Plume*. These productions are fairly faithful to Poe's stories, and they do not resort to the use of stagy Gothic settings and effects. The best of the three is the adaptation of "The System of Doctor Tarr and Professor Fether," directed by Claude Chabrol, which creates a sumptuously baroque atmosphere of increasing madness. In this French version, the fact that Monsieur Maillard repeatedly demonstrates that he does not know how to pour, much less drink, good wine is a clear hint that he is, in fact, insane.

Finally, it should be pointed out that the film medium has also been used to produce documentaries of Poe's life and works for general audiences. *Edgar Allan Poe* (A&E, 1994), part of its "Biography" series, and *Edgar Allan Poe: Terror of the Soul* (PBS, 1995) point up the fact, once again, that Poe continues to provoke interest and curiosity. Furthermore, and perhaps somewhat surprisingly, the porous border between Poe's life and writings can be seen even in these serious productions. The A&E program, for example, explains to viewers that "Poe, like his characters, was forever caught in a struggle between rationality and irrationality, order and chaos." The PBS version includes dramatizations of several of Poe's works and repeatedly interrupts them with comments on the author's life, providing an implicit and intimate link between the two. In the international sphere one could mention a recent German documentary, *Edgar Allan Poe: Visionär des Unwirklichen* (*Edgar Allan Poe: Visionary of the Unreal*, 1999), which, like the other two productions, makes use of period costumes and also slips back and forth between Poe's life and his writings, melting them together in the cauldron of the Poe myth.

Music and dramatic performances

Other genres have found inspiration in Poe and his works. Given the stress he placed on the musicality of his poetry, it is not surprising that Poe has frequently been adapted by composers and songwriters. Adaptations based on Poe, however, go well beyond a simple setting of his poems to music. For example, Claude Debussy wrote two one-act operas based on Poe stories, and Sergei Rachmaninoff's *The Bells*, written in 1913, is a four-movement choral symphony (each movement corresponding to one of the poem's stanzas) that lasts over half an hour. A more traditional and certainly more popular treatment can be seen in Joan Baez's somewhat shrill version of "Annabel Lee." One of the most ambitious adaptations of Poe in popular music is the Alan Parson Project's 1976 concept rock album, *Tales of Mystery and*

Imagination: Edgar Allan Poe. The 1987 re-released version includes the added attraction of previously recorded narration by Orson Welles (who thus returns from the dead to perform on the album). The work includes renditions of the poems "A Dream within a Dream," "The Raven," and "To One in Paradise" and tracks inspired by "The Tell-Tale Heart," "The Cask of Amontillado" and "The System of Doctor Tarr and Professor Fether." The most successful of these, perhaps, is "The Cask of Amontillado," in which sonorous lyrics contrast with the story of cold-blooded revenge.

Poe has also attracted various artists to perform dramatic readings of his works or to provide one-man shows mingling vignettes of various aspects of Poe's life with excerpts from his writings. Probably the most notable recent example of the first type is the 1997 double-CD album *Closed on Account of Rabies: Poems and Tales of Edgar Allan Poe*, which includes Iggy Pop reading "The Tell-Tale Heart" and a Marianne Faithful rendition of "Annabel Lee." While the work does include sung versions of "To Helen" and "The Haunted Palace" and a "performed" version of "The City and the Sea" (apparently an unintentional deformation of Poe's "The City in the Sea"), it is otherwise composed exclusively of readings. The album's title attests to the continuing interest in Poe's death, rabies being one of the more recent explanations put forward to explain the mystery. David Keltz has also recorded readings of Poe's poetry and tales; in addition, however, dressed as Poe, he does performances based on the author's life and works. Keltz appeared at the 1999 Poe festival in Prague, as did Kevin Mitchell Martin, who has his own act using the same basic format. The most famous participant in this genre is probably John Astin, who played Gomez in the 1960s television series *The Addams Family*. Astin has toured the United States and Canada in *Edgar Allan Poe: Once Upon a Midnight*, a play which incorporates quotations from over forty of Poe's works into the story of the author's life. Other similar efforts include John Matthews's *"Nevermore": An Evening with Poe* and Mel Harold's various programs such as *What is POE-try* and *In Search of Poe*. Harold's work, much of which is aimed at adolescents and teenagers, can provide an appropriate conclusion to this section as it harks back to the tradition of distortions begun by Griswold. The performer advertises that his presentations have "a strong antidrug message," and in the two programs mentioned above he explains "how Poe battled alcoholism and died from a drug overdose." He also discourses on "Poe's problems with peer pressure, self esteem, and alcohol." If Harold's use of Poe helps keep youngsters from the clutches of substance abuse, so much the better, but the fact that he also claims to work at "debunking rumors and misinformation about Poe, his life, death, and psychological battles" leaves one's head spinning since he need look no further than his own interpretations to find such twisting of the details of Poe's life.

The thrilling conclusion

So why has Poe remained such a prominent figure in popular culture? I have already suggested a few possible answers to this question, but it seems clear that there is no simple or definitive response. Poe's own seeking after popularity and his assimilation of the popular culture of his own day no doubt made his works likely candidates for later adaptation and exploitation. The appeal of the romantic tragedy of his life and the myths surrounding it as well as the seeming effortlessness with which popular culture has been able to meld these elements into adaptations of Poe's works provide another at least partial response. The fact that many people are first introduced to Poe at a young age and thus have associations with him related to childhood also probably goes a long way in explaining Poe's prominent place in popular culture. Furthermore, the facility with which Poe's stories lend themselves to illustration and to Hollywood-style exploitation also certainly figures into the equation. Somewhat more profoundly, the fact that Poe's stories negotiate the middle ground between lowbrow and highbrow culture, on the one hand, and the presence in his works of the uncanny, on the other, may also help in understanding the phenomenon of Poe in popular culture. Both of these aspects give a fundamentally ambiguous dimension to the writings that simultaneously reassures and excites. This equivocal quality, I would argue, has made Poe a natural target for appropriation by popular culture. Moreover, in a very real way, the adaptations of Poe I have discussed in this essay reenact and thus reinforce this ambiguity on at least two levels. Most of them are forms of lowbrow culture that implicitly remind their audience that their inspiration is highbrow (or at least from a source with enough cultural sanction to be able to claim that status). They thus insist on the fact that their audience can have its culture both ways, so to speak. Secondly, the popular exploitation of Poe can be seen as adding another dimension to the element of the uncanny already present in the author's writings since these productions are all strangely Poe and not Poe at the same time. The atmosphere evoked by the juxtaposition of the familiar and the foreign, so common in the tales and poetry, is perhaps part of the slightly bizarre attraction of a football team called the Ravens or a brightly-colored children's illustrated version of *The Bells* or a movie, with a hackneyed Gothic horror theme, entitled *The Black Cat* or a rock version of "The Cask of Amontillado" or an actor entertaining audiences with an impersonation of Edgar Allan Poe, but who isn't really Poe at all.

NOTES

1. Poe to Washington Irving, 12 October 1839, *Letters*, 2: 690.
2. Kenneth Silverman, *Edgar A. Poe: Mournful and Never-Ending Remembrance* (New York: HarperCollins, 1991), p. 198.
3. Silverman, *Edgar A. Poe*, pp. 111–112.
4. Killis Campbell, "Introduction," *Poe's Short Stories* (New York: Harcourt, Brace, 1927), p. xviii.
5. Jonathan Elmer, *Reading at the Social Limit: Affect, Mass Culture, and Edgar Allan Poe* (Stanford University Press, 1995), p. 4.
6. Elmer, *Reading at the Social Limit*, pp. 11, 19, 26–27.
7. Sigmund Freud, "The 'Uncanny,'" *Writings on Art and Literature* (Stanford University Press, 1997), pp. 226–227.
8. Elmer, *Reading at the Social Limit*, pp. 4–12.
9. See, for example, John Evangelist Walsh, *Midnight Dreary: the Mysterious Death of Edgar Allan Poe* (New York: St. Martin's Minotaur, 2000).
10. Rufus W. Griswold, "Memoir of the Author," *The Works of Edgar Allan Poe* (New York: W. J. Widdleton, 1867), pp. xxv, xxx.
11. Griswold, "Memoir," p. liv.
12. James L. Roberts, *Cliffs Notes on Poe's Short Stories* (Lincoln, Nebraska: Cliffs Notes, 1980), p. 5.
13. Laurie E. Rozakis, *The Complete Idiot's Guide to American Literature* (New York: Alpha, 1999), p. 62.
14. Griswold, "Memoir," p. lv.
15. Kurt Vonnegut, Jr., *Slaughter-House Five, or the Children's Crusade* (New York: Delacorte Press, 1969), p. 33.
16. Burton R. Pollin, *Images of Poe's Works: A Comprehensive Descriptive Catalogue of Illustrations* (New York: Greenwood, 1989), p. 2. Roy Gasson, ed., *The Illustrated Edgar Allan Poe* (London: Jupiter Books, 1976), reprints many illustrations from the 1850s to the 1930s, as well as film stills from movie versions of the 1920s to the 1970s. Peter Haining, ed., *The Edgar Allan Poe Scrapbook* (London: New English Library, 1977), which also reprints several illustrations of Poe's works, offers a good starting point for general information about Poe and popular culture.
17. Lafcadio Hearn, "The Raven," reprinted in Haining, ed., *Edgar Allan Poe Scrapbook*, originally appeared in the *New Orleans Times-Democrat*, 2 December 1883, p. 86.
18. Brod Bagert, ed., *Edgar Allan Poe* (New York: Sterling, 1995), pp. 27, 31, 33, 7.
19. Edgar Allan Poe, *Tales of Mystery and Terror* (London: Puffin, 1994), unpaginated.
20. Silverman, *Edgar A. Poe*, pp. 434–435.
21. Pollin, *Images of Poe's Works*, includes some comic book adaptations in his catalogue; however, this dimension of his work is clearly incomplete. Additionally, the fact that the comic book entries are mixed in with the others makes the work impractical for anyone seeking information about this specific genre.
22. *Classics Illustrated: Stories by Poe* (New York: Acclaim, 1997) includes "The Adventures of Hans Pfall," "The Tell-Tale Heart," and "The Cask of Amontillado." *Classics Illustrated: More Stories by Poe* (New York: Acclaim, 1997)

includes "The Pit and the Pendulum," "The Murders in the Rue Morgue," "The Fall of the House of Usher," and "The Raven." These are computer re-colored reprints of earlier editions.

23. *The Murders in the Rue Morgue and Other Stories* (Newbury Park, California: Eternity Comics, 1989) includes its title story preceded by "The Cask of Amontillado," and "MS. Found in a Bottle." *The Tell-Tale Heart and Other Stories* (Newbury Park, California: Eternity Comics, 1988) includes its title story preceded by "William Wilson" and followed by "The Facts in the Case of M. Valdemar." These are reprints of earlier editions.

24. Ron Haydock, "Poe, Corman and Price: A Tale of Terrors," in Haining, ed., *Edgar Allan Poe Scrapbook*, p. 135.

25. American International Pictures made two other Poe films without Price: *The Premature Burial* (with Ray Milland, 1962) and *Murders in the Rue Morgue* (with Jason Robards, 1971). Corman directed eight of the total thirteen AIP Poe films, seven of which starred Price.

26. Haydock, "Poe, Corman and Price," p. 134.

27. Denis Gifford, *Books and Plays in Films, 1896–1915: Literary, Theatrical and Artistic Sources of the First Twenty Years of Motion Pictures* (London: Mansell, 1991), p. 120.

28. Pollin, *Images of Poe's Works*, p. 335, following Walt Lee, *Reference Guide to Fantastic Films* (Los Angeles: Chelsea-Lee Books, 1972–1974), lists *Le Scarabée d'Or* as an adaptation of "The Gold Bug," but James S. McQuade's detailed review, " 'The Golden Beetle': An Exciting Photoplay of Adventure in the Wilds of Hindostan," *Moving Picture World* 22 (24 October 1914): 477, clarifies that the film has nothing to do with Poe's tale.

29. Tom Milne, *Horror*, vol. 3 of *The Aurum Film Encyclopedia* (London: Aurum, 1985), p. 17; Denis Gifford, "Pictures of Poe: A Survey of the Silent Film Era 1909–1929," in Haining, ed., *The Edgar Allan Poe Scrapbook*, p. 131.

30. Jean Renoir, *Oeuvres de Cinéma Inédites*, ed. Claude Gauteur (Paris: Gallimard, 1981), pp. 329–338.

14

KEVIN J. HAYES

One-man modernist

During the mid-1970s, Robert Motherwell created a series of Abstract-Expressionist collages inspired by the works of Edgar Allan Poe as well as a lithograph entitled *Poe's Abyss*.[1] These creative efforts indicate Motherwell's lifelong fascination with Poe's writings, which he first encountered in his youth and returned to as a young man after discovering Charles Baudelaire and Stephane Mallarmé, both of whom also received homage at Motherwell's hands. Being interviewed near the end of his life, Motherwell reiterated his devotion to Poe, naming him as a poet with whom he felt especially close.

"He keeps coming back, doesn't he?" the interviewer, aware of Motherwell's longstanding interest in Poe, observed. "What do you care especially for: the tales, the poetry?"

"Everything, really, the whole man," Motherwell responded. "I think he was a one-man modernist, at a moment when America was moving in the opposite direction. His English is so alive, sophisticated."[2]

That Motherwell, a major figure in the Abstract Expressionist movement, should convey such fondness for Poe is unsurprising, for major figures in virtually every artistic movement since the mid-nineteenth century have conveyed their indebtedness to Poe in word and image. Few, however, have put their appreciation of Poe so eloquently. Motherwell's epithet, which lends itself to the title of this chapter, conveys his belief that Poe was doing something that no one else at the time was doing. Motherwell did not elaborate his ideas in this interview, but he seems to have been suggesting that Poe had taken an avant-garde approach in his work that anticipated modern art. Whereas Poe's contemporaries continued to insist on the requirement that art both delight and instruct, the forward-thinking Poe, synthesizing the thought of European philosophers before him, set forth the idea of art for art's sake.[3] While this phrase has been variously attributed to Algernon Charles Swinburne and Walter Pater, both of whom used it in print in 1868,[4] Poe adumbrated it in his review of R. H. Horne's *Orion* in 1844, in which he insisted, "that under the sun there exists no work more intrinsically noble, than this very poem *written solely for the poem's sake*" (*E&R*, 295). While this essay did not receive much attention, Poe reused the phrase again in the posthumously-published essay, "The Poetic Principle," which was widely read during the nineteenth century. Well before he wrote either essay, however, Poe had exemplified this aesthetic in his imaginative writings and anticipated it in one of his earliest critical pieces, the introduction to the 1831 *Poems*, "Letter to Mr. —," which has a manifesto-like quality. The French formulation of the idea – *l'art pour l'art* – is generally given precedence over the English, yet Poe's use of the concept in this 1831 essay antedates the earliest printed use of the French phrase in 1833.

Like Motherwell, many artists have recognized the importance of Poe's aesthetic theory through the agency of Baudelaire and Mallarmé. Most who encounter Poe do so in their adolescence, and some, to their loss, leave him there. Many who return to Poe as adults recognize both the literary complexity and aesthetic ramifications of his work. Edward Hopper, for one, drew illustrations of "The Raven" and "The Bells" in his youth and, later in life, read and reread Baudelaire and Mallarmé on Poe.[5] Besides being Poe's greatest translator, Baudelaire was a fine art critic, too, and his interest in Poe often spilled over into his art criticism. "The Man of the Crowd," for instance, helped Baudelaire articulate his appreciation for the Parisian artist Constantin Guys. Writing his essay, "The Painting of Modern Life," Baudelaire asked his readers, "Do you remember a picture (it really is a picture!), painted – or rather written – by the most powerful pen of our age, and entitled 'The Man of the Crowd'?"[6] Not only did Baudelaire associate Poe's tale with painting, he also recognized both Poe and Guys as painters of modern life, for both of their works exemplified the modern urban spectator, the flaneur, a notion that numerous others, most notably Walter Benjamin, have expanded and refined. Baudelaire's translations of Poe's theoretical work, "The Philosophy of Composition" and "The Poetic Principle," however, may have had a greater influence on those working in the visual arts. Baudelaire identified with the second essay to such an extent that he incorporated much of it into his preface without attributing it to Poe and therefore led readers to believe that the ideas expressed were his own. Though Baudelaire translated Poe's imaginative prose and some of his critical writings, he published few translations of Poe's verse. After Baudelaire's death, Mallarmé, who undertook the task of translating the poetry, influenced the art world in terms of both personal agency – he was close friends with Edouard Manet and Paul Gauguin – and through his translations and critical writings, which also reflect the influence of Poe's aesthetic theory.

Mallarmé first met Manet in 1873, and the two quickly became close. After an unduly harsh critique of Manet's work appeared in early 1874, Mallarmé boldly defended him in print. By this time, the two may have already begun work on their collaborative Poe project. The result was *Le Corbeau*, which contained Poe's English text of "The Raven," Mallarmé's French translation, and Manet's illustrations, all done up in a handsome folio edition (see Figure 14.1). At the time of its publication in 1875, *Le Corbeau* was generally well received by the critics. *Paris-Journal* especially enjoyed Manet's illustrations:

> The artist has translated, by means of a remarkably vigorous handling of the black and white medium, the multiple, fantastic shapes of the sinister bird. Through the apparent but carefully calculated roughness and lack of finish in the technique, through the interplay of abrupt silhouettes and threatening shadows, M. Manet has transposed from one art into another the nightmare atmosphere and hallucinations that are so powerfully expressed in the works of Edgar Poe.[7]

Such critical praise did not, however, translate into sales. Regardless of its aesthetic success, *Le Corbeau* was a commercial flop. Both Mallarmé and Manet devoted some effort trying to generate support for the edition in England and the United States, yet these efforts, too, were largely unsuccessful. Edmund Gosse, who acquired a copy shortly after its publication, recalled the volume many years later describing it as a "famous folio . . . illustrated in the most intimidating style by Manet, who was then still an acquired taste. We should to-day admire these illustrations, no doubt, very much; I am afraid that in 1875, in perfidious Albion, they awakened among the few who saw them undying mirth."[8] The publication was, as Juliet Wilson-Barreau and Breon Mitchell have observed in their meticulous study of *Le Corbeau*, "dauntingly avant-garde."[9]

By definition, the avant-garde challenges contemporary notions of art. In so doing, however, it nearly always meets with belligerence. One way to help make an aesthetically challenging work of art acceptable to the contemporary public is to piggyback it, so to speak, atop an already accepted work. Before *Le Corbeau* appeared, Poe, largely through the efforts of Baudelaire, was thoroughly accepted in France and had achieved status equal to that of a great national author. Illustrating an edition of "The Raven," Manet used Poe as a way to make his own forward-thinking visual aesthetic more acceptable. The ploy did not work, yet it did establish a pattern other artists would follow in the years and decades to come. The visually innovative film, *The Cabinet of Dr. Caligari* (1920), for example, achieved contemporary acceptance, in part, because of its similarity to Poe's work. P. F. Reniers, who could not decide whether *Caligari* was Dadaist or Cubist or Futurist, did find one way to categorize it, for he grouped it with "The Murders in the Rue Morgue."[10]

Figure 14.1   Edouard Manet, *At the Window*, plate 3 from Le Corbeau, 1875. Courtesy
of the Harry Ransom Humanities Research Center, Austin, Texas.

Subsequently, James Sibley Watson, Jr. and Melville Webber created *The Fall of the House of Usher* (1928), choosing to adapt a work from Poe as a way to make their avant-garde filmmaking style more acceptable.

Odile Redon also invoked the specter of Poe to help his own work gain acceptance, for Redon entitled his 1882 lithographic album, *À Edgar Poe*. The title seems to offer a profound homage, yet at the time Redon denied Poe's influence and asserted that he so named the collection of images to capitalize on Poe's French fame. Redon's denial, however, directly contradicted Poe's obvious influence on him. Even before Redon had published *À Edgar Poe*, others had recognized similarities between his work and Poe's in terms of shared themes, motifs, and fantastic elements. Jules Boissé, for one, had recognized the artist's debt to Poe in a review of Redon's earlier collection of drawings, *Dans le Rêve* (*In Dreams*, 1879). Joris Karl Huysmans also recognized similarities between the two and suggested that Redon's title echoed the preface to *Eureka*: "I offer this Book to those who put faith in dreams as the only realities."[11] Redon later began preparing a series of drawings inspired by Poe's short fiction, possibly to accompany a translation by Emile Hennequin. The appearance of the 1884 Quantin editions of Baudelaire's *Histoires Extraordinaires* and *Nouvelles Histoires Extraordinaires* profusely illustrated by a number of artists including, most notably, François-Nicolas Chifflart, whose earlier work may have influenced Redon, rendered Redon's album of lithographs commercially unviable, however.[12]

Unpublished at the time, Redon's illustrations of Poe have survived and offer insight into his understanding of Poe. *The Teeth* (1883), a charcoal and black chalk drawing inspired by "Berenice," depicts a full set of teeth suspended in the air and radiating light. In the background are two bookshelves, the top one full yet cast in shadow and the bottom one with a few books whose bindings reflect the glow of the teeth. The drawing makes palpable the visions of Egaeus after he has become obsessed with Berenice's teeth: "The teeth! – the teeth! – they were here, and there, and every where, and visibly and palpably before me; long, narrow, and excessively white, with the pale lips writhing about them, as in the very moment of their first terrible development" (*P&T*, 230). Before his marriage Egaeus had fixed his attention on one or another of his books and would "muse for long unwearied hours with my attention riveted to some frivolous device on the margin, or in the typography of a book" (*P&T*, 226–227). Juxtaposing rows of teeth with rows of books, Redon thematically paralleled Egaeus's obsessions.

In *The Tell-Tale Heart* (1883), Redon imaginatively recalled Poe's story of the same name and, as Fred Leeman has noted, the drawing's modernity foreshadows Max Ernst's *frottage* technique (see Figure 14.2). Deceptively

Figure 14.2   Odile Redon, *The Tell-Tale Heart*, 1883. Santa Barbara Museum of Art,
Museum Purchase.

simple, Redon's charcoal drawing captures many of the tale's linked associations as it depicts a single eye gazing through a crack in the floorboards,
which appear parallel to the plane of the picture. Recognizing the difficulty
of rendering the sound of the beating heart visually, Redon chose to depict
another of the old man's organs, the one that initially provokes the narrator's
ire. When he first spies on the old man, the narrator of the story focuses a
lantern beam so that "a single thin ray fell upon the vulture eye" (*P&T*, 555).
The old man thus appears as an eye illuminated in the darkness. As he did in

The Teeth, Redon linked the action from the beginning of Poe's tale with its end and paralleled the two. Redon's drawing also establishes other parallels. First spying on the old man in "The Tell-Tale Heart," the narrator opens the door to his room slowly, so slowly that his own eye would have appeared through the crack in the door in much the same way Redon depicted the eye through the floorboards. Also, the large knot in one floorboard is shaped similarly to the eye and, therefore, parallels the structure of the dwelling with its inhabitants and, much like "The Fall of the House of Usher," suggests that there is a sentience in all inanimate things.

Among those recognizing Poe and Redon as kindred spirits was Paul Gauguin, who associated the two in his essay, "On Reading": "Do not think of reading Edgar Poe anywhere but in a very comforting place. And though you may be very brave, if you were only a little so (as Verlaine said), you'd be cooked. And, above all, do not try to go to sleep after looking at an Odilon Redon."[13] Continuing his essay after the reference to Redon, Gauguin recalled something that had occurred in 1880, when he and his wife were sitting together in front of the fireplace in a home they had rented from artist Félix Jobbé-Duval. While reading "The Black Cat," she temporarily set aside the volume of Poe stories she was reading to get some coal from the cellar:

> On the steps, a frightened black cat leapt: my wife, too. Nevertheless, after some hesitation, she kept on going. Two shovelfuls of coal, then a skull came loose from the coal pile. Overcome with fear, my wife left everything in the cellar and rushed back upstairs, finally fainting in the room. I went down next and, wanting to get more coal, I uncovered an entire skeleton.
>
> All together, it was an old articulated skeleton used by Jobbé-Duval, the painter, who had thrown it into the cellar when it had fallen to pieces.
>
> As you see, it is extremely simple; but the coincidence is nonetheless bizarre. Beware of Edgar Poe.[14]

The fact that the Gauguins had a volume of Poe in their home in 1880 suggests that they, too, had become caught up in the enthusiasm for Poe that Baudelaire's translations had generated. Gauguin also knew Mallarmé's translation of Poe's verse and counted him among his close friends. His portrait of Mallarmé indicates how closely Gauguin linked him with Poe, for Mallarmé appears with his hair, parted in the center and looking very like the leaves of an open book as a menacing raven appears over his shoulder with its beak above and therefore both paralleling and framing the top of his head. Mallarmé presided at the farewell banquet before Gauguin left France in 1891 for the South Seas, and on the occasion, someone saw fit to recite passages from *Le Corbeau*.[15]

Lines from Poe echoed in Gauguin's mind during his stay in the South Pacific. He was particularly moved by the paradox Poe attributed to Francis Bacon and articulated in "Ligeia" that great beauty requires a certain "*strangeness* in the proportion" (*P&T*, 263). Regarding one of the first paintings he did in Tahiti, *Vahine no te Tiare* (*Woman with a Flower*, 1891), Gauguin wrote, "And her forehead ... with the majesty of upsweeping lines, reminded me of that saying of Poe's, 'There is no perfect beauty without a certain singularity in the proportions.'"[16] Gauguin was not alone in his admiration of this idea. Decades earlier, Eugène Delacroix had copied the same passage from "Ligeia" into his journal.[17] This notion significantly influenced Gauguin's paintings of women in the South Seas, one of which he titled *Nevermore*, a painting that features a voluptuous woman in the foreground with much significant detail in the background. Though nude, the woman does not provoke arousal. Rather, the look on her face offers a mix of sadness and suspicion. Lying on her left side, her eyes gaze toward her right and, implicitly behind her, thus conveying her awareness of what is occurring in the background. The straight, vertical lines in the background contrast the curving lines of her body. In the top left of the painting, Gauguin has lettered its title in capitals: NEVERMORE. A strange tropical bird is poised on the nearby windowsill. "That bird," Gauguin later wrote, "is not the raven of Edgar Poe but the bird of the Devil biding his time."[18] Gauguin's words hint that the woman has committed an unpardonable sin, something the painting only hints at. Outside the doorframe, two women engage in close conversation. Possibly they are gossiping about the woman, and their barely audible conversation has evoked her suspicions. Borrowing his title from Poe, Gauguin juxtaposed the loud yet inherently meaningless call of Poe's raven with the quiet yet meaningful gossip of the village women. Gauguin's use of Poe's text also parallels his application of Milton's *Paradise Lost*. Once lost, nevermore can paradise be regained. After Gauguin's death, according to his biographer, *Nevermore* "achieved the status of an avant-garde icon," influencing, among others, Henri Matisse and Pablo Picasso.[19] The history of art, it would seem, offers an object demonstration of "The Power of Words," Poe metaphysical dialogue which suggests that once a word is uttered, it continues to exist and have influence across the infinity of space. With Gauguin's painting, the famous call of Poe's raven rippled over the world of modern art.

The Poe Centenary in 1909 reminded many people of his significance and prompted them to reread and reconsider Poe's work. Many Europeans, especially Germans, found his writings absolutely appropriate to modern times. In his Centenary lecture, "Poe in Germany," Georg Edward argued that German readers regarded Poe as a thoroughly modern author. During the opening years of the twentieth century, German authors and artists were beginning to distance themselves from realism and naturalism and sought new forms of creative expression. Edward labelled this new impulse "Nervosity" and defined it as a quest to record the "infinitely subtle variations of feeling which come surging in upon the modern individual."[20] According to Edward, Poe's work offered a model for those seeking to break from naturalism because he sought to express whatever "moved his inner soul." The literary forms that sufficed for his contemporaries Poe found insufficient. Far ahead of his own age, Poe conceived many ideas which he did not articulate fully himself, Edward argued, and his conceptions offered great creative opportunities for subsequent authors.[21]

Several new German editions of Poe's works appeared in or shortly after the Poe Centenary. Among the most notable are a series of collections of separate works published in Munich and Leipzig by Georg Müller and translated by Gisela Etzel, among others. The Müller Poe editions were products of good bookmanship. Well bound and finely printed on good quality paper with generous leading and rubricated title pages, they also contained handsome illustrations by Alfred Kubin, who had found in Poe a kindred spirit. Kubin's early experience predisposed him to the Poesque. His emotional instability prompted him to attempt suicide before he was out of his teens and resulted in a nervous collapse shortly after he entered his twenties. His early drawings are filled with fantastic monsters and deformed humans, both indicative of his predilection for the macabre, a predilection that would draw him to Poe's works. Other books Kubin illustrated reveal similar interests. In 1913, he illustrated new editions of E. T. A. Hoffman's *Nachtstücke* and Dostoyevsky's *Die Doppelgänger*. As Christoph Brockhaus has observed, the books Kubin chose to illustrate allowed him to indulge his taste for the fantastic and the bizarre.[22]

Like the works of any good illustrator of classic literature, Kubin's drawings mediated between texts from the literary past and contemporary times. In his illustration of "The Man of the Crowd," for example, Kubin depicted a dark-visaged man, bearded and hawk-nosed on a crowded street (see Figure 14.3). Literally head and shoulders above the rest of the crowd, he walks among them as a giant. His face expresses no emotion, nor do the faces of the other members of the crowd. Those nearest him have fairly well-defined facial features, but radiating out from him, the crowd's faces lose distinction. Some appear almost skull-like. Those in the extreme foreground consist of little more than a single line to show the contours of the nose and chin. In the background there appears a sprawling, four-story block of flats, each containing windows of identical size and shape, the architectural equivalent to the crowd below. Among members of the crowd, all torsos

Figure 14.3   Alfred Kubin, *The Man of the Crowd*. From *Das Feuerpferd und andere Novellen* (München: G. Müller, 1910).

lean forward, clearly indicating their movement. Though the man towers above the crowd, he is still of the crowd, for his posture is identical to theirs. His torso, too, is pitched forward, revealing that he moves with the crowd. He may be able to see above the crowd, yet he is powerless to escape it. Illustrating Poe's works and, in so doing, giving them a dynamic quality and imbuing them with a modernist sensibility, Kubin prepared the way for artists to follow.

The Müller editions of Poe with Kubin's illustrations influenced German Expressionism in multiple ways. In the second decade of the twentieth century Expressionism came to dominate the avant-garde in all German arts, and George Grosz, for one, came under its influence and began creating Expressionist drawings depicting brawls, sex murders, and suicides in a style reminiscent of Kubin's.[23] Long a devotee of lurid pulp fiction, Grosz found Poe's tales, especially the detective fiction, provocative and inspiring. He titled one drawing *Double Murder in the Rue Morgue* and dedicated it to

Poe. Grosz's other drawings of the period depicting murdersome gorillas and decapitated females clearly reveal the influence of "The Murders in the Rue Morgue."

Expressionist cinema, too, came under Poe's influence. *The Student of Prague* (1913), sometimes considered the first Expressionist film, was scripted by Hanns Heinz Ewers, a long-time Poe enthusiast, and clearly echoes "William Wilson."[24] *The Cabinet of Dr. Caligari* reflects the combined influence of Poe, Kubin, and Grosz. The attempted murder of Jane (Lil Dagover) is reminiscent of Grosz's depiction of sex murders; the film's visual imagery recalls Kubin; and the story of a somnambulist echoes two Poe stories, "Mesmeric Revelation" and "The Facts in the Case of M. Valdemar." In the second, the title character, having been mesmerized immediately prior to death, falls into a condition Poe described as "sleep-waking," which Gisela Etzel mistranslated as *Somnambulen* or sleepwalking.[25] "Valdemar," Kubin, and Grosz supplied the connections leading from Poe to *Caligari*.

"And Surrealism?" asked Alfred Hitchcock in an essay treating Poe's influence on himself specifically and, more generally, on art, literature, and film. Answering his own question with a question, Hitchcock responded, "Wasn't it, too, born from the work of Poe as much as from Lautréamont?"[26] Hitchcock might just as easily have mentioned André Breton as Lautréamont, for both were instrumental to the founding of Surrealism. The publication of Breton's first *Manifesto of Surrealism* (1924) is generally considered to mark the start of Surrealism, yet, as Breton admitted in the *Manifesto*, a number of others prefigured the movement, including Poe, whom Breton labelled a "Surrealist in adventure."[27] Among those who joined the Surrealist movement, few were more important than Max Ernst, who named Poe one of his favorite poets.[28]

None of Poe's works more significantly influenced Ernst than "Berenice," whose influence appears in his collages, paintings, and critical writings. In an early collage entitled *Microgramme Arp 1: 25,000* (1921), Ernst combined six cut-outs from a geological wall-chart with a written text consisting of six numbered phrases keyed to each cut-out. The last numbered phrase ends by mentioning "le cheveu de Bérenice."[29] With this phrase, Ernst recalled that part of Poe's story when its narrator, Egaeus, recognized how Berenice's appearance had drastically changed, her "once jetty hair" having given way to "innumerable ringlets now of a vivid yellow, and jarring discordantly, in their fantastic character, with the reigning melancholy of the countenance" (*P&T*, 230). The sight of her hair ultimately draws Egaeus's attention to her teeth, and Ernst seems to have followed course. An untitled collage he created the same year as *Microgramme Arp* depicts an arrangement of multiple sets of teeth. The image clearly echoes Egaeus's obsession in "Berenice."[30]

Ernst would reiterate Poe's influence and reuse the motif of Berenice's hair in his painting of the same name, *Berenice* (1935). At first glance, the painting would seem to have little to do with the story. Depicting two long-armed, long-legged figures Ernst invoked a favorite misogynistic image of the Surrealists, the praying mantis, a species whose female was known to devour the male after intercourse. The earlier reference to Berenice's hair in *Microgramme Arp* offers an interpretive link between Ernst's *Berenice* and Poe's. The hair of the figure on top – long and flowing in multiple ringlets that extend the length of the torso, clearly identifies the figure as the female. In the painting, Berenice's hair stands in for her teeth. Ernst expressed the idea the teeth in Poe's story implied – the devouring female – by depicting the female figure in the dominant position atop the male.

The profound influence of "Berenice" on Ernst also shows in his 1933 essay, "Comment on Force l'Inspiration," later translated into English as part of *Beyond Painting*, a collection of essays edited by Robert Motherwell. As Breton had advocated automatic writing as central to Surrealist literature, Ernst set forth automatic methods for painting, which involved a kind of obsessional staring reminiscent of Egaeus's behavior in "Berenice." Ernst explained that he had been "brought under the direct influence of the information concerning the mechanism of inspiration that is provided in the *Manifesto of Surrealism*. This process rests on nothing other than the *intensification of the mind's powers of irritability*, and in view of its technical features I have dubbed it *frottage* (rubbing), and it has had in my own personal development an even larger share than *collage*, from which I do not believe it differs *fundamentally*."[31] In his original French text, Ernst used the phrase "l'irritabilité des faculté de l'esprit," which he borrowed from Poe by way of Baudelaire. In Baudelaire's translation of "Berenice," Egaeaus had experienced "une irritabilité morbide des faculté de l'esprit."[32] Ernst took not only themes and motifs from "Berenice," he found in the story a fundamental approach to his Surrealist aesthetic. Put simply, "Berenice" facilitated Ernst's transition from collage to *frottage*.

Marie Bonaparte's *Edgar Poe, Étude Psychanalytique*, first published in Paris in 1933, generated much talk and, in so doing, greatly influenced the Surrealists. Salvador Dali recalled that Bonaparte's work was discussed in Paris cafés for quite some time after its publication.[33] It is not hard to imagine the numerous conversations about Poe taking place among the Surrealists in 1930s Paris, for, among the artists clustered there, several had been or would be influenced by Poe. Italian painter and engraver Alberto Martini, who had already created over a hundred illustrations of Poe's works and whose illustrations anticipated Surrealism, lived in Paris from 1928, where he became well acquainted with André Breton.[34] Mario Prassinos, who became

acquainted with Eluard, Breton, and Dali in 1934, experimented with proce-
dures of automaticism, which he continued in his later work, including illustrations for a Paris edition of *Pym* and an edition of "The Raven."[35] After her
first one-woman Paris show in 1935, Léonor Fini became acquainted with
Eluard and Ernst, who brought her in close contact with other Surrealists.
She never fully accepted the tenets of Surrealism, yet her subsequent work reflects its influence. In 1966, she illustrated a six-volume Paris edition of Poe's
works.[36]

Among those whose works reflect Poe's influence, few were more important than René Magritte, who sustained a lifelong enthusiasm for Poe. Near
the end of his life Magritte and his wife Georgette visited New York for the
opening of a Museum of Modern Art exhibition of his work. While there,
they visited Fordham Cottage, where Magritte was moved to tears. Writing
friends, he described the trip: "Poe's house is the most beautiful in the USA.
A raven greets you from the top of a narrow wardrobe, his desk and his
meagre, admirable furniture (and an old coal stove, like in Picardy) are still
there. Georgette and I spent a long time feeling the back of a chair that had
held him."[37] Returning home from the trip, Magritte told an interviewer,
"I love Edgar Poe; he has always been a very great importance for me."[38]
Magritte used the title of one of Poe's works – *The Narrative of Arthur
Gordon Pym* – in one painting, *Not to Be Reproduced* (1937), and he borrowed the title of two others to name his own works. He created multiple
paintings named *The Domain of Arnheim* (1938, 1949, 1950, 1962), and one
named after the title of the French translation of "The Imp of the Perverse,"
The Demon of Perversity (1928). Rather than images of Poe's tales, Magritte's
works represent images inspired by Poe. One of the paintings entitled *The
Domain of Arnheim*, for example, Magritte called the "realization of a vision" Poe would have liked.[39] Magritte's *Domain of Arnheim* recalls Poe's,
for, as Fred Miller Robinson observed, both express the "vast contradiction
between the natural and the artificial that is nevertheless an expression of
the affinity between the two."[40] Magritte's fondness for "The Imp of the
Perverse" is understandable, for Poe's story anticipated important Surrealist
impulses, which are analogous to the impulses of all avant-garde movements:
to pervert accepted notions of art and try new approaches and techniques,
to juxtapose unexpected images, to defy rational expectations, to celebrate
the absurd.

Marcel Duchamp, like Ernst and Magritte, was among the most important
and influential artists of the twentieth century, yet unlike the other two
Duchamp did not express a debt to Poe or allude to his writings within his
works (though, as David Hopkins has provocatively suggested, one of
Duchamp's ready-mades – the comb – combines the motifs of hair and

teeth and may, therefore, recall the obsession Egaeus has for Berenice's hair and teeth[41]). Duchamp's oeuvre reflects Poe's influence in a general way, however. Recently, T. J. Clark called Marcel Duchamp "the Edgar Allan Poe of the twentieth century." Explaining the comment, Clark paralleled the two. Like Poe's writings Duchamp's art was "an instigation to work by others that lies at the heart of modernism."[42] Describing his approach to writing short stories, Poe emphasized his attempts to write in a variety of different approaches and uniquely combine a variety of poetic devices, modes of discourse, and literary genres. Poe's experiments, combined with his obsession with originality, led to his creation of unique verse forms and new literary genres. In so doing, he created works which others could take for inspiration. Poe's various creative efforts allowed artists to pick and choose from his works to find those which suited their tastes and predilections. The wide-ranging work of those who came under Poe's spell indicate the diversity of his influence. The finest artists used Poe's imaginative works as a basis for their aesthetic theories. Redon found in Poe a precedent for his fantastic visions. Gauguin found in "Ligeia" an approach for his depiction of women. Ernst found Egaeus's obsessional behavior inspiration for his *frottage* technique. And Magritte found the spirit of Surrealism present in "The Imp of the Perverse." Put simply, Poe's writings have instigated generations of others in a variety of creative disciplines to advance their art and their aesthetic.

NOTES

1. Burton R. Pollin, *Images of Poe's Works: A Comprehensive Descriptive Catalogue of Illustrations* (New York: Greenwood, 1989), nos. 1472, 1476.
2. Mary Ann Caws, *Robert Motherwell: What Art Holds* (New York: Columbia University Press, 1996), pp. 197–198.
3. Rachel Polonsky, "Poe's Aesthetic Theory," above.
4. Hilary Morgan, "Art for Art's Sake," in *Dictionary of Art*, ed. Jane Turner, 34 vols. (New York: Grove, 1996), 2: 530.
5. Gail Levin, *Edward Hopper: An Intimate Biography* (New York: Alfred A. Knopf, 1995), pp. 46, 311.
6. Charles Baudelaire, "The Painter of Modern Life," in *The Painter of Modern Life and Other Essays*, trans. and ed. Jonathan Mayne (1964; reprinted, London: Phaidon, 1995), p. 7.
7. Juliet Wilson-Bareau, and Breon Mitchell, "Tales of a Raven: The Origins and Fate of *Le Corbeau* by Mallarmé and Manet," *Printer Quarterly* 6 (1989): 265.
8. Edmund Gosse, *French Profiles* (New York: Dodd, Mead, 1925), p. 306.
9. Wilson-Bareau and Mitchell, "Tales of a Raven," p. 266.
10. P. F. Reniers, "The Screen," *New York Evening Post*, 4 April 1921, p. 9.

11. Douglas W. Druick, and Peter Kort Zegers, "In the Public Eye," in *Odile Redon: Prince of Dreams, 1840–1916*, ed. Douglas W. Druick (Chicago and New York: Art Institute of Chicago and Harry N. Abrams, 1994), p. 134.
12. Fred Leeman, "Odile Redon: The Image and the Text," in *Odile Redon: Prince of Dreams*, 183; Michael Howard, "Chifflart, François(-Nicolas)," in *Dictionary of Art*, 6: 582.
13. Paul Gauguin, "On Reading," in *Gauguin: A Retrospective*, eds. Marla Prather and Charles F. Stuckey (New York: Hugh Lauter Levin Associates, 1987), p. 39.
14. Gauguin, "On Reading," 39–40.
15. Wayne Andersen, *Gauguin's Paradise Lost* (New York: Viking, 1971), p. 148.
16. Quoted in Belinda Thomson, *Gauguin* (London: Thames and Hudson, 1987), p. 138.
17. Eugène Delacroix, *The Journal of Eugène Delacroix*, trans. Walter Pach (New York: Crown, 1948), p. 510.
18. Quoted in Andersen, *Gauguin's Paradise Lost*, p. 184.
19. David Sweetman, *Paul Gauguin: A Life* (New York: Simon and Schuster, 1995), p. 439.
20. Georg Edward, "Poe in Germany," in *The Book of the Poe Centenary: A Record of the Exercises at the University of Virginia January 16–19, 1909, in Commemoration of the One Hundredth Birthday of Edgar Allan Poe*, ed. Charles W. Kent and John S. Patton (Charlottesville: University of Virginia, 1909), p. 85.
21. Edward, "Poe in Germany," pp. 87, 91.
22. Christoph Brockhaus, "Kubin, Alfred," in *Dictionary of Art*, 18: 490–491.
23. *The Berlin of George Grosz: Drawings, Watercolours, and Prints, 1912–1930* (London and New Haven: Royal Academy of Arts and Yale University Press, 1997), p. 5.
24. Hert L. Wegner, "Literary Influences on the Earliest Expressionist Film: *Der Student von Prag*," *Philological Papers* 26 (1980): 1–6; Heide Schlüpmann, "The First German Art Film: Rye's *The Student of Prague* (1913)," trans. Jan-Christopher Horak, in *German Film and Literature: Adaptations and Transformations*, ed. Eric Rentschler (New York: Methuen, 1986), pp. 9–24.
25. Edgar Allan Poe, *Das Feuerpferd und Andere Novellen*, trans. Gisela Etzel (Munich and Leipzig: George Müller, 1910), 60.
26. Quoted in Donald Spoto, *The Dark Side of Genius: The Life of Alfred Hitchcock* (Boston: Little, Brown, 1983), p. 40.
27. André Breton, *Manifestoes of Surrealism*, trans. Richard Seaver and Helen R. Lane (Ann Arbor: University of Michigan Press, 1969), p. 27.
28. Max Ernst, *Max Ernst: Beyond Painting*, ed. Robert Motherwell (New York: Wittenborn, Schultz, 1948), p. 6.
29. David Hopkins, *Marcel Duchamp and Max Ernst: The Bride Shared* (Oxford: Clarendon Press, 1998), p. 161.
30. Hopkins, *Marcel Duchamp and Max Ernest*, p. 162.
31. Ernst, *Beyond Painting*, p. 24.
32. Robert Belton, "Edgar Allan Poe and the Surrealists' Image of Women," *Woman's Art Journal* 8 (Spring/Summer 1987): 12.
33. Belton, "Edgar Allan Poe and the Surrealists' Image of Women," 13.
34. "Martini, Alberto," in *Dictionary of Art*, 20: 503.

35. Athena S. E. Leoussi, "Prassinos, Mario," in *Dictionary of Art*, 25: 450.
36. Whitney Chadwick, "Fini, Léonor," in *Dictionary of Art*, 11: 85.
37. René Magritte to Louis Scutenaire and Irène Hamoir, 17 December 1965, in *Magritte: Ideas and Images*, ed., Harry Torczyner, trans. Richard Miller (New York: Harry N. Abrams, 1977), p. 258.
38. René Magritte, *Écrits Complets*, ed. André Blavier (Paris: Flammarion, 1979), p. 619.
39. René Magritte, "The Lifeline," in *Magritte: Ideas and Images*, p. 216.
40. Fred Miller Robinson, "The Wizard Proprieties of Poe and Magritte," *Word and Image* 3 (April–June 1987): 157.
41. Hopkins, *Marcel Duchamp and Max Ernst*, p. 162.
42. T. J. Clark, "All the Things I Said about Duchamp: A Response to Benjamin Buchloh," in *The Duchamp Effect*, ed. Martha Buskirk and Mignon Nixon (Cambridge, MA: MIT Press, 1996), p. 225.

SELECT BIBLIOGRAPHY

Scholarly editions of Poe's writings

When James A. Harrison completed his seventeen-volume edition of Poe's works in 1902, he may not have realized that, a century later, his work would remain the single most complete edition of Poe. Thomas Ollive Mabbott, who imagined a thoroughly annotated, scholarly edition of Poe's works through much of his life, never fully brought the project to completion. Mabbott edited *Politan*, Poe's unfinished drama, as his doctoral dissertation at Columbia University in 1923, and he was preparing an edition of the poems and tales at the time of his death in 1968, which appeared posthumously in three volumes. Ostensibly continuing Mabbott's editorial work, Burton R. Pollin has edited several more volumes of Poe texts, which contain much valuable annotation, but whose overall quality is uneven. The two Library of America editions offer good collections of Poe's imaginative and critical writings. Due to their accessibility and general overall quality, *The Cambridge Companion to Poe* cites these two volumes primarily. Readers, however, should consult the Mabbott and Pollin editions for their detailed annotations. Though John Ostrom has edited Poe's letters, a thorough edition of Poe's correspondence remains a desideratum of Poe scholarship. For letters to Poe, readers should consult the last volume of Harrison's edition.

The Brevities: Pinakidia, Marginalia, Fifty Suggestions, and Other Works. Ed. Burton R. Pollin. New York: Gordian Press, 1985.

Collected Works of Edgar Allan Poe. Ed. Thomas Ollive Mabbott. 3 vols. Cambridge: Belknap Press of Harvard University Press, 1969–1978.

Complete Works of Edgar Allan Poe. Ed. James A. Harrison. 17 vols. New York: Thomas Y. Crowell, 1902.

Doings of Gotham: Poe's Contributions to The Columbia Spy. Ed. Jacob E. Spannuth and Thomas Ollive Mabbott. Pottsville, PA: Jacob E. Spannuth, 1929.

Edgar Allan Poe: Essays and Reviews. Ed. G. R. Thompson. New York: Library of America, 1984.

Edgar Allan Poe: Poetry and Tales. Ed. Patrick F. Quinn. New York: Library of America, 1984.

Edgar Allan Poe's Contributions to Alexander's Weekly Messenger. Ed. Charles S. Brigham. Worcester, MA: American Antiquarian Society, 1943.

The Imaginary Voyages: The Narrative of Arthur Gordon Pym, The Unparalleled Adventure of One Hans Pfaall, The Journal of Julius Rodman. Ed. Burton R. Pollin. Boston: Twayne, 1981.

The Letters of Edgar Allan Poe. Ed. John Ward Ostrom. 1948. Reprinted, with supplement. 2 vols. New York: Gordian, 1966.

Politan: An Unfinished Tragedy. Ed. Thomas Ollive Mabbott. Menasha, WS: Collegiate Press, 1923.

Writings in The Broadway Journal: Nonfictional Prose. Ed. Burton R. Pollin. 2 vols. New York: Gordian, 1986.

Bibliographies and reference guides

Many reference works exist for the study of Poe's writings. A thorough primary bibliography remains a desideratum, however. In lieu of that, multiple bibliographies must be consulted – the *Bibliography of American Literature (BAL)*, the *National Union Catalogue (NUC)*, and the Poe bibliography by Heartman and Canny – for a full view of Poe's writings. A thorough secondary bibliography is another desideratum of Poe scholarship, yet preparing such a work is an especially daunting task given Poe's enormous popularity and worldwide reputation. The current secondary bibliographies leave much to be desired. The Dameron and Cauthen bibliography, though quite thorough for its time, only goes through 1967. Also, its poor organization and annotations make it difficult to use. Hyneman's bibliography, much less thorough, is organized differently (though not necessarily better), and its annotations are also skimpy. The best source for secondary works published from 1963 is the annual *American Literary Scholarship*, yet its editors, while sometimes giving Poe his due, have, at other times, treated him as a poor cousin to his contemporaries, Nathaniel Hawthorne and Herman Melville. Besides bibliographies, the following list includes a number of other guides useful for studying Poe.

American Literary Scholarship: An Annual, 1963-. Ed. James Woodress, and others. Durham, NC: Duke University Press, 1965-. 36 vols. to date.

Blanck, Jacob, and Michael Winship. *Bibliography of American Literature*. 9 vols. New Haven: Yale University Press, 1955–1991. 7: 115–154.

Dameron, J. Lasley, and Irby B. Cauthen, Jr. *Edgar Allan Poe: A Bibliography of Criticism, 1827–1967*. Charlottesville: for the Bibliographical Society of the University of Virginia by the University Press, of Virginia, 1974.

Deas, Michael. *The Portraits and Daguerreotypes of Edgar Allan Poe*. Charlottesville: University Press of Virginia, 1989.

Frank, Frederick S., and Anthony Magistrale. *The Poe Encyclopedia*. Westport, CT: Greenwood Press, 1997.

Heartman, Charles F, and James R. Canny. *A Bibliography of First Printings of the Writings of Edgar Allan Poe; Together with a Record of First and Contemporary Later Printings of His Contributions to Annuals, Anthologies, Periodicals and Newspapers Issued During His Lifetime, Also Some Spurious Poeana and Fakes*. Rev. ed. Hattiesburg, Miss.: The Book Farm, 1943.

Hyneman, Esther F. *Edgar Allan Poe: An Annotated Bibliography of Books and Articles in English, 1827–1973*. Boston: G. K. Hall, 1974.

Kennedy, J. Gerald, ed. *A Historical Guide to Edgar Allan Poe*. New York: Oxford University Press, 2000.

Ljungquist, Kent P. "Edgar Allan Poe." In *Prospects for the Study of American Literature: A Guide for Scholars and Students*. Ed. Richard Kopley. New York University Press, 1997. 39–57.

National Union Catalog: Pre-1956 Imprints. 754 vols. London: Mansell, 1968–1981.

Pollin, Burton R. *Dictionary of Names and Titles in Poe's Collected Works*. New York: Da Capo Press, 1968.

Pollin, Burton R. *Images of Poe's Works: A Comprehensive Descriptive Catalogue of Illustrations*. New York: Greenwood Press, 1989.

Pollin, Burton R. *Word Index to Poe's Fiction*. New York: Gordian Press, 1982.

Vines, Lois Davis, ed. *Poe Abroad: Influence, Reputation, Affinities*. University of Iowa Press, 1999.

Walker, I. M., ed. *Edgar Allan Poe: The Critical Heritage*. New York: Routledge & Kegan Paul, 1986.

Wiley, Elizabeth. *Concordance to the Poetry of Edgar Allan Poe*. Selinsgrove: Susquehanna University Press, 1989.

Biographical studies and resources

Numerous biographies of Poe have been written but by common consent, Arthur Hobson Quinn's remains the finest. Readers willing to forego discursive biography for documentary history, however, may prefer *The Poe Log*, the single most important collection of biographical information about Poe. Works by Moss and Miller offer more specific collections of documents useful for reconstructing Poe's life. The definitive biography remains to be written.

Bondurant, Agnes M. *Poe's Richmond*. Richmond: Garrett and Massie, 1942.

Miller, John Carl. *Building Poe Biography*. Baton Rouge: Louisiana State University Press, 1977.

Moss, Sidney P. *Poe's Literary Battles: The Critic in the Context of His Literary Milieu*. Durham: Duke University Press, 1963.

Moss, Sidney P. *Poe's Major Crisis: His Libel Suit and New York's Literary World*. Durham: Duke University Press, 1970.

Quinn, Arthur Hobson. *Edgar Allan Poe: A Critical Biography*. 1941. Reprinted, Baltimore: Johns Hopkins University Press, 1998.

Silverman, Kenneth. *Edgar A. Poe: Mournful and Never-Ending Remembrance*. New York: HarperCollins, 1991.

Thomas, Dwight and David K. Jackson. *The Poe Log: A Documentary Life of Edgar Allan Poe 1809–1849*. Boston: G. K. Hall, 1987.

Walsh, John Evangelist. *Midnight Dreary: The Mysterious Death of Edgar Allan Poe*. New Brunswick: Rutgers University Press, 1998.

Whitman, Sarah Helen. *Poe's Helen Remembers*. Ed. John Carl Miller. Charlottesville: University Press of Virginia, 1979.

Collections of critical essays

Alexander, Jean, ed. *Affidavits of Genius: Edgar Allan Poe and the French Critics, 1847–1924*. Port Washington, NY: Kennikat Press, 1971.

Budd, Louis J., and Edwin Harrison Cady. *On Poe*. Durham: Duke University Press, 1993.

Carlson, Eric W. *A Companion to Poe Studies*. Westport, CT: Greenwood Press, 1996.

Carlson, Eric W., ed. *The Recognition of Edgar Allan Poe: Selected Criticism since 1829*. Ann Arbor: University of Michigan Press, 1966.

Clarke, Graham, ed. *Edgar Allan Poe: Critical Assessments*. 4 vols. New York: Routledge, 1991.

Eddings, Dennis W. *The Naiad Voice: Essays on Poe's Satiric Hoaxing*. Port Washington, NY: Associated Faculty Press, 1983.

Fisher, Benjamin Franklin, IV, ed. *Poe and His Times: The Artist and His Milieu*. Baltimore: Edgar Allan Poe Society, 1990.

Fisher, Benjamin Franklin, IV, ed. *Poe and Our Times: Influences and Affinities*. Baltimore: Edgar Allan Poe Society, 1986.

Fisher, Benjamin Franklin, IV, ed. *Poe at Work: Seven Textual Studies*. Baltimore: The Edgar Allan Poe Society, 1978.

Kent, Charles W., and John S. Patton, eds. *The Book of the Poe Centenary: A Record of the Exercises at the University of Virginia January 16–19, 1909, in Commemoration of the One Hundredth Birthday of Edgar Allan Poe*. Charlottesville: University of Virginia, 1909.

Kopley, Richard, ed. *Poe's Pym: Critical Explorations*. Durham: Duke University Press, 1992.

Merivale, Patricia, and Susan Elizabeth Sweeney, eds. *Detecting Texts: The Metaphysical Detective Story from Poe to Postmodernism*. Philadelphia: University of Pennsylvania Press, 1999.

Muller, John P., and William J. Richardson, eds. *The Purloined Poe: Lacan, Derrida, and Psychoanalytic Reading*. Baltimore: Johns Hopkins University Press, 1988.

Silverman, Kenneth, ed. *New Essays on Poe's Major Tales*. New York: Cambridge University Press, 1993.

Veler, Richard, ed. *Papers on Poe: Essays in Honor of John Ward Ostrom*. Springfield, OH: Chantry Music Press, 1972.

Book-length critical studies

Allen, Michael. *Poe and the British Magazine Tradition*. New York: Oxford University Press, 1969.

Alterton, Margaret. *The Origins of Poe's Critical Theory*. Iowa City: University of Iowa Press, 1925.

Baudelaire, Charles. *Edgar Allan Poe: Sa Vie et ses Ouvrages*. Ed. W. T. Bandy. University of Toronto Press, 1973.

Bonaparte, Marie. *The Life and Works of Edgar Allan Poe: A Psycho-Analytic Interpretation*. Trans. John Rodker. 1949. Reprinted. London: The Hogarth Press, 1971.

Campbell, Killis. *The Mind of Poe, and Other Studies*. Cambridge, MA: Harvard University Press, 1933.

Davidson, Edward H. *Poe: A Critical Study*. Cambridge, MA: The Belknap Press of Harvard University Press, 1957.

Dayan, Joan. *Fables of Mind: An Inquiry into Poe's Fiction*. New York: Oxford University Press, 1987.

Fagin, N. Bryllion. *The Histrionic Mr. Poe*. Baltimore: Johns Hopkins University Press, 1949.

Goddu, Teresa A. *Gothic America: Narrative, History, and Nation*. New York: Columbia, 1997.

Halliburton, David. *Edgar Allan Poe: a Phenomenological View*. Princeton University Press, 1973.

Harvey, Ronald C. *The Critical History of Edgar Allan Poe's The Narrative of Arthur Gordon Pym: "A Dialogue with Unreason."* New York: Garland, 1998.

Hayes, Kevin J. *Poe and the Printed Word*. New York: Cambridge University Press, 2000.

Hoffman, Daniel. *Poe Poe Poe Poe Poe Poe Poe*. 1972. Reprinted. Baton Rouge: Louisiana University Press, 1998.

Irwin, John T. *American Hieroglyphics: The Symbol of the Egyptian Hieroglyphics in the American Renaissance*. Baltimore: Johns Hopkins University Press, 1980.

Irwin, John T. *The Mystery to a Solution: Poe, Borges, and the Analytic Detective Story*. Baltimore: Johns Hopkins University Press, 1994.

Jacobs, Robert D. *Poe: Journalist and Critic*. Baton Rouge: Louisiana State University Press, 1969.

Kennedy, J. Gerald. *The Narrative of Arthur Gordon Pym and the Abyss of Interpretation*. New York: Twayne, 1995.

Kennedy, J. Gerald. *Poe, Death, and the Life of Writing*. New Haven: Yale University Press, 1987.

Levin, Harry. *The Power of Blackness: Hawthorne, Poe, Melville*. New York: Knopf 1958.

May, Charles E. *Edgar Allan Poe: A Study of the Short Fiction*. Boston: Twayne, 1991.

Pahl, Dennis. *Architects of the Abyss: The Indeterminate Fictions of Poe, Hawthorne, and Melville*. Columbia: University of Missouri Press, 1989.

Parks, Edd Winfield. *Edgar Allan Poe as Literary Critic*. Athens: University of Georgia Press, 1964.

Peeples, Scott. *Edgar Allan Poe Revisited*. New York: Twayne, 1998.

Polonsky, Rachel. *English Literature and the Russian Aesthetic Renaissance*. Cambridge University Press, 1998.

Quinn, Patrick F. *The French Face of Edgar Poe*. Carbondale: Southern Illinois University Press, 1957.

Richard, Claude. *Edgar Allan Poe: Journaliste et Critique*. Paris: Librarie C. Klincksieck, 1978.

Rosenheim, Shawn. *The Cryptographic Imagination: Secret Writing from Edgar Poe to the Internet*. Baltimore: Johns Hopkins University Press, 1997.

Stovall, Floyd. *Edgar Poe the Poet*. Charlottesville: University Press of Virginia, 1969.

Thompson, G. R. *Poe's Fiction: Romantic Irony in the Gothic Tales*. Madison: University of Wisconsin Press, 1973.

Thoms, Peter. *Detection and Its Designs: Narrative and Power in Nineteenth-Century Detective Fiction*. Athens: Ohio University Press, 1998.

Walsh, John Evangelist. *Poe the Detective: The Curious Circumstances behind the Mystery of Marie Roget*. New Brunswick: Rutgers University Press, 1967.

Whalen, Terence. *Edgar Allan Poe and the Masses: The Political Economy of Literature in Antebellum America*. Princeton University Press, 1999.

INDEX